Visual Communication and the Graphic Arts

Visual Communication and the Graphic Arts

Photographic Technologies in the Nineteenth Century

Estelle Jussim

With a Foreword by Beaumont Newhall

R. R. Bowker Company
New York and London, 1983

Published by R. R. Bowker Company
1180 Avenue of the Americas, New York, N.Y. 10036
Copyright © 1974, 1983 by Estelle Jussim
All rights reserved
Printed and bound in the United States of America

Library of Congress Cataloging in Publication Data

Jussim, Estelle.
    Visual communication and the graphic arts.

    Reprint. Originally published: New York: R.R.
Bowker, 1974. With rev. preface.
    Bibliography: p.
    Includes index.
    1. Photography—History. 2. Photomechanical
processes—History. 3. Graphics arts—History.
I. Title.
[TR15.J87   1983]   760   82-20194
ISBN 0-8352-1674-8 (pbk.)

Contents

Foreword

The world's first photographic process was the invention by the Frenchman Joseph Nicéphore Niépce around 1826 of a way to make an intaglio printing plate from an engraving. He discovered that a certain form of bitumen, normally soluble in an animal oil, became insoluble on exposure to light. He coated a metal plate with this material, laid an engraved print upon it, and exposed it to the sun's rays. Each inked line of the print held back the light; the bare paper allowed light to harden the coating behind it. He removed the original print, washed out the unhardened bitumen with his solvent, and etched the plate in acid, which bit into the metal beneath each inked line of the original. Thus was born what came to be called a photomechanical plate, which could be inked and printed to produce unlimited facsimiles of the original. Niépce named his process "Heliography," and used it for yet another purpose: fixing the image of a camera. In 1827 he produced a crude, but wonderfully prophetic, photograph of the view of his farmyard from his study window.

Thus from the very outset the photographic process was used for two distinct but closely interrelated purposes: the *reproduction* of existing pictorial images and the *production*, or generation, of records of the evanescent, elusive images of whatever lay within the focus of the lens—in other words, photographs.

Most histories of photography concern themselves with camera pictures as original works of art or visual documents. Little attention, surprisingly, has been paid to the way the public over the past century and a half have *seen* photographs. Of the uncountable millions that have been produced, by far the majority have been seen, not in their original form, but in reproductions in books and, especially, illustrated periodicals. Furthermore, illustrations of all types, both factual and fictive, in other media are for the most part known not from the original drawing or painting, but from reproductions on the printed page.

How phototechnology revolutionized the graphic arts and greatly enhanced visual communication is demonstrated by Dr. Jussim with meticulous documentation and copious illustration. She traces the development of reproductive printmaking from a handcraft to the first successful photomechanical halftone techniques that were perfected by the turn of the century. Her exposition of these often complex techniques is lucid and thorough. Using the language of current information theory, she shows that each medium has its own "code" by which the message is conveyed. Of particular interest is her discussion of the consequences of the impact of phototechnology on the quality and faithfulness to the original.

Before the 1880s photographs could only be reproduced in quantities by manual printmaking techniques. Even the most skillful draftsman and painstaking engraver necessarily, if unconsciously, imposed his personality upon the copy. Artist-illustrators were constrained to produce originals that would conform to the limitations of the printing process. The problems facing the illustrator are vividly recounted in Dr. Jussim's profiles of three of the most famous: Howard Pyle, William Hamilton Gibson, and Frederick Remington.

This book is a major contribution to our knowledge and appreciation of photography as a creative medium and as a reproductive technique.

BEAUMONT NEWHALL

Preface to the Paperback Edition

In the nine years since *Visual Communication and the Graphic Arts* was first published, interest in the history of photography has increased exponentially. Not only has the discipline called "history of photography" found acceptance in art departments at colleges and universities, but the implications of photography have reached across disciplines into almost every aspect of human communication.

Cultural anthropologists, sociologists, historians of art and politics, mass media and propaganda specialists, perceptual psychologists, and information theorists have discovered that photography—through all its attendant technologies—has permanently altered modern society.

In its simplest terms, this book is an investigation into the steps by which photography became the dominant mode of visual communication. It attempts to answer two fundamental questions concerning the impact of photography on the nineteenth century: What alterations occurred in the capacities of visual media for "artistic expression" and "information transfer"? What happened to our conceptions of art and information as we began to interpret "Nature" through photography in its published forms? In other words, what happened to human thought and perception as photography gradually vanquished the traditional graphic arts?

Applying concepts from the fields of information science, communication theory, visual perception, and social psychology as it applies to mass communication, this book is an extension of the pioneering insights of William Ivins, Jr., author of the influential *Prints and Visual Communication*. It augments, corrects, and expands the theories of Ivins, and relates these to Marshall McLuhan's extrapolations in *Understanding Media*. Using Ivins as a departure point, this book ventures into an in-depth exploration of the impact of photography and its related technologies on the graphic arts.

In the preface to the first edition, I explained that this book is not simply a "history of events," although it examines specific time sequences in order to verify trends. The approach is more issue-oriented than chronological, except where chronology elucidates an issue. Each of three artists—Howard Pyle, Frederic Remington, and William Hamilton Gibson—represents a new step in the intermix of photography and communication: imagination subjected to technology, photography in the service of the illustrator, and, finally, the displacement of the artist by the camera. Along the way, the role of the interpretative wood engraver is examined in detail.

Since the 1840s publication of Henry Fox Talbot's *The Pencil of Nature*, the photographic image has always found its widest distribution through books and periodicals. Fox Talbot quickly discovered, however, the paradoxical inability of photography to reproduce itself in a form suited to the printing processes of the mid-nineteenth century. Inventors were forced to seek ingenious methods of transforming photography into relief, intaglio, or planographic plates. *Visual Communication and the Graphic Arts* details the technological advances toward that goal.

One of the most important contributions I believe this volume makes is the presentation of illustrations *in their original size* as they appeared in books and periodicals, especially since several of Ivins' theories were distorted by an unscientific variation of size and enlargement of originals. Whenever possible, I wanted to present a series in different graphic media on the same kinds of subjects: the nineteenth century "lovely lady," animals, landscapes, objets d'art; these series keep a sharp focus on graphic capabilities. Unfortunately, despite the amazing ingenuity of twentieth-century printers, there is always a slight loss in the re-reproduction of original illustrations. Readers should seek out and examine originals themselves, especially in media like etching or photogravure where ink quality is vital. Information about the location of at least one copy of each book or print has been supplied.

In some cases, very few copies of original editions have survived, and it is hoped that this paperback edition will continue to encourage the preservation of the incunabula of photographic technologies.

Because no corrections could be made in the original plates of the first edition text, I must apologize for any errors which remain. One minor confusion deserves clarification. To the best of my recollection, various plates in the later Muybridge multiples series, such as Plate 91, were issued in both photogravure and collotype. That fact does not, in any way, alter my conclusions as to the trends in the use of photogravure, as these conclusions were based on hundreds of other examples.

Acknowledgments

I continue to be indebted to the following individuals and institutions for their assistance or counsel:

Dr. Elizabeth Lindquist-Cock, Art Historian, for permission to pursue some of her own research discoveries, and for acting as adviser both in the history of art and of photography; Ellen K. Shaffer, now Curator of the Robert Louis Stevenson Museum in St. Helena, California, and formerly Head of the Rare Books Department of the Free Library of Philadelphia, for exceptional generosity of access to collections and for encouragement; Professor Jack Dalton, then Dean of the Columbia University School of Library Service, and other members of the faculty of that school, as well as Dr. David Rosand of the Art History Department; also of Columbia University, Kenneth Lohf, Librarian for Rare Books and Manuscripts in Special Collections; Anne Carey Edmonds, Librarian, Mount Holyoke College, for permission to borrow the unusually fine nineteenth-century materials of that college; Nancy Devine, Reference Librarian, Mount Holyoke College; Violet Durgin and Stanley Greenberg, Reference Librarians, the Forbes Library in Northampton, Massachusetts, for assistance with the Kingsley archives; Roland Elzea, Curator of Collections; Phyllis Nixon, Librarian; Helen Farr Sloan, Curator of the John Sloan Memorial Collection, all at the Wilmington Society of the Fine Arts, Delaware Art Center; Tony Landini, Manager, Wagner

Photoprint Company in New York City, for assistance in the reproduction of difficult originals.

Permission to quote extensively from William Ivins' *Prints and Visual Communication* was granted by DaCapo Press, reprinters of the original Routledge and Kegan Paul edition of 1953. Margaret Van Brunt of Wilmington, Delaware, graciously permitted access to the extensive manuscripts and prints of her grandfather, Albert Munford Lindsay. Permission was granted by Houghton Mifflin Company for the use of materials from James J. Gibson's *The Perception of the Visual World* (© 1950, renewed 1977 by Houghton Mifflin Company; text now available from Greenwood Press, Westport, Conn.). Permission to quote from *The History of Photography* by Helmut Gernsheim, London & New York 1955 (new edition 1969), is by courtesy of the author.

A special note of thanks to Jean Peters of the R.R. Bowker Company for her patience and encouragement.

ESTELLE JUSSIM

October 1982

List of Illustrations

Visual Communication and the Graphic Arts

Introduction

This work is intended as a contribution to the understanding of an important modern phenomenon: the alteration of visual perception and visual habits through the impact of photography on the graphic arts.

Since it has specific goals in explicating visual communication and will be reformulating previous vocabularies which dealt with the graphic arts, the reader may find it useful to know in advance the methodology, scope, and terms or definitions of the book.

After assessing the achievements of William Ivins, Jr. in defining the nature of the graphic arts and visual communication, especially in the area of the influence of photography, I will demonstrate how the invention of photography in the third decade of the nineteenth century significantly transformed the capabilities of graphic media for what I shall call "artistic expression" and "information transfer." We shall see how artists responded to the new challenges of phototechnologies and whether or not the ability to transmit information through the mass media of graphic arts and book illustration was substantially improved by the availability of photography and photomechanical techniques.

We shall explore as the capabilities for *artistic expression* of a graphic process: (1) its autographic qualities, those qualities which permit direct creation by an artist without the intervention of a technician; (2) its appropriateness to the physical channel and the code, or message units (discussed in detail in Chapter 1) for the transmission of information about the "originals" of book illustration of an imaginative, fictive nature; (3) its quantitative capacity, informational bits per square inch, or tendency toward subliminal or other optical characteristics, judged visually rather than strictly mathematically.

We shall explore, as the capabilities for *information transfer* of a graphic process: (1) its capacity to transmit the characteristics of an object, individual, or event in Nature; (2) its quantitative capacities, as in (3) above. Rigorous standards for visual representation will be applied, using the psychologist's formulations—especially those of James J. Gibson—of the major elements of human perception. Information not specifically related to the capabilities of the graphic processes will be included where such data tends to shed light on the adoption of the graphic processes by the publishing trades.

In examining the capabilities of graphic media for artistic expression and information transfer, it should be recognized that these are not considered here to be strictly separate entities, nor is it pretended that they rarely occur together. This terminology is a matter of convenience and emphasis, a matter of placement along a continuum of communication. Under the rubric of "artistic information," we discuss imaginative, fictive works of art designed primarily to illustrate books and periodicals for the purpose of enhancing the pleasure of readers. The emphasis is on the *subjective manipulations* of the artist. Under the rubric "information transfer" falls what might be called "the visual report of the real world"—art history, natural sciences, travel, biography—whose accuracy may be crucial.

This book is not intended to be an exhaustive, chronological history of the photomechanical media, however useful such a history might be for other purposes. The concentration here has been to select meaningful samples from the enormous field of mass visual images for the purposes of accurately estimating the major steps in the transformation of the art and manufacture of the graphic arts as applied to book and periodical illustration from a specialized handcraft trade to a vast industrial enterprise, an enterprise whose manipulations of symbolic representations are important links in human communications.

THREE APPROACHES

The effects of the introduction of phototechnologies on the capacities of graphic media for both artistic expression and information transfer are examined here in three ways.

Capabilities for Artistic Expression

The first part of the book, a discussion of what graphic effects were available to American illustrators before and after the advent of photography, is followed by a brief presentation of the career of Felix Octavius Darley, whose work depended almost entirely on hand-reproduction, although it paralleled the development of the phototechnologies. Then follows a study of the careers of three major illustrators who are amply representative of the transition between the old and new technologies: Howard Pyle, William Hamilton Gibson, and Frederic Remington.

These three artists were exceptionally productive over much of the period which concerns us. Each was primarily an illustrator—an originator of messages specifically intended to be transmitted through the graphic arts—rather than a painter who only occasionally indulged in the graphic arts. Each produced the originals of his illustrations in many painting and drawing media. Pyle, Gibson, and Remington were reproduced over the years by the major nonphotographic and photographic media; the absence of certain established media in either category from their history is as telling as the presence of others. They were exceedingly popular and highly acclaimed, and therefore may be considered as representing what was admired, and therefore demanded, in illustration at the time. Each artist happened to be not only an illustrator, but an illustrator-author, who not only wrote and illustrated his own stories and articles, but who illustrated the works of other authors. Despite these basic similarities, each was vividly different from the other, and together they offer three diversified approaches to this study.

Howard Pyle (1853–1911) epitomized the imaginative, fictive aspects of illustration. He created legendary characters, magical landscapes, animals, and objects, and recreated historical personages and events. Amazingly versatile, he ran the gamut of illustrational possibilities, from comic fantasies for children to narratives of adult human relationships rendered with a realist's accuracy of detail and a romanticist's passion for color and mood.

William Hamilton Gibson (1850–1896) was considered in his day as the artist par excellence of the most ephemeral aspects of the miniature world of flowers, birds, and insects. Admired for the beauty and precision of his perceptions of the woods and fields of New England, his work not only permits us to study the expressive codes of natural history before and after the introduction of photomechanical reproductive media, but it leads us into an unexpected encounter with what the printing theorist, Victor Strauss, has called "the zone of interchangeability"[1] in the graphic arts. Gibson experimented with artistic media, and early introduced photographs into his book designs.

Frederic Remington (1861–1909) was unquestionably but perhaps not justifiably the most famous recorder of the life of the American Indian and the cowboy. Essentially a reporter of action, it has been said that to study Remington is to study one subject only: the horse. It would be more accurate to say that to study Remington is to study the rise of the portable camera and instantaneous photography. Indeed, Remington's oeuvre is so interconnected with the development of phototechnology that his contribution to American illustration consisted largely of his acting as an intermediary between the camera image and the printed page.

As the work of these three men, commonly considered to be "artists," reveals, the intermix of both "artistic expression" and "information transfer" occurs perhaps even more frequently in illustration than might be expected. An obvious example of the intermix can be discovered, for instance, when an imaginative artist like Howard Pyle copied authentic historical costumes and furniture as models for his illustrations about the life of George Washington. The informational content of such illustrations is considered by the publisher, the illustrator, the author, the historian, and the general public, to be measurable in terms of accuracy, or fidelity to some original. Since today we can see neither Washington's courtship of his wife or photographs of that courtship, we must content ourselves with the imaginative constructs of either Washington's contemporaries or other artists who will *recreate* the scene. This informational aspect is a legitimate and influential function of printmaking and book illustration, and its potential for structuring future thought about an event is evident in one of William Ivins' most significant observations: "At any given moment the accepted report of an event is of greater importance than the event, for what we think about and act upon is the symbolic report and not the concrete event itself."[2]

Now an important theoretical paradox occurs, for whatever the purported information to be transmitted between an artist and his audience, it must be accepted that the primary informational content of any reproduction of a picture by Howard Pyle, for instance, is the *picture*, and *not* the recreated or imaginary event portrayed. Unless the physical channel of the graphic medium, and its particular message structures, permits the representation of the image of the picture to be transmitted in a clear and nondistorting manner, we can't even begin to judge the "message" of Pyle's picture. *We must have information about Pyle's picture before Pyle's picture can deliver his message* about a recreated or imaginary event. Chapter 1 continues the discussion of this necessity as basic terms used by William Ivins are reformulated to conform to new theories concerning the nature of information.

Comments on the difference between a visual image, or picture, and information about that image should assist the reader in understanding that this book is concerned with the transmission of information about objects, individuals, or events in Nature, including ideational objects, like fictive book illustration, which achieve physical status, rather than with "meaning." "Meaning" has a complex cultural milieu as the matrix of its interpretation. This is a difficult issue. As the information scientist and aesthetician, Abraham Moles, indicated:

> Information differs essentially from meaning: Information is only a measure of complexity. To transmit a message is to make more complex the space-time surrounding the point of reception; it is to produce a micro-replica of the complexity created at the origin of transmission. Meaning rests on a set of conventions which are a priori common to the receptor and transmitter. Thus it is not *transmitted;* potentially, it pre-exists the message . . .[3]

In the case offered above, that of Pyle's courtship of Washington's wife, the message of any graphic medium is, strictly speaking, only that picture by Pyle. The *meaning* of Pyle's picture would differ, obviously, if the receiver of a graphic message about that picture had no idea of who George Washington was, when he lived, what a powdered wig was, why the lady was so encumbered by so much yardage of cloth goods, what candlelight was, or even painted walls, moldings, drapes, buckled shoes, and so on. Meanings exist in specific cultural thesauri, a matrix of agreement on objects, symbols, events; the dictionary is one such thesaurus of verbal meanings, but all societies have tremendously exact thesauri of the meanings of gesture, the visual arts, and the unspoken physical relationship between hierarchies. It should be stressed, for the sake of clarity, that we are not using the word "message" here as it is used to describe a "message play," where critics often have confused the two words, "message" and "meaning." In this book, the term "message" signifies only that which is to be transmitted to an audience, namely, information about an original object, individual, or event in Nature or in imagination.

In terms of the discussion on the capabilities of the graphic media for "artistic expression," no other single factor will be as significant as the correct transmission of information, for unless the information about a picture is transmitted correctly, "meaning" may be either unavailable or seriously distorted.

Information Transfer Capabilities

It should have become evident by now that the problem of communicating a fictive message by an artist like Howard Pyle is exactly analogous to the problem of communicating the "real world" of art history, except that the usual purpose of a painter, sculptor, or architect has been to create a complex object and not necessarily to illustrate a book or periodical. Aside from the many cases in the eighteenth or nineteenth centuries where an artist painted a picture specifically for the sake of receiving royalties or payment for graphic arts representations of it, the reproductions of most artistic creations become mass-distributed visual images, or "illustrations," only inadvertently.

Art history, as the one major subject field selected for study here, was chosen almost automatically, not only because it had been the primary motivation for the investigations of William Ivins in his widely known *Prints and Visual Communication,* but because there can be no question that the development of the graphic arts has been bound up with the reproduction of art objects from their very beginning. It has been one of the major functions of the graphic arts through the past four centuries to duplicate, disseminate, and popularize watercolors, oil paintings, views of architecture, and objets d'art. The other major function of the graphic media, of course, has been to provide vehicles for direct artistic autographic expression.

Art history also offers special advantages in the study of visual media. The objects of study—the originals—are in many shapes, sizes, textures, posing problems of reproduction ranging from those related to rendering the tone and color of the flat surface of paintings, to those encountered in "reproducing" the giant three-dimensional structures of architecture and sculpture. For this study, successive editions of art history books were sought and, failing their availability, successive versions of the same art original reproduced in different media in different books. Reproductions for comparative purposes were sought in the same size, for considerations of density, and in differing sizes, for considerations of scale and the obliteration of detail.

In art history, we are presumably seeking information about the thing in itself, the "original." Ivins was not the only person concerned about the distortions transmitted about art objects. It was likewise the major input of André Malraux's *Museum without Walls*, a volume of his *Psychology of Art*, in which Malraux expounded on the problems raised by the photographic duplication of objects as mementos of works of art universally available from all cultures and all times. The burden of Ivins' most influential work, *Prints and Visual Communication*, was to deliver evidence for the superiority of photographic media as transmitters of information about art objects. Today, we are perhaps more conscious of the concept of "messages about originals" when we look at reproductions of art than when we look at imaginative mass-distributed illustration, but this is a modern perception. It was Ivins' interesting observation that, up to the time of the introduction of photography,

> . . . very few people had been aware of the difference between pictorial expression and pictorial communication of statements of fact. The profound difference between creating something and making a statement about the quality and character of something had not been perceived. The men who did these things had gone to the same art schools and learned the same techniques and disciplines. They were all classified as artists and the public accepted them all as such, even if it did distinguish between those it regarded as good and as poor artists. The difference between the two groups of artists was generally considered to be merely a matter of their comparative skill. They all drew and they all made pictures. But photography and its processes quietly stepped in and by taking over one of the two fields for its own made the distinction that the world had failed to see.[4]

That field was information transfer, and the task of taking it over was long, and difficult, and by no means a complete victory.

Illustration by Chronological Section

Aside from the specifics of the careers of artists, or the specifics of one major subject area, art history, this book attempts to provide the reader with indications of what happened to mass-distributed visual images in general. An exploration of nineteenth-century critics' comments offers one approach. Another arises from two historical events which produced a significant outpouring of books for comparison. These were the Philadelphia Centennial Exhibition of 1876, and the World's Columbian Exposition at Chicago, in 1893. The many illustrated books[5] published in connection with these two international fairs demonstrate conclusively the radical change between the wood-and-steel engraving era and the overwhelming success of the photograph expressed in photomechanical terms. With these fairs, we find confirmation of the ouster of both hand-drawn and hand-produced illustration—the "syntax" of the subjective eye and the subjective hand—by mechanically "drawn" and mechanically produced images in the "syntax" of so-called objective reality.

As a further check on any developments which might have been missed, a selection of books published between 1876 and 1893 was examined, books incorporating the new media simultaneously with the old, and which therefore afforded opportunities for direct study of contrasting effects within one unit. Several hundreds of books were examined, especially in the areas of travel and geography, biography, local history, and poetry and poetry anthologies. Successive editions of the works of Washington Irving, Oliver Wendell Holmes, Henry Wadsworth Longfellow, and others in this period were also studied. Books and prints which could be discovered to have been the product of media innovators, like John Moss, William Kurtz, or James Osgood (as a publisher) were extensively searched. Always, the impact of developments in the mass image markets were studied for their influence on the traditional functions and characteristics of the graphic arts as prints.

As these studies developed, it was verified that periodicals were as overwhelmingly important in the history of American mass-distributed visual images as they had been in the dissemination of verbal information. In fact, it may even be said that the history of American book illustration in the second half of the nineteenth century was merely the history of magazine illustration, degraded and at one remove. For what came out one month in *Harper's New Monthly Magazine* came out the next as a monograph by Harper Brothers. Most graphic arts theory has neglected to study the consequences of what happened to the scale and textural details of originals of illustrations as they went through the publishing mill, from magazine to book and sometimes back again, changing size and shape and medium in ways which William Ivins, for example, ignored to the detriment of his contention that phototechnology was the supreme and omnipotent graphic art.

The reader may wish to consult Victor Strauss' magnificent compendium of modern graphic arts information, *The Printing Industry*, for terminology and definitions beyond the scope of the glossary offered here, especially for formulations like this:

> If we want to compare different printing processes and methods as to their ability to produce various aesthetic effects, we can do so best by establishing three different zones for every printing process or method. These zones can be designated as (1) the zone of uniqueness, (2) the zone of interchangeability, and (3) the zone of inability.
>
> In *the zone of uniqueness* we put effects and results which are peculiar to a printing method, which depend on its intrinsic nature, or, to be practical, on existing equipment, and cannot be duplicated by any other process or method. In *the zone of interchangeability*, we can place such effects and results as can be produced more or less equally well by two or more printing methods. In *the zone of disability* belong effects and tasks for which a given method is not suitable at all.[6]

Such definitions, as well as descriptions of processes in Helmut Gernsheim's *History of Photography,* are useful in understanding the capacity of visual media for informational communication.

1

Visual Information
and the Graphic Arts:
The Impact of Photography

The exigencies of the channel often require coding because it is only in a coded form that the signal can actually travel over it.[1]

Dots for the eye (photograph) and dots for the ear (telegraph) . . . .[2]

In terms of the graphic arts, the nineteenth century was a battleground where competing visual media were vanquished by a brash newcomer, photography. Economically, it was a fierce war, but economics was only the gross underpinning of a series of victories in which aesthetics, visual expectations, artistic predilections, traditional communications functions, social demands, and the technological availability of certain materials, all clashed head-on in the field. The challenges and capabilities of photography enraged purists and humanists, forcing the revival of moribund graphic arts, such as etching, as a revolt against what was perceived as a mechanization of the artist. Critics such as John Ruskin sped from enchantment with the labor-saving recording capabilities of photography to a bitter disillusionment with the havoc the new medium caused among all the visual arts. Baudelaire, seeing that the vast majority—the "masses"—sought only verisimilitude in art, scoffed that photography was the public's new Messiah. Not since the invention of printing itself had so much controversy raged over a new communications medium.

Yet few could argue over some of photography's conspicuous advantages. Through photography we could capture light directly from the stars, enlarge the picture of a distant nebula to be studied at leisure, stop the motion of animals in midair, secretly snap the visage of an unsuspecting "savage," sell the idea of national parks to the congressmen back in Washington, even become instantaneous artists by making portraits of our soldier sons with a little black box. The study of the arts could at last proceed with some assurance of accuracy, the sciences rejoiced in a remarkable new tool, and the politicians began to worry about their physiognomies, as the camera seemed implacable, unflattering, and ultimately ubiquitous. These were among the great and well-known accomplishments of nineteenth-century photography, and its rout of the older graphic media seemed complete and, to some, infinitely desirable.

What is perhaps less well known is that photography and its accompanying phototechnologies more or less completely redefined the nature of artistic expression and of information transfer. The fact that the camera seemed to be a scientifically reliable intermediary between the three-dimensional world and the media which multiplied its images had a profound and unquestionably unforeseen impact on our conceptions of "truth," "knowledge," and "reality."

We have had a recent example of media competition which ended, not only in the ousting of the older medium, but in restructuring of thought and expectation concerning the nature of "reality" and "truth." When the world-famous photographic weekly journal, *Life* magazine, decided in 1972 that it could no longer continue operations, there was widespread speculation that it had been the success of another visual medium, television, which had forced the issue. It seemed clear to a generation of television watchers that the mission of *Life* magazine, which had been to deliver accurate and up-to-the-minute news pictures to a mass audience, had become an anachronism. Television could perform that task with far greater simultaneity for a far larger public than any other visual carrier.

To any student of the evolution of media, the demise of *Life* magazine signaled the end of an unexpectedly short era. In the space of thirty-six years, between November of 1936 and December of 1972, *Life* had not only invented a new art of mass documentary photographic journalism, but had brought that art to the apogee of perfection, raising many lesser journals with it to the heights of its specific genre. The capacity of that genre, the photographically illustrated pictorial press, to deliver visual information about the sciences and the arts had been rivaled by only one other mass photographic medium, the motion picture.

What seems ironic about the death of such a magazine was that it had represented the final and spectacular success of a century-old struggle to transmit the information contained in photographs to the public *via the printed page.* It had represented the culmination of a supreme effort to perfect color printing, and through its glorious four-color halftones, many Americans enjoyed the delights of Renaissance painting or the complex aesthetics of body tattooing for the first time in their lives. Photographers such as Margaret Bourke-White and Eliot Elisofon, to name only two of dozens, made their names and fortunes through it. Yet from the time of Daguerre and Fox Talbot in the 1840s to the first decades of the twentieth century, the message of photography, the art of photographers, and the arts which only photography could accurately reproduce, all eluded efforts to find a way to transmit them to the public, in a compatible format, simultaneously with words that were transformed into metal type for printing in books, periodicals, or newspapers. A succession of processes—the mounted print, the collotype, photogravure, the woodburytype, the Moss process, the Ives process—were all devoted to the transmission of photography. For it was discovered that, while photography seemed the ultimate in the mechanization of visual information, it could not itself be easily mechanized. This, despite the fact that the photograph represented the successful mechanization of a human drive toward mass communication of visual information which the graphic arts had pursued since the fifteenth century, and which the recording aspects of all visual arts had pursued from the beginning of history.

THE CONTRIBUTIONS OF WILLIAM IVINS

That photography was the end product, and in many ways the very goal of all the previous graphic arts—not a separate entity, not a special case, not some sort of happy accident—was one of the insights offered by an outstanding theoretician and historian of the graphic arts, William Ivins, Jr. In his influential and pioneering work, *Prints and Visual Communication,* Ivins revealed that his creative energies had been devoted for much of his life to a "long endeavor to find a pattern of significance to the story of prints." [3] Unlike most connoisseurs of rare aesthetic items, Ivins, who had been Curator of Prints at New York's Metropolitan Museum of Art, was more interested in the visual communication aspects of his charges than in their rarity or preciousness. Early in his career, he had observed that

> . . . the backward countries of the world are and have been those that have not learned to take advantage of the possibilities of pictorial statement and communication, and that many of the most characteristic ideas and abilities of our western civilization have been intimately related to our skills exactly to repeat pictorial statements and communications. [4]

He saw that "Far from being merely minor works of art, prints are among the most important and powerful tools of modern life and thought." [5] *Prints* are not merely pictures produced by some special techniques, but are exactly repeatable visual statements capable of communicating complex ideas, with "limitations which their techniques have imposed on them as conveyors of information and on us as receivers of that information." [6]

As Marshall McLuhan was to acknowledge, Ivins' pioneering explorations of the sociological and psychological aspects of the graphic arts as communications carriers were a major source of inspiration for his own controversial *Understanding Media,* in which, unfortunately perhaps, he seemed neither to question Ivins' assumptions nor to document his conclusions. But we should not consider that Marshall McLuhan, however important and stimulating have been his contributions, was the first major media theorist. Ivins, of course, preceded him; but probably the work of Lewis Mumford, especially his *Technics and Civilization* (1934) and his *Art and Technics* (1952) should be regarded as the prime ancestor of media theory in the twentieth century. Even Mumford, however, did not invent the study of the interplay between technologies and society. Note the McLuhanesque title and scope of the subtitle of George Iles' *Flame, Electricity and the Camera: Man's Progress from the First Kindling of Fire to the Wireless Telegraph and the Photography of Color.* Published first by Doubleday & McLure in the year 1900, Iles' book also saw a 1904 deluxe edition by J. A. Hill in which Iles's stern and intent face is transmitted to us via a frontispiece on whose tissue cover it is explained, "Photogravure from a Photograph." We will pursue many of the reasons why it was necessary for publishers to "explain" the reproduction of a photograph.

Flame, Electricity and the Camera suggested that the human making of visual images had substantially preceded the articulation of spoken symbols, and Iles lauded the accomplishments of the visual artist in terms which strangely match the nineteenth century's eulogy of the photographer. For example:

> Ages after his death his pictures, images, reliefs remained to echo his voice
> to men who had never looked upon his face, and this, perchance, on shores

many leagues removed from the artist's home or grave. Art had begun its victory over time and space.[7]

But George Iles, whose ideas were much like those which William Ivins expressed in *Prints and Visual Communication*, believed that visual artists had their severe limitations.

> All the company of artists, recent and remote, glorious and inglorious alike, from the earliest to the latest, had but one method in copying nature — to express, line by line, stroke by stroke, what their eyes saw before them. By all this did reproduction fall short of its original, or erroneously surpass it, and set down falsity instead of truth. It was left for the nineteenth century to make the faithful touch of light limn its own impressions with more and more accuracy of form and of colour, with illusions, too, of relief and motion. . . .[8]

That "faithful touch of light"—the rays acting upon the photographic plate—could prove false. Once again, however, like William Ivins, George Iles saw photography as the outcome of a historical process, its culmination:

> The human hand has had no higher office than to depict what the eye can see; that service was to rise to a plane loftier still on the memorable day when, at the bidding of Niépce, it obliged light to print its own images, to be limner as well as revealer.[9]

Whether William Ivins developed his concepts independently of previous theorists is not important for our purposes. What is important is that probably nowhere better than in his *Prints and Visual Communication* are most—not all, by any means—of the problems concerning graphic arts theory articulated. Despite certain inadequacies of his documentation, which will be discussed shortly, and certain characteristics of his definitions which can be improved upon, his formulations present the inevitable starting place for any investigation into the specific relationships of phototechnology and visual communication. It is by expanding his research and his conclusions that we may find new aspects of significance concerning the impact of the graphic arts and of photography on human thought and perception.

For Ivins, it was "hardly too much to say that since the invention of writing there has been no more important invention than that of the exactly repeatable pictorial statement."[10] Where the medieval manuscript artist had perforce perpetuated subjective pictorial distortions of the three-dimensional world by hand copying each picture, the invention of *exactly repeatable printed pictures* to accompany *exactly repeatable printed words* provided the beginnings of precise communication, so basic to science and technology. Yet even here there were serious drawbacks. For a visual idea to be communicated through any printing medium, it had first to be symbolized by an artist according to the visual conventions of his time, then transferred to a printing surface by a hand engraver who superimposed on the original idea not only the technological limitations of the medium, but the specific rules of the mechanics of his trade.

According to Ivins, the invention of photography in the nineteenth century gave us the first and only graphic medium in which images

> . . . were not subject to the omissions, the distortions, and the subjective difficulties that are inherent in all pictures in which draughtsmanship plays a part. Here were exactly repeatable visual images made without any of the syntactical elements implicit in all hand-made pictures.[11]

Ivins used the word *syntactical* here because he had already defined all arbitrary formalizations, from the culturally determined modes of representation (e.g., an artist's selection of "realism") to the economically or technologically determined modes of reproduction (e.g., the "web of lines" on a copperplate engraving, or the lozenge-and-dot rationalizations of the same), as elements of *visual syntax*. Ivins was positive that photography was "pictorial statement without syntax." [12] For Ivins, in other words, all photographs provide what he called the visual report of nature, or man-made objects, without the distortions of artificial or subjective modes of communication.

He went even further; he specifically claimed that the process halftone engraving—a photomechanical invention of the late nineteenth century whereby reproduction is accomplished on a relief surface by exposing a light-sensitive emulsion on a metal plate to an original viewed through a finely apertured screen—was the most valuable of all the photographic technologies:

> The great importance of the halftone lay in its syntactical difference from the older hand-made processes of printing pictures in printer's ink. In the old processes, the report started by a syntactical analysis of the thing seen, which was followed by its symbolic statement in the language of drawn lines. This translation was then translated into the very different analysis and syntax of the process. The lines and dots in the old reports were not only insistent in claiming visual attention, but they, their character, and their symbolism of statement, had been determined more by the two superimposed analyses and syntaxes than by the particularities of the thing seen. In the improved halftone process there was no preliminary syntactical analysis of the thing seen into lines and dots, and the rules lines and dots of the process had fallen below the threshold of normal vision. Such lines and dots as were to be seen in the report had been provided by the thing seen and were not those of any syntactical analysis. [13]

What Ivins seems to be saying here is this: since the lines and dots of the perfected fine-line halftone process, such as it existed in the pages of *Life* magazine, are (1) below the range of normal vision, and (2) provided by the "thing" viewed by the camera, *there is no syntax involved* in a reproduction of an original. Implicitly, therefore, the halftone process is equivalent to normal vision, to all intents and purposes equivalent to direct contact with an object, free of all the symbolic interferences which older hand processes had inflicted on the visual world.

One sentence separates the long quotation just presented and Ivins' summation in the following words: "At last man had discovered a way to make visual reports in printer's ink without syntax, and without the distorting analyses of form that syntax necessitated." [14] If this is indeed the fact, then what shall we make of that intervening sentence thus far omitted? Here it is: "If there remained the same complete transposition of colour and loss of scale that had marked the older processes, the preliminary syntactical analyses and their effects had been done away with, and the transposition of colours was uniform." [15]

How is "the same complete transposition of colour and loss of scale" accomplished if there is no "syntax"? How can something be "transposed" without a structure or syntax with which to transpose it? Is a halftone process engraving *not* a symbolic representation? Are there any symbolic representations which do *not* employ syntax? Is not even a subliminal mesh of lines and dots a syntax of some sort?

The basic question becomes inevitable: what does William Ivins really mean by "syntax"? Would it be possible to redefine his terms without demolishing either his theoretical structure or his conclusions? This problem of "transposition" cannot be ignored, for more serious reasons than simply to catch another theorist in a contradiction. If we are to understand the problems of visual communication, we should seek as many avenues as possible, especially any other scientific analysis or theoretical structuring which has concentrated on the grammar of all communication. Such a focus is available to us through the constructs of information theory, which offers a vocabulary by which the substructures of communication can be investigated.

William Ivins wrote *Prints and Visual Communication* when information theory was in its infancy, when cybernetics was still an esoteric subject far removed from the concerns of the philosophy of art. Even Abraham Moles' *Théorie de l'information et perception esthetique* did not appear until 1958 (with its first American translation produced in 1966), although E. H. Gombrich, Rudolph Arnheim, Charles Biederman, Richard Bernheimer, and others (see the Bibliography) had already contributed to a new field of interest which encompassed the psychology, sociology, philosophy, and information theory of art and visual experience. The contribution of Abraham Moles which proved useful for our purposes was the notion that quantitative aspects of information governing perception and appreciation were applicable to the arts.

Unquestionably, Ivins would have benefited from the new vocabulary and insights of the communications scientists, since these would have liberated him from some of the very verbal traps which he had blamed the older graphic arts for inadvertently perpetuating. Once we abandon the clumsy concept of *syntax*, and replace it with what we offer here as a new application of communication vocabulary, we find that Ivins could have presented his case far more convincingly, with less internal contradiction, if he had used the concepts of *message, channel,* and *code.*

INFORMATION THEORY: A NEW APPROACH TO THE GRAPHIC ARTS

A *channel*, obviously, is the physical medium of communication. A *code* is the structure imposed upon a message which permits that message to be transmitted. A *code* can be said to be composed of *message units* which are appropriate to transmission via a specific physical channel. Not all aspects of codes, however, are predetermined solely by the characteristics of physical channels, but result from a complex of national stylistic developments, individual idiosyncracies in the case of handcrafted visual messages, or economics.

In all forms of communication, the *channel* and the *code* together form the *medium*. In the case of the graphic arts, the channels of wood, metal, paper, ink, in combination with lines, dots, halftones, or solid areas, provide the characteristic effects of what we label wood engraving, etching, and so on.

A visual code transmits a visual *message*, the meaning of which rests upon many predetermined factors, e.g., culturally accepted symbolism or socially structured kinesic responses. The *meanings* transmitted do not concern us here. What does concern us is the manner in which the channel and the code together structure the transmission of visual messages, and what the influence of that structuring is on our ability to receive and respond to such messages. What particularly concerns us in this book is the transmission of visual information through the kind of visual messages which have characteristically accompanied the verbal texts of printed books and periodicals.

Books have contained visual messages, or illustrations, for a variety of reasons, of which the primary among these may be said to be: (a) to increase the sales and therefore the profits of a publisher by capturing the attention of a potential reader, or by appealing to a reader's desire for conspicuous consumption; (b) to assist in the imaginative discourse between author and reader by providing visual points of reference, especially for children or other verbally underdeveloped or inexperienced readers; (c) to convey information concerning the three-dimensional "real" world which words alone cannot convey as economically or as usefully; (d) to provide visual mementos of objects which have already been seen or are to be seen, for purposes of pleasure or study; (e) to satisfy the impulse of an author-artist to create a completely personalized visual-verbal entity; (f) to satisfy a human need to decorate manufactures of any sort.

Illustration, like all communication, is not a bodiless abstraction; it is material. It consists of the production of images through graphic media on appropriate surfaces. These images are symbols: they stand for, or represent, either creations of the imagination or objective paradigms of "reality." Whether imaginative (fictive) or reality-oriented, these images are, quite literally, what you see on the page. They are the lines, dots, tones, colors— in other words, patterns of ink or other coloring matter—which a graphic medium has somehow deposited on a surface.

Book illustration, periodical illustration, prints, should all be understood to be modes of communication which have required the development of appropriate codes for the effective transmission of messages. In the course of the following chapters, we shall be examining book and other illustration as communications channels, attempting to distinguish the characteristics of the codes developed for this channel by the introduction of photographic technologies in the nineteenth century. In essence, we will find ourselves exploring the implications of a statement originally made in another context:

> The materiality of communication implies that communication must obey the fundamental physical laws governing all objects. Among the first of these is the *approximation* caused by the quantification due to perceptual thresholds, and the *destruction* caused by noise, which creates uncertainty in the message.[16]

Messages, as Marshall McLuhan reminded us, cannot be extracted *pure* from media. In his overly quoted and often misunderstood dictum, "The medium is the message," McLuhan was observing that the use of each medium by a society tends to restructure the social organization of that society and the psychology of the individuals living in it. That restructuring and reconditioning is the "message" of the medium; we are ordinarily unaware of this message because the media environment is so pervasive it is like the air we breathe. We continue on ordinarily attending only to the overt *content* of a mediated event such as a poem, play, telecast, film, musical recording, or the presence or absence of electric light—"pure message," as McLuhan called the latter. In a sense, all the research involved in the preparation of this book grew out of an intellectual concern with the possibility of testing a statement such as "the medium is the message." Curiously enough, by concentrating on a seemingly small issue, for example, that of *the message of the medium itself,* the statistical concepts of Shannon and other strictly materialistic theorists and technicians are verified, and McLuhan receives support for some of his large and seemingly grandiose general theories.

Obviously, the message of a visual medium itself can sometimes interfere seriously with the message which a sender desires to transmit, whether it is a passage of evanescent charm in a fictive illustration or a unit of cold scientific fact. The essence of the problem is that visual communication, like all other forms of communication, has a material base. While an illustration purports to convey to us the Raphael painting of St. Cecilia, what we actually experience is a black smear of ink on yellowed paper, or a complex network of crosslines within which certain larger or smaller blobs of ink convey to our minds certain visual implications. These implications are perceived through learned habit, just as all sight may be said to be learned. Just as we somehow learn to rectify the upside-downness of our retinal images, and do so without consciously paying attention to such a miracle, so we piece together the dots and lines—the codes—of our culture's graphic media. We learn to interpret the stylistic conventions of each new visual mode of communication.

As Ivins demonstrated in both *Prints and Visual Communication* and *How Prints Look* (1943), each graphic medium possesses its own graphic syntax, its own mode of structuring visual experience for transmission purposes. And, just as the very structure and vocabulary of the English language impose both potentialities and limitations on thought and expression, so too the structure and vocabulary of visual codes impose their own potentialities on visual communication.

Let us take one of Ivins' basic contentions and see what can be done by applying our new vocabulary:

Ivins' Version

The invention of the ruled cross-line halftone screen was a device which made it possible to make a printing surface for a pictorial report in which neither the draughtsman nor the engraver had had a hand. Its great importance lay in the fact that *the lines of the process as distinct from the lines of the visual report* [italics added] could be below the threshold of human vision. In the old hand-made processes the lines of the process and the lines of the report were the same lines, and *the process counted for more than the report in the character of the lines and statements they made* [italics added].[17]

New Version

The invention of the ruled crossline halftone screen provided both a channel and a code which made it possible to manufacture a printing medium for a pictorial message in which neither the draughtsman (primary codifier) nor the hand engraver (secondary codifier) had a part. Its great importance lay in the fact that the *code* as distinct from the *message* could be below the threshold of human vision. In the old hand-made processes, once the visual message had been translated into the code, the message units of the code appeared to be synonymous with the message itself, and these units preempted attention as objects of aesthetic interest per se.

While this is by no means perfect, intensive study of Ivins indicates that he would have accepted such a reformulation, probably welcoming it for the flexibility which words like *code, channel,* and *message* would have offered him. In the case where he might have wanted to discuss an etching by Winslow Homer from one of his own paintings, instead of the circumlocution, "the lines of the etching process as distinct from the lines of the visual report of Homer's painting," he would have been able to say, simply, "the etching codes as distinct from the message about Homer's painting."

Other terms from the repertory of information theory are applicable to the study of the graphic arts, especially *fidelity, distortion,* and *"noise."* Messages suffer loss of fidelity with respect to the characteristics of an *original* to be transmitted; they can be distorted in transmission, and the "noise" of a code or the inadequacy of a channel can obliterate them partially or entirely. As Moles put it, "A noise is a signal that the sender does not want to transmit." [18]

QUESTIONS UNANSWERED BY IVINS

To recapitulate briefly, William Ivins contended that the hand processes of the graphic arts imposed codes which were (1) subjectively distorted, because the artist-illustrator, or draughtsman—the "packager" of information, or the primary codifier—had to *draw* by hand an object about which information was to be transmitted, and had to rely upon the artistic and visual conventions of his time to do so; (2) technologically distorted, because a hand engraver—the secondary codifier—had to translate the message which the artist-illustrator had given him to transmit to the public, into codes suitable for the physical channels chosen for the transmission, and that none of these media was free of interferences with the message.

According to Ivins, with the invention of photography and photomechanical graphic media, "Man had at last achieved a way of making visual reports that had no interfering symbolic linear syntax of their own." [19] In the new vocabulary, this would read, "Humanity had at last achieved a way of transmitting visual messages in non-interfering codes." Furthermore, especially concerning the halftone process, Ivins believed "Such lines and dots as were to be seen in the report had been provided by the thing seen and were not those of any syntactical analysis." [20] This led him into a logical contradiction, since all processes require "transposition" for the transmission of messages.

Ivins tended to regard photography and photomechanical technologies as practical equivalents. This implication was reinforced by his documentation. Because of the grand scope of his work, he offered only two short chapters on the advent of photography and photomechanical processes. In these two chapters, he mentions the process of photogravure exactly once, and scants all other processes except the halftone relief engraving which he insisted was "the greatest and most valuable of all the photomechanical processes." [21] This was because he believed it was completely type-compatible, and could be published jointly with metal type.

The joke was, of course, that in the first edition of his own book, *Prints and Visual Communication,* the very book in which Ivins made this laudatory claim, the exigencies of publishing technology had made it necessary to print his visual documentation—that is, photographs of art—separately from and on different paper from the text. The photomechanical engravings were of too fine a screen to be printed on the coarse, cheaper text paper. This might seem like a minor point, except for the fact that Ivins stressed it so much, with the strong implication that with the coming of the fine-screen halftone process, all of the communications problems concerned with transmitting the information contained in photographs were solved for all time.

Genius that he was, Ivins was so intent on his overall story, so intent on demonstrating that each of the nonphotographic processes had, indeed, possessed highly interfering codes, that he further imperiled his credibility by documenting his book almost entirely with enlargements of the specimens of the nonphotographic codes. Since he stated explicitly that the fine-screen halftone process was superior to all others in that the lines and dots of the process were subliminal, i.e., below the threshold of human vision, he made it difficult to accept his evidence since we cannot see for ourselves, by examining the reproductions he offered, *whether or not any of these processes had subliminal effects as well.* While he informed the reader that economic considerations on the part of the publisher prevented him from including all the pictorial documentation he had amassed, he did not, however, specify what this documentation might have been. And, alas, he did not provide methodically sampled comparisons of photographic with nonphotographic processes nor did he differentiate between different photographic processes. Even his informative Laocoön series invites suspicion, as some of the reproductions are enlargements and others are reductions.

As we reread the Preface of *Prints and Visual Communication*, we find that Ivins acknowledged writing the book from memory,[22] with a minimum of checking, and it seems unmistakable that the book is less the scientific testing of a hypothesis than the philosophical conclusions of years of observations and deductions. That his memory and experience were formidable cannot be denied; indeed, we can only admire his tremendous and stimulating erudition and intuitive grasp of possible truths. But there can be no doubt that many questions remain unanswered, and—perhaps even more importantly—many crucial questions remain unformulated.

To begin, if photography is as objective as Ivins claimed it to be, were all problems of visual communication solved with the advent of the photo-technologies? If not, which problems were resolved and which problems continued to interfere with ideal communication? Were all the photo-technologies equally capable of transmitting codes suited for mass distribution through books and periodicals? Were any of them more capable than the others, and, if so, for what reason?

Furthermore, is there anything to be learned from examining the history of the development of these codes and their relationship to the history of the transmission of visual messages through illustration? How did these new codes come to be accepted? What were the barriers or encouragements to their acceptance? If, as Ivins suggested, photography abolished the need for the preliminary artist-illustrator's "syntactical translation" (i.e., his use of artistic codes of rendering), what were the effects of the phototechnologies on the illustrators, and why did they continue to be needed? What were the effects of the photographic technologies on the illustrators whose fictive work was destined to be communicated to the public through new visual systems? Was there a discernible difference in any aspect of the communication of information between the pre- and nonphotographic media and the new photographic media? Was there any way to document changes in the transmission qualities of visual messages which we call book illustration?

These questions ultimately resolve themselves into a single general question: *In what ways did the introduction of photographic technologies alter the artistic and informational capabilities of the graphic arts?* As a subset of that question, it becomes necessary also to ask: *In what ways did the capabilities of the photographic technologies for artistic expression and information transfer differ not only from the nonphotographic processes but from each other?*

In any attempt to respond to questions as large as these, a strong research focus is required. For that reason, the field of American book and periodical illustration, as well as interrelated aspects of the graphic arts in general, was selected as a historical area which pinpoints many significant issues, particularly in the exploration of the crucial years between 1865 and 1905, the years which could be named "The Forty Years War of the Media"— literally the years of a life-and-death struggle for survival among competing graphic channels and codes. Why certain visual media became favored over certain others during this period, how certain graphic codes forced their competitors to imitate their effects in the fight for cultural and economic survival, what the interaction was between photography per se and illustration per se, these are the primary concerns of this book, especially as they tend to support some of the hypotheses of information theory applied to visual communication: the "quantitative aspect of information." [23]

SUMMARY

In order to assess the impact of photography on the graphic arts, it becomes necessary to seek the comparative precision of the constructs and vocabulary of information theory. These constructs make it considerably easier to examine the hidden implications of many statements by the pioneer of graphic arts theory, William Ivins, especially where these implications misleadingly imply that photography totally lacks "syntax" or a transpositional structure. We posit that there is an original object, individual, or event in Nature about which an artist (primary codifier) wishes to communicate via a visual message to the public. These messages must be codified into message units suitable for selected communications channels, and this process ordinarily involves a secondary codifier, a technician, unless the channel permits direct autographic manipulation. Photography and its allied technologies seemed at first glance to have obviated the need for any consideration of transmitting codes and their appropriateness to channels, since the message was derived directly from Nature without intervening subjective distortions. An investigation of a specific field of the graphic arts—American illustration—should make it possible to demonstrate the accuracy of Ivins' observations, or to modify them in accordance with new findings arising from the application of information theory.

2

The Major Codes of the Graphic Arts: Theory and History

> In the Graphic Arts you *cannot* get rid of matter. Every drawing is *in* a substance and *on* a substance. Every substance used in drawing has its own special and peculiar relations both to nature and to the human mind.[1]

If we were to imagine communicating in a world without visual symbols, we would be forced to dismiss not only the pictures which are ubiquitously present in our publications, but the alphabet itself. Those magical twenty-six letters of our own alphabet, or the many thousand ideograms of the Chinese language, are visual codes which man developed for the communication of sounds. Both the Roman alphabet and the Chinese ideogram may perform the same function, yet it is not difficult to recognize the visual difference between one speech code and another. When one sense, the eye, serves as the translator of a symbolic code for another sense, the ear, we readily accept the idea that a transaction of some sort has occurred.

What the alphabet itself represents, namely, speech, is, of course, twice removed from "reality," since speech itself is merely a conglomeration of culturally determined sounds which have been assigned to stand for specific events, objects, or ideas. For various reasons,[2] it is less easy to grasp this idea of once removed and twice removed when the eye must interpret a visual code for itself rather than for another sense, as this seems to pose the existentialist conundrum of not being able to think about thinking while you are thinking. Certainly, we rely on certain minute muscular contractions of our eyes to provide clues concerning the contradictions we perceive, for example, between the flat surface of a painting and the modeled three-dimensional illusionism of space which it depicts, even if we are not conscious of the perceptual processes involved.

Yet it is not difficult to recognize differences in visual codes once we accept the fact that humanity communicates with as great a variety of visual codes as it does with codes dealing with the aural world. The difference between these two sets of codes is, primarily, that the aural is recognizably symbolic and the visual fools us. We may confuse the distant babble of children's voices with the distant babble of brooks, but we are not likely to confuse the distant babble of children's voices with the three-dimensional children themselves. We are not so safe in the visual world, where a cleverly painted representation of a child might very well confuse us. Illusion both plagues and helps us in making symbolic visual representations; plagues us in that we may confuse a message about reality with reality itself, helps us in that it makes possible the communication of certain messages themselves.

All visual communications which attempt to recreate, or represent, a three-dimensional world where forms are made known to us through light, shade, and color, are attempting to fool our eyes to a greater or lesser extent. For example, visual communications which transmit messages resembling Nature are, of course, not transmitting "Nature" at all, but some sort of code which attempts to imitate the effects of Nature, the outward appearance, the show.

Before proceeding to compare the effectiveness of various graphic codes, an attempt should be made to understand what it is that these graphic codes try to transmit, namely, some imitation of the retinal images which we call the visual world.

THE THEORETICAL CONSTRUCTS OF JAMES GIBSON

In his basic text on *The Perception of the Visual World,* James J. Gibson offered considerable substantiation for his hypothesis that the "object possessing the greatest importance for vision [is] the single element of the texture of a surface." [3] Gibson was formulating a ground theory of our perception of the visual world, and indirectly provides us with the basis for understanding the illusions which artists can create on two-dimensional surfaces.

> The grain or structure of a surface is made up of units of one kind or another which are repeated over the entire surface. These units are characteristic of the physical substances in question. They determine an array of light reflections from the surface which can be focused as an image. [4]

The number of these units tends to be evenly distributed over a surface. Closely packed units tend to be considered as "smooth"; somewhat more separated units are called "rough." These units obey the laws of perspective.

In addition to the perspective which the Renaissance artists and scientists taught us to project along the edges of surfaces, Gibson demonstrated that there is a *perspective of texture* on surfaces which can be perceived as a foreshortening of the textural elements, so that the units of an overall pattern (e.g., the weave of a particular cloth) appear more closely packed when further away from us, and less dense near us, while the dots or individual items of the texture shift in size and shape as they recede or approach the eye. The so-called "Op" artists of recent decades have taken advantage of this perspective of texture to fool the eye into believing that it is perceiving undulations on what is a two-dimensional surface.

We have only to imagine a field of grass, in which the near blades are large and distinct, the far blades diminishing in both size and clarity, and the view of the blades shifting from an angle almost on top of them directly at our feet, to an angle which progressively becomes more vertical as our eyes look upward toward the horizon. If the field undulated, there would be corresponding shifts of angle, density, size, and other clues, like light and shadow, which would demarcate the ground contours beneath our grass texture.

These characteristics of what Gibson calls "Texture Gradients"[5] are summarized by him as follows: ". . . the gradient of density in a projection of a physical surface bears a fixed relation to the slant and facing of the physical surface projected."[6] We perceive corners, edges, contours, by variations in texture gradients.

But texture alone does not offer us all the needed clues, since "no surface can be seen unless it is illuminated to some degree."[7] We are so accustomed to this idea that we take largely for granted what Gibson has formulated: "The illumination of a given section of surface . . . *is a function of the orientation of the surface toward or away from the source of light.*"[8]

What we need of Gibson's perception theory may be summed up in his own words:

> The gradient of texture . . . is a function of the slant of a physical surface away from the observer and the density of the texture varies with physical distance. Variation in shading, on the other hand, is a function of the physical orientation of the surface to the light source. It varies not with distance but with the curving or bending of the surface relative to the direction of illumination. Even the slightest curve or bend, insufficient to make much difference in a texture gradient, can produce a variation in shading if the direction of the light is favorable. Hence arises the capacity of light and shade to give what artists call relief to a surface, and to supplement the modelling of the surface in three dimensions.[9]

Gibson's theory leads to the conclusion that if a graphic art is to create an illusion of the three-dimensional world, it must possess a channel and a code which can *simultaneously* transmit accurate messages about:

(1) *texture gradients*
(2) *chiaroscuro* (variations in light and shade)
(3) *undulations of both surface and contour.*

And we should add another most important element of perception and correct analysis of transmitted information:

(4) *color,* both in local areas and as a function of distance (so-called aerial perspective).

Obviously, if what is required is an illusion of reality—a "faithful" copy of an original—these characteristics must be transmitted whether the original of the message is a "flat" painting, a contoured landscape, or a young lady in ball dress. The accuracy of transmission of these characteristics would ensure the accuracy of what we term information transfer. The history of the graphic arts is largely a record of the attempts to develop visual communications media which could imitate as closely as possible all the effects of "Nature,"[10] and that history is precisely the record of the struggles by artists and engravers to transmit texture gradients, chiaroscuro, undulations of surface and contour, and color. Exceptions to such imitators were creative artists like Rembrandt who were engaged in direct artistic expression through printmaking and who were, therefore, far more concerned with an increasingly separate vocabulary of effects for increasingly select audiences.

HISTORICAL DEVELOPMENT OF THE GRAPHIC ARTS

When a trained and talented artist creates an original message, e.g., an oil painting or a drawing, he or she can include sufficient data in this single transmission to create a credible illusion of Nature. We have only to think of the *trompe l'oeil* paintings of Hans Holbein or Will Harnett as examples.

But the artist, however prodigiously talented, could not replicate his original many hundreds of times without herculean effort and a prohibitive expenditure of time. The entire history of the graphic arts demonstrates that man came to recognize that he could not replicate large numbers of an original message *by hand* with any significant measure of accuracy, economy, or simultaneity of transmission. Visual messages had to be subjected to a manufacturing process which would ensure widespread distribution and reliable reception, and this manufacturing process, in turn, had to transform what E. H. Gombrich called "the ambiguities of the third dimension"[11] into universally accepted codes.

Any graphic art—that is, any manufacturing process which attempts to duplicate large numbers of an artist's original—constitutes *a message about a message*, unless it is possible for the artist to make his statements *directly* in the duplicating medium. For certain kinds of symbolic statements which did not rely upon illusionistic copying of the effects of Nature, the early codes of the graphic arts proved adequate. But when the demand arose for greater and greater amounts of information about the real world in all visual transmissions, the artist who drew the original message came to rely more and more upon a growing corps of manufacturing technicians, both for the sake of protecting his creative energies from the labor of translating his ideas into the stubborn limitations of metal and wood, and for the economic advantages of the division of labor into design and reproduction.

As with other manufacturing processes, this labor of translation grew into big business. The marketing of duplicated visual messages, whether in books or as prints, depended upon the efficiency and skill of the hand engravers, who began to specialize not only in certain reproductive media, but in specific kinds of translations, whether of landscape or portraits. The reproduction of oil paintings and other objets d'art became the staple product of many manufacturers, indirectly encouraging artists to create original messages specifically intended for reproduction and multiple sales. The spread of public education, and the growth of a general reading public by the late eighteenth century, coincided not only with the rise of the bourgeoisie but with technological advances which made more rapid book and print production both feasible and mandatory.

The historian and the scientist, however, remained at the mercy of the economics of engraving and publishing until the dawn of the nineteenth century, when a medium was invented which offered the simultaneous advantages of cheap and direct duplication of an artist's original, vast edition capacity, and a hitherto unattainable range of codes. This astonishing medium was lithography, and we shall see that it was under the impetus to further mechanize, or automate, visual replication through lithography that the first successful steps were taken toward photography.

Visually, we can recapitulate the capsule history of the graphic arts in the Western world by examining a series of "lovely ladies" produced in each of the major prephotographic codes. By doing so, we can familiarize ourselves with the capacities of each for the transmission of information about the texture gradients, chiaroscuro, undulations of surface or contour, and color, of the originals of messages. After we have studied these basic characteristics of prephotographic codes, we will make a preliminary assessment of the pioneering hypotheses of William Ivins whose influential theories in *Prints and Visual Communication* can be refined here in the languages of both (a) the psychology of vision, as defined by James Gibson, and (b) definitions used in information theory, specifically as these help to test the applicability of new models in reviewing the history of the graphic arts.

THE MAJOR CODES OF PREPHOTOGRAPHY

In his own way, a major nineteenth-century theorist of the graphic arts, Philip Gilbert Hamerton, formulated the questions that are being addressed here: the capabilities of the various graphic media for information transfer and artistic expression. Hamerton observed:

> The two questions about each of these arts are, "Can it interpret nature?" and "Can it express human thought and emotion?" The answer to these questions in every case is, "Yes; within certain limits fixed by the nature of the material and the process." And then comes the further question, "What are those limits?" [12]

This chapter offers a series of eight plates which were carefully selected as typical examples of the codes of pre- or nonphotographic "graphic arts" of the nineteenth century. They are, as follows:

Black-line wood engraving: "Lady Geraldine" (Plate 1)

Mezzotint: "Forget-Me-Not" (Plate 2)

Stipple "engraving": "Castella" (Plate 3)

Metal line engraving: "The Strawberry Girl" (Plate 4)

Combined black-line, white-line wood engraving, old "syntax": "Major Ringgold Mortally Wounded" (Plate 5)

Metal line and stipple engraving: "Lionel Lincoln" (Plate 6)

Etching: "Sarah Bernhardt" (Plate 7)

Lithography: "Madame Dorus Gras" (Plate 8)

These examples, reproduced as close to the size of the originals as possible, were selected to demonstrate not only the general characteristics of the codes usually employed in various media, but to serve as examples of the potentiality of each medium for illusion.[13]

We can probably best explore the relevant characteristics of these codes by comparing our "lovely ladies" and "bold soldiers" in pairs.

Pair I. "Lady Geraldine" and "Forget-Me-Not"

It seems obvious that "Lady Geraldine" (Plate 1) and "Forget-Me-Not" (Plate 2) exemplify opposite ends of the spectrum of representationalism or illusionism. "Lady Geraldine," using codes in one of the oldest traditions of the graphic arts—those of the black-line woodcut—must rely upon artistic conventions for delineating contour, i.e., the outer edge of objects as determined by cross section or profile at their maximum extension in space, rather than on the illusionistic definition of either surface textures, surface undulations, or light and shade.

Symbol and Illusion

"Forget-Me-Not," on the other hand, achieves almost all its effects by contrasts of light and shade, and the smooth chiaroscuro of the flesh tones, especially, present the most marked contrast to the frightful splotches on poor Lady Geraldine's face. Unlike "Lady Geraldine," the mezzotint does provide us with clues about the nature of fabrics: we "see" a gauzy, diaphanous veil in the one, in the other an opaque shawl which might as well be made of wood, for all we can tell; we "see" a patterned, shining gown in the one, a white shape scarred with coarse black lines in the other.

PLATE 1. *Lady Geraldine.* *Black-line wood engraving by W. J. Linton, illustration by Hennessy. Reproduced here the same size as the original, page 33, in Elizabeth Barrett Browning,* Lady Geraldine's Courtship *(New York: Scribner, 1870), from a copy owned by E. Jussim.*

She would break out, on a sudden, in a gush of woodland singing.

PLATE 2. ***Forget-Me-Not.*** *Mezzotint by H. W. Smith from a painting by Schlesinger. Reproduced here the same size as the frontispiece for* The Lily of the Valley for 1852 (*Boston: Greene, 1851*), *from the copy owned by the Forbes Library, Northampton, Mass.*

We can imagine glancing out of a distant window at dusk and seeing "Forget-Me-Not"; except for the absence of natural color, we might think she were real. We would find it hard to accept finding "Lady Geraldine" sitting there. "Lady Geraldine" is not an illusion; she is a symbolic representation. In an arbitrary code which provided opportunity for neither subliminal characteristics or much textural differentiation, "Lady Geraldine" can be considered to fit Marshall McLuhan's definition of "cool," since, in his terminology, she requires a great deal of intellectual interpretation whereby we contribute significantly to the message.

Technological Considerations

Both of these ladies were originally nothing but ink on paper,[14] yet the manner of their production was vastly different.

"Lady Geraldine" was an illustration for a book publication, in 1870, of a long poem by Elizabeth Barrett Browning. The publisher, Scribner, hired the artist, W. J. Hennessy,[15] to conjure up the imaginary lady in the title, and to prepare these drawings suitably for engraving on wood, since this most economical and convenient medium could be printed simultaneously with the words of the poem transformed into metal type. Upon approval of his drawings, which most probably were drawn directly upon the blocks themselves (in exactly the size you see here, but in reverse) the engraver, W. J. Linton, undertook to cut the drawings in his own inimitable style. We cannot surmise what the original drawings looked like, or what their medium—whether pencil or pen-and-ink or gouache or ink washes. We have only what we see here, and we can only presume that we are seeing at least some likeness of the Hennessy drawing. We assume that Hennessy's drawing was technically adequate for the engraver to follow without further adjustment for the sake of the reproductive medium, although such two-step codification is in the tradition of the medium. Indeed, the two-step is quite old; Ivins himself notes this in the famous *De Stirpium Historia* of Fuchs (1542). In that work, the first artist (primary codifier) sketched from living plants. Another artist copied these drawings onto the woodblocks, in such a way that the woodcutter simply had to facsimile his lines, a practice which lasted well into the nineteenth century. *De Stirpium Historia* was

> . . . the first time that both artist and woodcutter are given full recognition in the informational book they concerted to illustrate, and it is the first specific statement of the fact that the drawing on the block was not made by the original draughtsman but was a revised version of his drawing made by a specialist whose business it was to draw with lines that were suitable for their technical purpose.[16]

What is curious about W. J. Linton's translation of Hennessy's original is that the engraver did *not* use lines that were suitable to their technical purpose, but merely followed tradition, for the most part, despite the fact that his channel—boxwood end-grain—had far more capability for high-density information transfer than had the woodcut channel of the sixteenth century. Linton was perpetuating a code which had originated in a channel where each black line required a cut of the knife on each side of the line, and another series of cuts to free the slivers of wood between one line and the next, or to free a proposed dot from its encircling wood. Nevertheless, Linton at least partially utilized the capability of the new channel by using a graver, not a knife, to flick out small white areas in the surrounding blacks of the tree trunks, for example. He also saved himself much trouble by simply incising the face and neck dots with the graver cross-hatching at right angles. What happened to Linton's textures with the advent of photography-on-the-block and illusionistic white-line wood engraving will be discussed in considerable detail in forthcoming chapters.

When Linton had completed his work, the block was sent to the printer to be locked into forms with the type. Both type and block were simultaneously inked with greasy black which adhered to the relief surfaces of both picture and words, and white paper was imprinted with these lines in what might be called an upside-down stamping process.

Since not all graphic communication must rely upon illusion, and certain classes of information can be "almost purely schematic, for the thing it is intended to symbolize is not any particular instance of the shape of a concrete leaf or muscle, but a broad general class of shape," [17] the codes of the black-line woodcut were at least minimally adequate. For other classes of information, especially art history or biographic portraiture, the woodcut was inadequate, since "what is desired is a visual statement of the characteristics or qualities which differentiate" [18] each work of art and each person.

It was precisely for portraiture and for the reproduction of paintings that the mezzotint was best suited. Invented in mid-seventeenth century, but coming into prominence in the eighteenth and early nineteenth centuries, this first true chiaroscuro code was "peculiarly fitted for the reproduction of the air of distinction and stately grace that marked both the method and the subjects of the canvases [of] the great portrait painters . . . Reynolds, Gainsborough, Hopper, Romney. . . ." [19]

Mezzotint had such a range of halftones that it can be called the reproductive medium par excellence for oil paintings, which, indeed, it was for much of its career. Such is our little "Forget-Me-Not": not an illustration for a specific literary work, it was, rather, the transmission of an original message (an oil painting) by Schlesinger, who may or may not have been attempting to transmit information about a particular model; and the printed mezzotint served merely as a decorative frontispiece for one of the typical American miscellanies called "ladies' annuals" or gift albums, in this case, *The Lily of the Valley* for 1852.

To manufacture this frontispiece, a painting was chosen, perhaps even commissioned especially for the publication, which would be sure to appeal to the sentiments of the subscribers. The painting was copied by either the painter or the engraver, or, as previously suggested, by a trained middleman, onto a sheet of paper small enough to serve as easy reference for the engraver, who had previously prepared a copper or steel plate by working all over its surface with a "rocker," a tool which produces "lines of dots crossing and re-crossing each other [which create] innumerable minute hollows separated by thin walls of metal"; [20] such a burred and pocked intaglio plate would print a velvety, solid black if untouched. Smith, the engraver, then used a scraper to remove "both hollows and burrs altogether for the very highest lights, and less and less" [21] for the middle tones. By providing the capacity to describe the *lights* which fall on forms, rather than to fill up a space with schematicized black lines or visible black dots, the mezzotint could transmit a "resounding gamut of mellow lights and soft transitions and unctuous, translucent shadows." [22]

"Forget-Me-Not" was sent to a printer who probably specialized in intaglio processes, for the inking of such a plate was crucial to its success. In fact, there may have been more than one plate called "Forget-Me-Not," each prepared by Smith, since the soft burrs raised by the rocker wore away so quickly that it was impossible to print large editions from mezzotints unless they were steel plated. Unlike "Lady Geraldine," a relief plate in a

PLATE 3. *Castella.* *Stipple "engraving" by G. Parker, from a portrait by H. Inman. Reproduced here the same size as the plate facing page 58 in* The Magnolia for 1837 *(New York: 1836), from the copy owned by Mount Holyoke College.*

PLATE 4. *The Strawberry Girl.* *Steel line engraving by Smith from a painting by Dec-oninck. Reproduced here the same size as the plate in G. W. Sheldon,* Hours with Art and Artists *(New York: Appleton, 1882), from a copy owned by E. Jussim.*

sturdy material, "Forget-Me-Not" could not be replicated by electro-typing.

The inked plate, wiped free of surface excess, was subjected to considerable pressure to squeeze out the ink from its pocks and hollows onto a dampened sheet. Such ink deposits are characterized by a richness which the stamping quality of relief processes cannot match, and this specific quality of intaglio processes actually enhanced the range of its codes for illusionistic effects. This enhancement will be discussed further in connection with metal line engraving.

The separate prints of "Forget-Me-Not," for such they were, were delivered to the binder, who sewed a copy, and perhaps a dozen such mezzo-tints, into the folded pages of the printed words, the latter usually on lighter weight and less expensive paper than the so-called "illustrations."

Commentary   On balance, if "Lady Geraldine" is overly repetitive in its scratchy textures, and singularly lacking in smooth transitions from light to dark, we may criticize "Forget-Me-Not" for achieving an opposite extreme of an almost suspicious smoothness, which envelops the trees as well as the gown with an unnatural silkiness. As a master of textural variety indicated, "nature does not repeat herself, and no one given surface of a picture should be like another." [23] While the wood engraver, Linton, apparently believed that his work was technologically appropriate, despite the fact that he was following tradition, it is probable that not much more textural variety could have been achieved by the mezzotinter, who had reached the limits of the technological capacity of his medium.

Codes, then, can be a combination of both intellectual preconceptions and technological limitations.

Pair II. "Castella" and "The Strawberry Girl"

Subliminality and Scale   With Plates 3 and 4, we enter into an area hardly touched upon by William Ivins, who claimed the superiority of the subliminal character of photographic codes, and of one phototechnological code in particular, namely, process halftone engraving, without exploring or clarifying some important aspects of pre- or nonphotographic codes.

Very simply put, the subliminality of a code is a function not only of the actual, measurable size of its structural elements, but of the position of the viewer relative to the transmission channel.[24] In the case of the two "book illustrations" under comparison here, we may perform three simple actions which will dispel any doubts as to the relativity of "subliminality."

First: Glance from "Castella" to "The Strawberry Girl" with the pages held about 12 to 14 inches from the eyes. A slight overall graininess should be visible in "Castella." A complex and extensive web of crisscrossed lines should be visible in "The Strawberry Girl."

Second: Move as close to "Castella" as focus will permit, about 4 to 6 inches away, and the graininess reveals itself as distinguishable dots, even in our screened halftone process copy of it, with extremely fine lines describing the hair and fabric. Even this proximity should not disturb the overall sense of chiaroscuro.

Third: Move back from "The Strawberry Girl" about 3 or 4 feet from the picture. Not only will the web of lines disappear from the flesh areas, but a spectacular improvement in contrast of light and dark should result, with areas of the blouse and bonnet suddenly resembling brushwork, rather than masses of lines. The further back from "The Strawberry Girl," the greater is the chiaroscuro effect, and, with severe limitations, the greater is the textural differentiation.

There are two conclusions to be drawn from the results of these actions. The first is that if we are to succeed in judging the effectiveness of visual codes for illusion, we must set a standard distance for reception for them. For the purposes of our investigation here, we suggest 8 to 12 inches, or normal book-reading range. The second is that we should not judge codes that were meant to be suitable for framing prints, i.e., prints to be hung on walls and viewed from a distance, by the standards we set for book illustration. It is true that "The Strawberry Girl" appeared bound into a book with many other engravings whose skeins of lines are simply so much "noise" when viewed too closely. But these engravings were "art" engravings, typically culled from the stock of framing print selections, much as we today hear of books advertised with "pictures suitable for framing." Since one of William Ivins' major contentions was that photography possessed, among other attributes, a unique subliminal code, and as he particularly excoriated message-sending via linear engraving codes, condemning them as "conventional, artificial, linear systems," [25] we should recognize that his assumptions need to be examined with extreme care.

Plates 5 and 6, which are not in the series of "lovely ladies," demonstrate the remarkable versatility and high-density textures of the same codes which produced "The Strawberry Girl."

Plate 6, "Lionel Lincoln," a steel line engraving from a drawing by F. O. C. Darley, shares with "The Strawberry Girl" one of the oldest graphic traditions. To produce chiaroscuro, textural gradients, undulations of surface and contour (leaving aside color for the moment), the engravers of either "Lionel Lincoln" or "The Strawberry Girl" could rely upon codes which had seen a steady intensification of illusionistic effects from the sixteenth century to the nineteenth century. Pushing a special metal tool called a graver, or burin, along and into the surface of a burnished metal plate (copper at first, later steel), the line engravers created V-shaped furrows which shifted smoothly from thin to thick and back again, not only along the surface but in depth below the surface. Engraving, or "pushing" the tool, encounters the intractability of the metal in a way that encouraged the development of comparatively ordered and methodically codified (what Ivins called "rationalized") schemata for representation. A portion of a recipe for such methodical codes follows:

Technological Considerations

> Let us suppose that the engraver wishes to reproduce a half-draped figure. After making a drawing of it, he traces this drawing upon the copper or steel, marking by a succession of points, the contours of the figures, the strongest shadows, even the half tints. Then with the graver, he masses the shadows by means of a series of cuttings that are called *first,* and which, following the projections and depressions of the muscles or folds, become more slender, and are further apart near the light, while they are crowded together and thickened in the shadows.[26] This first work not sufficing . . . the engraver blots out the white by crossing the first lines with more slender *second* lines. . . . Sometimes instead of crossing the first, the engraver slips in intercalary lines which, allowing the passage of slender threads of light, suit the imitation of polished, shining bodies.
>
> According as the second lines cross the first obliquely or at right angles, they produce lozenges or squares that may be cut anew by a third line. All these crossings form little luminous triangles that prevent the shadows from growing heavy. . . . The lozenge, when oblong, produces a sort of undulation

PLATE 5. *Major Ringgold Mortally Wounded.* *Originally, black-line combined with white-line wood engraving; reproduced here the same size as either an electrotype of the original block, or a photomechanical line engraving made from a print of the original which appeared early in the 1850s, in Henry Northrup,* The New Century History of Our Country (*Philadelphia: Moore, 1900*), *from the copy owned by E. Jussim.*

not suitable for flesh, making it resemble a moired ribbon, but in drapery it gives the aspect of cloth hot pressed.[27]

That lozenge is all too obvious in "The Strawberry Girl," so obvious that it is difficult to believe that a magnifying glass applied to the two largest faces in "Lionel Lincoln" will reveal precisely the same kind of lozenges, produced in exactly the same manner. At a distance of about 12 inches, the crisscrossed lines and center flicks which form the lozenges are well-nigh subliminal. The intractable metal, steel, was dense enough to maintain the V-shaped furrows even very lightly and narrowly applied.

We should note here that our photographic copy of the original steel engraving can only hint at one of its most important code characteristics: the varying density of ink, a dimension of added light and shade which no relief process can match. If we compare "Lionel Lincoln" with Plate 5, "Major Ringgold Mortally Wounded," we will see not only the differing capabilities for illusion of the two media, but the limitations of black-line wood engraving, which (like the woodcut) could rely only on flat black areas suitable for the stamping character of the printing press. Metal line engraving, like all intaglio media, can summon up the added resources of a thick-

and-thin deposit of ink. Even without this added dimension, the one-stroke positive black-line manipulation of the steel engraving far exceeded the two-stroke-for-each-side-of-a-black-line manipulation of black-line wood engraving for high density detail, and, just as importantly, for variety of texture. Note how skillfully the engraver of the Darley illustration, Plate 6, uses pure line to model and describe the solidity of legs, boots, coats.

In our previously quoted recipe for this method, by Charles Blanc in 1874, the theory behind what he called the first and second lines was perhaps better expressed by a writer who was still paying attention to such problems at the very moment when phototechnology was permanently displacing the hand crafts. In 1892, John Whitfield Harland wrote:

> Line is capable of expressing the perspective of all surfaces. . . . If the outlines of a table or other receding surface be drawn, and then horizontal lines be ruled, commencing with the most distant edge, in a very light fine line, gradually making the lines thicker and further apart until the whole surface is covered, it will at once be apparent that the fine lines look much further off than the nearer part where the lines are bolder.[28]

PLATE 6. *Lionel Lincoln. Steel engraving by Thomas Phillibrown, from a drawing by F. O. C. Darley. Reproduced here the same size as the frontispiece of J. Fenimore Cooper,* Lionel Lincoln *(New York: Townsend, 1859), from the copy owned by E. Jussim.*

Harland's theorizing sounds very like Gibson's:

> . . . the object itself is imagined to be covered with lines equidistant and equal in breadth. This great fundamental principle is capable of endless extension, for every curved surface or plane, no matter at what angle it is presented to the eye, must be treated exactly in the same manner. Undulating surfaces obey the same law, each part of such being in reality part of a curved surface. A rough surface is simply an agglomeration of small surfaces at various angles to one another. Folds in drapery are nothing more or less than curved or undulating surfaces, and must be expressed in line perspectively correct.[29]

A perfect model of the theory could be constructed as follows:

> Suppose a bust to be carved in wood of a portrait, head and face, and the wood in which it was carved to be alternately composed of thin veneers of black and white wood alternately in layers. These veneers could represent our ideal lines, and a photograph of this bust would give precisely all the varied undulations or modellings for the engravers to follow . . . the lines would again have to be thickened or thinned in an exaggerated manner, so as to also express the proportionate amount of light and shade, as well as the direction and the perspective undulations.[30]

Note that in the last paragraph a "photograph of this bust" is being suggested to perform the most basic codification of *all* the known graphic media: to translate a three-dimensional real object into the two dimensions of ink on flat paper.

The most noticeable textural differentiation in "Lionel Lincoln" occurs between the horse and all the other objects in the picture. The horse is *stippled,* but a magnifying glass soon reveals that his overall texture was created with short flicks or interrupted lines which follow the projections of the muscles or mold their roundness by crossing horizontally to the axis of each form. This particular kind of "stippling" with flicks of the burin was superseded by a far faster method which offered special advantages for our "lovely ladies." Some of those advantages can be observed by briefly reexamining Plate 3.

"Castella" was produced in one physical channel (a metal plate) by two different manipulations: stipple *etching*[31] for the flesh and amorphous background, and line *engraving* for the hair and cloth, as well as for the firm accents around the eyes and mouth.

Dots, "coarser or further apart, or finer and closer together, according to the strength and darkness, or the delicacy and light . . ."[32] constitute the major code of "Castella," permitting the smoothest textural gradient which competed with mezzotint for subtlety of chiaroscuro and subliminality. (Compare "Castella" with "Forget-Me-Not.") But, since *dots* could not serve to indicate the typical texture of hair, *line* was called upon. Channels, or the physical carriers of codes, do not necessarily limit the variety of codes. Indeed, it became typical of the nineteenth century to indulge in such a multiplicity of codes on one piece of metal that it is almost impossible to judge by what physical manipulations certain illustrations were produced. Yet, it may be a truism to note that media tend to become identified with a specific range of codes, and we shall see in the chapter on William Hamilton Gibson that it was not a simple matter for the practitioners of one code to relinquish or to change what they consider to be "appropriate."

To reproduce the painting by Henry Inman, the engraver Parker, pointed his dots through to the surface of a copper plate which had been prepared with an acid resist, using one or two sharp instruments bound tightly together. The plate was then exposed to acid, and the dots etched to the desired depth. After augmenting various dots with a special curved graver, the lines for the hair and cloth accents were incised. Again, as with "Forget-Me-Not" and "The Strawberry Girl," a special intaglio press had to be employed to squeeze the ink from the pits and furrows onto heavy damp paper, and again, bound as "prints" into body text, in this case, *The Magnolia for 1837.*

> In portraits . . . stipple found its most appropriate application, its peculiar soft qualities appearing to best advantage in lighter tones. But it has also been employed to reproduce paintings by old masters, where its weakness in expressing variety of color and texture is more apparent.[33]

Weak or not, its success in chiaroscuro effects on flesh sustained stipple etching as the typical biographic portrait medium of the nineteenth century in America. From the all-stipple portraits of *Delaplaine's Repository* (1815), through the *National Portrait Gallery* (1834–1839), with its stipple faces and engraved clothing, on into Harriet Beecher Stowe's *Men of Our Times* (1868), and as the steel-engraved frontispiece for many a distinguished biography of the 1880s, stipple was so unsurpassed for facial modulations that it was used to reproduce portraits based on both daguerreotypes and photographs.

Commentary

Whatever their individual excellences in dealing with the problems of illusion, neither "Castella" nor "The Strawberry Girl" transmit the characteristics of their originals, namely, the paintings by Inman and Deconinck which they purport to reproduce. True, the iconography is presented to us: a girl in such and such a costume and in such and such a pose; but we cannot begin to guess whether Inman used transparent glazes or Deconinck painted thick impasto strokes. We must recognize, therefore, that for all intents and purposes, no matter how detailed and finished their originals were, the painters of these two "lovely ladies" merely supplied the designs for the engravers. *It is the engravers' pictures which we see, not the picture painted by the original artist.* We shall be concerned to see whether or not phototechnology could improve upon this situation, as William Ivins strongly contended it did.

Whatever their individual deficiencies in terms of our four Gibsonian criteria, by comparison with "Lady Geraldine" (or "Major Ringgold"), "Castella" and "The Strawberry Girl" (and "Lionel Lincoln") represent tremendous human achievements on the road to high fidelity transmission of visual messages. They can help us to understand the justice of one of Ivins' contentions:

> The principal function of illustration has been the conveyance of information. The graphic processes and techniques have grown and developed to the end of conveying information. The illustration that has contained the greatest amount of information, i.e. of detail, has been the one most in demand. As a result of this, the graphic processes have shown an ever increasing fineness of texture.[34]

Pair III. "Sarah Bernhardt" and "Mme. Dorus Gras"

Three of the codes thus far examined were produced by human hands: routing wood ("Lady Geraldine"), incising V-shaped troughs in metal ("The Strawberry Girl" and the hair in "Castella"), and scraping down the

Autographic Spontaneity and Chemistry

Bastien-Lepage pinx.

R de Los Rios sc.

PLATE 7. *Portrait of Madame Sarah Bernhardt.* *Etching by de Los Rios, from a painting by Bastien-Lepage. Reproduced here the same size as Plate XVI in John M. Mollett,* Etched Examples of Paintings Old and New *(London: Sampson Low, 1885), from the copy owned by the Forbes Library.*

raised walls of minute metal burrs ("Forget-Me-Not"). The fourth created its dots first by the delicate pressure of a pointed tool downward through a thin layer of acid resist until bare metal was touched, and second, by exposing those dots to the action of an acid. This represents the first application in the graphic arts of chemistry for its labor-saving action, and the corrosive action of various acids is still very much a part of modern graphic technology. Indeed, corrosive acid may be said to provide the indispensable mechanizing, or automating, element in two of the major photographic technologies (halftone process engraving, and photogravure).

"Sarah Bernhardt" (Plate 7) exemplifies the spontaneous dash and rush of personal gesture which etching made possible. Instead of the laborious pushing of the burin to rout out V-shaped furrows, now thick, now thin, now shaved from the top layer of the metal, now gouged deeply into the metal, the hand of the artist can skim over the surface, much as it does with a pencil or certain pens.

> It will be seen that in etching, where a blunt instrument is employed to skate over the surface of the plate, removing the covering of the ground but not penetrating the metal below, there can be no emphasis from the action of the hand in drawing. Provided that the touch be firm enough to remove all the wax, so that the acid may reach the metal at all, the strength of line and "colour" is controlled entirely by the *mordant,* and contrast in depth depends upon the length of time that some parts are permitted to bite in relation to other parts. This is controlled as a rule by "stopping-out" those parts which have been sufficiently bitten, by covering them with an acid-proof varnish; then continuing the biting of the unprotected parts, and so on to the last and heaviest bitings of all. In etching, therefore, there can be no "touch." [35]

If there can be no "touch," as E. S. Lumsden insists, then we must more than ever admire the etcher de Los Rios for his bravura treatment of "Sarah Bernhardt." Any reader who knows anything about the tempestuous career of the actress, Madame Sarah Bernhardt, can scarcely disagree that her temperament suited not only the bravura treatment by de Los Rios but the essentially bravura character of etching (in the following, called aquafortis) itself:

> As the graver with its regular steps, its methodical elegance, befits solemn compositions, ideal figures and the nude, so aquafortis in its capricious march, suits familiar or rustic things, savage landscapes, picturesque ruins. . . . The graver renders by slow strokes the chefs d'oeuvres of sculpture and monumental painting; the aquafortis recalls . . . the varied phenomena of real life, or the fancies of a day. The graver, in a word, corresponds to the majesty of art and the severe eloquence of drawing; the aquafortis represents improvisation, liberty and color. . . . Aquafortis . . . attaches itself from choice to all that is irregular, fantastic, unfinished, or in ruins. [36]

The editor of the book in which the etching of the portrait of Sarah Bernhardt appeared remarked:

> Evidently in this extraordinary portrait, characteristic rather than beautiful, we have a record rather of the eccentricities than of the genius and personal attractions of the gifted artist whom it is intended to represent. . . . The half-closed, expressionless eyes, the open mouth, the ungraceful attitude, the hideous bunch of hair, are not to be compensated by the skillful execution of detail. The artist appears here as one of those who, taking the most material view of his art, cares nothing for the expression of genius and intellectual beauty in a comparison with the delicate and skillful elaboration of textures. [37]

The extraordinary thing about this statement is that we cannot be sure whether the editor is chastising the *painter,* Bastien-Lepage, or the *etcher,* de Los Rios, although the context of the statement indicates clearly that it is the *etcher* who is being condemned *as if* he were the painter! But we know nothing of the textures of the original. We have only the brilliant textures of the etching, for surely the painter did not stripe Madame Bernhardt's face—or did he? Mollett's comment is typical, however, and should serve to warn us that it is extremely easy to mistake a codified transmission for the original of the message; this is a major problem in all communications, of a significance only beginning to be recognized, for, as William Ivins suggested: ". . . at any given moment the accepted report of an event is of greater importance than the event, for what we think about and act upon is the symbolic report and not the concrete event itself." [38]

Much of our exploration will be concerned with presenting evidence which tends to demonstrate that photography was instrumental in making us aware that there is a difference, and a vastly important one, between making a creative statement, such as de Los Rios is here making about an oil painting, and making a statement of fact.

"Aquafortis . . . attaches itself from choice to all that is irregular, fantastic . . ." as Blanc said. But it is not *from choice* at all. Although codes can be interchanged to a considerable degree from channel to channel, there are some codes which are almost uniquely wedded to their physical carriers. Such is pure line etching, the limitations of which were justly described by Philip Hamerton:

> The strong points of etching in comparison with other arts are its great freedom, precision and power. Its weak points may be reduced to a single head. The accurate subdivisions of delicate tones, or, in two words, perfect tonality, is very difficult in etching; so that perfect modelling is very rare in the art. . . .[39]

Specifically, pure line etching usually represents forms by (a) direction of line to create contour; (b) blank, or white areas, outlined with varying thickness of line and placed against massed lines which stand for midtones; (c) a kind of aerial perspective, hinted at by Blanc and Harland: that the thinner of two lines placed side by side will appear further away, as the eye tends to interpret smaller objects as being more distant from it than larger objects; and (d) black masses placed against paler tones, or against pale outline structures, so the darker object tends to be interpreted as being closer to the eye than the lighter object, especially if the principal of overlapping planes is used. Such means could not compete with stipple etching.

No matter how "free" and autographic line etching was, and even adding stipple to its repertory, or the chalklike capabilities of so-called "soft-ground" etching, the medium had its distinct limitations for reproduction, and, in terms of Gibsonian illusionism, definite limitations for autographic statements about three-dimensional objects.

Further Application of Acid as a Labor-Saving Device

An ingenious application of the principles of etching secured the best solution of its time—the mid-eighteenth century—to "the long endeavor of the reproductive engraver to represent tone otherwise than by webs of lines." [40] Aquatint, as it was called for its superior capabilities in the imitation of the textures of watercolor drawings, speeded the production of tints far beyond either mezzotint or stipple, for large flat areas could be etched rapidly: "Minute particles of a resinous substance are deposited on a copper plate. The latter is then placed in a bath of acid, which eats into the copper wherever it is not protected by the resinous particles." [41] Each of the two ways of applying the "resinous substance" will be seen as having vast importance to the future of phototechnology:

Method 1: "A fine powder is allowed to settle on the plate inside of a box in which it has been stirred up and thrown into the air by a special contrivance. The quantity of powder may be regulated by taking the plate out, covering with paper the portions which have been sufficiently powdered, and then replacing it in the box." [42]

Method 2: ". . . the particles [of resin] are held in suspension in alcohol which is poured over the plate. As this coating dries, it crackles, leaving little fissures." [43]

In both methods, the acid bath is the same. The acid bath produced minute pits or dots or irregular fine webs of crackles (like a sun-baked mud flat) over any surface prepared with the resin. The longer the acid bath, the deeper the pits, and the more ink will be deposited. Producing flat tints, "rather sharply circumscribed and consequently without gradation," [44] aquatint could not provide delicate transitions or well-modulated chiaroscuro. But, since it could provide the opportunity for layers of tints, in separate colors if desired, it greatly enlarged the vocabulary of graphic communication. With plate capacity large enough to accommodate even the grand designs of Audubon's *Birds of America* (1830–1839), it was immediately pressed into use for English book publishing and print manufacture, especially for street views (as in *The Microcosm of London*), and was widely used in costume books, sporting albums, and for reproductions in such works as the *Liber Studiorum* of Claude Lorrain (republished in 1840). In America, "the art was not firmly established until John Hill came to New York (from London) in 1816." [45] Neither easily autographic nor type-compatible, as it was an intaglio process, aquatint saw little service in American book publishing beyond contributing to mixed media illustrations in which it provided the basic division of light and dark for purposes of hand coloring. Nevertheless, for the purposes of our discussion, aquatint was perhaps the most important single advance in the graphic arts before lithography, for the idea of chemically manipulating fine-grained surfaces for the direct production of images was a necessary precedent for lithography, and, ultimately, for phototechnology.

"Madame Dorus Gras" (Plate 8) has been waiting discreetly while the center of the stage has been preempted by "Sarah Bernhardt." Yet the modest bourgeoise represents the ultimate, and almost miraculous, breakthrough of the graphic arts into the duplication, as opposed to the reproduction (or translation), of images. Reduced to its simplest terms, "Madame Dorus Gras" came and posed for the artist, Charles Vogt, who codified the young lady directly from life onto a replicating surface:

Direct Production of Images: Lithography

> The drawing is applied with a greasy crayon or tusche to a calcium carbonate stone — which can either be polished smooth or left with a granular surface. After it has been drawn on, the surface is covered with a solution of gum arabic containing a small quantity of nitric acid. When this is dry, the surface gum . . . is washed off. Then the damp stone is rolled [with ink], but only the drawing receives the ink; the other parts repel it. In other words, the process relies on the natural antipathy of grease to water. [46]

This deceptively simple process, for which Alois Senefelder labored so many years before he discovered it in 1796, was the result of a search for a

PLATE 8. ***Madame Dorus Gras.*** *Lith-ograph by Ch. Vogt from life. Reproduced here the same size as a plate of unknown provenance, owned by the Forbes Library.*

prosaic labor-saving device for the publication of musical scores. The versatility of the medium is so enormous that it has probably not been completely exploited even to this day. The range of codes is unbelievable, compared to other media, since the codes of almost any other medium can be either duplicated directly by the transfer method (shortly to be described) or closely imitated, depending on different treatments of the carrier. If toothed stone is used, with grease crayon, "Mme. Dorus Gras" is the result. If polished stone is used, with a thick ink called tusche, drawings with pen-and-ink or brush are facilely rendered; indeed, the hair net which Mme. Gras wears, and the accents around her flowered coiffure, her eyes, touches on the brooch, are undoubtedly rendered with tusche, which permitted jet black, untextured effects. If the stone is prepared with gum and acid before drawing, and wetted thoroughly, its entire surface will reject ink; therefore, scratching through the preparation will produce lines which *will* accept ink. Drawings produced in this manner will print black on white paper, just as if they had been drawn positively, and often closely resemble the swelling thick-and-thin line of metal engraving. This incised version of lithography, or pseudoengraving, was used with stunning success by Felix Darley, whose fame rested in great measure upon a series of large albums of outline drawings, like the *Scenes of Indian Life* (1843), and the *Compositions* published to accompany Washington Irving's *Legend of Sleepy Hollow* and Judd's *Margaret* (1856).

Lithography is so versatile that etching grounds laid upon the stone will permit of direct etching techniques, including aquatinting. Most importantly, the transfer process expanded the potentialities of the medium far beyond the *duplication* of designs drawn upon the stone, into the realm of reproduction, or *replication* of other media.

> The transfer process is also applied to place on the stone characters which have been written with a pen in the ordinary manner on prepared paper. In this way a person's handwriting is so accurately reproduced in the impressions that it is often very difficult to detect the interposition of the lithographic stone, and the impression often passes as the immediate production of the writer's pen. It is obvious that drawings etched with the pen on transfer-paper can be printed from in the same manner. And line engravings, which have been originally produced by cutting hollow lines on polished plates of copper, can be printed lithographically by transferring an impression to the stone. By transfer also the impressions of raised types or of woodcuts can be printed when desirable.[47]

Robert Routledge describes the process in detail:

> The process of *transferring* is practiced by the aid of a certain paper specially prepared by a coating of paste. On this a proof is taken from the original drawing on the stone, and the still moist sheet is then applied to another stone, with the face downwards, and passed under the press. The effect of the pressure is to cause the adherence of the layer of paste to the stone; and when the paper has been thoroughly wetted at the back, it may be removed, leaving the paste still adhering to the stone, with the impression beneath it. When water is applied, the paste is washed off, while the ink of the impression remains attached to the stone, there reproducing the design drawn on the first stone. . . . The transferred drawing may be made to yield another transfer, and so on indefinitely. . . . In this way as many as 70,000 copies have been taken from a single drawing without there showing any marked difference in the character of the impressions.[48]

We should note here that prepared zinc often substituted for the heavy stones, and while it was somewhat harsher in overall effect, it was otherwise capable of almost every effect of lithography, perfectly adapted to speedy reproduction of line work.

Although transfer paper and the entire transfer process were not really perfected until the third quarter of the nineteenth century, the transferable capabilities of the process were immense, and the fact that it could reproduce the impressions of raised types or woodcuts had a tremendous and still unappreciated impact on the development of the nineteenth-century book into an inexpensive mass medium, especially after photographic technologies were available to mechanize the transfer of already printed matter into new editions.

Pure line, crosshatching, shading, a wide range of halftones, pure blacks, the codes of other media through transfer, all combined to make lithography an outstanding medium for information transfer as well as for direct autographic self-expression. If it could not duplicate the rich, embossed character of the intaglio methods, it could at least reproduce what had been drawn in them, as it would for the etchings of Cruikshank and Phiz in book illustration.[49] In the most popular and widespread technique, the crayon manner, it is true that the graininess of the stone tends to impose similar textural surfaces on all forms, and that exceptional ability is needed to overcome this slight drawback.

From the first, lithography had been put to work "to make faithful reproductions of art treasures available to the public fairly cheaply,"[50] and it soon attracted the attention of some of the greatest artists of the century, notably Daumier, Gericault, and Delacroix. In the creation of his magnificent lithographic illustrations for Goethe's *Faust* (Paris, 1827), Delacroix is considered to have "originated the pictorial interpretation of literary works."[51]

Lithographic illustration in America was innocent of any such extraordinary achievements before the Civil War, however widespread became its acceptance for commercial purposes, for the framing prints of Currier and Ives, or as chromolithographed frontispieces for the myriad gift albums. The first American lithograph was a small sketch in the *Analectic Magazine* for July, 1819. The *Port Folio* occasionally carried small lithographs of landscapes, and certainly the painter Henry Inman (see Plate 3, "Castella") who contributed heavily to the gift albums, mastered the art of small portraiture suitable for book illustration. "One might have expected work of this quality to compete formidably with the popular steel engraving, but the fashion was too strongly set to be easily changed, and lithography was long regarded either as a curiosity or as a convenience for commercial reproduction."[52]

Color lithography in American books was primarily a post-photographic phenomenon, "the first fully illustrated book by this process in the United States, 'Wild Scenes and Wild Hunters'"[53] not appearing until Max Rosenthal's chromolithographic plates were perfected in Philadelphia in 1849. Chromolithography is discussed further in a unified section on color codes in Chapter 3.

Commentary   If the autographic spontaneity of a medium like pure line etching was a stunning addition to the range of artistic alternatives for self-expression, the technological limitations of the medium prevented its use for high fidelity information transfer, since the codes available or possible could not imitate the dense structure of "natural" effects. A more fragile medium than metal line engraving, etching was more suited to deluxe editions than to mass publication, especially since the ink deposit demanded good quality paper, preferably with a high rag content. It was lithography that replicated the etchings of Cruikshank in American editions of Dickens, lithography through the transfer process. Both autographic and reproductive, lithography became the vehicle for simultaneous typographic and illustrative materials, with the serious limitation that it could not, before photography, duplicate the extensive textural differentiations or delicate chiaroscuro of oil paintings.

That lithography did not see more service in American book publishing before the Civil War was because of a scarcity of trained technicians and a predisposition of public and publisher alike to already established visual codes and to inexpensive manufacturing procedures.

SUMMARY: THE MAJOR CODES OF PREPHOTOTECHNOLOGY

Our six "lovely ladies" and two "bold soldiers" have introduced us to the characteristics of the most prevalent codes used by the graphic arts before photography. Whether produced by hand or with the aid of chemistry, each code manifested certain strengths or inadequacies with reference to the imitation of the textural gradients, chiaroscuro, and modulations of surface and contour of Nature. Even the most versatile medium, lithography, had technological limitations, most particularly in the areas of textural differentiation and perfect modeling of chiaroscuro. Yet lithography could perform the miracle which no other graphic art before it could perform: to directly duplicate the effects of other media, through the transfer process—provided (and this is crucial) that these media were primarily in *line and dot codes.*

Lithography was such a major advance over the limitations of other media that William Ivins called its effects: THE TYRANNY BROKEN.[54] It offered to the autographic artist the ability to create a print that would be practically identical with his original. Depending on his talents and inclinations, it provided a superb range of tones between white, gray, and black, with the possibilities of working in a sketchy or tightly modeled manner. But most importantly, it seemed to be promising an almost "pure" method of communication:

> It completely did away with any need for the translator-middle-man engraver with his inevitable systematized grammar and syntax of linear webbing. Its defect was that, like the copper-plate processes, it had to be printed in a different press than that which printed type, and thus called for two separate printings if it were to be used as a book illustration.[55]

It has already been noted that it was possible to take proofs from metal type and transfer the coded sounds we call words onto either stone or prepared zinc; although two processes were combined, lithographically printed books were one-step processes. But that is a minor cavil with Ivins. There is a more important question.

Were all our "lovely ladies" produced by a *"translator-middle-man engraver with his inevitable systematized grammar and syntax of linear webbing?"* Not "Madame Dorus Gras," to be sure; she was a lithograph codified directly from the model. All the others happen to be two-step codifications, with an artist providing the primary codification, or design, and an engraver recodifying for the technology. But can we really accuse either "Castella" or "Forget-Me-Not" of representing "systematized grammar and syntax of linear webbing"? It has been mentioned before that both the stipple engraving or the stipple etching and the mezzotint possessed significant qualities for illusion. Their codes were subliminal, the mezzotint possessing no visible, separable code elements even under a ten-power magnifying glass.

Even "Sarah Bernhardt" relied more upon imitative strokes than on a "systematized grammar and syntax of linear webbing." Surely Ivins was mistaken, or else guilty of a curious unscholarly myopia, in insisting that all media, save lithography (and later, photography), are cursed with the close-up convolutions, lozenges, and other peculiarities of "The Strawberry Girl." Even those, when reduced to the scale and distancing of "Lionel Lincoln," prove to possess subliminal characteristics which contribute to at least partial illusion.

If there already existed codes with subliminal characteristics which could tolerably well imitate the effects of Nature, and if lithography had provided the release from an interference on the part of the engraver, then there could remain but one exclusive contribution to be provided by the invention of photography: the elimination of the artist as the primary codifier of information.

The Major Codes of Phototechnology and Their Development as Publishing Media

Photography is the blackening and decomposition of a salt by *some* of the solar rays . . . it is *not* drawing by light, and the word photography is a misnomer.[1]

The nineteenth century began by believing that what was reasonable was true and it wound up believing that what it saw a photograph of was true—from the finish of a horse race to the nebulae in the sky.[2]

We must pause before proceeding to examine the individual phototechnological processes in terms of a second series of "lovely ladies," since they can be more profitably explored in the context of their interrelationships with the demands of publishing. In effect, photography could not serve the mass manufacture of visual messages integrated with sound-into-typographic-code texts until it had been transformed from the mere "blackening and decomposition of a salt" [3] into a medium compatible with printer's ink. So that we can better understand why such a transformation was necessary, let us review the prior relationship of the graphic arts to publishing.

THE GRAPHIC ARTS AND PUBLISHING

The technological processes which we generally label *photography* appeared at a moment in history when, as we saw with our first series of "lovely ladies," the graphic arts in the Western world were already enjoying a considerable range of pictorial codes. Within his own lifetime, the pioneer of the inventions which led to the daguerreotype, Joseph Nicéphore Niépce (1765–1833), saw not only the full development and wide adoption of the mezzotint, the aquatint, and the stipple engraving, but also the introduction of white-line wood engraving, and the completely new and revolutionary process of lithography, a planographic chemical process offering numerical superiority of impressions through mechanical transference.

Lithography, moreover, could be adapted to reproducing typography. For book publishers, the lack of type-compatible intaglio processes had been a major economic concern, since pictorial communications multiplied by any of the intaglio methods had to be manufactured separately from verbal communications.

According to David Bland, much of the creative inventiveness of the eighteenth century in the graphic arts began with a fashion indulged by both French and English artists, of

> . . . issuing volumes of reproductions of paintings. . . . For the first thirty years or so of the century, illustrations were more often than not a set of plates bound up with the text, their styles reminiscent of paintings, their relevance not immediately apparent.[4]

Encouraged by the profitable sale of prints to the middle classes, artists sought media which could reproduce the subtle chiaroscuro of oil paintings, or the crisp washes of watercolor, or the chalky freedom of crayon drawings.

But the publishers of prints did not suffer the technological restrictions of book publishers. A *print,* after all, is an individually manufactured impression in ink of a master plate, often pulled in limited editions on expensive paper. For a book publisher to utilize a print as an illustration, he could (a) mount it on his book pages; (b) sew the print into the book, treating it as a foreign body which must be grafted onto the structure of the binding; or (c) copy the print in a graphic medium which not only could be printed simultaneously with metal type, but which could reproduce adequately on the text paper selected for a specific publication.

It was by no means an automatic benefit to *book* publishers that the mezzotint was adept in chiaroscuro, or that the aquatint could be colored neatly, or that stipple was useful for portraits. What had plagued the book publisher since Gutenberg was the technological need to discover typographically compatible illustration media. As we shall see, the advent of photography did not automatically or altogether alleviate this problem, and several of the more delicate and aesthetically satisfying of the photo-technologies, like collotype and photogravure, raised as many problems as they solved.

While the lack of type-compatible media had not deterred seventeenth-century publishers from amalgamating prints and type pages into one unit, the eighteenth-century dissatisfaction with the aesthetic and technical disharmonies led to the desperate expedient embodied in John Pine's *Horace,* which was an attempt to create a harmonious whole by engraving both text and picture together on one plate. Engraving a *text,* however, was clearly a regression, a flight from the advantages of movable type, a return to the principles of the xylographic book, where text and picture were cut together out of blocks of wood to make a continuous relief printing surface. William Blake's ingenious expedient of drawing and writing on a copper plate by using the acid resist itself as the graphic medium, and then etching away the negative space around the forms drawn by the artist, was essentially the production of a "block book." In Blake's case, it was a solution to the private expense of movable metal type and its lack of unity with intaglio plates. Publishers who had access to the established manufacture of types were seeking the opposite goal; for their ordinary trade publications, they wanted type-compatible illustration media, and this demand for a relief medium dominated and ultimately conquered almost all other considerations.

Lithography, as we have noted, offered a solution to these dilemmas in an inexpensive form. Freshly inked reproduction proofs could be pulled from type blocks and transferred to the stone; the same stone could also transmit a line drawing, a crayon drawing, or a transfer from some other medium—*provided* a freshly inked reproduction proof could be pulled from a relief, intaglio, or other planographic surface. *If there was no way to supply greasy ink to the stone, there was no way to automatically transfer a previously printed picture.* The immediate stimulus for the development of the first successful process of photography was the goal of circumventing human intervention in the duplicative processes of lithography.

THE FIRST SUCCESSFUL PROCESS
OF PHOTOGRAPHY

Joseph Nicéphore Niépce was a generalist genius. Having applied himself to everything from one of the earliest steamboats to the production of dyes for artists' pastels, Niépce became excited by the commercial possibilities of lithography. He became obsessed, in fact, with "finding a substitute for the lithographic chalk with which the designs were drawn, and the almost fantastic idea took possession of his mind that they might be done by light itself." [5] Actually, there was nothing fantastic in such a notion, for the experiments with light-sensitive materials by Wedgwood and Davy, among others, were widely published, and Niépce was certainly keeping up with the advances in chemistry.

Since Niépce did not want to copy pictures by hand either on lithographic stones or on transfer paper, the latter marvel was of no use to him. One version of the story goes:

> When the craze for the newly invented art of lithography swept France, in 1813, it naturally attracted the attention of Niépce. Isidore [his] son, made the drawings on stone while his father attended to the chemical side. Not being able to obtain proper lithographic limestone locally, they soon changed over to pewter plates. The following year, Isidore joined the army, and Niépce père, *unable to draw well* [italics added], placed engravings made transparent, on plates coated with various light-sensitive varnishes of his own composition and exposed them to sunlight. Though these attempts do not seem to have been crowned with success, Niépce's ideas progressed beyond merely copying drawings to the thought of fixing the very image of Nature. Thus lithography led to what Niépce later terms "heliography"—sun-drawing.[6]

Niépce's fanatical devotion to bypassing that very autographic property which had so endeared lithography [7] to the early romantic French artists led him, after many failures with silver chloride salts, to the discovery that bitumen of Judea, an acid resist used both in etching and lithography, had two useful characteristics: (a) it hardened with exposure to light, and this exposure to light could be selectively controlled; and (b) what had not been exposed to light, and therefore not hardened, could be dissolved and washed away, leaving a slight relief surface of a design. With bitumen of Judea, Niépce succeeded in producing the first photomechanical pictorial statements; they were reproductions of engravings, not surprisingly. As Marshall McLuhan has noted, the content of the new medium is the old medium.[8]

Niépce was not satisfied. He became intrigued with a problem whose solution had eluded artists and inventors alike: the fixing of the image of the camera obscura, an instrument—essentially a box with a hole in one side, later fitted with a lens—which had been used for centuries for copying landscapes, portraits, and objects by tracing the images cast on paper, canvas, or even walls. By increasing the power of available lenses, and gradually increasing the sensitivity of the bitumen, Niépce at last secured what is considered to be the world's first photograph from Nature, most probably in 1826.

Fixing the image of the camera obscura had, meanwhile, also become the overpowering obsession of a noted artist and scenic illusionist, Louis Jacques Daguerre (1787–1851). Daguerre was not only the creator of the world-famous Diorama, an entertainment hall established in 1822, whose offerings were large-scale theatrical *trompe l'oeil* productions whose sole criterion of excellence became fidelity to Nature. He had also been one of the first contributors to "absolutely the most ambitious publication illustrated by lithography, in France—or in the world,"[9] Baron Taylor's *Voyages pittoresques et romantiques dans l'ancienne regime,* which commenced its long career in 1820. Daguerre may be considered to epitomize the spirit of his age, for the essence of the illusions he created in the Diorama were not only sentimental, grandiose, operatic, but they were famous for three-dimensional illusionism. Driven by his own needs to perfect some means of creating absolutely authentic, three-dimensional, optically correct vistas to amuse the public, Daguerre sought out Niépce, going into partnership with him in 1829. Just before Niépce's death in 1833, Daguerre discovered that "an image could be produced on a silver plate which had been exposed to the action of iodine";[10] after Niépce's death, Daguerre discovered—by a famous happy accident and much labor—the secrets of the latent image formed by light on an emulsion of silver iodide, and how to develop this latent image by exposure to mercury vapor.

Even before Daguerre announced his momentous discovery to the Academy of Sciences, his pictures were seen by another scientist-inventor-artist. In 1839, Samuel F. B. Morse, the American portrait painter and recent inventor of the electric telegraph, was in Paris to present his own remarkable transmitting device to the same Academy. Morse enthused to his brother about daguerreotypes:

> They are produced on a metallic surface, the principal pieces about 7 inches by 5, and they resemble aquatint engravings; for they are in simple chiaroscuro, and not in colors, but the exquisite minuteness of the delineation cannot be conceived. No painting or engraving ever approached it. . . . In a view up the street, the distant sign could be perceived, and the eye could just discern that there were lines of letters upon it. . . . By the assistance of a powerful lens which magnified fifty times . . . every letter was clearly and distinctly legible, and so also were the minutest breaks and lines in the walls of the buildings; and the pavements of the streets.[11]

A medium had been discovered which bypassed the artist and the engraver, relying upon Nature itself for codifying the message to be transmitted, and possessing characteristics far beyond the powers of normal vision.

In the midst of the wild and amazed enthusiasm which greeted Daguerre's announcement on both sides of the Atlantic, several drawbacks to the process were noted at once: (a) the image on the plate was fragile, and had to be protected by glass; (b) the image could be seen only by holding the plate at a certain angle; (c) the image was reversed (later corrected by installing a mirror in the camera itself); and (d) the image could not be used to reproduce itself directly. This latter characteristic meant that each daguerreotype was, of necessity, unique, each plate requiring a new exposure, while the goal of the graphic arts had been precisely to produce *one* plate which could print *many* exactly repeatable images. The daguerreotype, itself the child of the graphic arts, seemed to represent per se an absolutely sterile dead end for the graphic arts, a paradox which Joseph Nicéphore Niépce could not have anticipated.

Nothing daunted, inventors promptly began to seek methods of converting daguerreotypes into printing plates. On April 18, 1840, Dr. Joseph Berres (1796–1844), of Vienna, announced "the first publication with photo-mechanically produced illustrations," [12] the result of ingeniously etching solid silver daguerreotypes prepared with resist. The following year, Hippolyte Fizeau (1819–1896) produced facsimile printing plates by electrotyping daguerreotypes.

Two of Fizeau's photoetchings appeared in the *Excursions daguerriennes*,[13] one of the first of a long line of distinguished travel books illustrated directly or indirectly by a photographic process. The older graphic arts played their usual role, however:

> Most of the full-page illustrations are lithographed from daguerreotypes, some engraved on copper and some etched by hand. . . . There are others, however, which are produced by Fizeau's direct-etching process on metallic daguerreotype plates, although in part very extensively worked over by a copperplate engraver.[14]

The complex history of the interrelationships of photographic technologies with the graphic arts began, as it would continue, with a simultaneous interest in the capturing of the image of the three-dimensional world and the transformation of that image into printable surfaces.

NEGATIVE/POSITIVE PAPER PHOTOGRAPHY

In 1833, the year of Niépce's death, an Englishman named William Henry Fox Talbot (1800–1877) was on a tour of Europe with his family. A chemist and a "gentleman scientist" of sorts, he also enjoyed landscapes, and tried to copy the charming scenes of Italy with the aid of both the camera obscura and a totally unrelated instrument, the so-called camera lucida, which was essentially nothing but a prism on an extending support.[15] Like Niépce, he could not draw well, and, as he later related, in the frustration of his own artistic impotence, he was led to

> . . . reflect on the inimitable beauty of the pictures of Nature's painting which the glass lens of the camera throws upon the paper in its focus—fairy pictures, creations of a moment, and destined as rapidly to fade away. It was during these thoughts that the idea occurred to me how charming it would be if it were possible to cause these natural images to imprint themselves durably and remain fixed upon the paper. . . .[16]

As silver nitrate was known to be light-sensitive, Fox Talbot began to experiment with various silver compounds *on paper,* and, by so doing, instead of working with metal, Talbot went straight to the end product of all the previous graphic arts: an image which could be combined with text to make a book.[17] Finally he succeeded in producing a paper negative from which paper positives could be made. To accomplish this feat, he devised a tiny camera obscura which could focus intense sunlight so that an exposure of reasonable length could be achieved.[18] In August of 1835, before Daguerre had even discovered the latent image and subsequently the development of it, Fox Talbot produced what is called the "first paper negative and the second surviving photograph in the world." [19]

We might expect that Talbot would have rushed to publish such a fantastic discovery. But Fox Talbot was a gentleman of means; he was in no hurry. Four years passed in other pursuits, and it was with considerable shock that he learned of Daguerre's imminent pronouncements. Alarmed lest he lose his rights of priority of invention, Talbot hurriedly published his results. In absolute contradistinction to the foresightedness [20] and generosity of the French government, which paid Daguerre a pension for the right to make his process public, the English government permitted Fox Talbot to secure patents which were so restrictive that the possible benefits of paper photography in terms of public use and book illustration (and, therefore, mass distribution of a new kind of visual communication) were seriously delayed.[21] The effect of his strangulation over use of this first invention of his was to permit the dominance of the daguerreotype throughout Europe and America for more than a decade. In all fairness to Fox Talbot, however, we must applaud the genius who laid the foundation of modern photography: "a negative which can be used for the production of an unlimited number of positive copies."[22]

The daguerreotype had been a direct-positive process, that is, it had coded certain of the effects of Nature in a direct equivalence of light and dark. Fox Talbot's paper photography, on the other hand, used a negative code, whereby what was light in Nature darkened the salts on the paper, and what had been dark in Nature did not register. To make a positive, light again was used, through this paper negative, to do the same trick again; only this time the lights and darks reversed themselves, and a simulacrum of "Nature" appeared on the second sheet of paper. Invariably, during the early years of the so-called calotype process, the texture of the paper was visible, and the soft finish of the print paper produced fuzzy contours.

To promote the sale of licenses for his patent, and to demonstrate the superiority of his invention over Daguerre's in the matter of duplication and publication, Fox Talbot wrote and published what he called *The first photographically illustrated book. The Pencil of Nature,* issued in six parts, beginning June 22, 1844, and ending April 23, 1846. Since it has already been noted that *Excursions daguerriennes,* for one, had appeared in 1841–1842, and that it contained at least two photoetchings direct from Nature, and a considerable number of plates copied lithographically after daguerreotypes, we shall have to redefine Talbot's title. *The Pencil of Nature* was the first book of any importance which contained mounted positive prints made from negatives that had been produced by exposing a treated paper to the light focused by a camera obscura aimed at the three-dimensional world. This is precisely what we know today to be "photography"—yet, because we are so accustomed to the products of photographic technologies, we tend to confuse books whose illustrations mechanically reproduce "photography" with those in which photographic prints are actually mounted. We think of them both as "photographically illustrated." The two are not the same. But, to Talbot, to whom all of this was a new and bewildering miracle, it was perhaps legitimate to think of *The Pencil of Nature* as the "first photographically-illustrated book." He had no experience, nor had anyone else for that matter, with an entire book containing text and pictures which were paper object-symbols of the "real world."[23] The confusion attendant on the presentation of such a new medium to the public is exemplified by Talbot's insertion of a slip marked: "Notice to the Reader. . . . The plates in the present work are impressed by the agency of light alone, without any aid from the artist's pencil. They are the sun pictures themselves, and not, as some persons have imagined, engravings in imitation."[24]

Was this to answer public doubts that the pictures in *The Pencil of Nature* were truly unlike the steel engravings, copperplates, and lithographs in *Excursions daguerriennes,* and not mere copies after Nature studies? Or was this an indication of how far other graphic media, notably the mezzo-tint, had progressed toward well-developed chiaroscuro and the approximation of the texture of Nature's objects? Samuel F. B. Morse had even described the first daguerreotypes as resembling aquatint prints. We contend that Talbot's first calotypes can easily have been confused with mezzotints. Consider this late nineteenth-century opinion:

> Mezzotint appears of all processes the best adapted to reproduce photo-graphs, if it could in any way be utilized. . . . Mezzotint, before even the advent of the now obsolete daguerreotype. . . gave to the world the nearest and best expression of soft washes capable of being printed.[25]

Was it only Talbot's naiveté or a general public skepticism which occasioned his reassurance: "Groups of figures take no longer time to obtain than single figures would require, since the camera depicts them all at once, however numerous they may be." [26]

Since this was a characteristic of the daguerreotype as well—or of any light-drawing (photographic) process—we may infer that either Talbot was treating the daguerreotype as if it did not exist, or that he was genuinely bewildered and awed by the unexpected capabilities of his own invention. Or he may have been simply huckstering his own wares.

In *The Pencil of Nature*, Talbot demonstrated the wide range of applications of the paper print: architectural views, landscapes, photographs of sculpture, reproductions of engravings, photogenic [27] silhouettes of botanical specimens and fabrics; and, indeed, his book was a prophetic and accurate prediction of only a few of the future applications of his invention. In an advertisement of 1846 for the talbotype, or calotype as he also called it, he claimed that:

> *Authors* and *Publishers* will find the Photographic process in many cases far preferable to engraving for illustrating their Works, especially when faithful representations of Nature are sought, as this alone can be depended upon for accuracy.[28]

This statement was even more prophetic. Eventually, publishers were to insist on one or another "photographic process" for illustrating books and newspapers and periodicals. Quite literally and abruptly, with the appearance of *The Pencil of Nature*, the myriad graphic artists who had perfected the marvels of mezzotint, aquatint, copper and steel engraving, etching, wood engraving, lithography, and all the complex beauties of processes which we have perforce neglected to mention, e.g., the Baxter color processes, stood now in imminent danger of losing their livelihoods. What saved them from immediate catastrophe was a combination of unexpected technical dilemmas.

These dilemmas can be summarized as follows: (1) Each print had to be manufactured individually from separate sheets rather than from continuous rolls of paper; (2) pasting, mounting on text paper in manufactured books, ironing the prints dry, were all time consuming and exacting, therefore expensive; (3) like copperplate engravings or etchings, the prints were not part of a unified typographic form; therefore, like other prephotographic books produced by multiple processes (relief for text, intaglio for picture), there was no immediate technical advantage to using paper prints instead of other media, and the economic advantages of bypassing a hand engraver were balanced by other factors; (4) most importantly, if the prints were not washed properly, ensuring the removal of every last particle of silver iodine, the photograph would gradually fade away.[29] It was especially the threat of impermanency, coupled with Talbot's restrictive patents, which kept the paper photographic print from immediately driving all other black-and-white media out of the market.

Despite the understandable hesitancy of the public in buying books whose pictures might turn to blank pages, it has been estimated that at least one thousand books with mounted photographic prints for illustrations were published between 1844 and 1890.[30] But even Talbot saw the limitations of his first invention, and, along with many other scientists of the day, set to work to invent a permanent photography which would be printing-compatible.

"PERMANENT" PHOTOGRAPHY: "LOVELY LADIES" SERIES TWO

There were two basic avenues of pursuit open to Talbot and his contemporaries. The first was simply to discover some superior chemistry for the original patent. Such a solution would not solve the problem of unifying picture and text. The second, with far-reaching implications, was to find some means of converting the photographic negative or positive into a printing channel. Publishing, which had developed reliably permanent printing inks and rapid presses which used rapidly moving rolls of paper, could settle for nothing less.

This chapter offers a second series of illustrations which have been selected as typical examples of the major codes of phototechnology. These include lovely ladies, couples, and a portrait of Abraham Lincoln which caused a sensation. The plates are as follows:

Heliotype: "Portrait from Life" (Plate 9)

Photogravure: "Benedick and Beatrice" (Plate 10)

White-line Tonal Wood Engraving via Photography-on-the-Block: "Modjeska as Juliet" engraved by Timothy Cole (Plate 11)

Facsimile Wood Engraving of Line Drawing via Photography-on-the-Block: "Portrait of A. Lincoln" engraved by Timothy Cole (Plate 12)

Moss Process Line Engraving: "The Princess Finds Her Prince" by Howard Pyle (Plate 13)

Heliotype Reproducing Lithography: "The Courtin'" by Winslow Homer (Plate 14)

Process Halftone Engraving: "Madame Modjeska as Juliet" (Plate 15)

Once again, these examples were selected to demonstrate the characteristics of the codes available to each medium and their capacities for illusion.

The Heliotype Process: "Portrait from Life"

Lithography Applied to Photography

This first of our second series was the outcome of an application of the very first approach to photography, by which Niépce succeeded in capitalizing on the characteristics of bitumen of Judea, noted earlier, that (a) it hardened with exposure to light, and this exposure could be selectively controlled by a camera; and (b) what had not been exposed to light, and therefore not hardened, could be dissolved away, leaving a slight relief surface of a design. In 1855, Alphonse Poitevin (1819–1882) introduced a method of obtaining permanent ink impressions of a photograph taken

from Nature using lithographic principles. He had discovered that a substance called "bichromated gelatine"

> . . . became not only insoluble when acted on by light, but also water
> repellent, whilst the parts unaffected by light retain their normal property
> of absorbing water. He found further that when such a coating, after exposure
> to a negative, was moistened and greasy lithographic ink applied, it adhered
> to those parts which had been acted on by light and which were water repel-
> lent, but not to those which were unaffected by light and therefore moist.[31]

Only partially successful in the first decade of application, Poitevin's
discovery nevertheless led to the development in 1868 of a trio of similar
processes which are generally called *collotype.*

> Collotype is a process by which a film of gelatine is made selective of either
> greasy ink or water so that it may be printed from in a lithographic manner.
> The gelatine is sensitized with a bichromate and *given a grain* [italics added] in
> drying. This sensitized gelatine is exposed under an ordinary photographic
> negative, washed and dried, and then treated somewhat similar to a litho-
> graphic stone, to which it shows corresponding properties.
> The results produced by Collotype printing can have *all the gradations of
> the photograph, from which it is difficult sometimes to distinguish it* [italics added]
> though it has the advantage that it is in permanent printing-ink, so that for
> fine book illustration and permanent records such as government publica-
> tions, and for small and choice editions of illustrated work, it cannot be ap-
> proached by typographic methods.[32]

Our "lovely lady" called "Portrait from Life" (Plate 9) was manufactured
by a modification of this collotype process:

> In the Heliotype, a modified collotype introduced by the London portrait
> photographer ERNEST EDWARDS (1837–1903) in December, 1869, the sensitive
> coating of bichromated gelatine, which contained chrome alum to harden it
> and prevent the unexposed gelatine from swelling, was formed on a waxed
> glass plate, and then stripped off. The film was given a short exposure on the
> *back* of the coating to harden it, either before or after exposure under a re-
> versed negative. It was attached by rubber solution to a pewter plate for
> development with warm water, and printing. Two printings were made—
> with thick ink for the shadows, and thin ink for the halftones. . . . One
> thousand five hundred impressions could be obtained from a single plate at
> the rate of 200–300 impressions a day.[33]

"Portrait from Life" was produced by exposing a sensitized gelatin film
to the light reflected from a "Lovely Lady" and converting it into lithography! It is perhaps difficult to accept the fact that such subliminality of
code was the result of a lithographic process, and perhaps even harder to
imagine how such a printing code could have been developed without the
precedent of the invention of lithography. The slight grain, introduced
into the gelatin for the purposes of breaking up the image into manageable
message units, hardly interferes with the transmission.

The first book illustrated by the heliotype process was Charles Darwin's
The Expression of the Emotions in Man and Animals (1872), with twenty plates
inserted mainly from negatives by the renowned narrative photographer,
O. G. Rejlander, who also posed for some of the more expressive pictures.
The utility of photography to the sciences was evident from the start, but
the heliotype had its own problems.

Like lithography, the heliotype could be used as a transfer process for
typography. Unfortunately, however, not only did the heliotype require
two printings, but each picture had to be printed separately from metal

PLATE 9. *Portrait from Life.* *Heliotype reproducing a photograph from life. Reproduced here the same size as Plate 13, in Ernest Edwards,* The Heliotype Process *(Boston: Osgood, 1876), from the copy in the Columbia University Graphic Arts Collection.*

PLATE 10. **Benedick and Beatrice.** *Goupil photogravure from a painting by H. Merle.*
Reproduced here the same size as the plate in Strahan and Walton, Selected Pictures from
Public and Private Collections in the United States (*Philadelphia: Barrie, 1888*),
from the copy owned by E. Jussim.

relief type. However beautiful the results, therefore, it was doomed to a short, active life, assisting, as we shall see, in the production of a most important American book. Its parent, the collotype, remains to this day a European-based manufacturing process for small special editions and art reproductions; apparently the humid climate of the United States has not favored collotype, as the process depends on the moisture-absorption of water by glue.

> The collographic processes have suffered more than any others from the mania for high-sounding names. The prints resulting from them have been dubbed gelatine prints—which, being English and simplest, would be better even than collographs or collotypes—phototypes, heliotypes, albertypes, autotypes, indotints, photophanes, glyptographs, and worse than all, *photogravures* [italics added] this latter in the attempt to make them pass for what they are not i.e., prints from intaglio plates. The beauty of the results . . . makes it evident that such deception is wholly unnecessary.[34]

These remarks lead up directly to a consideration of what might *photogravure* have to offer that heliotype did not, and how the intaglio methods fared under photography.

Photogravure: "Benedick and Beatrice"

Aquatint Applied to Photography

The "lovely lady" of Plate 10, "Benedick and Beatrice," is the ultimate development of Joseph Nicéphore Niépce's first copying success:

> When Nicéphore Niépce, in 1824, coated a metal plate with a solution of asphalt and exposed it to light under a positive engraving and then developed and etched that portrait of Cardinal d'Amboise, he had discovered the whole application of photography to intaglio engraving.[35]

"Photo-Aquatint" was the name given to the photogravure process in a historic exhibition at the Boston Museum of Fine Arts in 1892. The name went rapidly out of use, but the basis in aquatint remained. The following description will serve to remind us once again that some sort of grain or texture is necessary as a unit of coding:

> Gelatin bichromatized is the medium by means of which the photogravure plate is produced; but as the screen is not used in ordinary work, it is necessary to produce an ink holding grain in some way upon the plate. This is done by allowing a cloud of bitumen dust, raised inside a box, to settle upon the surface of a copper plate; it is fixed by heat, which, though insufficient to melt it, is enough to attach the fine grains to the plate. Over this prepared surface is laid the film of bichromatized gelatin, upon which is printed the subject through a glass positive; the usual hardening process takes place by the action of light, followed by a washing out of the unhardened portions of the gelatin. The plate is exposed to the action of ferric chloride, which attacks it most strongly in the least exposed parts, but which cannot eat it away in broad flat masses of dark, even in the non-exposed portions, owing to the existence of the bitumen granulation, which ensures the keeping of a grained surface even in the darkest passages.[36]

The grained message units of photogravure are far more densely packed than those even of the heliotype, and some photogravures yield more information upon enlargement than in the original size of the transmission. The heliotype, on the other hand, loses clarity when enlarged. (But the reader should remember that it has been necessary to screen the heliotypes and photogravures here presented, as there is no other way to transmit them. A magnifying glass here will prove misleading. The reference is to the originals.)

Stephen Horgan, one of the fathers of the rival medium, the so-called process halftone engraving, titled a chapter in his handbook: "PHOTO-GRAVURE. BY ALL ART LOVERS RECOGNIZED AS THE MOST BEAUTIFUL OF ALL PHOTOMECHANICAL PROCESSES." [37] It seems strange, therefore, that William Ivins mentions photogravure only once in his *Prints and Visual Communication,* and completely ignored it in his eulogy of process halftone. Yet plates like the "Benedick and Beatrice" were far more important in the history of art history in the late nineteenth century than any other process, and, more importantly, photogravure remains with us today as the intaglio process of such beauty and warmth of ink impression that book designers are willing to forego perfect typographic reproduction for the sake of reproducing pictures as richly as possible. Before the invention of photographic typography, however, the text of any verbal communication had still to be set in metal; reproduction proofs would be pulled and then photographically copied onto glass negatives. This was expensive; therefore, for most purposes, photogravure could not be considered perfectly type-compatible. Indeed, it was, like the heliotype, expensive to produce and difficult to print, often requiring duplicate plates to finish out a production run.

". . . up to the end of the century one photogravure plate cost as much as the printing of a whole edition of the same picture by one of the other reproduction processes, such as collotype or Woodburytype." [38] The beauties of "Benedick and Beatrice" were therefore beyond the reach of the ordinary trade publication, and were reserved for deluxe editions or folios of reproductions suitable for framing.

The Woodburytype: A Brilliant Detour into a Dead End

A short discussion of the woodburytype is included here without any example for the reader to view, since it is too important to ignore and not sufficiently different in its codes to need visual documentation. Long obsolete, the woodburytype was used extensively for book publication "from about 1875 to the end of the century." [39] The process was ingenious, involving the fact that lead metal is soft enough to receive an impression, even of a substance as seemingly fragile as a hardened gelatin relief plate—given sufficient pressure. An intaglio mold was created from this pressure. Colored gelatin was poured in; then paper was spread over it, with another application of pressure. "When set, the gelatine impression adhered firmly to the paper, and only required hardening in an alum bath. The resulting picture . . . consisted of coloured gelatine in relief, the thickest parts being the darkest." [40] The superlative continuous halftones of the woodburytype perhaps would have driven all other competitors from the market, save for its one failing. Like Talbot's photographic prints, it had to be mounted, and could not be printed directly on the page.

> The Woodburytype process offers valuable facilities for the production of copies of photographs in comparatively large numbers; but for the illustration of books this will not suffice, and we require a process which will give us prints in ink, capable of being inserted among the pages of a book without incongruity, or obvious unfitness for their position.[41]

The "Book Stereoscope" and Mounted Stereographs

The dual images of the stereoscopic print, which depend on a viewing instrument to fuse their two sides into one three-dimensional illusion, seem peculiarly unsuited to the printed page, yet the stereograph appeared in countless volumes, beginning with a book printed in 1858 which mounted both sides of the picture. This was Charles Piazzi Smyth's *Teneriffe, an Astronomer's Experiment,* in which the publisher, Mr. Lowell Reeve, offered for sale his convenient new invention, the *Book Stereoscope,* so that viewers could enjoy the stereographs as they were intended to be seen—in three dimensions. But despite such inventions, publishers usually transmitted the stereograph as if it were a single-view photograph, copying it into wood engraving for mass distribution in periodicals, or simply cutting the twin views apart and mounting them as halves. The tremendous impact of stereographs on nineteenth-century visual habits came through their use as slides, not as book illustration, even though examples of such book use continued into the twentieth century.

The Essential Problem for the Publisher

Mounting prints, no matter how permanent, was an unsatisfactory procedure for book publishing. Besides the expense of the additional labor involved, the weight of any object mounted in a book contributes materially to deterioration of the binding and of individual pages. The desire for a relief halftone process which could be printed simultaneously with raised metal types was not satisfied by the softness of the heliotype, the economy of the woodburytype, or the rich ink impressions of the intaglio photogravure. The problem in achieving such a relief halftone printing surface is evident in the following:

> It is, of course, an easy matter to make from a positive a negative, or from a negative a positive, broken up into isolated dots. We may draw lines on the original crossing one another, or we may perforate it, or we may lay some kind of netting upon it. . . . The result, however, will be a picture in *dots of equal size but differing in intensity,* that is to say, some black, some dark grey, some lighter grey, and so on. Here is a photograph of this kind made by Mr. Thomas Gaffield quite a number of years ago, before anyone, at least in this country, was thinking of half-tone relief blocks. It is distinctly *broken up into dots, but they are equal in size but different* only in intensity . . . a negative of this kind will not do for the making of relief blocks, since grey lines or dots will either not reproduce at all, or will be rotten, or will come up a solid black. . . . It was this experience, as we saw, that led to special methods of drawing for process work. What is wanted is a negative having dots not of the *same size and differing in intensity,* but on the contrary, *differing in size and of the same intensity.*[42]

As the woodblock had long served for the production of type-compatible pictures, it was logical that some attempt would be made to use it for cutting dots "differing in size and of the same intensity."

White-Line Wood Engraving via Photography-on-the Block: Timothy Cole's "Modjeska as Juliet"

Photography Applied to Wood Engraving

It may be surprising to learn that some of the same tools and exactly the same kind of woodblock, end-grain boxwood, were used to produce W. J. Linton's "Lady Geraldine" (Plate 1) and Timothy Cole's "Modjeska as Juliet" (Plate 11). The codes are so dissimilar that it would be extremely easy to ascribe entirely different channels. Obviously, there were significant variances, crucially so in the matter of an ideological posture toward the transmission of messages.

Linton engraved "Lady Geraldine" following a *drawing* on the block. Cole worked from a *photographic portrait* printed on the block, a portrait which was clearly the same as that which served for the process halftone engraving of Plate 15. Linton not only regarded himself as a creative artist following in the great black-line tradition of Dürer, but considered the work of the preliminary draftsman as a mere starting point for his own embellish-

PLATE 11. ***Modjeska as Juliet.*** *White-line wood engraving by Timothy Cole, from the photograph by Scholl. Reproduced here the same size as the plate on page 665, in* Scribner's Monthly, *March 1879; this was copied from W. J. Linton's* History of Wood-Engraving *(1882) in the Free Library of Philadelphia.*

ments. He was translating a symbolic statement without regard for illusion. Cole, on the other hand, was almost solely pursuing illusion, the illusion of Nature, with its variable textural gradients, chiaroscuro, undulating contours, and so on. His ideology might be considered allied with that of the mezzotinters: he removed the darks, "drawing" with white into the black — by using the graver to remove tiny slivers of wood, routing out dots and flicks to describe the *light falling on objects*. He worked with a fine magnifying glass to do this precise, patient routing, creating with a manual dexterity that is still amazing a very considerable range of blacks through grays to pure whites. The dots and flicks were of differing size, but, because the ink rolled over the block like a steamroller on a flat plane (with a few subtle distinctions too difficult to discuss at this point), they were of the same intensity. This meant, very simply, that the woodblock engraved by Timothy Cole went through the press with the type (or an electroplate of the entire form), receiving but one inking; the message about a photograph of Madame Modjeska, a famous nineteenth-century Polish actress, reached the public with only a few confusions about the braids in her coiffure and the exceptional soulfulness of her eyes.

Cole could do all this not only because he had invented an exquisite code for the transmission of photographs, but because he could work from the photography printed on the block, thus bypassing the need for a preliminary draftsman to transfer his own rendering of the photograph. There was a technical difficulty in this photography on wood: it "was to secure a material which would hold the sensitive silver salt to the wood and yet not impair the lines of the wood engraving itself." [43]

When photography-on-the-block was introduced shortly before the Civil War, the new process was used simply to facilitate the cutting of artist's designs.

> The method, which apparently was used quite extensively, was to photograph on glass with wet collodion in the usual way. The film was then stripped from the glass, transferred to the wood block and solvents employed to dissolve out the collodion. This left the black silver image upon the wood itself and served as the guide to the engraver. [44]

But after the war, when W. J. Linton arrived from England, engravers had already begun to insist that mere facsimile work was beneath the dignity of true professionals. We have already noted that "Lady Geraldine" bears the unique stamp of Linton's translation. Moreover, the new capability of transferring originals to wood opened a kind of technological Pandora's box:

> The very fact of photographing all kinds of subjects and textures on the wood, destroyed the old landmarks, and tempted the trying of anything the artist most desired. . . .
> The only limit in the matter was the ability to print the engraving when it reached the magazine presses. [45]

The artists of original illustrations no longer wanted to be confined to the demands of preparing copy that an engraver *could* transmit. As we will discuss this rivalry between two schools of wood engraving in our chapter on William Hamilton Gibson, we can observe now that this "trying of anything the artist most wanted" did not have the effect of liberating the engraver to do the same. On the contrary, the new freedom which photography-on-the-block provided in copying fictive illustration was put in the service of accuracy in the transmission of originals. That is, for the first time in history, there was an attempt to transmit by hand (albeit with the essential aid of photography) a message which dealt with more than just the iconography or subject matter of an illustration or painting. Suddenly there was the recognition, rather amazing, that an illustration or a painting was the original of a *message* to a mass audience, a message which had to be transmitted with all its particularities and individual textures. As William Ivins observed, without having documented this significant event himself:

> Up to that time very few people had been aware of the difference between pictorial expression and pictorial communication of statements of fact. The profound difference between creating something and making a statement about the quality and character of something had not been perceived.[46]

W. J. Linton had not perceived this difference; Cole had. Today we are so conditioned by photographic technologies that we take for granted that "reproductions" of pictures, whether of line or wash drawings or of oil paintings or photographs, will resemble the originals, but this alteration of perception and expectation represents a true revolution in human communication.

We can see some of the characteristic befuddlement which greeted this new perception in one of W. J. Linton's statements concerning what he believed was appropriate to wood engraving and what was not:

> Though I have placed Mr. Cole at the head of the new school, Mr. Juengling is its most remarkable exponent. With his name also . . . I find . . . the tendency to sacrifice form and meaning to mere chiaro-scuro, of which I am always complaining. A portrait of *Edison in his Workshop*, drawn by Muhrman (*Harper's Weekly*, Vol. XXIII, p. 601) may emphasize my meaning. The picture is effective and vigorously drawn. Edison is working at a charcoal fire. The rays of light are just as solid and tangible as the man's hair, while a glass bottle on the bench is as woolly as his coat, which again is no woolier than his face. In a small or hurried work no difference of material had perhaps been looked for. But in this front page of the paper, very elaborately engraved, with endless cross-line, black-and-white, we have a right to expect definition, detail, and some expression of material (not only of the material of the drawing, which may have been only a copy or photograph of our favorite crayon drawing, but of the differences that do subsist between light and hair and wood and glass and wool and flesh).[47]

What is so astonishing here is that Linton is acknowledging that the Muhrman is "our favorite crayon drawing." Yet he is demanding of the wood engraver, Juengling, that he deliver "definition, detail and some expression of material" not only of the material of the drawing itself, namely crayon and paper, but of the real materials which existed, the original models which Muhrman's artistic crayon codes had rendered in the specific characteristics of that medium. In other words, Linton is demanding that Juengling ignore the specific textures of the drawing which he was being paid to transmit via a wood engraving in order to transmit the real-life characteristics of what would have amounted to a photograph of the *original scene*. Juengling might have been happy to comply, except for the fact that the only reason he had been hired to make a wood engraving from a crayon drawing was that there had probably been no photograph available, and, even if one had been available, there was no way for *Harper's Weekly* to reproduce it without having a hand engraving made.

Timothy Cole was not engraving a crayon drawing for this portrait of "Modjeska as Juliet." He was engraving a photograph-on-the-block, bending his ingenuity to the characteristics of the photograph while keeping firmly in mind the demands of press runs in 1879. Cole had such unusual

PLATE 12. *Portrait of A. Lincoln.*
Facsimile of a pen-and-ink drawing by
Wyatt Eaton, engraved by Timothy Cole
via photography-on-the-block. Repro-
duced here the same size as the frontis-
piece, in Scribner's Monthly, *bound*
volume for November 1877–April 1878
(vol. 15), from the copy owned by E.
Jussim.

facility with transmitting the textures of originals that he had created quite a stir the year before:

> So many questions have been asked about the methods of producing the portrait of Lincoln, printed as a frontispiece to the Midwinter number, and so many theories have been set afloat as to "material" and "processes" that it may as well be told that Mr. Wyatt Eaton made the original drawing (from the photograph), less than half life-size, on white paper, with India ink, with a Chinese brush. This drawing was photographed on the block, and engraved by Mr. T. Cole, who engraved in the same number, "A Moose-Flight," "A Girl of the Mexican Camp," "A Wedding Under the Directory," and St. Gaudens' panel of "Angels." For its proper effect, the engraving should be held at a greater distance from the eye than is necessary with most magazine illustrations.[48]

Here was a photograph of President Lincoln which was redrawn by a portrait artist in pen and ink. This drawing was photographed on the block, and then facsimiled by a master wood engraver in the same code, a code apparently unsuited to our standard recommended distance for viewing. We can see the product of these various steps in Plate 12, "Portrait of A. Lincoln," by Wyatt Eaton, engraved by Timothy Cole. Why a pen-and-ink drawing, which is a statement coded in terms of pure black and white lines, flicks, and dots, had to be laboriously hand engraved when there was a photographic process which could accomplish the same objective easily and economically is difficult to understand.

MOSS PROCESS LINE ENGRAVING: HOWARD PYLE'S "THE PRINCESS FINDS HER PRINCE"

In the *Publishers' Weekly* for June 10, 1876 (p. 777), an advertisement read:

> Relief Plates: For Newspaper, Book and Catalogue Illustration, Engraved in hard Type metal by a new Photographic and Chemical Method, from all kinds of Prints, Pen-and-Ink drawings, Original designs, Photographs, &c. much cheaper than Wood-cuts. These plates have a printing surface as smooth as glass, the lines are deeper than those in hand-cut engravings, and we guarantee them to print perfectly clean and sharp, on wet or dry paper, and on any press where type or woodcuts can be so printed. Electrotypes or Stereotypes can be made from them in the usual way.

The man whose company published this advertisement is one of the neglected heroes of American graphic arts. John Calvin Moss (1838–1892), after a faltering start in 1871—the year of the founding of his Actinic Engraving Company—established the Photoengraving Company, destined to become the largest and most influential concern devoted to the various phototechnological inventions of its founder.

Ignored by most conventional publishing or printing histories, Moss deserves to be remembered not only for the Moss process, a method of reproducing line drawings (see Plate 13, "The Princess Finds Her Prince") but for training an entire generation of artists in the fine points of pen-and-ink drawing for reproduction, an accomplishment which will be discussed in detail in the chapters on "Illustrators and Photography" and on Pyle. The fact that the Moss process is largely unknown and certainly not featured in any histories of rare books has contributed to the profoundly mistaken idea that many of the pen-and-ink drawings of the 1870s and 1880s were reproduced in magazines by facsimile wood engraving, as in the Cole-Wyatt Eaton production. The most famous example of this confusion involves no less a celebrity of the book world than Howard Pyle's *Robin Hood*.

he Princess finds her Prince.

PLATE 13. *The Princess Finds Her Prince.* *Process line engraving from pen-and-ink drawing by Howard Pyle. Reproduced here the same size as the plate facing page 74, in Pyle's* The Wonder Clock *(New York: Harper, 1887), from a 1915 reissue owned by E. Jussim.*

The Moss line process had strict limitations, relying, in fact, on the principle presented earlier, that of having the capacity to reproduce dots of different size but of the same intensity. As a photographic process, resembling a European counterpart invented by Gillot, it partook of what Victor Strauss has called the *zone of interchangeability*, a phenomenon which can be illustrated as follows. Plate 14 offers "The Courtin'," a silhouette by Winslow Homer; the credit lines indicate that it was first printed from stone and then heliotyped by James Osgood, to appear, as it happens, in the sales catalog by Ernest Edwards for his heliotype process. The original of the Homer, then, was a lithograph. The heliotype, employing the principles of lithography, could copy these solid blacks without difficulty. The Moss line process could take this heliotype of a lithograph and re-reproduce it. In other words, three dissimilar processes could display exactly the same graphic characteristics.

However, another heliotype, the "Portrait from Life" (Plate 9), originally a photograph from Nature, could *not* be reproduced by the Moss *line* process without undergoing a translation into a line or dot code. The heliotype offered a superb range of halftones: subliminal microscopic dots which were of differing intensity, requiring one printing for the shadows and one for the lighter tones. Photographic portraits such as these were ordinarily given by Moss to one of his trained artists, in the form of photographic paper positives, so that they could be rendered in codes resembling copperplate or black-line engraving. Using pen and ink on the photo-

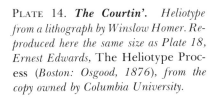

PLATE 14. ***The Courtin'.*** *Heliotype from a lithograph by Winslow Homer. Reproduced here the same size as Plate 18, Ernest Edwards,* The Heliotype Process *(Boston: Osgood, 1876), from the copy owned by Columbia University.*

graphic print itself, portrait faces were dotted in imitation of stipple engraving, clothing lined thick-and-thin in imitation of copperplate engraving. Then the emulsion of the print was bleached away, leaving the sharply defined black-and-white pen dots and lines which the camera could capture for the Moss so-called "line" process because the code was all of the same intensity.

As we shall see in the chapter on William Hamilton Gibson, Moss attempted to discover some means of securing halftones in relief form, and succeeded after a fashion. It was not Moss, however, but another American, Frederick Ives (1856–1937), who solved the problem of making *dots* differing in size but equal in intensity *directly* from photographs, for it was the dot, not the line, which offered the greatest hope for imitating the textural gradients of a Nature in which the objects to be found now included photographs and the products of phototechnologies. The secret lay in discovering some means by which the dot could be made small enough to transmit visual information without distorting that information with the specific characteristics of an interfering code.

Process Halftone Engraving: "Madame Modjeska as Juliet"

Photography and Metal Etching

By the beginning of the 1880s, the manufacture of mass visual communications had available the heliotype, photogravure, photography-on-the-block, and the Moss line process. And others were appearing rapidly. In 1882, J. Comyns Carr noted:

> That these processes should already occupy an important place as a means of book illustration is scarcely remarkable, seeing that they can be employed at a cost very much lower than is required even for the commonest and coarsest wood-blocks. . . . Within the past few years, nearly all these different processes have been developed with remarkable rapidity and success, and I believe it probable that, before long, results will be obtained such as even the most delicate wood block cannot rival. All these processes . . . have been the outcome of the invention of photography.[49]

Obviously, white-line wood engraving had reached such perfection that it was regarded as the measure of all the other reproductive arts. It was doomed, nevertheless, even at the apogee of its glory. Only one year after the Carr lectures on book illustration were published, the very first issue of the *Inland Printer* (September, 1883) devoted a long editorial to begging its readers—printers and wood engravers—not to worry about technological unemployment.

What had probably precipitated the dire prophecies of Comyns Carr, and the editorial in the *Inland Printer*, was the patent issued to Frederick Eugene Ives in August of 1881, for a process by an inventor which would ultimately make possible the high-density scanning characteristics of "Madame Modjeska as Juliet" (Plate 15). This first Ives patent represents one of the most complex recodings of the continuous halftones, or chiaroscuro, of Nature into "dots for the eye" ever achieved by the graphic arts. We offer here the enthusiastic description of R. R. Bowker in 1887:

> . . . the gelatine picture is swelled till the light parts . . . stand out in hilly contour . . . while the black parts remain as valleys. By taking a plaster cast from this the dark parts become the hills and the light parts the valleys. The ingenious part of the Ives process, most difficult to describe, is the inking method, for which the elastic "composition" of glue and molasses used in

PLATE 15. *Madame Modjeska as Juliet.* *Process halftone engraving from a soft-focus photograph by Scholl; highlight "engraved" by H. Davidson. Reproduced here the same size as the plate on page 200, in the* Century Magazine, *December 1909, from a copy owned by E. Jussim.*

inking rollers is made in flat sheets, furrowed by V-shaped ditches, which are crossed by other lines of ditches not so deeply furrowed. This leaves the inking surface a series of tiny pyramids close together, and the ink is pressed on so that it not only inks the tops of the pyramids, but their sides and the ditches between. This inked surface is now turned on its face and pressed upon the white plaster cast. Where this cast is high (the darks of the original picture) the inked pyramids are flattened out against it by the pressure, and leave a broad square of ink; where it is low (the lights of the original picture) only the tiny tops of the pyramids touch the cast, and the merest point of ink is left. . . . When the inking surface is removed, the eyes see on the plaster almost an exact reproduction of the original picture, in little blocks instead of in continuous tone. This is taken off the plaster by a collodion film or photographed directly, and the relief plate is made easily. . . .[50]

This negative/positive, back-and-forth procedure produced a number of plates in various periodicals in the United States. Obviously, it depended for its ultimate transposition to the printed page on some equivalent of the Moss line process, for in the modern graphic arts, "line" is interpreted as signifying anything of a solid, uniform density, whether actually, descriptively, a line or a dot.

To some extent, Ives' prodigious ingenuity was wasted, for in 1882 the Munich engraver, Georg Meisenbach (1841–1912) also patented his process, keeping it secret from any American competition until it was made public in 1886. Meisenbach's method consisted

. . . in photographing the original picture as seen through a so-called "grating," made by coating glass with an opaque film, through which transparent lines were cut. By placing this "grating" a little distance in front of the picture a curious optical effect of translating the darker portions of the picture into thicker lines is produced. From this line effect a relief plate is produced.[51]

Ives introduced an improvement on this single line screen in 1886, with the crossline screen. From there on, numerous small improvements, including the invention of Stephen Horgan's varied apertures, the Levy Brothers black-line screen, led gradually to the presumed apex of perfection represented by "Madame Modjeska as Juliet" (Plate 15). She is the personification of the development toward "dots of differing size but equal in intensity." A magnifying glass quickly reveals "Madame Modjeska's" structure (in the original; it has here perforce needed rescreening to be transmitted). The code is so gross that magnification supplies no further detail, as it could with photogravure or the daguerreotype. Yet, for all its crudity by present-day standards, it managed to transmit more condensed accurate information than even the genius of Timothy Cole, who clearly had felt it necessary to finish off all the details of Modjeska's costume even if the original photograph had displayed her bathed in detail-destroying light.

The dots of "Madame Modjeska" were created by exposing a light-sensitive emulsion, an acid-resisting material, on a copper plate, to the light reflected through a screen from a *photograph,* not from the original of the message, namely, Madame herself. The dots were then "cut" from their background by the adaptation of the very method which William Blake had invented a hundred years before: *etching* the negative spaces around positive areas. In this sense, "Madame Modjeska" is drawn with acid resist, just as Blake's books were drawn. The dots stand out in clear relief, just as did the pyramids of Ives' first process, and are inked with a roller. The plate is mounted type-high, then locked into forms with metal typography, and can be printed simultaneously.

It seemed for the moment that the ultimate medium had been found, until it was discovered, as pointed out in the chapter on art history, that relief pictures do not necessarily print clearly on the same text paper which bears the heavy stamping pressure of typography. The original of our copy of "Madame Modjeska" was printed on coated paper; indeed, it could not have been printed otherwise, unless the screen were considerably coarser. As we noted earlier, the stamping character of relief printing methods leaves a flat, easily smeared ink impression. The paper surface was discovered to be so crucial to the final effect that publishers who had been longing for a text-paper-compatible medium discovered to their sorrow that they must still print their fine-screen plates on a different paper, usually a supercalendered or "glossy" stock, inserting them into the collation of the book or periodical just as they had inserted other "prints." One solution, of course, was to print *both* text and pictures on glossy stock, with the eye-straining dazzle which we can all remember from the "slick" magazines. Another solution was to use coarser screens which could print more acceptably on text-finished papers, thereby necessarily and unfortunately decreasing the subliminal effects of pictures and increasing the presence of the code itself as a part of the transmission.

Before we summarize this investigation of the second series of "lovely ladies," we should briefly survey the major problems encountered by the phototechnologies as they entered the area of the transmission of color information.

CODES FOR THE TRANSMISSION OF COLOR

The problems of color transmission are so vast and complex that we have limited ourselves until now to the consideration of black-and-white "transpositions," as William Ivins called them. The Western world was thoroughly accustomed to these black-and-white illusions and had no difficulty accepting the lack of natural color either in daguerreotypes or in paper photography.

> It is a theory held by some that, to a highly-trained imaginative artistic mind, line will almost supply the place of colour, if it be only carried out very carefully and intelligently. While we cannot go practically as far as this, still we have seen skies so beautifully engraved in horizontal and oblique lines that we had no hesitation in saying which were the azure-blue parts and which the grey, and could almost fancy we saw a faint tinge of these colours.[52]

This attitude was by no means unusual. Oliver Wendell Holmes commented: "But color is, after all, a very secondary quality compared with form . . . the color of a landscape varies perpetually, with the season, with the hour of the day, with the weather, and as seen by sunlight or moonlight. . . ."[53] Color was not a customary part of mass-produced transmissions through book illustration in the first three centuries of printing history. "It was seldom printed until about 1840"[54] when lithotinted and lithographed books by Thomas Shotter Boys and Hullmandel in England became remarkable for their ability to render effects like aquatint. The success of Owen Jones with chromolithography was a strong impetus to American firms to develop color craftsmanship, but this progress was slow in terms of book publication. As usual, the problems of cost, lack of type compatibility, the physical difficulties of insertion of what amounted to separate "prints," all combined to slow the appearance of chromolithography in books, although many fine examples of frontispieces by firms like T. Sinclair of Philadelphia can be found by mid-century.[55]

Quoting the painter Longhi's assessment of the engraver Le Blon's first color prints, Charles Blanc noted:

> "Colored prints, never able to be what is really necessary, are mere puerilities." As compensation: in rendering intelligible to the eye scientific works, books upon natural history, anatomy, architecture, or polychrome ornamentation, a print in colors becomes a very valuable auxiliary.[56]

Blanc agreed with Longhi that color prints should not be considered the equivalents of oil paintings; yet color was clearly invaluable in matters of information transfer. In medical books, color was not a luxury but a necessity. But in chromolithography—which was attempting to advance beyond Owen Jones' stained-glass window technique, whereby each flat color was neatly divided from its neighbor by a strong black line—the problems of superimposition and the exact registration of each color made even necessity hazardous:

> It has been for a considerable time rather the fashion to decry the art of Chromolithography, and to assert that it can at the best render but a faulty and feeble representation of highly executed watercolour drawings. That this is a fallacy is becoming daily more apparent. . . . It is a mistake to suppose that Chromolithography cannot grasp elaborate designs. . . . The absence of proper shading—the unseemly blotches which so painfully mar the effect of the reproduction, and the unnatural blending of colours, which either struggle out pale and indistinct, or startle by emphatic but unintelligible results—are faults that should not be pointed to as affording evidence to depreciate Chromolithography as an art, but should rather be attributed to the true causes, namely, an insufficient number of stones to work upon, an improper mixing of the colours, or careless, and, above all, hasty printing.[57]

The advantages of transfer paper in achieving exact duplication of a design from stone to stone (or zinc plate to zinc plate) were counterbalanced by the need for scrupulous care in presswork, otherwise red lips might be imprinted on pink cheeks or blue rivers in the midst of wastelands.

> As is generally the case, the merit of these reproductions is more apparent in Landscape than in Figure drawing. The extreme nicety of treatment is not so requisite in one as in the other, indeed the subject does not require it. An irregular, misplaced line, caused by carelessness in fitting the stones, will no doubt produce an awkward effect in the landscape; but one, perhaps, apparent only to an artist; whereas, a similar misfortune in the formation of a figure will at once appeal to the eye of the most uninitiated.[58]

Color demanded precise simultaneous transmission of *all* the Gibsonian criteria for the imitation of natural effects. We have used chromolithography as the paradigm of the problems of such simultaneity.

From the time of William Savage's *Practical Hints on Decorative Printing* (1823), which had featured pictures produced by the juxtaposition and superimposition of innumerable woodblocks, publishers and engravers had sought a relief process which would ensure a thick, oil ink deposit, close register, and, if possible, halftones. Savage's techniques were an unlikely solution, however handsome the effects, for it was not likely that ordinary trade publishers could economically accept illustrations for which *each* of the following colors represented a separate plate impression.

> Collins' "Ode to Mercy" . . . perhaps the most complicated job ever printed in colours from wood blocks . . . the tints employed, in the order in which

they were used . . . four sepias, yellow, puce, blue, red, dark grey, yellow, light grey, light yellow, two reds, mauve, light blue, two blue-greys, three shades of pale pink, green, greyish-blue, light blue, a purplish red and a grey red (on different parts of the same block), blue, a pale reddish-grey and light brown. . . .[59]

Such extravagances as *twenty-nine* impressions for a single colored picture were obviously out of the question for mass media transmissions by publishers. Attempts were made, therefore, to cut wood engravings according to the three-color principles defined by Isaac Newton and essayed by Le Blon in the seventeenth century; that is, by superimposing the three primary colors. Again, problems of simultaneity of transmission were seemingly insurmountable; the woodblock codes were insufficiently flexible to match the results of chromolithography:

> Many attempts have been made to cut blocks for colour, and this has been even partially successful, but nothing as yet seems to produce a result at all approaching the perfection of chromolithography. The reason is because half-tints of colour have to be represented by lines, and when two colours cross each other it is evident that the same direction cannot be preserved by both. There is a direct invasion of the principle of direction; a surface which ought to be horizontally expressed must, for instance, be treated differently in each colour, marring both texture and effect; indeed, too often the texture of a "parti-coloured" tweed is the result all over. When dots are employed the interstices which should be occupied by dots in another colour too often remain white by reason of the dots not falling in the right place, but upon other dots, thus blurring them. . . .[60]

James Gibson might have called such destruction of natural texture gradients the single greatest obstacle to illusion in the graphic arts. And not even the genius of George Baxter, who combined many media in his "oil" prints, solved the problem of relief printing in color.

Photography in the nineteenth century was black-and-white, and, as will be discussed later, was only a black-and-white equivalent of some of the colors of Nature, as early emulsions were largely color-blind. Hand coloring was applied to photographs and daguerreotypes from the beginning, later to heliotypes and other collotypes, as chemistry seemed to be failing in the search for directly sensitive color exposures. Clerk Maxwell fell back on the Newtonian idea for his 1855 concept of three-color photographic reproduction, and Louis Ducos du Hauron continued experimentation along these lines between 1859 and 1869. But a solution to color separation had to wait for Dr. Hermann Wilhelm Vogel (1834–1893) and his discovery in 1871 of color sensitizers for photographic plates. Color photogravures were available from Goupil & Co. at about the same time, but the plates were not strictly speaking three-color separations; they were

> inked by hand, from a standard coloured copy which the inker has beside him for reference. As the colouring is entirely at the discretion of the artist, and not dependent upon colour selection by the camera, the scheme can of course be modified or extended, according to the nature of the work and the price the producer of the plates is going to get for them.[61]

It would hardly appear that photography had automatically and permanently bypassed either the artist or the engraver, and three-color photogravures, based on separation by the camera into primary color negatives, were not perfected until the turn of the twentieth century.

In 1893, the *Engraver and Printer* of Boston published a frontispiece entitled:

"Photography in Colors. Taken from Nature by W. Kurtz, Madison Square, New York. Printed in Three Colors on the Steam Press." This was a fruit-piece printed from three single-line blocks and proved to the whole printing world that reproductions of colors by photography into three half-tone blocks to be printed in colored inks had arrived.[62]

Not Kurtz, however, but Frederick Ives deserves to be considered the father of the three-color process, for as early as 1881—the same year in which he patented his first Ives process halftone—he had shown "a three-colour reproduction of a chromolithograph, produced by the aid of three screens."[63] Like Fox Talbot, unfortunately, Ives did not recognize the importance of his own invention, not taking the trouble to patent it, "so that the most prominent colour illustrative method of the age has always been public property."[64]

Lest we be deluded that there was any magical direct transmission involved even in the finest-screen halftone color plates, we may be reminded of the translation into codes by the following explanation by Stephen Horgan:

> Let it be remembered that in making a negative of a black-and-white subject, for ordinary photoengraving and printing in black ink, the black in the copy does not affect the sensitive plate; it is represented by the transparent parts of the negative. It is only the white and the lighter shades that form the deposit in the negative, and these are not printed in the printing process. It is the same in three-color record negative-making. The color that is recorded on a color-record negative is the one that is cut off by the filter and not allowed to reach the sensitive plate, or, the color for which the plate is sensitive. . . . The negatives in three-color work have no color in themselves, but record the amount and gradations of each of the primary colors found in that which is photographed. Hence they are properly termed color-record negatives and sometimes color separation negatives.[65]

Kurtz's first attempts were applications of collotype, which unfortunately, as noted earlier, was not able to "be worked successfully in America, owing to climatic conditions, and therefore Kurtz had to apply the process to letterpress printing."[66] Kurtz gradually perfected this process, so that in the late 1890s, duotone relief blocks reproduced illustrations in the picture journals, and by 1902, genuine three-color halftone blocks were widespread. *Colliers'* magazine thought so highly of the process that it put several famous illustrators, including Frederic Remington, under contract to paint originals just for the purpose of color reproduction, both in the publication itself and as separately purchasable prints.

There was a parallel development for simple black-and-white illustrations, for Dr. Vogel had not only invented color-separation negatives, but he had found a way to expand the color blindness of early films by the orthochromatic process.

The most important American publication to take advantage of the new multicolor capabilities was *The Art of the World, Illustrated in the Paintings, Statuary, and Architecture of the World's Columbian Exposition* (New York: Appleton, 1893), a folio series like the parts issued by Strahan in 1888. For this series, the successors of Goupil & Co., i.e., Boussod, Valadon, & Co. of Paris, were the manufacturers, and so far had the century progressed toward an understanding of the need for the accurate transmission of messages that

> Appreciating the magnitude and beauty of this work, many of the leading artists of France, Holland, and America have painted replicas of the pictures selected which have been sent to Boussod, Valadon & Co . . . whose processes

are conceded to be unapproached, in order to insure exact reproductions in color. For no art work ever published has this been done before, and the preparation of these costly color models for this work marks a new departure in the making of art books.[67]

These effects of photography on art history will be pursued further in a later chapter.

Unquestionably, the year 1893 definitely marks the emergence of expectations on the part of public and publisher alike that, henceforth, accuracy of transmission was of primary concern. By 1905, the year of the *Colliers'* contracts mentioned above, color came to dominate those expectations, and the complex development of appropriate codes for the transmission of color messages has been the subject of many twentieth-century investigations into what is, essentially, a twentieth-century achievement.

SUMMARY

The graphic arts are technological processes utilizing physical channels which permit physical codes to transmit *multiple* messages about some type of "reality," whether that reality is a fictive portrait, an artist's creative evocation of a mood, or a photograph from Nature. Prephotographic, or nonphotographic, messages relied upon a packager of information, called an illustrator, to codify what his own idiosyncrasies recorded of three-dimensional reality, using artistic media in a way largely dictated by the artistic conventions of his day. The artist's drawing or painting was then given into the hands of an engraver, who also operated with graphic codes dictated by the graphic conventions of the day and subject to sometimes stern technological restrictions. The final printed messages were perforce at least three times removed from reality, and must be viewed as symbolic representations of ideas which we interpret.

The advent of photography seemingly had the potential to abolish at least the preliminary artist's intervention, yet the camera itself was merely a mechanical message-taker, or codifier into molecular codes, and its products did not lend themselves to publishing. Even the mechanical message-taker had defects of distortion through lenses, color blindness in the emulsions (of which more in the chapter on Gibson), and relied upon human operators to regulate its focus, position, and replication. When negative/positive paper photography failed to meet publishing requirements, it became necessary to invent codes for the transmission of what we must recognize are messages about photographs, instead of messages about "reality," even where an original negative exposed to Nature can be used directly in the plate-making operations.

The success or failure of transmission, which used to be judged as an aesthetic characteristic of the older media, was a judgment now based on the subliminality of the codes carrying the information, although pre-photographic codes of considerable subliminality had been employed over long periods of time. The optimum condition for the employment of any particular medium was type-compatibility, since publishers of ordinary trade books, or publishers of magazines, demanded an all-at-once printing operation whenever possible. Process halftone offered a potential for both subliminality and type-compatibility, but it was certainly not the first subliminal process, nor was it capable of the softness and molecular compression of detail which was an outstanding feature of photogravure, nor did it automatically solve the problems of simultaneous text-and-picture printing.

If we pause for a moment and review our second series of "lovely ladies," we should be able to characterize the major differences of nineteenth-century phototechnological media. Like our first series of "lovely ladies," the heliotype "Portrait from Life" (Plate 9), the white-line wood engraving by Timothy Cole, "Modjeska as Juliet" (Plate 11), the photogravure "Benedick and Beatrice" (Plate 10), and the fine-line process halftone "Madame Modjeska as Juliet" (Plate 15), were all selected as typical of the capabilities of each process to transmit the textural gradients, chiaroscuro, contour, and surface modulations (leaving aside only color) of "Nature."

"Portrait from Life," the heliotype, was essentially a lithograph from a photographic negative/positive process made possible by the happy propensity of bichromatized gelatin to harden upon exposure to light. Somewhat more compressed in detail than the mezzotint, "Forget-Me-Not" (Plate 2), and exceeding all the prephotographic technologies for softness and range of chiaroscuro, it is, nevertheless, somewhat grainy, and enlargement of any detail does not provide the hidden delights of information which Samuel F. B. Morse had noted in the daguerreotype. Nontype-compatible, it was nevertheless the first major phototechnological product which did not require mounting on text paper.

"Modjeska as Juliet" (Plate 11) one of the master creations of the engraver Timothy Cole, represents the most purely imitative moment in the history of wood engraving. If we admire it for its almost daguerreotype precision, a comparison with the process halftone, "Madame Modjeska as Juliet" (Plate 15), swiftly reveals it as a travesty of the original *photograph*. Working on a print of the negative (either made by the original photographer or copied by the Scribner's staff photographer) directly on the woodblock, Cole's graver was too rigidly limited to specific types of excavations to be able to transmit the softness of tones or the auras of light present in the original. Cole chose, apparently, to capitalize on the precision inherent in the wood-engraving medium, rather than to risk failure by attempting to rival the new soft-focus photography, introduced in the 1880s, of which the Modjeska portrait is a typical example.[68] For photographers by Cole's time were no longer or necessarily pursuing the microscopically fine detail which had so splendidly characterized the daguerreotype. They were no longer interested in the total transmission of information about Nature. In their new goal of seeking acceptance of themselves as artists in their own right, rather than mere mechanics, photographers had begun to envelop their subjects in haze, flattering their female patrons with an out-of-focus or selectively focused lens, a trick well known to Hollywood cameramen of today. We can see, therefore, that Timothy Cole was forced by the exigencies of his medium into attempting to transmit a totality of information which was both anachronistic, unfashionable, and, in a very specific sense, inaccurate.

While looking at the process halftone engraving (Plate 15), it must be kept firmly in mind that this is *not* the original photograph. Not only are we *not* looking directly at Madame Modjeska, in or out of focus, but we are not even seeing the photographer Scholl's print. Even a low-powered magnifying glass reveals the original engraving of "Madame Modjeska as Juliet" as a mesh of fine dots: printing ink on paper, the end of a complex transmission about "reality," aided by a hand engraver, as we see in the caption, "Halftone engraved by H. Davidson." This is a sad indication of where many of the talented wood engravers terminated their careers, as "finishers" of the very process which had technologically displaced them.

Actually, Davidson's "engraving" here consists merely of picking away at some highlights to remove the heavy-handed effects of the screen, or filing down some of the dark dots to print more cleanly. But even if there was no significant interference by the hand engraver, and even if hand engravers have passed into craftsmanlike anonymity today, it is unavoidably true that the process halftone represented no magical bypassing of the entire technical configuration which can be subsumed under the word *engraving*.

When we turn from "Portrait from Life" and the two Modjeskas to the photogravure, "Benedick and Beatrice," we are turning from transmission of messages about what is easily defined as "reality," to the transmission of messages about realities which happen to be fictions. Thereby some interesting questions arise which bear upon our future discussion of Pyle, Gibson, and Remington. For "Benedick and Beatrice" is not a portrait from life; it is a transmission about a *painting* which represented imaginary people, although the painter, Merle, may well have posed models for it. It was not painted as an illustration *for* a book, although it appeared as a transmission *in* a book. The painting was an object to be considered as a specific event in the space-time continuum, just as was the model who sat for the heliotype, "Portrait from Life." But while we can guess the size and other physical characteristics of the models who sat for the heliotype and the Modjeskas, we cannot guess the size of the original "model" of the reproduction of "Benedick and Beatrice" simply because the "model" which sat for this photogravure is a painting, not two people in fancy costumes. We may make certain conjectures based on the compression of details, or the information about the textures of the original which the photogravure transmits with its subliminal and noninterfering grain (see especially the man's fur collar)—but we must admit that conjecture is still only conjecture. There are, therefore, several levels of human interpretation involved in "Benedick and Beatrice"; we "see" an imaginary discourse between two handsome figures garbed in costumes not of our own century; we "see" a painting by Merle, whoever he might be; we "see" a complex technological artifact which has required many stages of manufacture, including the difficult attempt in the present book to reproduce as many of the original's characteristics as possible given the limitations of economics, paper availability, and so on. What we "see" at any moment, then, is entirely the result of a decision to focus now on this, now on that. Under certain circumstances, we can imagine a situation where even a fiction like "Benedick and Beatrice" might fool the eye into "seeing reality."

If "Benedick and Beatrice" are compared with all the rest of the "lovely ladies," both prephotographic and photographic, we should be able to agree that it transmits a higher density of information, both sharp detail and soft halftone transition, and interferes with neither the texture of flesh (as painted), nor fur, nor feathers. But we must keep in mind that the reason it far exceeds the detail of the process halftone "Madame Modjeska as Juliet" (Plate 15) is because the original was a "sharp-focus" painting, while the original of the second "Madame Modjeska" was a "soft-focus" photograph. In the course of this book, many more comparisons between photogravures and process halftones will be presented which should enable us to make a more just comparison of their capabilities.

Let us now reread the major Ivins hypothesis, and determine what our "lovely ladies" have brought into the argument:

> The great importance of the half-tone lay in its syntactical difference from the older hand-made processes of printing pictures in printer's ink. In the old processes, the report started by a syntactical analysis of the thing seen,

which was followed by its symbolic statement in the language of drawn lines. This translation was then translated into the very different analysis and syntax of the process. The lines and dots in the old reports were not only insistent in claiming visual attention, but they, their character, and their symbolism of statement, had been determined more by the two superimposed analyses and syntaxes than by the particularities of the thing seen. In the improved half-tone process there was no preliminary syntactical analysis of the thing see into lines and dots, and the rules, lines and dots of the process had fallen below the threshold of normal vision. Such lines and dots as were to be seen in the report had been provided by the thing seen and were not those of any syntactical analysis. If there remained the same complete transposition of colour and loss of scale that had marked the older processes, the preliminary syntactical analyses and their effects had been done away with, and the transposition of colours was uniform. At last men had discovered a way to make visual reports in printer's ink without syntax, and without the distorting analyses of form that syntax necessitated.[69]

We have surely seen that the preliminary artist, or first packager of information, had been replaced by the photographer, who could submit reality to soft- or hard-focus manipulation. Photography itself was a molecular coding of certain limited aspects of reality, hardly those of the third dimension, and hardly three-dimensional even in today's high-fidelity color transmissions. Ivins' underlying assumption, that photography itself lacks "syntax," is what provided the basis for his ensuing thesis, that the screened process halftone was so subliminal in its effects that it, too, lacked "syntax." In his shorter statement of this thesis, he made this point quite clear: "The invention of the ruled crossline halftone screen was a device which made it possible to make a printing surface for a pictorial report in which neither the draughtsman nor the engraver had had a hand." [70] The implication that the ruled cross-line halftone screen made the printing of photography from Nature possible, and that no other medium provided such services, is unmistakable — and, obviously, as has been preliminarily demonstrated, mistaken.

> Its great importance lay in the fact that the lines of the process as distinct from the lines of the visual report could be below the threshold of human vision. In the old hand-made processes the lines of the process and the lines of the report were the same lines; and the process counted for more than the report in the character of the lines and the statements they made.[71]

We have seen, however, that several prephotographic processes, namely, the stipple engraving and the mezzotint, had subliminal effects, that the heliotype had subliminal effects based on fine-grain and multilevel transformations, and that the codes of photogravure can hardly be seen by the unaided eye. We intend to demonstrate that the codes of process halftone engraving were considered to be extremely "noisy," and that, far from replacing the artist in the transmission process, it only helped photography in general to demonstrate the difference between fact and fancy. Far from replacing the "syntactical" interference by the hand engraver, it merely substituted a new set of transmission problems.

4

*Illustrators and the
Photographic Media*

How these technical and economical questions interfere, in the fine
arts, with the free choice of means! [1]

. . . The confounded camera, that dulls all the crispness of my highlights and blurs all my blacks. [2]

THE PENCIL OF NATURE

The major concern of William Ivins in *Prints and Visual Communication*
was with the development of visual media which would interfere least with
the transmission of informational messages. When that concern touched
upon the reproduction of art objects, Ivins excoriated the intervention of
both "illustrators" (in our terms, the *primary codifiers* of information) and
hand engravers (in our terms, the *secondary codifiers* of information). For
Ivins, each of these codifications represented the imposition of either subjective or arbitrary "syntaxes" on Nature (conceived both as natural and as
man-made objects).

In commenting on Sir Henry Fox Talbot's invention of paper negative/
positive photography and on its description in *The Pencil of Nature* (1844;
subtitled: Some Account of the Art of Photogenic Drawing, or The Process
by which Natural Objects may be made to Delineate Themselves without
the Aid of the Artist's Pencil),[3] Ivins says:

> In other words, he fully realized that these images which he made were not
> subject to the omissions, the distortions, and the subjective difficulties that
> are inherent in all pictures in which draughtsmanship plays a part. Here
> were exactly repeatable visual images made without any of the syntactical
> elements implicit in all hand-made pictures. Had Talbot been an accom-
> plished draughtsman instead of an incompetent one he would probably not
> have recognized this fact, even if he had discovered how to make the images.[4]

Now, much of this line of conjecture can be demolished very easily, by
pointing to the example of Daguerre. Daguerre was a genius at illusionistic
representationalism in theatrical settings. He, too, had been obsessed with
discovering some means to permanently fix the images of the *camera
obscura*. Fox Talbot, as indicated earlier, was hastening to get into a lucrative
competition with Daguerre. But even if it must be recognized that Ivins
was putting words—not to mention rather complex ideas—into Talbot's

head, he opens a line of investigation which proves useful in demonstrating the accuracy of one of his own major hypotheses.

Is there a difference between an "artist" and a "draughtsman"? Was Talbot talking about the former or the latter, or was there some confusion in his mind about the identity of the two functions? After all, Talbot's initial desire to discover a process to fix the images of the *camera lucida* had originated not out of a creative desire to paint some tremendous and moving image of the Italian campagna, but simply out of a desire to copy, and then to capture, an image cast by a prism on a piece of paper, an image he had wanted primarily as the memento of a pretty scene. "Art" had photographic or retinal-recording intentions before photography was invented. Indeed, much of the history of Western art, from the Renaissance struggle with perspective to the exclusive retinism of the Impressionists in the nineteenth century, was the result of an obsession with naturalistic and illusionistic representationalism, as opposed to the symbolic representationalism of Eastern cultures.[5] "Art," of course, had had expressive intentions as well, but it was the advent of photography which eventually made the two sets of intentions more sharply defined. As Ivins observed:

> Up to that time very few people had been aware of the difference between pictorial expression and pictorial communication of statements of fact. . . . The men who did these things had gone to the same art schools and learned the same techniques and disciplines. . . . The differences between the two groups of artists were generally considered to be merely a matter of their comparative skill.[6]

When photography and phototechnologies arrived, they inevitably took over the role of the pictorial communication of statements of fact, making a distinction between the two roles of artists which continues to be observed today. If it is doubtful that Henry Fox Talbot was as keenly aware of this distinction as Ivins, it is because he had no aspiration to being what we today call an "artist," that is, someone involved in self-expression. Very probably, he was only aware that the "artist" of his day—someone who could draw superbly well, well enough to copy anything quite accurately out of "Nature" using the visual codes of Western European nineteenth-century art—was at last faced with some competition. He may have been boasting about the sublimity of his invention: that a mere chemical transformation could accomplish what years of training were needed to accomplish in the artist's eye, brain, and hand. We may verify the justice of this interpretation as against Ivins' notion of Talbot as someone who had "fully realized" the *subjectivity* of an artist's delineations, by examining the history of the first photographically assisted American book, John L. Stephens' *Incidents of Travel in Yucatán* (New York: Harper, 1843).

The Artist and the Camera

Yucatán was the first important book to be illustrated by benefit of camera. Not that halftones were used . . . but before Stephens departed for Yucatan in 1841, he and his associate, Frederick Catherwood, learned photography from Professor John W. Draper, of the University of the City of New York, who had made the first photograph of a human face. . . . They brought back a lot of daguerreotypes, which enabled Catherwood to check his drawings of artifacts, the most exact that had ever appeared in archaeological work.[7]

More accurate details are available in the Stephens account itself:

> At Uxmal, Mr. Catherwood began taking views, but the results were not sufficiently perfect to suit his ideas. At times the projecting cornices and

ornaments threw parts of the subject in shade, while others were in broad sunshine; so that, while parts were brought out well, other parts required pencil drawings to supply their defects. They give a general idea of the character of the building, but would not do to put into the hands of the engravers without copying the views on paper . . . which would require more labor than that of making at once complete original drawings. He therefore completed everything with his pencil and camera lucida, while Dr. Cabot . . . and myself took up the Daguerreotype; and, in order to ensure the utmost accuracy, the Daguerreotype views were placed with the drawings in the hands of the engravers for their guidance.[8]

There are several important implications here which need to be spelled out, as they will help establish a basis for ensuing discussion: (a) the artist, who happened to be an exceptionally gifted draughtsman and architectural visionary, learned how to use, and used, the daguerreotype apparatus; (b) the daguerreotype, despite its vaunted "accuracy," was not amenable to exact control over the scene or object which the artist wished to transmit as a message, since the light-sensitive materials could not simultaneously expose correctly for both shadows and lights—a problem which continues to plague photography today; (c) the artist saw nothing "wrong" with transmitting a factual message through the aid of photography or directly through photography, as he "perfected" the drawings primarily because of the mechanical defects and limitations of a specific photographic process; (d) other individuals could secure the pictures, and, in a sense, supplement what the artist drew by supplying him with plates to follow for drawings; in a very real sense, the "artist" had no argument with a mechanical device, since his objectives were precisely those of the camera, namely, the objective recording of the real visual world; and (e) neither his own drawings nor his daguerreotypes (or any others) could be used for direct reproduction, since both "subjective" drawing and "objective" daguerreotype had to be submitted to a hand engraver for the purposes of publication. All of these implications, crucial to our understanding of developments in the nineteenth century, will be further elaborated and documented in our discussions of Frederic Remington and William Hamilton Gibson.

When the explorer Stephens failed to get financial backing for his idea for "a great work on *American Antiquities* to contain 100 or 200 engravings (folio) to be issued . . . quarterly,"[9] his artist, Frederick Catherwood, invested on his own in the publication of several large drawings he made after the trip. With the last of his savings, he went to England,

> . . . employed the finest of London's artists, and thus published the magnificent collection of lithographs on the Maya civilization. In March, 1844, Catherwood's *Views of Ancient Monuments in Central America, Chiapas, and Yucatán* was published in London.[10]

Aside from implications of the poor state of lithography in the United States in 1844, we see that Catherwood did not transfer his own drawings to the stones, but required "the finest of London's artists" to do so. This man, whom we would today call merely a copyist, was then called "an artist." An artist was simply someone who had been trained to use his eyes and hands in the act of either reproduction or representation. No wonder that our engraver of "Lady Geraldine," William James Linton, became so confused about the proper role of reproductive engraving: a copyist was an artist, a draughtsman was an artist, and a man who drew things out of his imagination was also an artist; why should not the engraver be an artist as well?

PLATE 16. *Monjas—Chichen Itza.*
Combined etching-engraving based on
daguerreotype, probably by Frederick
Catherwood, who corrected the image with
a camera lucida, adding the figures free-
hand. Reproduced here slightly reduced
from the original, in John L. Stephens,
Incidents of Travel in Yucatán (*New*
York: Harper, 1843). *Courtesy of Colum-*
bia University Libraries.

In the Catherwood lithographs, quaint native figures have been added to what were originally camera lucida "copies" from Mayan monuments (see Plate 16, "Monjas—Chichen Itza"). These figures constitute an aspect of "artistic expression," or form of fictive manipulation for the sake of an interesting composition, human identification, or a sense of scale of a temple. "Artistic expression" is a somewhat elusive quality, although we will attempt to develop an example of its meaning seen in a role of "addition" to a seemingly straightforward example of information transfer in our discussion of William Hamilton Gibson.

Gyorgy Kepes, a distinguished educator [11] and artist, has defined "artistic expression" as: "the ordering of a visual impression into a coherent, complete living form." [12] This may begin to define what it was that William Hamilton Gibson and Frederic Remington did when they integrated visual perceptions into reproducible and communicable form, but it must be further defined if we would understand the work of Howard Pyle, or any other primarily fictive artist. If the Kepes statement read, "the ordering of a visual *idea* into *communicable form* by the subjective manipulations of an individual trained in the use of appropriate codes," we begin to have a definition suitable for the purposes of our broad discussion since it provides a definition of the process called "artistic expression" as it relates specifically to illustration. We have already indicated that there is a difference between the codifying of a visual idea by the so-called "fine artist," whose purpose is to create an object not necessarily destined to become an illustration in a book or periodical, and the "illustrator," whose purpose is precisely to create an object suitable for reproduction. Nothing prevents an individual from performing both of these functions, but our major concern here is with illustration as it signifies purposefully created visual communications destined specifically for reproduction, usually in direct connection with a printed verbal fiction or nonfiction.

The illustrator, before the nineteenth century, was the primary codifier of visual ideas. In the early years of the graphic arts, he often worked directly on the printing surface, on the woodcut or the steel engraving, sometimes simply as the draughtsman who put down the marks for the engraver to follow, sometimes, like Dürer, cutting his own plates. Often there were three men involved, as Ivins has presented an example from the sixteenth century:

> The illustrations were drawn from the actual plants by an artist named Albert Mayer, whose drawings were then copied on the blocks, and doubtless given their schematic form, by Heinrich Fullmaurer, after which the wood-cutter, Hans Rudolph Speckle, did his work of cutting the blocks. [13]

Three times removed from reality, the cut was printed and distributed to readers or viewers. The sequence is not so different for Frederick Catherwood: he had made the drawings from Nature himself; then he redrew them larger for the sake of making them "artistic"; and another man recopied these for the sake of reproduction.

Was this sequence as destructive for the man who was more interested in "artistic expression" than in "information transfer"? Was the artist who had only his own imaginative designs destined for reproduction as illustration, rather than representations from Nature, as concerned with the problems of reproduction?

What shall we make of a statement like this? ". . . the crisp touch of Felix O. Darley (1822–88) was not wholly betrayed by the engraver in his re-creations of scenes from Cooper, Irving, and Dickens. . . ." [14]

Perhaps an answer lies in this comment by Helmut Lehmann-Haupt:

> . . . only gradually were the new opportunities of photography recognized. The fact that an illustrator's first, free sketches, in all their freshness and spontaneity, could be reproduced without that further elaboration which Cruikshank and Leech had so resented was not immediately clear. Perhaps it is not even fully realized today. . . .[15]

This can only be a partial answer, if an answer at all, since Catherwood had certainly recognized the assets of photography almost as soon as it had arrived in America.

THE EXAMPLE OF F. O. C. DARLEY

The applications of photography to reproduction became available in the following roughly chronological order: (1) the daguerreotype, essentially—despite valiant attempts—nonreproducible through itself; (2) paper negative/positive photography, impermanent, requiring mounting, nontype-compatible; (3) photolithography, slow of application in the United States, between 1858, with the exception of isolated instances, and 1880, the date of Stephen Horgan's success in the *Daily Graphic*, capable of effects in line rather than halftone; (4) photography-on-the-block, from 1855 to 1876 in the service of black-line facsimile reproduction rather than of tonal, textural effects; (5) the woodburytype and carbon prints, requiring mounting into books, nontype-compatible, although superbly beautiful in effect and possessing true subliminal photographic characteristics; (6) the heliotype of the early 1870s, not requiring mounting but not type-compatible either, therefore not destined to take over the field of book or magazine publication, despite its depth of tone and high fidelity to photographic originals; (7) process line engraving, like the Moss process of the 1870s, which produced type-compatible blocks without true halftones; (8) photogravure, a secret process dominated by Parisian and Viennese firms, available after 1876; (9) process halftone engraving, utilizing screens to codify dots of differing sizes but of the same intensity, gradually perfected from 1881 to 1893; (10) color processes of various types, in a progression from chromolithography in the 1840s to the imported heliogravures of the early 1890s and the three-color process halftone plates manufactured on the Ives-Kurtz principles in the late 1890s into the twentieth century. "Never before in the relationship of artist and printer had such a variety of reproductive processes been available than in the 19th century, and never before had such radical changes taken place in so rapid a succession."[16]

There was certainly a tremendous variety of reproductive processes: all those developed in previous centuries, and all the new applications of photography. Yet, of all these, the illustration career of one of America's greatest and most famous graphic artists, Felix Octavius Carr Darley, encompasses only the following media (excepting those prints meant specifically as "framing prints"):

a. Incised Lithography, known as "etching on stone," as in the *Scenes of Indian Life* (1843), *Illustrations of Rip Van Winkle* (1848), with the most famous example being that of his *Compositions in Outline from Judd's Margaret* (1856).

b. Black-Line Facsimile Wood Engraving, as in Irving's *Sketch Book of Geoffroy Crayon* (1848), or the 250 illustrations for the *Library of Humorous American Works* (1846–1853), or his own *Sketches Abroad with Pen and Pencil* (1869); see Plate 36, "Dutch Fishermen."

c. Black-Line Tonal Wood Engraving, as in the illustration for "The Song of Hiawatha," in the Houghton, Osgood edition of Longfellow (1879–1880); see Plate 79.

d. Black-Line Wood Engravings with Lithotint Backgrounds, as in many of the over five hundred illustrations for Benson J. Lossing's *Our Country* (1876–1878).

e. Steel Engravings, as in the well-known series of frontispieces and added title pages for both Cooper's *Novels* (Townsend, 1859–1861) and for the fifty-five volumes of *The Works of Charles Dickens* (Townsend, 1862–1865; Hurd & Houghton, 1866); see Plate 6, "Lionel Lincoln."

While it is not only possible but extremely probable that many of the later black-line wood engravings were assisted by photography-on-the-block, it is not until 1879 that any sign of photographic reproduction for Darley appears:

f. Photogravure, as in (1) *Compositions in Outline from Hawthorne's Scarlet Letter* (Boston: Houghton, Osgood, 1879), issued both bound and loose; (2) Longfellow's *Evangeline* (Boston: Houghton Mifflin, 1883); "designs different from those in Evangeline, 1867"; [17] (3) *The Complete Works of William Shakespeare*, ed. by William Cullen Bryant (New York: Amies, 1888), illustrated by Darley and Chappell; "30 photogravure reproductions of wash drawings by Darley"; [18] and, last (4) *Character Sketches from the Works of Charles Dickens* (Philadelphia: Porter & Coates, c.1888).

Immediately after Darley's death, several of his "illustrations" appeared in Walter Montgomery's *American Art and American Art Collections*, which was "fully-illustrated with etchings, photo-etchings, photogravures, photo-types, and engravings on steel and wood," [19] in the form of photoetchings. But these were no longer illustrations by Felix O. Darley intended for reproduction in connection with a specific book or event; these were now reproductions of Darley's works used as illustrations for a new book, and using—not the old plates, as would have been necessary before the age either of lithography or of photography—brand new plates. These photo-etchings, which have the same texture as photogravures, were printed in dark green ink, a characteristic embellishment of many books of the transitional and multimedia era of the late 1880s.

Two of the photoetchings were from the originals of illustrations; the other two re-reproductions were apparently in some process line medium, greatly reducing original illustrations as they appeared in Judd's *Margaret* and *Compositions to Accompany the Scarlet Letter,* both originally in incised lithography.

Darley's career offers us a nutshell glimpse of the typical American illustrational career in terms of the reproductive media employed before, during, and after the struggle between nonphotographic and photographic media, with the notable feature that he was apparently never asked to produce original art scheduled for reproduction in its first appearance through the medium of process halftone engraving. His career ended before the perfection and the assumed triumph of that medium in the late 1880s and early 1890s, but it was typical of the careers of many other illustrators of his time. For example, we recognize that before the success of the various photographic media, he was at the mercy of the engravers; not *one* engraver, but an endless succession of them. His vignette illustrations for Cooper and Dickens were "cleanly and understandingly reproduced by J. D. Smillie, Hinshelwood, Hollyer, A. V. Baulch, Schoff, C. Rose and others. . . ." [20]

In [*The Knickerbocker History*] one may indulge in interesting comparisons of Childs and Herrick (somewhat addicted to inky shadows) and speculations as to the extent to which the manner of the individual engraver may have modified the design of the illustrator.[21]

It is difficult now to answer such speculations, for very often a few sketches for an original Darley illustration are all that is left. If the medium was wood engraving, most often he drew directly on the block, the engraver either facsimiled the drawing or "improved it," depending largely on whether the Darley drawing was in line or wash; the drawing was then gone forever, except as it reappeared in reproduction. Certainly we can judge from all of this that it was not only the artist who was guilty of subjective distortions: an engraver could "cleanly and understandingly" reproduce an artist's work, or he could "modify the design of the illustrator."

As we shall see with Pyle, Gibson, and Remington, this was a matter of considerable concern for both expressive and informative illustrators, for just as long as the hand engraver was a necessary intercessor in the publication process, the illustrator was judged by the end result, not by his original. We shall also see that photography did not automatically solve this problem, despite what seemed to be implied in a mechanical process.

THE CAMERA VERSUS THE SKILLED CRAFTSMAN

At least one critic insisted that even the precision of process line engraving, largely used to reproduce pen-and-ink drawings from the 1870s on, was not equal to a hand product:

These drawings have been reproduced by Louis Chefdeville, and, like all his reproductions, are better than the work of any other reproductive engraver today. He has not only reproduced the drawing excellently but he has kept the quality of the line which each man used. The reason for this is not difficult to find. Chefdeville was an artist and reproduced drawings in an artistic manner; that is, he sought to reproduce the character of the draughtsman's work. His rendering of separate lines is infinitely better than that of any photoengraver.[22]

This accolade to a great craftsman was nothing compared to the enthusiasm which greeted Timothy Cole and other members of what became known as the New School of Engraving. Chefdeville could *not* have "reproduced drawings in an artistic manner" if he had been denied the assistance of photography-on-the-block, for the drawings mentioned above are pen-and-inks of Remington, Frost, and Kemble, executed not on the block but on separate sheets of paper. In the "old days," when blocks were cut apart for assembly-line tactics, as one master wood engraver recalled:

The first step in making the illustration was to draw a rough sketch on paper the exact size of the composite wood block. From this a tracing was made, which was rubbed down reversed on the block. . . . After the tracing on the block was completed one of the men, with a brush and India ink, laid in the main broad shadows. Before the "figure man" outlined his people on his horses . . . or whatever details were to form the main subject of the picture, the two, three, or even four men who were to work on the drawing would get together and determine how deep a tone was to pervade the whole composition. Each man had to carry this in mind, else the picture when completed would never hold together. . . .[23]

It was standard practice for *Harper's Weekly* and the other news-slanted illustrated journals to send out a pair of specialists on assignment:

Many a night out on the road we juggled architecture and figures back and forth on a wood block under a single gas jet in a hotel bedroom. . . . All that is a thing of the past; now a photographer goes out with his camera and click—he has it all in half the wink of an eye.[24]

If subtlety of translation of a simple news drawing was likely to suffer under such circumstances, we can imagine what such hackwork did to sensitive egos of artists like Winslow Homer, whose work of the prephotographic era reproduced in jobbed-out blocks as described above was recently criticized by John Canaday as being "boring." What Canaday seemed to have forgotten was that it was not Winslow Homer that he saw in those excruciating black-line botches of Civil War Days, but the hasty "universal" engraving codes at work.

When photography-on-the-block successfully managed to copy almost any original artistic medium for the wood engraver to follow, it was possible for the New School of Engraving to erupt with a textural revolution.

All the various kinds of textures served the useful purpose of bringing the artist and engraver in contact, giving each the chance to find an affinity, and gradually the best possible results came out of it. Artists who never thought of being represented came forward to try the new engraving.[25]

The author of that opinion was the leader of the New School, Elbridge Kingsley (1842–1918), and he was not as pleased with photography-on-the-block when it concerned engraving from a photograph from Nature rather than reproducing an artist's illustration. Writing about the early 1880s, Kingsley remarked:

I speak of photographs gotten to illustrate special articles *from a distance* [italics added], where perhaps no other material was available. They might be turned over to an artist to make an outline drawing, and be reproduced by mechanical means, or if important, a black and white drawing would be made for engraving. Sometimes the engraving might be made directly from the photograph. Here I had some experiences a little peculiar. . . . Mr. Frazer showed me an engraving that had been produced with infinite labor, taking a long time. Also it was unsatisfactory. The trouble with it was that the photograph had been carefully followed, and like most of such material, accentuating detail that happened to be in focus, with nothing but white for the sky and meaningless black for the foreground.[26]

In the days before orthochromatic film, when greens printed black (as they still do if filters are not judiciously used), and blue dropped away white, and yellows and reds turned pitch, when copy might have been provided by an amateur equipped with an inexpensive "detective" camera, the middleman between the message and the engraver was still needed. Kingsley admitted that he did not do very well with an engraving if he had only a photograph to go by, especially if he were unfamiliar with the material it represented.

There were other difficulties with photography-on-the-block, even though the following specifies its major utility: "Reducing engravings to any size for wood engravers is one of the most useful applications of photography. All the illustrated papers and the lithographers have their original sketches and designs photographed to the proper size. . . ."[27] As we shall see in our discussion of Gibson, there is some question as to the universality of the practice; but the problem of reduction from an original was a serious one. For example, in response to W. J. Linton's harsh criticism of the New School of Engraving, Kingsley defended the new techniques:

> There is one element that is generally overlooked, when complaining of the extreme fineness of the new engraving. An artist making a drawing of any size or in any medium that he chooses, generally overlooks the fact that if his drawing is reduced very much it crowds the detail to such an extent, that it can become a different picture in the process.[28]

What an astonishing statement this is, if we can understand for the moment that photography was making something possible which had been a major source of difficulty in the graphic arts from the very beginning: the transference of an artist's drawing "of any size or in any medium that he chooses"! What a liberation of "artistic expression" this should have foretold, and what a Pandora's box of evils it turned out to be!

These evils arising from a supposedly complete liberation of the artist from any concern over reproduction in a specific circumstance were not immediately visible, especially so long as the hand engraver was still the middle man. Men like Elbridge Kingsley and Timothy Cole were as liberated as the artists themselves, since they abandoned Mr. Linton's orthodoxy of reproduction in order to pursue textures that would adequately render the textures of originals. When an original by an artist was so much reduced in transferring it to the block that it crowded the details, these men of the New School of Engraving restored a sense of scale, opened up the crowded areas, used what can only be described as artistic discretion. Far from being mere hack copyists, they were inventing whatever code was needed to translate an original into an appropriate surface for printing which would convey as much of an accurate impression of the original as was possible in black-and-white and in small size. The trained craftsman had an advantage over the early phototechnologist:

> Photography cannot always claim the absolute veracity which is sometimes attributed to it. It inevitably coarsens to some extent, even the simple lines of a pen and ink drawing. . . . The photographic engraver can distinguish between a broad line and a thin line . . . but he is . . . powerless to effect any distinction between a dark line and a light one.[29]

Some of these distinctions were achieved by Kingsley and the others of his New School by lowering the surface of the block to regulate the amount of ink it would receive.

Even as the art of photomechanical process line engraving progressively improved under the tutelage of its American leader, John Calvin Moss, certain illustrators found they could not adapt to the rigid strictures of creating designs in absolutely solid black ink lines of photographable dimension. Edwin Austin Abbey (1852–1911), an outstanding book and magazine illustrator whose calligraphic hand was notoriously "itchy," was a prime example (see Plate 17, "The Violinist" by Abbey):

> Now, it would drive any wood engraver on earth raving crazy to follow in and out around each one of these delicate, fibrous blacks, as soft as the hairs on a spider's legs. Even the direct photographic process itself stops short of the exact result; and one of Abbey's recent trips from London here was to see if, among some of the newer processes, something might not be found to obviate these difficulties. The engraver couldn't and the process wouldn't.[30]

Abbey was not being arbitrary or whimful:

> Abbey never drew a clear, clean-cut line in his life even with his pen—his chief medium of expression—and he never will. If he did, he would never be what he is. Examine any one of Abbey's pen-and-inks under a magnifying glass and you will find that every line, seemingly clear and flowing, is made up of many little, niggling touches, ragging the main line into exquisite softness.

PLATE 17. ***The Violinist.*** *Process line engraving from pen-and-ink by Edwin A. Abbey. Reproduced here the same size as the illustration for "The Deserted Village," in* Harper's Monthly Magazine *105 (August 1902): 461; from the copy owned by E. Jussim.*

This is not a trick of his; it is the outcome of his peculiarly nervous, high-strung temperament, expressing itself in this unique way. The artist in him led him to this touch, and he was too wise ever afterward to attempt to learn anything different.[31]

Here, for the first time in history, since for the first time in history it was becoming possible technologically, an artist was insisting that the engraver find some method of reproducing his original—rather than the engraver forcing the artist to prepare a suitable drawing.

> . . . for whereas, before, there was a special class of designers who mastered the technique of drawing for the engraver, and rarely painted at all, now not a painter but could see his work engraved even though he never put pencil to block, and that without the perilous aid of a draughtsman.[32]

A genius in line art could perhaps demand that engravers follow him, rather than vice versa, but the young and inexperienced artist (as we shall see with Remington) had only his ideas and not much else:

> . . . the plea put forth, that it is better to have the facsimile of the artist's work, pure and simple, without the intervention of the engraver, is a questionable one, and is not the fact in the majority of cases. The artist may be a master of the technique of painting, colour, effect, feeling, &c. and yet be the veriest tyro in the domain of line. His drawings would gain, in ninety-nine cases out of a hundred, by being translated into line by an engraver whose life study has been devoted to a subject of which but few artists know the slightest rudiments. . . .[33]

Artists were expected to know enough about many, many other things to satisfy the requirements of the authors of their books and articles. In a typical example, Thomas Hardy wrote to James Osgood, on December 6, 1888, concerning a story of his due to be illustrated for *Harper's Magazine:*

> The artist for the Christmas story should have special skill in the following—the delineation of old English manor-house architecture, and woodland scenery, with large gnarled oaks, etc., besides, of course, figures, in the costume of George the Second's reign—the date of the story being about 1740. . . . I do not know whether the artist would like to see the place. . . .[34]

Osgood had been one of the enterprising publishers who had set out to establish a business based on a specific phototechnology, in his case, the heliotype. It was he who published Ernest Edwards' *The Heliotype Process* in 1876, in an attempt to capitalize on the interest generated at the Philadelphia Centennial in the new processes. It was Osgood who had published

PLATE 18. *I Tell You This . . . Heliotype from a gouache and chalk original painting by Elihu Vedder, with his hand lettering. Reproduced here slightly reduced from the full-page plate in Vedder's edition of the* Rubaiyat of Omar Khayyam *(Boston: James Osgood, 1884). Courtesy of Samuel and Mary R. Bancroft Collection, Delaware Art Center, Wilmington.*

34

I tell you this—When, started from the Goal,
Over the flaming shoulders of the Foal
 Of Heav'n Parwín and Mushtári they flung,
In my predestin'd Plot of Dust and Soul

35

The Vine had struck a fibre: which about
If clings my Being—let the Dervish flout;
 Of my Base metal may be filed a Key,
That shall unlock the Door he howls without.

36

And this I know: whether the one True Light
Kindle to Love, or Wrath-consume me quite,
 One Flash of It within the Tavern caught
Better than in the Temple lost outright.

the sumptuous Elihu Vedder drawings to accompany the *Rubaiyat of Omar Khayyam*, in 1884, using folio heliotypes for both text and picture. Now a classic of American illustration, and a great rarity, the Vedder designs

> . . . beside their merit and value as illustrative drawings, gain much also from the circumstance that each page of the book is drawn, text as well as the surrounding design, by the same hand. That emphasizes the advantage and importance of having the book, as a mechanical product, one connected whole, "cast in one piece." Text and illustration are thus in harmony, instead of having the latter in no relation to the type, a separateness today emphasized by the frequent appearance of the plate as something extraneous to the book, on a sheet of different paper to hold the halftone, tipped in loosely and coming out all too easily.[35]

This aesthetic appreciation aside, the Vedder book was, unquestionably, a return to the idea of the "block-book" using the heliotype as the medium instead of woodcuts, or, as in the case of William Blake, of whole-page etchings of text and illustration together (see Plate 18, "I Tell You This," by Vedder). The heaviness of the pages, the difficulty caused by the requirements of two ink impressions—one for the lights, one for the shadows, as previously noted—marked this as a singularly ambitious aesthetic achievement, and a failure for the future of book illustration.

When fires and other catastrophes forced Osgood to close his publishing business, the critic George A. Townsend wrote, in the Boston Sunday *Globe* for May 10, 1885:

> The failure of Osgood in Boston . . . calls a halt upon so much sensuousness in our literature. . . . Instead of making strong books and strong meat for the mind, our publishers have been giving us decorative books, all bursting with illustrations . . . that catch the eye and do not minister to the soul. You cannot make a literature . . . with pictures.[36]

Whether this is a Victorian reaction against pretty pictures, or a portent of the nonbook proliferating in our own time, it was an unfair judgment of the accomplishment of J. Osgood and Co., under whose aegis important advances were made in the fields of art history and motion analysis. While Osgood went on to function as Harper's literary agent abroad, book illustration went on in search of the perfect medium.

LIBERATION OR NEW ENSLAVEMENT TO TECHNOLOGY

We have noted that Townsend (quoted above), chastised publishers for producing "decorative books, all bursting with illustrations." It was true that the phototechnologies, even before the perfection of the type-compatible process halftone, were tending to cheapen manufacture and production, and, perhaps inadvertently, cheapening the quality of artist's work as well. "Photo-mechanical processes of reproduction were invented by men who sought, not to create an art, not to help art in any way, but only to cheapen the cost of reproduction." [37]

Ivins thought that only hand engraving imposed restrictions on artists. But for every sensitive and high-standard-setting artist such as Edwin Austin Abbey,

> The mere journeymen among illustrators have "drawn for process" in the worst and most commercial sense of the term, and have set down their lines after the hard-and-fast rules which were formulated for their guidance. For years after the invention of zincography, artists who were induced to

make drawings for the new methods of engraving worked in a dull round of routine; for in those days the process-man was not less, but more, tyrannical than his predecessor, the wood-engraver; his yoke was, for a time, harder to bear.[38]

We recall that even with the application of photography to lithography, or zincography, only *line* could be reproduced. The strictures were specific:

> One was enjoined to make pen-drawings with only the blackest of Indian ink, upon Bristol-board of the thickest and smoothest and whitest kind. . . . he should draw lines thick and wide apart and firm, and that his drawings should be made with a view to, preferably, a reduction in scale of one-third. Also that by no means should his lines run together by any chance, except in the matter of a coarse and obvious cross-hatch. . . . The man who then drew with a view to reproduction squirmed on the very edge of his chair, and with compressed lips, and his heart in his mouth, drew upon his Bristol-board slowly and carefully, and with so heavy a hand, that presently his wrist ached consumedly, and his drawing became stilted in the extreme.[39]

Perhaps only someone like Howard Pyle could withstand such strictures and still produce a *Robin Hood* or an *Otto of the Silver Hand*.

We saw that Darley had his outline drawings for several books reproduced by photogravure from 1879 to 1888. This was also the process insisted upon by Abbey for his deluxe edition of the oversized, richly embellished *She Stoops to Conquer,* of 1886.[40] Halftone was still in its experimental stages, although that year Frederick Ives patented his second screen process. Even with the advent of this perfected screen, which seemed to promise so much, the artist discovered that very exacting procedures were to be followed, if he desired any success in reproduction at all:

> . . . if you wish to work in oil I would suggest that you work in monochrome, and further I would advise you to make your designs in simple black and white—that is if the reproduction is to be printed with black ink; for the nearer your original is to the colour in which it is printed, the nearer will the engraver and printer be able to approach it. I would also suggest that perfectly dead colours should be used, because varnish or any sort of glaze, shine or glitter, will tell in the photograph, and even the most careful engravers are rather given to reproducing the photographic copy than the original. . . .
>
> Body colour and gouache are much used; the only thing to be remembered is that you should keep to the same colours and the same method of work all the way through each drawing. It is very interesting to combine body colour with wash; often in the original design the combination is most pleasing, but the camera does not approve of it, and frequently plays the most unexpected tricks with these combinations.[41]

The poor illustrator, who was expecting photography to liberate him forever from the technological restrictions of hand engravers and the older media, discovered to his chagrin that he must conform or fail.

> In this pure wash work you should be careful, very careful, not to let any meaningless pencil lines show through, as they always photograph, cannot be taken out, and at times spoil the whole effect; in fact, imperfections in wash drawings always reproduce more perfectly than the perfections themselves, and it is well to keep your paper reasonably clean, to avoid smudging, blots and lines, or otherwise you will be disappointed in the result. . . .[42]

The mixtures of techniques, the ignominious disasters of untalented men who thought the new halftone process could automatically ensure success in the way the old engravers had done, can be judged in one of the Moss halftones (see Plate 62, Chapter 6).

PLATE 19. *Engraving from Nature.*
Tonal white-line wood engraving by
Elbridge Kingsley, working directly on
the block from Nature. Reproduced here
the same size as the plate on Japan tissue
in F. Hopkinson Smith, American Illustrators *(New York: Scribner, 1892)*
from the copy owned by Mount Holyoke
College.

It is rather difficult to explain this, but the screen produces white lines in the darks and dark lines in the whites; you can see them by looking at any block. . . . This reproduction of wash work is very uncertain; good effects are obtained, about as often as failures. The delicate tones are not infrequently altogether lost. There are no positive blacks or whites, but a uniform grey tint covers the entire block. . . . Therefore, to get a good effect, when printed, the drawing should be simply made, that is if it is for cheap engraving and rapid printing; but if for the best books and magazines, wood engravers may be employed to remedy the imperfections of the photograph and the mistakes of the etcher.[43]

The idea that the "screen produces white lines in the darks and dark lines in the the whites" and that "a uniform grey tint covers the entire block" certainly verifies the coding processes of early halftone reproduction, and is counterindicative of Ivins' contention that "syntax," as he put it, was missing or so subliminal as not to matter. We shall see verified many times that it was the continuing presence of a necessary syntax (the code suited to a particular channel) which permitted the hand engravers to compete with the new media during the 1880s. Indeed, it was the ability of the practitioners of the tonal achievements of the New School of Engraving to surpass with infinite superiority the mean, gray effects of process halftone, that led to a fascinating transformation: the *secondary* codifier of information could so well outperform most of the *primary* codifiers of transmissions about Nature that the engraver became the illustrator.

THE ENGRAVER AS ILLUSTRATOR: THE EXAMPLE OF ELBRIDGE KINGSLEY

Some of the more astute, most amusing, and informative commentary about the state of the illustrator's art can be found in F. Hopkinson Smith's *American Illustrators* (1892), an invaluable document which was written in the form of imaginary dialogues about general questions of concern to artists and evaluations of how well contemporary artists were faring under the new reign of phototechnology. *American Illustrators* also presented a variety of the new media as "illustrations" of what the major American artist-illustrators were producing: a photogravure of Howard Pyle's "A Wounded Enemy," a heliotype of Will Low's "Narcissus" and another of Winslow Homer's "The Rower," an albertype of Kenyon Cox's "Lilith," photochromolithographs of Abbey's "The Two Sisters," and Frederic Remington's "A Russian Cossack," with the final plate being a "Japan proof" by Elbridge Kingsley of "Engraving from Nature" (Plate 19).

Now, what is astounding about this inclusion of Kingsley is that he had been an engraver for most of his professional career, in other words, he had dutifully reproduced the designs of illustrators. He was not functioning in *American Illustrators* as the originator of a message which another engraver had transcribed. His role was unique: he had somehow become an engraver-illustrator, and, curiously enough, it was photography which had accomplished this fact.

Kingsley's "Engraving from Nature" (Plate 19), was an outgrowth of many conditions which characterized the decade from 1882 to 1892. One of the masters of the New School of Engraving which had originated as a result of the proficiency and range of opportunity provided by photography-on-the-block, Kingsley may be said to have been the first American painter-wood engraver, in the same sense that the fine artist, James Whistler, was a painter-etcher. An outstanding practitioner of the art of reproduction (a subject to be discussed further in Chapter 8), Kingsley was quick to see the advantages of a new kind of paper imported into the United States in the early 1880s. This paper was transparent, lightweight, and seemingly fragile, yet it was the very paper which had made possible the many excellences of the Japanese woodblock art.

With "Japan paper," great delicacy of detail in wood engraving became possible. The publishing houses, whose autocratic possession of the block and all proofs therefrom had previously denied engravers any "framing print" use of their handiwork, were now persuaded to supply their loyal engravers not only a few Japan proofs of their own plates, but access to paper and press to produce a few originals. With Japan proofs to sell, engravers believed they could branch out on their own and become entrepreneurs. But for Kingsley, this economic advantage—small, at best—was secondary to a genuine creative ambition. For the capabilities of Japan paper tempted Kingsley into something which seems never to have been done before: to engrave directly from Nature, that is, to go out into the field with his block of wood and to render the textures of landscape directly on it, just as would any other autographic painter-etcher or painter-engraver.

He arrived at this development not simply through the availability of Japan paper, but rather because it was the logical next step in his relationship to photography-on-the-block. As mentioned earlier, Kingsley had had a distinguished career as a reproductive engraver specializing in landscape. Illustrator's conceptions of landscape had been transferred onto his working blocks via photography for many years. It had been *his* textures, *his* interpretations, *his* manipulations of codes for these photographs-on-the-block which had transmitted the message of the photograph—namely, a landscape—to the public. The original illustrators had been working as close to Nature as possible, sketching out of doors and often relying on photographs from Nature to supply their basic designs. Not only that, but the photograph-on-the-block transferring the artists' designs constituted a message about Nature—that is, always defining "Nature" as including man-made objects which exist in the three-dimensional world. If Kingsley could render into printing codes a message about "Nature," why could he not, and why should he not, do it directly, instead of producing a message about a message, as Timothy Cole perforce had to do in his "Modjeska"?

According to Kingsley's autobiography, he had been reading Philip Gilbert Hamerton's *A Painter's Camp*, which advocated traveling and camping outdoors for close communion with Nature. Early in the 1880s, at about the same time that P. H. Emerson was advocating soft-focus photography, Kingsley and his brother outfitted a cart with photographic apparatus, making a portable darkroom with combined sleeping quarters, and they traveled the Pioneer Valley in Massachusetts seeking appropriate views and then photographing them directly onto woodblocks. Kingsley's artistic goals were impressionist, affiliated not only to the poetics of Emerson's soft-focus Nature scenes, but to the Barbizon masters whom Kingsley had been employed to transmit via tonal wood engraving for the national magazines. "Engraving from Nature" was one of many such plates which he produced from direct association with landscapes. But we must note here that he remained largely dependent upon photography as an easy way to transfer a view onto a printable surface. However, instead of remaining in a New York office or in his house to render the textures of reality, he could check his effects and constantly improve upon and alter the photograph-on-the-block in accordance with the textures and chiaroscuro he could directly perceive, since he did not leave a scene until he had almost finished a wood engraving of that scene.

Such devotion to the effects of Nature and to the accuracy of transmission was very much a nineteenth-century outcome of the general influence of photography on the visual arts. Kingsley soon attracted like minds, and the formation of the "Society of American Wood Engravers," of which he and Timothy Cole and men such as A. M. Lindsay and J. P. Davis were all members, stirred a considerable American interest in the possibilities of direct work in wood engraving. National magazines published articles by and about them; their work was in great demand for reproductions as well as for creation of originals. In 1889, Kingsley himself received the highest possible reward for his labors: the Gold Medal of the Paris Exposition for original work in his field. And then the axe dropped.

> The photographic process plate, with its cheapness and facility of production, presently began to make such inroads upon the livelihood of the engraver that the bulk of the profession was soon crowded out. . . . Kingsley's work for publishers practically ended in 1890 with a record of about three hundred plates. . . . Since 1890 his engraving has been mainly on large work for the Japan proof alone, concerning which the general public has little knowledge.[44]

In other words, by the time that Kingsley's "Engraving from Nature" appeared in *American Illustrators,* he was technologically unemployed, put out of business entirely by a code and a medium which he had tried to rival or surpass: the process halftone. The woodcut and the wood engraving, media which had been used in one way or another almost continuously for four hundred years, had been ousted from the mass communications processes, separated from their reproductive functions, and would be ignored until artists decided to revive them as autographic media for framing prints in the twentieth century. Photography-on-the-block had transmitted information about Nature in such a way as to encourage illusionistic codes; ultimately it had suggested that the engraver go directly to Nature. By so doing, the engraver became an illustrator producing framing prints. It was a convolution probably unforeseen in the history of the graphic arts, yet it was not only wood engraving which photography ousted. The phototechnologies managed to antagonize myriad artists in many media, and the convolution developed in the same manner for each graphic medium.

THE CAMERA AND THE GRAPHIC ARTS IN GENERAL

Not everyone suffered an abrupt termination of his services. Timothy Cole, for example, had achieved such éclat that he was kept on to reproduce the Old Masters—more of which, later. The less great, however, went to work for the process engravers, or quit the trade entirely. "The most serious impact thus far has been upon the art of engraving on steel, which indeed was at a somewhat low ebb when the photogravure process sprang into existence, and it is doubtful if it will ever recover its old standing."[45]

Steel engraving, except as a curiosity or for producing bookplates and other minor work, was dead. Etching, as the most autographic of all processes, had revived in the so-called "etching craze" of the 1870s and 1880s, when everyone from Edouard Manet to Winslow Homer busied himself with making etchings from his own paintings as a protest against the encroachments of the phototechnologies; as early as 1863, in fact, when carbon prints and other refinements were transmitting photography throughout the Western world, the Europeans had risen in protest:

> At this time when photography charms the mob by the mechanical fidelity of its reproductions, it is necessary to encourage an artistic trend in favor of free caprice and picturesque fantasy. The need to react against the positivism of the mirrorlike camera has forced more than one painter to take to the etcher's needle. . . . The Société des Aquafortistes was founded to combat photography, lithography, aqua-tint, and engravings . . . to combat regular, automatic work, without inspiration which denatures the very idea of the artist.[46]

American illustrators and artists, who saw the exhibition of the Aquafortistes at the Philadelphia Centennial in 1876, were spurred to return to the free dance of the etcher's needle. In terms of ordinary trade publications, use of etching as a reproductive or as an original medium was out of the question, unless it were reproduced through either photomechanical process line engraving or other facsimile methods which were type-compatible.

> It is a curious fact that the photograph and photomechanical processes of reproducing printed pictures, which spurred the revival of interest in etchings among the artists of the middle nineteenth century, were also responsible in the last decade of the century for bringing the revival of etching to a close. By the end of the century color printing processes had made it possible to make printed copies of paintings, in full color, making the reproductions of paintings by means of etching absolutely obsolete. And the photogravure reproduction of etchings and paintings made the production of pictures of this kind so cheap and plentiful the art of etching lost its appeal to most artists because they could no longer derive any income from it . . . in general, the photogravure and the chromolithographic printing processes brought "the etching craze" to a sudden halt.[47]

Except for isolated instances of etchings used as frontispieces, as in the Bibliophile Society's limited deluxe edition of the *Odes and Epodes* of Horace (1901), etching, too, was finished as a reproductive medium. It took John Sloan's genius in the etchings for the novels of Paul de Kock to revive it as an authentic autographic medium for the creation of original works.

THE CAMERA AS ILLUSTRATOR

"The etching craze" began with a kind of artists' revolt against technological unemployment. The camera was, indeed, quite a threat. Instead of their own works being bought by the public, etchers saw the profits going to the photographer and the publisher. The economics of publishing were pushing illustrators to look to their livelihoods:

> . . . the introduction of processes in connection with photography is leading to another result, which deserves to be considered with some care. The publisher, who is most frequently the plotter of illustrated books, has been a very interested observer of the changes which have been going on. The element of cost has been that which he has most closely studied. As the processes have been developed, he has seen with increasing gratification that he could get rid of the engraver, and so reduce greatly the expense of his plant and the amount of his risk. An immense addition of illustrated books, of every degree of slovenliness, bears witness to this activity of the publishing mind. Having rid himself of the engraver, he has speculated if he cannot rid himself of the artist also, and thus still further reduce the cost of manufacture. . . .[48]

Now, the photograph as an illustration medium per se had been tried over and over again, as mounted prints or re-reproduced through the heliotype or the woodburytype. For example, one of the first American works of literature to be illustrated entirely by mounted photographic prints (see Plate 20, "Sculptor's Studio") was Nathaniel Hawthorne's *Transformations; or, The Romance of Monte Beni* (Boston: Houghton Mifflin, 1860) in three volumes. Thirty years later, the same book, now called *The Marble Faun; or, The Romance of Monte Beni* (Boston: Houghton Mifflin, 1890) was republished, this time illustrated with photogravures.

Whether the photographs or the photogravures were true "illustrations," or not, we have the following comment in the *Atlantic Monthly* in January of 1891:

> As the preface of that book states, the scheme was suggested by the very common practice, indulged in by travelers to Rome and Florence, of binding in photographs of localities and monuments referred to in the tale, insomuch that booksellers in those cities did a thriving business in furnishing books thus extended, ready made for the tourist. . . .[49]

If the editors of the *Atlantic Monthly* seemed to be mistaken that the style for such a book had been set in the 1890s, they were not mistaken in their judgment of the aesthetic value of such conglomerates. Here they comment on George Eliot's *Romola*, reviewed with the Hawthorne:

> To take up these books and judge them by the illustrations alone, one would suppose they were histories of Florence in the time of Savonarola. . . .

PLATE 20. ***Sculptor's Studio.*** *Mounted photographic print, anonymous Italian photographer. Reproduced here slightly enlarged from a plate in Nathaniel Hawthorne,* Transformations: or, The Romance of Monte Beni *(Boston: Houghton Mifflin, 1860). Courtesy of Columbia University Libraries.*

> It is indeed a bit of irony that the writer who took the human soul for her subject . . . should be illustrated . . . by stone walls, and towers, and prisons. It is as if one asked to be shown a city, and was conducted to the cemetery.[50]

The 1860 version of *Monte Beni* was filled with vacuous prints of "natives," or empty streets, or famous monuments, with as much relation to the story as for the *Romola* indicated above. Whether plumped out with photographic prints or with photogravures from Nature, such books were not "in any true sense illustrated books; they are simply, in the parlance of the collector, extended books." [51]

Unfortunately, the editors of the *Atlantic* were oddly optimistic about the future of such monstrosities. In their opinion,

> . . . there are scarcely any limits to the extent to which photography may be employed for book illustration. It is a common enough occurrence for tableaux to be arranged illustrative of the successive scenes of a poem. How easy to reproduce these groups in a series of photographs, to pass the photographs through the photogravure process, and then to publish them as accompaniments to the text in a holiday edition! [52]

For anyone who has seen a Victorian tableau, such a suggestion must surely bring on a fit of the giggles. Even the greatest artists such as Julia Cameron and Oscar Rejlander had difficulties with the ineluctable realism of the camera's product. Photography had its own essence, both as an artistic medium presenting its own compositions from Nature, and as a reproductive medium transmitting other artistic codes. One has only to take "Portrait from Life" (Plate 9) and imagine the heliotyped lady therein as an illustration for an edition of, say, Edgar Allan Poe's *Annabel Lee,* or facing a discreet typographical setting of Shelley's "To . . . ," or taking her dotted Swiss netting into Henry James' *Maisie,* to see how hilarious this effect would be—at least to modern eyes. Yet funnier effects were perpetrated in all good conscience. A typical example of 1890s high camp is an article called "Models and Art," which appeared in *Metropolitan Magazine* 3 (July 1896). On page 444, there appeared a poem accompanying a picture of two plump ladies. The poem, by Harriet Osgood Lunt, reads: "To the eye of subtler sight / Crassness loses all its dross; / Bathed thou art in Fancy's light, / While mere earth is but thy loss. / / Brush and chisel are to thee / As the flame to feeding spark; / Time may waste and youth may flee, / But Art's image ne'er will cark. / / Above this gem, the two draped ladies can only be described as squatting lumpishly bathed in realism's blight. While the article, "Models and Art" purported to be offering good advice on how to pose and photograph tender subjects like dying ladies, "Fancy's light" was never dimmer.

Even the greatest of such attempts to use real models posed in tableaux instead of artists' fictions is inevitably the cause of much laughter, for the very specificity of the models as they appeared in the code of developed process halftone—sparing nothing, even with the most assiduous retouching of wrinkle and mole—denied the essential aspect of fictive illustration: the imagination set free.

The imaginative illustrator would seem, then, to have been in less danger of losing his job than the packager of information. But even to the imaginative illustrator there were dangers which one of the major designers and illustrators of the 1890s remarked; in discussing the overall effects of photography on illustration, Walter Crane observed:

> Its influence . . . on artistic style and treatment have been, to my mind, of . . . doubtful advantage. The effect on painting is palpable enough, but so

far as painting becomes photographic, the advantage is on the side of the photograph. It has led in illustrative work to the method of painting in black and white, which has taken the place very much of the use of line, and through this, and by reason of its having fostered and encouraged a different way of regarding nature—from the point of view of accidental aspect, light and shade, and tone, it has confused and deteriorated . . . the faculty of inventive design, and the sense of ornament and line; having concentrated artistic interest on the literal realization of certain aspects of superficial facts, and instantaneous impressions instead of ideas, and the abstract treatment of form and line.[53]

While it is not within the scope of our general discussion to explore in any depth the aesthetic consequences of photography on artistic style and treatment, except as such consequences have a direct bearing on our study of codes and messages, the reader may wish to keep in mind photography's "having fostered and encouraged a different way of regarding nature— from the point of view of accidental aspect, light and shade, and tone," thereby having "confused and deteriorated . . . the faculty of inventive design, and the sense of ornament and line," as this has specific bearing on the problems we are investigating. We shall see that in the career of Howard Pyle, for example, when he worked decoratively in line (as in *Robin Hood, Stops of Various Quills,* or even in *One Hoss Shay*) he experienced comparatively little difficulty in reproduction, once he had learned the ground rules from process line men such as Moss. However, when he worked in illusionistic modes (no matter how fantastic the subject matter) which required that he order "a visual impression into a coherent, complete living form," [54] by means of imitating the effects of light and shade in Nature, he had a much more difficult time. Where his hand seemed completely at home in pen-and-ink, it faltered and became clumsy in his first wash drawings. It was photogravure, not process, for which he painted in oils rather than in watercolors, that permitted him to orchestrate the spectrum of monochrome gray-through-blacks. *Color* process halftone again revived the decorative in him, and some of his greatest illustrations were produced in that medium.

The same applies in large measure to Frederic Remington, whose very worst work was produced for the black-and-white process screened halftone camera, when he depended on news photographs, with all their "accidental aspect," as Crane put it. The "painting in black and white" which Crane deplored, was largely in monochrome gouache, an opaque watercolor paint which dries matte, reflecting no glare into the camera, and which could take almost endless corrections. The transparent watercolor washes, which, when used as artistic media, are characterized by crisp edges, sparkling detail, and a spontaneous, autographic quality demanded of a quick-drying, yet flowing, medium, were transformed by the process halftone screen into muddy waters indeed. If we can imagine a generation of artists trained to produce nothing but monochrome black-and-white gouaches or watercolors, or monochrome oils, we can well understand why it was that a famous illustrator like Remington "did not experiment with colored oils until the early 1890's, and it took him several years to master the technique." [55]

Freedom of artistic expression, usually associated with free choice of artistic media to be manipulated in whatever manner the artist chooses, was certainly not *automatically* conferred upon illustration by phototechnology, even though it expanded the choices available, gradually including color in the repertory of effects. If we realize that "the printed image consists normally of ink and nothing else," [56] and the smoothness, brightness, whiteness, and gloss of paper contributes to the success of the ink image, and that a graphic medium must somehow combine channel, code, ink, and paper for the production of visual images which in some way resemble an original message, we can understand that expanded choices in artistic media alone do not always guarantee duplicative results. As Victor Strauss indicates, printing inks have color, gloss, and thickness, each of these factors influencing the ultimate printed message. The characteristics of printing inks for color process halftone must be transparency and richness of deposit, since the final effect depends upon the superimposition of three or four colors. The human factor cannot be overlooked, either:

> Before undertaking color process work of any kind it is advisable to have one's eyes examined by a specialist to learn if there is any defect in color perception.[57]
>
> The reproduction of colour is a fascinating subject; it involves physiology, psychology, physics, chemistry, and technology; it presents complexities which are well nigh unfathomable; it involves a wide variety of industrial enterprises; yet its climax is an event of the utmost commonplace, looking at pictures.[58]

Obviously, looking at a reproduction of an illustrator's work is not the same as looking at his original work. When we think about freedom of expression, we must take into consideration the technological demands which inevitably dictate the methods of the artist. Sometimes the artist cleverly capitalized on these very technological limitations; for example, on the fact that *red* is interpreted by photographic emulsions to be *black*. Thus, Howard Pyle, for example, in order to be able to judge his own results before sending them to the printer, developed a style of painting in red and black, distinguishing, say, the trickle of blood down a gladiator's arm by using red in the original, simply so that he could *see* what he was doing. It is perhaps like asking a great colorist like Rubens to paint his masterpieces in monochrome, differentiating each texture and material only by chiaroscuro and linear detailing.

It was mentioned in Chapter 3 that the first color experiments in engraving by Le Blon had been based on the Newtonian discovery that "there are but three primary colors, and that all the other colors and hues are mixtures of these three in varying proportions." [59] Thomas Young (1773–1829) also offered the hypothesis that the human eye contained at least three types of color receptors, "sensitive to red/yellow/blue. Later, he modified his hypothesis, suggesting red/green/purple as the primary set." [60] Various process halftone engraving schemes, as well as color heliogravure, were developed during the 1890s based on either of these schemes, but the three-color processes fell far short of what many considered the optimum of color reproduction.

> Whether to use three or four colours has long been one of the contest points in colour work. The theoretical advocates of three colours have stoutly held out for three-colour, but many practical men hold the faith that three colours can never give an entirely satisfactory rendering of the subject. The weakness of the three-colour process is chiefly found in the rendering of blue in all its gradations, in its inability to yield a good grey, and in the imperfection of the blacks, which according to theory should be formed by the superposing of the three colours in equal strength. The remedy proposed is to use a black or neutral grey as a fourth printing.[61]

Illustrators, naturally enough, became advocates of the various systems of color reproduction, all seeking for some correspondence between the flat ink impressions and the texture and impasto of their own work. Compared to the somewhat heavy-handed ordinary trade chromolithography, the perfected relief and intaglio processes were miracles of compression of detail, although the limitation of the latter processes to combinations of three and four primary colors, even in superimposition by fine screens, did not achieve the richness of chromolithography using up to twenty-five impressions from different plates. The illustrator was still at least partially limited by the circumstances of the technology.[62]

One of the least expected results of the technological deluge of the nineteenth century was the appearance of what became known as "The Illustrator," a new creature. In 1895, Joseph Pennell wrote:

> . . . the cause of this modern development is not hard to discover. It was the application of photography to the application of books and papers which established the art on a new basis. As the invention of printing gave the first great impetus to illustration, so surely and more importantly from the invention of photography . . . . Greater ease of reproduction, greater speed, greater economy of labour have been secured, as well as greater freedom for the artist, and greater justice in the reproduction of his design.[63]

Recognizing that cheap reproduction was "flooding the world with cheap and nasty illustrated books and periodicals," [64] Pennell nevertheless insisted that "not in the days of Dürer himself was so large a proportion of genuinely good work published." [65]

On balance, the Pennell of 1895 seemed to find "progress" in the vision of enlargement of potentialities through photography. We may contrast this with Joseph Pennell in 1920, looking back on the whole period we have been discussing and on its aftermath:

> The screen has been a great blessing and a great curse to illustration. By its use paintings can be reproduced and any sort of drawing; consequently a tribe of money grubbers have arisen who can't draw, can't paint, but they have formed a combine, and the screen and the artless editor are altogether responsible for the utter downfall of American illustration. For a while editors believed they could drive artists out of the magazines by photography. People got sick of it. But they have standardized and sterilized artists in a fashion to delight a prohibitionist.[66]

On the one hand, then, was the curse. Had there truly been a blessing? He thought, "Drawings . . . may be intelligently prepared for the half-tone process in wash or oil, but by either one the screen deadens, lowers, flattens them. . . ." [67] Perhaps color was the blessing?

> It is ridiculous to say color can be reproduced by the present mechanical methods. How can a painting, which has no pure red or blue or yellow in it, be copied by the use of raw reds, blues, and yellows? The engraver and printer must use the colors the artist used, and the artist must know what colors to use, what colors will reproduce and print. Both must study this in a technical school.[68]

Color was certainly *not* the blessing:

> To make color prints, as many blocks must be cut as there are colors. The artist must mix the colors himself and put them on one by one, colors that will print. This method can be employed for rapid printing. It is the only right one. The three-color scheme can be seen on the cover of any magazine, each more artless than the other. The artist must be prepared to have mean-

ingless, artless tints of blue, brown, or green stuck over his drawings by artless editors and printers, the drawing cut in half and put on two pages facing each other, bits cut clean off—in fact there is no end to the barbarities, vulgarities and inanities the art editor will perpetrate on an artist's design after it has left his hands.[69]

The "artless tints" were certainly perpetrated on Remington, for example, many of whose black-and-white gouaches or monochrome oils were given some window dressing by the addition of a color tint which was simply a percentage of a color solid produced by the relative density of a screen, producing a flat area of dots of color which was superimposed over, or sometimes printed under, the form-giving chiaroscuro. Remington did not ask for such treatment; it was simply doled out at their own discretion by the art editors. He did, however, cooperate in what is presently called "fake process," or the use of numbers of flat tints, printed at varying angles to avoid a moire pattern, to imitate what the true process halftone color camera did: to separate colors from an original by means of filters. In fake process, the method by which many of Remington's full-page and double-spread illustrations were produced for *Colliers'*, the following procedures were employed, using black-and-white copy as the original:

> To make color half-tones from an ordinary photograph that will be pleasing and yet not require too many printings, the following method will be found . . . quite superior . . . capable of much or little, depending upon the artist who lays out the colors, and is not very difficult. Four prints, if cleverly "laid out," will give nearly all the colors required in any portrait or landscape. A thoroughly good halftone negative and an etching on copper is the first requirement. From the same negative make three prints on zinc by the albumen process, and then powdered and burned in. Make a proof from the copper etching on calendered paper, and let the artist roughly color it so as to serve as a guide in preparing the plates. The first, or yellow plate, is to have all required solids painted in with etching ink that has been thinned. . . . All parts of the plate where no yellow should appear are now to be scraped away with a sharp scraper, cutting right through to the bare metal. This gives a plate composed of solids, middle tints, formed by the screen, and whites. If it is desired to produce any further gradation it is best done with a "Ben Day" machine. . . . The red and blue plates are to be treated in the same manner. . . . The yellow is to be printed first, the red next, followed by the blue, and over all the key plate is printed, either in a warm brown or in a combination of all three of the other inks, which will give an almost black impression. . . .[70]

By this method of "fake process," whether using one or more tints, a Remington appeared in "duotone"—brown and black—as early as September 20, 1890, in *Harper's Weekly*.

> He had, of course, to pay the penalty of the artist who turns from illustration in black-and-white to work in color. For a considerable time his pictures were invariably marked by a garishness not to be explained alone by the staccato effects of a landscape whelmed in a blaze of sunshine. I have seen paintings of his which were as hard as nails.[71]

Clearly, Remington—along with his contemporaries—was simply learning what he had to learn: how to put together color pictures the way they would print; in bright, flat tones, "hard as nails." It was only with the improvement of process engraving toward the end of his life in the first decade of the twentieth century that he was liberated from this illustrator's fate of being constrained by technology.

SUMMARY

It seems evident from the foregoing discussion that the primary codifiers of messages, namely, individuals who came to be called "illustrators," depended for the efficacy of their codes not purely on the secondary codifier, the engraver, but on a combination of technological insights and training. The illustrator was not simply free to "express himself" at any time, before or after the advent of photography, despite the fact that the phototechnologies enlarged his repertoire enormously. Indeed, his very professional status was considered by many to have been "brought into being by 'process' engraving—those modern methods of reproduction . . . which have completely revolutionized the Illustrator's practice." [72]

Before the phototechnologies, the Illustrator was

> . . . an obscure journeyman working at a poorly-considered craft. Distinction in handling—that which, in a word, we call nowadays "technique"— was so seldom thought of that the illustrator whose mere powers of draughtsmanship were assured was rarely troubled by his editor or his publisher on the score of style. As a matter of fact, the artist who attempted an individual method found his efforts thrown away on the wood-engravers, who promptly engraved all individual manner out of his drawing on the woodblock.[73]

We have a general idea, then, of the illustrator of the 1880s as an artist who was beginning to find a personality, and of the 1890s, as insisting on one. The wood engraver, on the other hand, who signed all his reproductive transmissions in an often conspicuous flourish during the 1880s, found himself by the late 1890s thrust into permanent anonymity.

But a personality—of an illustrator or of anyone else—is suitable only for "artistic expression," not for the objective communication of the visual world in some perfect transmission such as William Ivins seemed to desire. As Philip Hamerton remarked, "The natural material is in itself artistically as nothing; it only becomes something in the sensations of a human being." [74]

In terms of information transfer, therefore, personality was only a hindrance.

Apparently, an artist could not be expected to free himself, even if he could, from the trappings of personality. Worse, there was a natural ethnocentricity which befell his technique, approach, selection of codes, manner, in every detail. National academies had been established since the Renaissance; these perpetuated specific schemes for transmitting information which became more and more insular and idiosyncratic. "Much as he might want to, a German in the fifteenth or sixteenth century could not draw like an Italian, or *vice versa*. This meant that neither could say the same things in his drawings that the other could." [75]

If not only personality but nationality blocked objective statements about reality, there is the implication here that a mechanical process had to be found, one which could effectively bypass the subjective responses and the parochial training of all artists, or a reliable system of universal visual communication could not be developed.

One alternative which nineteenth-century illustrators pursued was to work from photographs. The reality depicted in these photographs was distorted by the lenses, by the inevitable compression of three-dimensional planes into a single plane on the paper, or by whatever obstruction happened to be either on the lens or on the negative at the time of the original exposure or of printing; and, as Pennell observed, drawings made by copying photographs

... even by the most skilful men, lack the go and life obtained when the work is done direct from nature, or at least without the photograph; and every true artist prefers nature to any photograph. There is nothing in the world more difficult to work from. One is confused by endless, unimportant, unselected details; the point of view is never that which one would have selected, and the result, save in the rarest instances, is dubbed photographic even by the artless.[76]

Yet, it was better to work from a photograph than from the imagination.

There were certain kinds of drawings which Ivins admitted justified the existence of "illustrators," drawings for which no photograph could supply the appropriate selected information: diagrams. "In fact, even today, when we want to give a statement not of personal characteristics but of abstracted generic form we still use drawings for our illustrations." [77]

For other reasons as well, such as the ludicrous inadequacies of attempting to illustrate fiction with the inescapable realism of the camera, illustrators could not be entirely replaced by photography from Nature.

THE INVESTIGATION OF SPECIFIC ILLUSTRATORS

A good test of much that we have been indicating thus far will naturally occur as we explore the work of three specific illustrators, and we should be able to see general results of the impact of photography on visual communication through such study. In fact, the examination of the careers of Howard Pyle, Frederic Remington, and William Hamilton Gibson can be expected to reveal far more detail and perhaps a different perspective or perhaps even different events or outcomes, even as we might suspect that much of what has been indicated here will be generally confirmed through their careers.

Several critical questions arise as we turn to these specific careers.

(a) Was there a close chronological relationship between the availability of photographic media and their use by illustrators, or did extraneous considerations delay the adoption of the new media?

(b) What circumstances dictated the choice of reproductive media and how did these influence the choice of the artistic medium of the original of an illustration?

(c) What were the illustrator's intellectual, emotional, and aesthetic responses to the new reproductive media, as evidenced in verbal comment or in departures from previous modes of pictorial expression?

(d) What differences, if any, can be discerned in the effects of the various reproductive media on the same illustration, whether re-reproduced in the same size or in different sizes, in terms of the accurate transmission of an artist's original?

(e) What, if any, new modes of pictorial expression were made possible by the illustrator's reliance on photography per se, either as a source for artistic inspiration or for visual documentation of "reality"?

(f) What were the reactions of readers, more specifically, book reviewers and art critics, to the illustrations by these artists reproduced in the new photomechanical media?

The answers to these questions provide some means of assessing the totality of responses to the new media, specifically in terms of their capabilities for artistic expression and for information transfer, permitting us to evaluate, or reevaluate, each of the three illustrators in question both as creators of expressive images and as technicians.

Howard Pyle (1853–1911): The Intermix of Imagination and Technology

It has been said that the highest aim of the photomechanical processes is to convert a photograph from any natural scene, or from a painting, into a printable block or plate, without the intervention of designer or engraver.[1]

Illustrators of fiction find themselves in very much the same circumstances as the directors of films. Both have to adhere to the general outlines of a writer's script, and their genius is expected to find expression in the *mise en scène,* the creation of visual realities through the appropriate lighting, costume, arrangement of dramatic interrelationships, mood, and the selection of revealing detail. While the director of a film concentrates on the placement of the actors and the pacing of the script, another skilled professional, the cameraman, is responsible for how the scene will materialize on the medium, film. Some great cameramen have quite literally created the masterpieces for which their directors received their accolades. It should not surprise us, therefore, that just as they suffered incorrect transmissions, illustrators of the nineteenth century often won praise for what was, essentially, the technical ingenuity of the hand engraver, who was, like the cameraman, the materializer of form in a specific medium.

Not all directors of films, of course, work from a writer's script. Some, like Sergei Eisenstein, Orson Welles, and Ingmar Bergman, have either dominated the script or invented it themselves. These are the masters of film, who work in a totality of visual-verbal interrelationships which are uniquely their own. Within the smaller world of illustration, which was, nevertheless, as potent a distributor of visual images for the nineteenth century as the movies have been for the twentieth, Howard Pyle represents the model for each kind of artist: simultaneously capable of creating his own stories and books and of visually dramatizing the verbal creations of others. In each instance, however, he was dependent on the skills of the transmitters of his ideas. Like the genuine nineteenth-century artist that he was, Pyle dreamed all his life of someday not only being free from the trammels of publishing, with its deadlines, demands, and difficulties, but also free from having to illustrate anything but his own ideas. In essence, he wanted to be a "fine artist," someone whom he conceived as working only toward the creation of individual, nonrepeatable works of art.

Pyle was exceptionally versatile, working with equal ease in themes from folk tales, high Gothic romance, Colonial history, classical Roman melodramas, seafaring adventures, and children's fantasies, and was in each genre, ultimately, a master of exquisite mood and powerful design. He demonstrated again and again that he could learn the technical demands of new media, even if, as time went on and the pressure of his own fame left him less time in which to cope with all the exploitative treatments of his work by publishers, toward the end of his life he tended to ignore the limitations of transmission media and asked for nothing better than to create compositions which could stand on their own as easel paintings. His career is of considerable interest to us, therefore, as he went from his early apprenticeship to the technical exigencies of the Moss process to his later grand-masterly waiving of publishing requirements. It was photography and phototechnology which made this transition possible, whether we consider it positively or negatively.

Pyle's career was a long one in which he served to creatively imagine for his public a host of lively characters, from Robin Hood to the Cock Lane Ghost. Working in a variety of media, from pen-and-ink to watercolor, oils both monochrome and full-color, and gouache, he also experienced a generous range of transmission media. As one commentator remarked:

> . . . remember, Pyle started out with direct reproduction. He was working at the time the half-tone process came in. He was the forerunner of the day when the two-color set came in, and was practically the first man who worked with the three-color plate when it appeared. . . .[2]

As each photomechanical medium appeared, Pyle had to restructure his thinking, and with some new media this proved to be felicitous, while in others, for example, with transparent watercolor reproduced in process halftone, he encountered artistic disaster. It was not enough to be able to draw interesting scenes or compose a telling anecdote. He was in the midst of a technological revolution in visual communication, and he was heir to all the difficulties which photography had engendered.

Born shortly after Sir Henry Fox Talbot discovered the principle of the screen for separating continuous tone into printable bits of information — something which the old gentleman got around to patenting and perfecting in 1858 — Pyle's early years in illustration parallel the early struggles of transmission media for mastery over the problems of transforming halftones into "dots" on the page. By the time Pyle was ready to seek his fortune as an illustrator, photographic transfer of originals to woodblocks was a commonplace, the woodburytype was being mounted into books, the heliotype had just been imported by Osgood, the *New York Daily Graphic* had already achieved an initial success with its 1873 modification of an "Albertotype" into intermediate tone printing via photolithography, and John Calvin Moss had already established what was to become America's largest photoengraving company of that generation. In 1876, when Howard Pyle left his native Wilmington for the publishing opportunities of New York City, he was to discover that mere drawing talent was scarcely a guarantee of employment. What had become mandatory in the year of the Philadelphia Centennial was an understanding of the technological demands of a new profession.

EARLY ENCOUNTERS WITH THE MOSS PROCESS
AND WOOD ENGRAVING

In the typical fashion of the day, Pyle began his career by submitting ideas for "compositions" to the art editors of the illustrated journals, as well as by illustrating his own poems and stories. From almost the very beginning, however, he encountered serious reproduction difficulties. While his first pen-and-ink outline drawings for his poem "The Magic Pill" (*Scribner's Monthly*, July 1876), were accepted without interference, his projected series of fables illustrated in outline ran afoul of John Moss and the rigid strictures of photomechanical line reproduction techniques:

> Nov. 17, 1876
>
> I went down to *Scribner's* yesterday to take my fable to Mrs. Dodge. There was, I believe, some little difficulty in regard to the blurring of the lines of my illustrations, since both the former and Mr. Drake, the Art Editor, suggested that I should go down and see the Photoengraving Company and obtain such suggestions as they might offer.[3]

"Mrs. Dodge" was, of course, Mary Mapes Dodge, then editor of *St. Nicholas*, a children's magazine of highest literary and artistic standards, published by *Scribner's*. "The Photoengraving Company" was another name for Moss, and Pyle must have obeyed Mrs. Dodge, for on the next day he could report in a letter to his mother that he had visited the Moss establishment and "received many valuable hints in regard to pen drawing." [4] That these hints could not be carried out either easily or quickly can be gleaned from the following:

> Dec. 15, 1876
>
> Still more reverses, and worse than before! I went down to see Mrs. Dodge yesterday morning to find out whether she had accepted my fairy tale or not . . . what worried me was the complaint that was made of my drawings for the fable; and they certainly do not look well in print. They seem coarse and cheap looking, more so than in the original drawings, for upon being reduced, they blotted and came up "black and heavy looking."
>
> Mrs. Dodge complained very much . . . "I am getting tired of these cheap looking actinics.[5] People are beginning to complain about them, and we shall have to use more wood-engraving." [6]

Here, "actinics," also known as "actinic engravings," after the fact that it was some of the sun's actinic rays which made photography possible at all, was yet another name for the Moss process line engraving. The word is no longer in use.

As for what Mrs. Dodge meant by her complaints, it is difficult to decide. Was she exonerating Pyle's craftsmanship while blaming Moss? Was she expressing concern that too much pure outline illustration was repelling readers, and that wood engravings—probably what we are calling tonal wood engravings, those attempting chiaroscuro renderings of painted illustrations—would satisfy these disgruntled readers? Or was she suggesting that even simple outline drawings could be better reproduced by the then obsolescing black-line wood-engraving technique, rather as Timothy Cole had laboriously wood engraved Wyatt Eaton's pen-and-ink portrait of Abraham Lincoln?

Whatever her exact meaning, we gather from this and other evidence that by December of 1876, *actinics* had already waged a successful battle to oust the older medium by virtue of cheapness and dispatch, if only in the reproduction of the simpler outline pen-and-ink drawings. Yet Pyle's difficulties were symptomatic of a technological transition. John Moss was only beginning to train the new breed of artists in the art of producing complex chiaroscuro through crosshatch shading with pen-and-ink, which he could reproduce photomechanically (more of this in the next chapter), nor were the newly introduced shading and stipple papers, used to simulate the codes of lithography through photomechanics, successfully attracting major talents or practitioners. Tonal wood engravings remained the major method of simulating halftones in the year of the Centennial. Moss may have owned the woodburytype patent in the United States, and James Osgood was making the heliotype widely available, but they were not suitable for periodical publication in large quantities, type-compatible, or appropriate for rotary presses. Photogravure was still a French monopoly.

Howard Pyle, therefore, thinking himself repudiated by Mrs. Dodge, forced himself to exert all his energies during 1877 to master two antithetical techniques: (a) the production of pen-and-ink outline drawings suitable for actinics; and (b) the rendering of monochrome chiaroscuro paintings suitable for tonal wood engraving via photography-on-the-block.

Despite his hard work, he suffered the customary humiliation of the young illustrator of the times: that of having the *Scribner's* staff artists redraw his sketches for his first accepted article, "Chincoteague" (April 1877).[7] It is unlikely that he supplied more than a sketch for his first full-page illustration in *Harper's Weekly* (May 12, 1877), "Queen of the May," rendered in tonal wood engraving from what a note in the study scrapbooks prepared by the Wilmington Society of Fine Arts indicates was a drawing on wood made with pencil and tinted with india ink. This plate is so large that a detail selected for this book would be nearly useless. His second full page, "Entangled" (January 19, 1878), was "Drawn by E. A. Abbey from a Sketch by H. Pyle," and it was not until his first gigantic double-page spread appeared (a singular honor for so young an artist), that he could convince Charles Parsons, then Art Editor of *Harper's Weekly,* to let him work up his own idea for reproduction. "Wreck in the Offing!" (March 9, 1878), painted in monochromatic opaque watercolors during the winter of 1877–1878, was photographed on an enormous woodblock (19.7 x 17.6 inches) and engraved in vigorous textures by an engraver called "Lagarde." Compared to the execrable rendering of "Queen of the May," in which the rain outside the window is exactly the same texture as the girl's clothing, "Wreck in the Offing!" displays some of the better characteristics of the black-line engraving codes.

Pyle was as disappointed with the general run of wood engravers as Mrs. Dodge had been with actinic engravers.

> Feb. 28, 1878
> . . . it would be useless to submit aforesaid criticisms to Mr. Parsons as they can't very well correct the expression of the face without doing another block over again, and there isn't time for that, as it is coming out this week. I will send you a proof of my Indian picture, so you can see how an engraver can knock spots out of a thing, and make allowances for my poor work accordingly.[8]

Some of the difficulties which even a competent wood engraver faced, however much he was aided by photographing an original drawing on the block, can be understood by comparing a Pyle original with the wood-engraving transmission of it. In a typical example, one of the illustrations for Rossiter Johnson's "Phaeton Rogers" (*St. Nicholas,* March 1881) the original gouache drawing owned by the Wilmington Society of Fine Arts

Willard Morse Collection (Plate 22) was almost twice the size of the wood engraving (Plate 21). It is a night scene, with figures rendered originally in blacks, grays, and a few whites, in an overall close harmony of tones somewhat compressed by reducing it for reproduction purposes here. The original (Plate 22) is a strong, well-realized composition. In the wood engraving, however, the overall effect is scratchy and fussy: detail which was comprehensible and purposeful in the original becomes destructive in the transmission to the public.

Comparing the vest and shirt of the central figure, for example, we can see that in the original, the vest is as dark as the shadow behind the inquiring policeman, while in the wood engraving the vest looks like a vertical striped fabric instead of solid color and is much lighter than it should be.

PLATE 21. *One of the Policemen . . . White-line wood engraving from illustration by Howard Pyle. Reproduced here the same size as a plate for Rossiter John-son's, "Phaeton Rogers," in* St. Nicholas Magazine, *January 1881, from the copy owned by the Forbes Library.*

PLATE 22. *One of the Policemen ...*
Gouache painting by Howard Pyle, orig-
inal for wood engraving; see Plate 21.
Reproduced here slightly reduced from
the original. Courtesy of the Willard S.
Morse Collection, Wilmington Society
of the Fine Arts.

In the original, the shirt is close in tone and clearly stands for "white" seen at night, actually a deep gray. In the wood engraving, the shirt is totally wrong, destroyed by the attempt to put in strong highlights, so that the white of the page must be used, as always in wood, to express a great range of grays. As for the face of the central figure: in the original, it is darker than the sky behind it, well realized, with a marked decorative effect, even a black outline to separate it strongly from the background. In the reproductive wood engraving, the face is the same "color" as the sky, lacks the decorative outline; the beard, which was a fairly solid tone in the original is here a scratchy, obscure mess lacking both strength and directional value.

The original of another illustration for this same serialized story, "Edmund Burton, you are a genius!" (*St. Nicholas*, January 1881) has delightful scumble and dry-brush effects which are totally lost in reproduction; touches of light on various surfaces are almost obliterated by the "diagonal stripe code" used by the engraver.

We shall find, again and again, that the problems of representing simultaneously the textures and details of execution of an original and its iconography constituted almost insuperable contradictions, and that these contradictions only became apparent with the arrival of photographic media.

PYLE AND CHROMOLITHOGRAPHY

Pyle returned to Wilmington in 1879, and it was here that he began to produce his first full-color illustrations for *Yankee Doodle* (Dodd, Mead, 1881), which were reproduced by chromolithography. A charming book, in the manner of Ralph Caldecott, the concept of the drawings and the manner in which they were reproduced seem to modern tastes so perfectly matched that the condemnation by Pyle's biographer seems totally unjustified: "It was done in color in a very crude way, for the methods of color reproduction were by no means refined in 1881."[9] But Abbott admits,

> It was full of a quaint and sprightly kind of humor, and was sufficiently successful to be followed up by *The Lady of Shalott*, done in the same manner. But whereas in so vigorous a subject as *Yankee Doodle* the imperfect coloring made little difference, in this next book with its romantic fervor and intensity, it meant a cheapening and vulgarizing of the pictures. *The Lady of Shalott* was a book which Howard Pyle always looked back upon with horror. Nothing could have suited him better than to see every copy destroyed.[10]

Where or when Howard Pyle expressed these sentiments has not been verified, but even the most cursory examination of *The Lady of Shalott* (Dodd, Mead, 1881), reveals sufficient reason for Pyle to have hated it, more out of a misunderstanding on his part than out of any essentially technological limitation. The book layout is extremely strange: on almost every left-hand page (see Plate 23A, "But in Her Web She Still Delights"), a stanza of the poem was hand-lettered, presumably, as in the case with medieval manuscripts, an integral part of the design. Yet the right-hand page (Plate 23B) supplies us with that same stanza again, this time in a monstrously ornate pseudo-Gothic, a horror out of the Victorian decadence of typography which has, at least, the virtue of being much more legible than Pyle's hand lettering! Perhaps Pyle had wanted the entire book to have the look of illuminated manuscripts, on the style of Owen Jones' chromolithographed reproductions in England. In any event, what is wrong with the book is certainly not the process per se, but rather the way

But in her web she still delights
To weave the mirror's magic sights,
For often thro' the silent nights
A funeral, with plumes and lights,
            And music, went to Camelot:
Or when the moon was overhead,
Came two young lovers lately wed;
'I am half sick of shadows,' said
            The Lady of Shalott.

in which the entire design was conceived. Those plates (see Plate 41, for example) which did not have to bear the burden of the inappropriate lettering are, at least, handsomely designed, even if some details printed poorly. Since Pyle so often did his own hand lettering, there is no reason to suppose that the inferior "manuscript" letters which so sadly mar his decorations are the work of another hand; but almost certainly it was not Pyle, after all, who did the color registration for the printing. That was, presumably, the job of the transfer artists at Brett Lithographic Company of New York. Perhaps Pyle had expected more color differentiation between the background designs and the lettering; otherwise, it is hard to imagine on what basis Pyle could have decided on this artistic scheme.

If the failure of *The Lady of Shalott* was all Pyle's fault, why did not the publisher restrain him? Or the color lithographer advise him, as Moss Engraving had advised him, that each medium has its specific characteristics, both advantages and limitations? In chromolithography, as in all

PLATE 24. *The Mighty Fight betwixt Little John and the Cook.* *Process line engraving from a pen-and-ink drawing by Howard Pyle. Reproduced here approximately one half of the size of the double spread in Pyle's* The Merry Adventures of Robin Hood (*New York: Scribner, 1883*). *Courtesy of the Free Library of Philadelphia, Rare Book Dept.*

HOW LITTLE JOHN LIVED AT THE SHERIFF'S HOUSE. 73

"Now, by my faith," cried the Cook, as he rattled the pottle against the sideboard, "I like that same song hugely, and eke the motive of it, which lieth like a sweet kernel in a hazel-nut."

"Now thou art a man of shrewd opinions," quoth Little John, "and I love thee truly as thou wert my brother."

"And I love thee, too. But the day draweth on, and I have my cooking to do ere our master cometh home; so let us e'en go and settle this brave fight we have in hand."

"Ay, marry," quoth Little John, "and that right speedily. Never have I been more laggard in fighting than in eating and drinking. So come thou straight forth into the passage-way, where there is good room to swing a sword, and I will try to serve thee."

Then they both stepped forth into the broad passage that led to the Steward's pantry, where each man drew his sword again, and without more ado fell upon the other as though he would hew his fellow limb from limb. Then their swords clashed upon one another with great din, and sparks flew from each blow in showers. So they fought up and down the hall for an *Little John and* hour and more, neither striking the other a blow, though they *the Cook fight.* strove their best to do so; for both were skilful at the fence; so nothing came of all their labor. Ever and anon they rested, panting; then, after getting their wind, at it they would go again more fiercely than ever. At last Little John cried aloud, "Hold, good Cook!" whereupon each rested upon his sword, panting.

"Now will I make my vow," quoth Little John, "thou art the very best swordsman that ever mine eyes beheld. Truly, I had thought to carve thee ere now."

"And I had thought to do the same by thee," quoth the Cook; "but I have missed the mark somehow."

"Now I have been thinking within myself," quoth Little John, "what we are fighting for; but albeit I do not rightly know."

"Why, no more do I," said the Cook. "I bear no love for that pursy Steward, but I thought that we had engaged to fight with one another, and that it must be done."

"Now," quoth Little John, "it doth seem to me that instead of striving to cut one another's throats, it were better for us to be boon companions. What sayst thou, jolly Cook, wilt thou go with me to Sherwood Forest and join with Robin Hood's band? Thou shalt live a merry life within the woodlands, and sevenscore good companions shalt thou have, one of whom is mine own self. Thou shalt have two suits of Lincoln green each year, and forty marks in pay."

color processes which depend upon the accuracy of successive impressions from stone or metal, one minor slip of plates too finely registered can cause catastrophe.

The major point about *The Lady of Shalott* is, as the writer Charles Blanc noted in another connection, "One principle is important to remember, we should not attempt by one method what can be better done by another." [11] Pyle was attempting to render a combination of powerful decorative design, modeled shapes conveying chiaroscuro, and superimposed lettering in a medium which needed a large number of stones to achieve any subtlety of effects, and in which, moreover, he had insufficient experience. Another book available in 1874, long before Pyle's efforts, Harriet Beecher Stowe's *Women in Sacred History* reveals that, given a sufficient number of stones with which to achieve its effects, chromolithography was capable of a considerable range of chiaroscuro and decorative effects. [12] But the fact that the Stowe book was illustrated with chromolithographs imported from France indicates that American color work was not up to European standards.

The numerous flat tones employed by chromolithography to simulate continuous tones, which had proved so successful for *Yankee Doodle,* had proved seriously inadequate for an adult theme designed by Pyle. And the lessons of *The Lady of Shalott* were not lost on Pyle. His particular and outstanding genius for color was thwarted by his own inability to design for an admittedly limited medium. Undaunted, he continued his pursuit of decorative expressiveness in black-and-white media, two years later achieving what was destined to become "a masterpiece of writing for children, and incidentally a masterpiece of printing and binding," [13] perhaps the greatest single work he ever produced in any medium, *The Merry Adventures of Robin Hood* (Scribner, 1883).

PYLE AND THE MOSS PROCESS TRIUMPH

Pyle's *Robin Hood,* limited to a code of pure blacks and whites, achieved all the variety of page layout, boldness of decorative effect, and accuracy of detail that had been denied him in *The Lady of Shalott.* Contrary to the information in various sources, ranging from his bibliographers, Morse and Brinckle, [14] to periodical articles and the opinions of several rare books librarians, the delightful illustrations for *Robin Hood* were reproduced not by facsimile wood engraving, as has been claimed, but by process line engraving (see Plate 24, "The Mighty Fight betwixt Little John and the Cook") just as his fables had been reproduced for *St. Nicholas* by Moss. [15]

It is possible that the confusion over which process reproduced these famous illustrations arose, not so much out of ignorance or inadequate research, but out of an identification of these illustrations with the techniques of another age. That Pyle had assiduously studied the graphic art of Albrecht Dürer is, of course, well known. Indeed, Joseph Pennell remarked about Pyle that, "I admit, with certain American critics whom I respect, that in some qualities it is very hard to tell where Dürer ends and Howard Pyle begins." [16] Pennell found the later *Otto of the Silver Hand* (Scribner, 1888) even more Dürer-esque than *Robin Hood:*

> . . . one finds the little tail-pieces there have much the same motives and are carried out in much the same spirit . . . while they are reproduced mechanically with an ease that would have surprised Dürer . . . the full pages, though reproduced by process, look like old wood blocks; the head and tail-pieces might be mistaken at a glance for Dürer's. [17]

There should be no surprise at this apparent paradox, that Pyle was imitating for another channel the codes of an earlier medium when he produced the pen-and-ink drawings [18] for the two books mentioned above. Dürer and his engravers had solved one of the most difficult tasks of the graphic arts: to distribute tiny black shapes over a white surface in such a way that each of the shapes printed legibly as a contribution to the construction of a larger symbol, e.g., a knight on horseback. They had also solved the problem of suitable directions of cutting, so that the lines of the code were themselves pleasing to the eye and not conflicting with the larger message, which had been planned with the code in mind.

A woodcut "is like a pen drawing with an added regularity of tone . . ." [19] and Pyle was by this time well versed in the strict necessity for conceiving his design in alternations of "regular tone," i.e., solid blacks and pure white. His teacher in this necessity had not been solely the masterly example of a great sixteenth-century artist, but, rather, as we have seen, the prosaic technological demands of John Moss and nineteenth-century photomechanical line engraving.

If sales of *Robin Hood* were slow at first, despite its artistic and literary merits, the ultimate success of the style and format of Pyle's design and illustration led him to formulate similar black-and-white illustrations for his other so-called medieval masterpieces, *Pepper and Salt* (Harper, 1886), *The Wonder Clock* (Plates 13 and 43), the aforementioned *Otto of the Silver Hand* (Scribner, 1888) and his *King Arthur* series (Scribner, 1903 and 1905). Gradually, he departed more and more from the Dürer prototype in favor of his own more decorative Art Nouveau impulses, closer to Burne-Jones, William Morris's artist for several major Kelmscott Press productions, including the famous Chaucer. Morris, however, is said to have considered *Robin Hood* the finest book to have come out of America. Whether this was because Pyle was duplicating Morris's own intentions of creating "perfect" books which featured decorative black-and-white illustrations combined with decorative typography, or because Pyle's subject matter suited Morris's Pre-Raphaelite inclinations, one cannot be sure. It is safe to say, however, that neither of them was visually recreating the "medieval book." On the contrary, it was the Renaissance book which influenced them, Morris leaning more toward the size and color of the large incunabula, Pyle, more toward the conglomerate effects of sixteenth-century printing, where woodblocks from different books were often reassembled in new combinations of an eclectic but often aesthetically satisfying effect.

Quite literally, Pyle's books were reassemblages. All of these "medieval" fables were first published in individual story form or installments in *Harper's Young People, St. Nicholas,* or other juvenile publications, with plates in these periodicals that were almost invariably larger than the ultimate reproductions for the book. With inexpensive photomechanical line engraving, which preserved Pyle's original drawing from use as an engraver's original on the block, it was quite easy to reduce Pyle's pen-and-inks to whatever size was wanted. While these bold drawings could tolerate up to about a fifty-percent reduction in size (and were, indeed, often planned from the beginning for such a reduction), without too great distortion of the artist's intentions or the destruction of legibility of forms, the practice of rephotographing either an original drawing first reproduced in a magazine, or proofs of that reproduction, for the purposes of illustrating books, was to prove extremely unsatisfactory as it was applied to tonal wood engravings, process halftones, or photogravures. Strictly speaking, since the illustrations for *Robin Hood* were designed for periodical publication first, can one say that Pyle was truly illustrating a *book?* Perhaps not in the modern sense, although with the so-called "medieval" books illustrated with pen-and-inks, he did a magnificent job of suturing the plates and the text together.

FURTHER ENCOUNTERS WITH WOOD ENGRAVING

Howard Pyle was an extraordinarily versatile artist. Not limited to any one technique or style, he could draw almost anything he set his mind to, in almost any way that he wanted. At the outset of his career he had to force himself to conquer two basic technical problems of reproduction: (a) the production of pen-and-ink outline or cross hatch drawings suitable for actinics; and (b) the rendering of monochrome chiaroscuro paintings suitable for tonal wood engraving through photography-on-the-block. With the success of *Robin Hood*, Pyle had proved his mastery over the first problem. But the illustrations for "Phaeton Rogers," previously discussed, were just the beginning of the struggle to master the second.

In 1884, Pyle produced several illustrations for a schoolbook, Horace E. Scudder's *A History of the United States* (New York: Taintor), among the earliest of his large Colonial-American oeuvres. These American history illustrations were from the very first inclined toward naturalistic representationalism rather than decoration. Full of meticulously researched detail, based on life studies or on photographs of models in costume, they were intended to be in the history-painting tradition of the English and French academics, continuing the idea of the representation of history as an enactment on a stage. "You-are-there" is the key to all his Colonial pictures.

For such minute precision, which was a typical outgrowth of photographic influence on the style of nineteenth-century painting, the codes of tonal wood engraving had distinct limitations. Since black-and-white photography had encouraged men to hope for achieving "true" reproduction of nature in all the graphic arts, wood engraving from W. J. Linton on had sought to refine and develop techniques of symbolizing chiaroscuro. Even as Pyle was struggling with monochrome modeling, engravers such as Timothy Cole and Elbridge Kingsley were beginning to liberate wood engraving from the continuing conservatism of W. J. Linton. These men invented new textures to imitate the characteristics of real objects, but no matter how ingeniously they could render certain subtleties of landscape, they could not find a solution to the problem of rendering details of anatomy, flesh, or costumes, *below a certain size of reproduction*, a problem which William Ivins overlooked for the most part. The need for excavation of the wood surface could not permit a small enough positive (black-line, rather than white-line) dot to render the details of faces. Compare, for example, Plate 25, "Dutch and Indians Trading," from the Scudder schoolbook, with Plate 26, "The Choicest Pieces of Her Cargo," engraved by Albert Munford Lindsay, for an article which appeared in *Harper's New Monthly Magazine* in 1895. Even the most advanced and almost unbelievably fine textures of Lindsay had perforce to be in the service of black-line positive rendering of facial details in tiny sizes. In Plate 25, "Dutch and Indians Trading," the engraver used white-line wherever possible, but he was forced to employ black-line to transmit shadows along noses, eyebrows, the outlines of eyes, and so on. Not all engravers solved these problems in similar ways.

the Hudson, and took possession of tracts of country as far south as Delaware Bay. They established trading-posts also on the Connecticut River.

16. The chief occupation of the Dutch, in the early days of the colony, was trade with the Indians, especially for furs; and the colony was composed, for the most

Dutch and Indians Trading.

PLATE 25. *Dutch and Indians Trading.* *Tonal white-line wood engraving by F. H. Wellington, from an illustration by Howard Pyle. Reproduced here the same size as the plate on page 58, in H. E. Scudder,* History of the United States of America *(New York: Taintor, 1884). Courtesy of the Willard S. Morse Collection, Wilmington Society of the Fine Arts.*

PLATE 26. *The Choicest Pieces of Her Cargo.* *Tonal white-line wood engraving by*
Albert Lindsay, from an illustration by Howard Pyle. Reproduced here the same size as the
plate for Thomas Janvier's "New York Slave Traders," Harper's New Monthly Magazine,
Jan. 1895; from a Japan tissue proof owned by Mrs. Margaret Van Brunt of Wilmington,
Del.

PLATE 27. *The Emperor Commodus.*
*Tonal wood engraving by Cowee from
the illustration by Howard Pyle. Reproduced here the same size as the plate
for C. Thaxter,* Verses *(Boston: Lothrop,
1891). Courtesy of the Free Library of
Philadelphia, Rare Book Dept.*

For another example, Plate 27, "The Emperor Commodus," [20] a wood
engraving which saw service in at least four books that had no other connection with Howard Pyle contains faces, in the upper-left-hand corner,
half again as small as those in Wellington's "Dutch and Indians Trading."
Examination of these tiny heads under a magnifying glass reveals some of
the technical contortions which the engraver, G. L. Cowee, was forced to
employ in an attempt to render both the overall tone of the original and
the suggestions of expressions on individual faces. That Pyle indicated
these faces in considerable detail in his originals may be safely surmised.
Pyle almost always painted or drew his originals at least twice as large as
the final result for transmission to the public would be, for ease of execution
and a crispness of detail which artists soon found was a completely delightful aspect of phototechnological reproduction.

Portrayal of tiny faces in sharp detail, seen in a crowd massed well back from the foreground of his pictures, with a significant disproportion between the sizes of the foreground figures and those in the background, was a stylistic trick of Howard Pyle in his illusionistic works. It was a successful means of creating a diagonal going back into an illusion of three-dimensional space. Yet it clearly posed serious difficulties for wood engravers, and, as we will see, did not fare well under early process halftone.

In Scudder's *History* of 1884, Pyle's work was transmitted via two different engravers, identified as Henry Marsh (Plate 28, "Whitman Starting for Washington"), and F. H. Wellington, who engraved the "Dutch and Indians Trading" which we have discussed. On the basis of the overall appearance of these two illustrations we could easily question whether the *originals* could have been produced by the same artist. Since Pyle had a distinctive style for all his American history subjects, it is extremely unlikely that the originals—unfortunately unavailable at this writing—were different in treatment or medium, both presumably having been rendered in opaque gouache. Yet we cannot fail to recognize that each of the engravers has developed his own codes, within which limitations it can be seen that we are nearing the downward borderline below which it is practically impossible to render anatomical or costume detail. Henry Marsh, whom we will encounter again in connection with William Hamilton Gibson, might be considered to belong to the "Closson" school of codes, named after a famous engraver who rendered almost all originals in a texture not unlike that of Persian lamb fur. Wellington's codes are more straightforward and lead to the achievements of men such as Lindsay. To compare Marsh's rendering of sky tones with his rendering of grass, thatched roof, or distant people, is to wonder whether he was aware of differentiated textural gradients defining three-dimensional realities. There is some directional texturing on the horse, and it is useful to compare this Marsh wood-engraving horse with another horse of almost exactly the same size and position which was transmitted through fine-screen process halftone.

Plate 29, "A Virginia Plantation Wharf," appeared in Woodrow Wilson's biography of *George Washington* (Harper, 1897). It was an oil painting originally, monochrome, about four times the size of the process halftone, employing the crisp detail which gave so much authority to Pyle's historical images. Once again, large foreground figures with tiny faces in the background, these now much more visible in detail than the Marsh "Whitman Starting for Washington" (Plate 28). Yet there is a dull sameness about the tonal differentiations, and there seems no way of telling from this engraving whether "A Virginia Plantation Wharf" was conceived as being in sunlight or in shade. Process halftone, by 1895, had achieved sufficient sophistication and subliminal capability to transmit many of the chiaroscuro aspects of "reality," but not a sufficient sense of contrast and light; the dots were too pervasively stamped on every aspect of the picture. It was the same with Pyle's beginnings with process halftone in 1887.

THE STRUGGLE BETWEEN PROCESS HALFTONE AND WOOD ENGRAVING

By 1887, it might have been expected that such problems of scale and compression of detail would have been vanquished by the first reproductions of any Pyle book illustration in a process halftone medium, especially since more and more technically advanced photoengravings had been appearing in the illustrated journals. It seems inexplicable that the

pushed on to St. Louis, and thence to Washington. There he found that the treaty had been signed, but that Oregon had been left out of the settlement altogether.

17. Dr. Whitman's errand was to make clear to the administration at Washington the value of Oregon, and

Whitman starting for Washington.

then to organize companies of emigrants. He did both. In the following summer he carried a great body of settlers over the mountains, and at the close of 1844 there were three thousand Americans within Oregon. The people were fast deciding the question.

PLATE 28. *Whitman Starting for Washington.* *Tonal white-line wood engraving by Henry Marsh, from the illustration by Howard Pyle. Reproduced here the same size as page 349, in H. E. Scudder,* History of the United States of America *(New York: Taintor, 1884). Courtesy of the Willard S. Morse Collection, Wilmington Society of the Fine Arts.*

PLATE 29. *A Virginia Plantation Wharf.* *Process halftone engraving from the illustration by Howard Pyle. Reproduced here the same size as the plate in Woodrow Wilson,* George Washington *(New York: Harper, 1897). Courtesy of the Free Library of Philadelphia, Rare Book Dept.*

process halftones used, say, by *Scribner's Magazine* during that same year are clear and unmuddied, yet that same publisher's production of James Baldwin's *A Story of the Golden Age* was a definite artistic disaster for Howard Pyle, despite the fact that these illustrations were prepared specifically for this book and only for this book.[21] (See Plate 42, "The Silver-Footed Thetis Rising from the Waves" which will be discussed again at the end of this chapter in a comparison with other media.) Pyle was clearly experiencing the same sort of harassing difficulties with a new medium which he had suffered with process line engravings and chromolithography. The scale of his illustrations for the Baldwin book is all wrong, and a non-Pyle-like murkiness weighs down the overall tone. Pyle had earlier, in 1882, illustrated Baldwin's *Story of Siegfried* for Scribner, and these illustrations had been reproduced in tonal wood engravings. The two Baldwin books offer a useful comparison of the artistic values of tonal wood engraving with the deadening literalness of reproduction of the early halftones.

The awkwardness of Pyle's artistic efforts for his first process halftones seems to indicate that his inspiration and talent failed him in a new medium. With the early halftone screen pressing inexorably down on every aspect of his drawing, unrelieved by the pure whites which engravers learned to master in the so-called "highlight halftone," and with a composition unaided by the skill of any tonal wood engraver—who would probably have "textured up" his monotonous backgrounds to relieve their tedium—Pyle's reputation would surely have foundered without the balancing excellence of his decorative line drawings.

But despite the artistic banality and technical failure of books such as *A Story of the Golden Age*, process halftone engraving was not to be halted. Publishers increasingly saw only the high cost of tonal wood engraving, which for them outweighed its tested printability. By 1889, the future availability of media for Pyle seemed set. From a letter by Smithwick, art editor of *Harper's,* and himself a great engraver, to Albert Munford Lindsay (1858–1940), we see the battle joining.

Sept. 24, 1889

Dear Mr. Lindsay
We send "the Pyle" today. I would like to please you with an estimate, but you must help me this time. I will do as much for you some other time.

(Confidential) This particular Pyle has a history, it was selected as a test for process—*and tested*—it didn't test with a copper[22]—and the result or lack "friscult"—turned the drawings for the two articles into the hands of the engravers. Now for the good of the "profesh," for the good of Pyle, and pro bono publico do your prettiest, and, in the words of the Irish saint—"My blessings on you"—and in the words of the French polisher, "nous verrons."[23]

Smithwick's joshing letter does not conceal his sympathetic alarm for the future livelihood of the wood engravers. The postscript to this same letter reveals that he was so concerned about the matter that he had already written another confidential note on the same day from his office.[24] Lindsay did do his "prettiest"—he may possibly have been the greatest of the Pyle engravers (see Plates 26 and 35), as well as an outstanding renderer of William Hamilton Gibson and Frederic Remington—but the increasing dependability of process halftone, plus its comparative cheapness, would make an irresistible combination. We note, as an aside here, that Lindsay, like so many others, kept expecting that the tide of photographic technology would be reversed; his bitterness and sorrow over the loss of a master craft are all too evident in the letters which remain, despite a gentlemanly politesse which he maintained with Smithwick. Eventually, driven to the wall economically, he became Art Editor for the *Ladies' Home Journal*, where he was daily forced to purchase and supervise illustrations in the very medium which had ousted him.

It was not only the engravers, however, who had cause for concern about the inexorable march of process halftone engraving, for it permitted publishers, once they had paid for an illustration, to use it again in whatever manner they chose, with results that could not have failed to displease a man with the high standards of Howard Pyle.

THE PUBLISHERS ILLUSTRATE PYLE'S BOOKS

With the next major book illustrated by Pyle and reproduced in process halftone, a new phase began in the war of the media. Harold Frederic's *In the Valley* (Scribner, 1890) contained sixteen Pyle illustrations which had already appeared as tonal wood engravings in *Scribner's Magazine* during 1889 and 1890. For the book publication, these wood engravings were abandoned in favor of reshooting the original black-and-white oil paintings—some of which are owned by the Wilmington Society of the Fine Arts, the Willard Morse collection—through a process camera for screened halftones. At least one of these paintings ran the gamut of the major media available in the 1890s. Variously called, "The Fallen Foe" or "My Hatred of Him . . . ," this scene of the hero accompanying his dying enemy in a canoe downriver was reprocessed also in Goupilgravure for F. Hopkinson Smith's *American Illustrators* (1892). In three basic translations, the original underwent such remarkable transformations that we can only wonder if Pyle was forced to redraw or repaint any details. In the tonal wood engraving that appeared in *Scribner's Magazine* for July 1890, the canoe and the men's faces seem quite different from the ensuing plates. In the smaller process engraving, on page 398 of *In the Valley,* the effects of overall mood and details seem submerged by the gray compression of information. In the large photogravure, Pyle's first reproduction in this expensive medium by Goupil, printed in blue and black, there is enough sensitivity of the gravure "dot" structure to indicate the texture and directional masses of brush strokes, as well as clearly defining the highlights.

If a viewer, who had never encountered the reputation of Pyle or any of his works, were to make his first acquaintance with him through each of these three different transmissions of the same original, it is safe to conjecture that (a) the wood engraving would convey some idea of Pyle's adequacy of draftsmanship and ability to model chiaroscuro; (b) the process illustration would convey utter mediocrity of both technique and idea; while (c) the photogravure would establish Pyle as a competent delineator of psychological nuance, naturalistic detail, and appropriateness of mood, besides indicating that he was capable of designing an original in the proper scale for reproduction through a specific medium. We are unable to reproduce these three plates here for a variety of technical reasons, but they would repay the reader's attention, as they offer verification for another of William Ivins' indications, to the effect that our aesthetic hierarchies, or what Charles Morris calls "values," depend to a critical degree on what a medium does to a message.

Perhaps it was the poor engravings purchased by Scribner's for *In the Valley* which prompted this note from Harper, the publisher of his next process halftone book; this is Smithwick again, who wrote to Albert

Lindsay on July 15, 1891, "Can you by cautious inquiry . . . procure for me the address of Mr. Ives, the inventor of 'Ives' process—a friend of mine, a process man in N.Y. desires the address. . . ."[25] It seems unfeeling of Smithwick to ask a tonal wood engraver to find the address of his nemesis, Frederick Ives, but we can only assume that Harper had good reasons for wanting to please its famous illustrator with the best available photo-mechanical transmission. Whether or not they used Ives for their first process halftone book with Pyle, *Flute and Violin* (1890) is not known.

Their second process book with Pyle, *Men of Iron* (1892), has been incorrectly called by his biographer, Abbott, the first Pyle-illustrated book to be reproduced by process halftones. To set the record straight, hopefully, Baldwin's *A Story of the Golden Age* (1887) was first; *In the Valley* (1890), second; *Flute and Violin* (Harper, 1890), third; *Men of Iron*, fourth.

When the latter appeared in 1892, Oliver Wendell Holmes wrote to Pyle, who had already illustrated this author and who was then beginning work on several Holmes books: "I have seen no book with such striking illustrations for a long while. There is none of the hurried slap-dash air which is so common since the 'impressionists' have splashed their colors about on the canvas, but honest work and careful study."[26] Holmes here revealed the prejudice of his time for the academic realism of Meissonier and Gérôme. Modern readers, however, may wonder if Holmes is talking about the originals or the reproductions, since these small process half-tones (e.g., Plate 30) are so clumsy, out-of-scale, heavy-handed, colorless, and poorly executed, that it may seem incomprehensible that they could attract any favorable opinion at all. Not only is there no aesthetic relationship in design between the large, fatuous schoolbook typography of the text with the illustrations, but the process halftone had not yet achieved any technical success with the problems of highlights, pure white, and solid black. Just as in *A Story of the Golden Age* and *In the Valley*, an unpleasant sea of gray dots engulfs these pictures. The plates were, moreover, separately printed on calendered stock; the text is a coarse woven paper. One must turn the book on its side in order to see many of the illustrations. Perhaps Holmes had seen the first reproductions in *Harper's Young People*, published between January 20 and June 9, 1891, which are right side up and larger. These seem rather worse than better, although their size improves the scale of the details.

In any case, Pyle must be excused for the poor design of the book, at least. This was no *Robin Hood*, carefully supervised in every detail by the master himself. *Men of Iron* was simply manufactured by a publisher from a serialized story without the need for Pyle's intervention. Pyle did not design *Men of Iron* or *In the Valley*, but he has no excuse for the illustrations for Baldwin's two books. Neither *The Story of Siegfried* (Scribner's, 1882), illustrated by tonal wood engravings, nor *A Story of the Golden Age* (Scribner's, 1887), illustrated by process halftones, appeared previously in any magazines. Yet each suffers this same design defect, that many of the pictures cannot be viewed without turning the text sideways. Since the preprocess books of the nineteenth century seem just as guilty of this fault, photographic technology cannot be solely the culprit. Poor taste, malignant haste on the part of the publishers, who undoubtedly decided that the juvenile market could tolerate slovenliness, and Pyle's seeming lack of interest, are to be blamed.

But why this lack of interest? Here Pyle stands revealed more than ever before in his role as picture maker, rather than as book illustrator, and it seems to have been the halftone processes, both screened and gravure, which at least partly encouraged him to forget his function as illustrator. No one who compares a typical double-page spread in *Robin Hood* (1883) (Plate 24) with a typical double-page spread in *Men of Iron* (1892) (Plate 30) can doubt that two vastly different standards of bookmaking are in evidence here. For *Robin Hood,* Pyle created imaginative solutions to the problems of size and shape of illustration, using borders, lettering, and so on, to maintain balance even when he was seeking horizontal rather than vertical solutions to compositions. In *Men of Iron,* there was no such attempt. Perhaps there could be none. Not only was the book manufactured from paintings already used in *Harper's Young People,* but technical factors like

PLATE 30. ***When Thou Strikest That Lower Cut . . .*** *Process halftone engraving from the illustration by Howard Pyle. Reproduced here approximately the same size as the original double spread in Pyle's* Men of Iron *(New York: Harper, 1892). Courtesy of the Free Library of Philadelphia, Rare Book Dept.*

Nevertheless he spoke up undauntedly as before. "Aye, marry, will I strike it again," said he; and this time he was able to recover guard quickly enough to turn Sir James's blow with his shield, instead of receiving it upon his head.

"So!" said Sir James. "Now mind thee of this, that when thou strikest that lower cut at the legs, recover thyself more quickly. Now, then, strike me it at the pel."

Gascoyne and other of the lads who were just then lying stretched out upon the grass beneath a tree at the edge of the open court where stood the pels, were interested spectators of the whole scene. Not one of them in their memory had heard Sir James so answered face to face as Myles had answered him; and, after all, perhaps the lad himself would not have done so had he been longer a resident in the squires' quarters at Devlen.

"By 'r Lady! thou art a cool blade, Myles," said Gascoyne, as they marched back to the armory again. "Never heard I one bespeak Sir James as thou hast done this day."

"And, after all," said another of the young squires, "old Bruin was not so ill-pleased, methinks. That was a shrewd blow he fetched thee on the crown, Falworth. Marry, I would not have had it on my own skull for a silver penny."

48

"When thou strikest that lower cut at the legs, recover thyself more quickly."

the difference in paper influenced the outcome. Just as in *A Story of the Golden Age*, where this same disjunction between typography, book layout, and illustration obtains, Pyle did not evince any interest in experimenting with the design of a total package of artistic expression using process half-tones, just as he had not bothered with books illustrated with tonal wood engravings. His *Rose of Paradise* (Harper, 1888), a typical "manufactured" book, appeared first in *Harper's Weekly*, June 11 to July 30, 1887. The large tonal wood engravings, successful in the journal, were reduced unconscionably and plopped into the book helter-skelter, sideways, without thought of design.

From 1892 on, whenever a book was illustrated in some artistic medium other than pure line, and with few exceptions indeed, Pyle seemed primarily concerned with creating works which could stand on their own as easel paintings. It was almost as if it was only in pure line that he would think decoratively, that the calligraphic qualities of his line pen-and-inks called his attention to a needed artistic relationship between typography, picture, and overall layout. It may be that process halftone suggested artistic media, watercolor, oils, gouache, which stimulated a response inappropriate to a flat surface and of a certain size, especially when he knew that the camera was increasingly capable of reproducing the kinds of chiaroscuro effects and precise detail that he admired in the academic painters.

Pyle's love of detail can be corroborated in his own words. From a letter to his engraver, Albert Lindsay, dated January 28, 1890:

My dear Mr. Lindsay
. . . Of the reproduction of my Jamaica sketches, I reckon those of yours among the best, and in the New York Tavern, I think you have wonderfully caught the painty effect of original. I mean by that the freedom—as well as the feeling.

I wish to express to you how much I appreciate your care of detail—the hands and feet and the little minor matters of this kind. Too often engravers aim for the general effect sacrificing all those lesser matters which are, after all, the heart and soul of true art.

My own thought has always been that the true interest of a picture lies in careful and conscientious finish. Of course that which catches the eye is the broad general feeling and effect. But in a little while the mind grows used to that and then seeks for something beyond. If it finds well studied detail it always returns refreshed to seek for something further; if not, the work soon seems flat and stale.[27]

The rest of this letter gives Lindsay very specific instructions on how to complete his engraving. This love of detail led Pyle on toward greater and greater compression of information, spurred on by the increasing ability of the phototechnologies to reproduce whatever he presented, even if with a general deadening of tone and contrast. Even in *Men of Iron*, for example, the tiny heads of the crowd are reproduced with far more "color," solidity, tone, shading, and sense of detail than the comparable heads in the Commodus engraving (Plate 27) already noted.

SHIFTS IN STYLE AND COMBINED OR NEW MEDIA

In 1892, 1893, and 1894, Pyle produced a series of book illustrations for works by Oliver Wendell Holmes. Those for *One Hoss Shay* (Houghton Mifflin, 1892) and *Dorothy Q* (Riverside Press, 1893) are pen-and-ink designs of a nature rather different from previous works in that medium. For

PLATE 31. *The Cock Lane Ghost.*
*Process line engraving from the brush
and pen-and-ink drawing by Howard
Pyle. Reproduced here the same size as
the plate for Pyle's "The Cock Lane
Ghost,"* Harper's New Monthly Magazine 87 *(August 1893): 331; from the
copy owned by E. Jussim.*

these, as well as for his own delightful story, "The Cock Lane Ghost"
(Plate 31), appearing in *Harper's New Monthly Magazine* for August 1893
Pyle abandoned his Düreresque line and the ponderous gouache style of
his early tonal wood engravings for a lively brush-and-ink and pen-and-ink
style which reproduced perfectly by process line engraving. If *Dorothy Q*
sported three small halftones as well, they were in appropriate and harmonious scale with the text, light in tone, without large areas of solid black,
and, even though they were conceived as rectangles (halftone media
simulating the conventional Renaissance window frame) they do not over-
burden the frame.

The frontispiece of *Dorothy Q* is probably the first illustration in which
Pyle ever attempted a combination pen-and-ink garland with a wash drawing. The garland, of necessity, was reproduced by process line; the wash
drawing, an oval portrait of *Dorothy* embellished with the garland, was
perforce in process halftone.[28] The paper used was fortunately successful
for both media, and the details of the little halftones reveal a screen
increasingly capable of rendering an artist's intentions without excess
distortion.

PLATE 32. *Into the River.* *Photogravure, on heavy woven stock, from the illustration by Howard Pyle. Reproduced here the same size as the plate facing page 276, in Oliver Wendell Holmes,* The Autocrat of the Breakfast Table *(Boston: Houghton Mifflin, 1894), vol. 2, from a copy in the University of Massachusetts Library, Amherst.*

In 1893, after these two Holmes books had received considerable acclaim, Pyle was persuaded to begin work on a third, a deluxe edition of *The Autocrat of the Breakfast Table* (Houghton Mifflin, 1894). After the success of his drawings in the new decorative style, one might expect that he would now choose the same medium for the numerous head- and tailpieces in the text, but, for reasons which now can only be surmised, Pyle or the publisher decided to produce these vignettes as monochrome watercolor originals, to be reproduced through tonal wood engravings. The full-page illustrations were oil paintings reproduced through the most expensive, but most eloquent medium, photogravure, printed on special paper differing from the text, with tipped on glassine covers bearing the captions for each picture (see Plate 32, "Into the River" and Plate 33, "*Autocrat of the Breakfast Table*—Headpiece Vignette." A comparison with Plate 34, "Stops of Various Quills—Headpiece Vignette," will be discussed shortly.)

It may have been the poor showing of process halftone plates on ordinary text paper that was the prime motivation for ordering the watercolors transmitted via tonal wood engraving. But it can be conjectured as well that certain aesthetic pressures came to bear for the production of a *deluxe* edition, as tonal wood engraving still stood at the top of the aesthetic hierarchy. Pyle was noted, however, for his insistence on different artistic media and styles as being appropriate for different subjects. It may well be that he believed a pen-and-ink style which could be reproduced by process line engraving, and therefore could be printed with the text, would not suit the warm color of the gravure ink impression. For a deluxe edition, at any rate, he could be expected to pay close attention to all details, unlike his usual attitude toward publisher-manufactured books.

The overall book designed for *The Autocrat of the Breakfast Table* proved to be excellent, with the Riverside Press supplying delicately appropriate typography, into which the vignetted tonal wood engravings seem to fit perfectly, both in mood and in color. Nevertheless, judging from the meticulous corrections he made on proof sheets,[29] Pyle still thought wood engravers "knocked spots" out of his work. For example, on the proof of the plate for a portrait of Benjamin Franklin—for which he had prepared a treatment exactly like that he had produced for the frontispiece of *Dorothy Q*, an oval portrait rendered in wash and decorated with a pen-and-ink garland background, but for which the reproduction was now tonal wood engraving instead of process halftone for the portrait, and outline wood

The Autocrat of the Breakfaſt-Table

VII

PLATE 33. *Autocrat of the Breakfast Table—Headpiece Vignette. Tonal wood engraving, engraver unknown, from the wash drawing by Howard Pyle. Reproduced here the same size as the plate on page 221, in Oliver Wendell Holmes,* Autocrat of the Breakfast Table *(Boston: Houghton Mifflin, 1894), vol. 2, from a copy in the University of Massachusetts Library, Amherst.*

THIS particular record is note-worthy principally for containing a paper by my friend, the Professor, with a poem or two annexed or intercalated. I would suggest to young persons that they should pass over it for the present, and read, instead of it, that story about the young man who was in love with the young lady, and in great trouble for something like nine pages, but happily married on the tenth page or thereabouts, which, I take it for granted, will be contained in the periodical where this is found, unless it differ from all other publications of the kind.

VOL. II.

SYMPATHY.

FRIEND, neighbor, stranger,
　　as the case may be,
　　You who are sitting in the
　　　stall next me,
And listening also to this pitiless
　　play
That says for me all that I would
　　not say,
And follows me, however I wind
　　about,
And seems to turn my whole life
　　inside out:
I wonder, should I speak and be
　　the first
To own just where in my soul it
　　hurt worst,
And you revealed in yours the spot
　　its flame
Scorched fiercest, if it might not be
　　the same.

PLATE 34. *Stops of Various Quills—Headpiece Vignette.* *Process line engraving from the brush-and-ink by Howard Pyle. Reproduced here the same size as the plate in William Dean Howell,* Stops of Various Quills *(New York: Harper, 1895), from a copy owned by Mount Holyoke College.*

engraving instead of process line engraving for the garland—Pyle wrote angrily:

> I like this less than anything the engraver has done on this set. A great deal of modelling is lost in the face and consequently the likeness is lost and then there is a lack of "crispness" in the decoration. KEEP THE BLACK OUTLINE I HAVE PUT INTO THE ORIGINAL.[30]

Very precisely, he enjoins the engraver to "Bring the shadow of the curve of the mouth a little more down and join it with the shadow at the side of the chin. This is *very* important." [31] We should note that the entire picture of Benjamin Franklin reproduces about two inches overall height; yet Pyle maintained this fanatical attention to detail.

How Pyle judged the gravure reproductions of the oil paintings is unfortunately not available at this writing, but it can hardly be doubted that he was enormously pleased. "Into the River" (Plate 32) beautifully renders both Pyle's sense of "what catches the eye" and "careful and conscientious detail," which he had lauded to Lindsay. In photogravure, with its softness, richness of ink impression, lack of visible screen, use of non-shiny stocks which process halftone required, Pyle could achieve a painterly effect *on the page*. Nothing of his craftsmanly devotion to detail, or his superior ability to handle close-set masses of faces, or to construct dramatic compositions utilizing a great range of chiaroscuro effects, nothing (except color) was lost in this monochrome illustration. It is almost as if a veil had been removed which previously had obscured all his intentions. For richness of reproduction, in which neither detail nor range of tonal values is marred either by an intervening engraver's hand or by the technological limitations of a medium, these gravure illustrations must stand at the top of any list of Pyle's works. Whether the purist taste of some modern bibliophiles might condemn both Pyle and the Riverside Press for using any medium other than outline wood engraving is not relevant; Pyle's intentions of creating the illustrational equivalent of easel painting were at last fulfilled. He could place these plates beside the gravure reproductions of Meissonier or Gérôme, produced for the World's Columbian Exposition of 1893, and he could see how closely his work resembled that of the European academics he revered for the same photographic realism which pervaded his own work.[32]

At the same time that *Autocrat* appeared, Harper's ground out still another "book" using one of the serials which had appeared in *Harper's Monthly* the year before, illustrated by tonal wood engravings from Pyle gouaches. For this book, Thomas Janvier's *In Old New York* (1894), the wood engravings were set aside once again in favor of considerably smaller halftone process plates shot directly from the originals.[33] One of the discarded tonal wood engraving plates (compare Plate 35 with Plate 37) was to call forth astonished enthusiasm from one of Pyle's most famous pupils, N. C. Wyeth. Fourteen years after it had first appeared in *Harper's Monthly*,[34] "A Privateersman Ashore" (Plate 35) was sent to Wyeth with a group of Japan proofs from Albert Lindsay, who had by then left the trade of tonal wood engraving far behind.

Sept. 26, 1907

My dear Mr. Lindsay:—
. . . the *qualities* that you have got into those pictures are marvelous and for the life of me, I cannot understand *why* such work shouldn't constitute the best and choicest of what magazines have to offer in the way of art. That one of the seaman smoking is a *wonder*. Never have I felt more exquisite light and atmosphere in a reproduction: and the wonderful textures, too.

Of course wood-engraving is all a grand mystery to me so excuse my enthusiasm. They came as such a surprise and a revelation that I must say something.

By sending these proofs to me you have completely restored a failing interest in Mr. Pyle in addition to confirming my opinion that the wood-engraving is the "highest" method of reproduction. . . .[35]

Looking back to black-line facsimile wood engraving in a similar subject, F. O. C. Darley's "Dutch Fishermen" (Plate 36), engraved by Bogert in 1869, we can see how much freedom illustrators had gained at the hands of interpreters like Albert Lindsay, and how much illustration had achieved

PLATE 35. *A Privateersman Ashore.* *Tonal white-line wood engraving by Albert Lindsay from the illustration by Howard Pyle. Reproduced here the same size as the plate for Thomas Janvier's "The Evolution of New York,"* Harper's New Monthly Magazine, *June 1893; from a Japan tissue proof, owned by Mrs. Margaret Van Brunt, Wilmington, Del.*

PLATE 36. *Dutch Fishermen.* *Facsimile wood engraving by Bogert from pen-and-ink or pencil sketch on the block, by F. O. C. Darley. Reproduced here the same size as the plate facing page 80, in Darley,* Sketches Abroad with Pen and Pencil *(New York: Hurd and Houghton, 1869), from the copy owned by the Forbes Library.*

through photography-on-the-block. The years from 1869 to 1893 had seen this linear symbolism give way to a significant amount of illusionism. Yet in the fourteen years since 1893, when Lindsay's "A Privateersman Ashore" appeared, this high accomplishment in human communication had been already forgotten. Can we imagine Wyeth raving so enthusiastically about the skimpy process halftone (see Plate 37, "A Privateersman Ashore") which Harper manufactured for another trade book? If Mr. Pyle had failed to keep Wyeth's attention in the year 1907, we may suspect that Pyle's reputation was not established or glorified by such pseudo illustrations, but was made precisely on his autographic pen-and-inks and by the skills of the great tonal wood engravers, as well as by illustrations where he could supervise the scale of reproduction for each specific medium.

Harper's redeemed itself in 1895 by publishing William Dean Howell's *Stops of Various Quills* with good process line and improved process halftone reproductions of Pyle illustrations which had already appeared in slightly larger form in the magazine. The decorative beauty of the headpieces (see Plate 34) and borders reminds us that

> . . . for abstract beauty, character, and the compelling force of decorative craftsmanship (three enduring virtues in art) Howard Pyle's pen drawings represent his highest artistic achievement. They stand with the greatest works of all time done in this medium.[36]

A comparison between the pallid tonal wood engravings of *The Autocrat of the Breakfast Table* (Plate 33) and these vigorous process line drawings, which mark Pyle's most mature style, reveals that Pyle thought most comfortably in pen- or brush-and-ink. For every superlative craftsman like Lindsay, there seemed to be a dozen hacks who would impose codes for which Pyle seemed unable to design.

As for process halftone, Pyle's work was to undergo yet another development, a development which also involved the hand engravers in the last decade of their activity before they sank into anonymous oblivion.

PLATE 37. *A Privateersman Ashore.* *Process halftone engraving, lightly retouched, from the illustration by Howard Pyle, possibly rescreened from another edition. Reproduced here the same size as page 65, Thomas Janvier,* In Old New York *(New York: Harper, 1894). Courtesy of the Free Library of Philadelphia, Rare Book Dept.*

PLATE 38. *In the Presence of Washington.* *Process halftone engraving retouched heavily to resemble white-line
wood engraving, from the illustration by
Howard Pyle. Reproduced here the same
size as the plate facing page 849, in S. W.
Mitchell's, "Hugh Wynne,"* Century
Magazine, *April 1897. Courtesy of the
Free Library of Philadelphia.*

THE HAND ENGRAVER IN THE SERVICE
OF PROCESS HALFTONE

The year 1897 saw five Pyle-illustrated books appear, three of them previously published in the illustrated journals.

Of these, S. Weir Mitchell's *Hugh Wynne, Free Quaker* (*Century Magazine,* November 1896–October 1897) transmitted Pyle paintings in a development which represented a kind of cross breeding between two media. At first glance, the magazine reproduction of "In the Presence of Washington" (Plate 38), appears to be exceptionally subtle tonal wood engraving, bearing, as it does, the seemingly usual directional roulette and graver marks. But even the unaided eye soon recognizes that the directional marks are not the usual furrows of black and white but are flecked into peculiar areas

PLATE 39. ***Peractum Est!*** *Photogravure from the two-color (red and black) oil painting by Howard Pyle. Reproduced here the same size as page 204, Henryk Sienkiewicz,* Quo Vadis, *translated by Jeremiah Curtin, new ed. (Boston: Little Brown, 1897), vol. II, from a copy owned by E. Jussim.*

PLATE 40. *Peractum Est!* *Process halftone engraving from the two-color oil painting by Howard Pyle. Reproduced here the same size as the plate facing page 424, Henryk Sienkiewicz,* Quo Vadis *(New York: Grosset and Dunlap, 1907), from a copy owned by E. Jussim.*

of "gray"—a gray which seems unaccounted for until the mysteries are examined with a magnifying glass. Now it can be seen that the "gray" is the result of a process halftone screen. The entire engraving had been worked over by a skillful hand—unidentified, but obviously belonging to someone well versed in the high arts of tonal wood engraving—which had knowledgeably managed to convey both reflected light in the shadows and soft highlights, something which the process plate alone had failed to accomplish. From the period of about 1897 to about 1905, this combination effect could be found in a preponderance of periodical engravings, sometimes signed but often as not simply the last visible vestige of the approximately 450 artist-craftsmen who had become technologically unemployed but who were kept on for a time in the service of the new phototechnologies.

In the first trade edition (Century, 1897), the illustration of "In the Presence of Washington" was, typically, considerably reduced for a small format volume. The original was not left entirely to the mercies of the process screen, however, but once again retouched by an engraver in order to provide some of the pure white highlights so vital to Pyle's mood, for example, in the candle flames and reflected on the buttons of the figure to the left. The hand engraver lacked the skill of the craftsman who had worked over Plate 38, and "In the Presence of Washington" became much darker and more ominous in the shadow behind the General, much brighter and therefore confusing in the foreground details of bedsheets and clothing, and it became difficult to make sense out of the expression on Washington's face. Pyle had never intended such reduction in size.

The same illustration appeared in two other trade editions (Century, 1899 and 1900). In the later of these editions, "In the Presence of Washington" was re-reproduced from the original in a somewhat larger size than in the second edition. With a screen of different texture this time, that is, a screen of different shape and aperture, Pyle's original improved considerably from the second edition, this time showing, even in a reduced size, the kindly light in the general's eyes. Undoubtedly, photogravure could have reproduced this illustration in a small size without loss, with a combination of perfect detail and depth of ink color, but it was much too expensive for the ordinary trade book.

How photogravure could have contributed to the effectiveness of "In the Presence of Washington" can be seen in the gravure plates for another of the books published in 1897, Sienkiewicz's *Quo Vadis.* In "Peractum Est!" (Plate 39), we can see the enormous capacity of photogravure for illusionism—given an illusionistic original—given its capacity for smoothly graduated chiaroscuro. No visible dot structure intervened. Much truer to Pyle's original—an oil painting in red and black[37]—the gravure clearly transmits Pyle's strong diagonal highlights on the arena floor, permitting these to function as directional forces in the design. In the process plate, (see Plate 40, from a cheap trade edition, 1907) there is such poor contrast between pure white and gray floor that these slashes of light lost their meaning, as does much of the clarity of form of the helmeted gladiator. In the later process plate, the exact meaning of Pennell's statement seems unmistakable: process screen is a steamroller.

PYLE AND THE COLOR TECHNOLOGIES

Howard Pyle's relationship with the color processes revealed him as a master designer, both for "fake process" utilizing flat tints and for the ultimate triumphs of the four-color halftone process. He was a decorative genius, as even the early plates for *The Lady of Shalott* (1881) had revealed. Even if we cannot here see him in color, we can compare some of the effects of four treatments of similar subject matter and thereby see how Pyle had responded to four different transmission technologies. These are (and for the sake of convenience, we are shortening the titles) "The Lady of Shalott" (Plate 41), "Thetis" (Plate 42), "A Princess" (Plate 43), and "Bertha" (Plate 44).

"The Lady of Shalott," a chromolithograph of 1881, is here seen to be a typical example of the kind of "artistic expression" which this medium enforced or encouraged: fairly flat decorative tones or tints, with chiaroscuro achieved by the superimposition of schematic areas of darker colors standing for shadow. The white line surrounding "The Lady" her-

PLATE 41. ***The Lady of Shalott.*** *Chromolithograph from the illustration by
Howard Pyle. Reproduced here the same
size as in Alfred Tennyson,* The Lady of
Shalott (*New York: Dodd Mead, 1881*),
from a copy owned by E. Jussim.

PLATE 42. *The Silver-Footed Thetis Rising from the Waves.* *Process half-tone engraving from the wash drawing by Howard Pyle. Reproduced here the same size as the plate facing page 96, in James Baldwin,* A Story of the Golden Age (*New York: Scribner, 1887*), *from a copy owned by the Boston Athenaeum (a 1907 reissue).*

self was successfully used by Pyle in other compositions, especially Baldwin's *Siegfried,* produced by tonal wood engravings, where it serves as an artificial but necessary expedient in the service of clarity, making for easier registration of the color tints here and a separation from the background tints. Well-conceived, dramatic, "The Lady of Shalott" has the charm of a Pre-Raphaelite dream, adapting here—unlike the pages in the same book which he ruined with hand lettering—directly to the technological requirements of chromolithography.

In the "Thetis" (1887), however, Pyle was hopelessly at sea in black-and-white watercolor wash and unaware of what the process halftone screen would do to his contrasts and details. The murkiness of the overall dot formation, an inevitable concomitant of the early process halftone, further dulled and obliterated any life which the original might have had. The decorative sureness of "The Lady" had capitulated to some kind of meager representationalism; furthermore, the scale was wrong, so that details are fussy and meaningless in terms of an overall effect. Technology here has tempted him to try effects he could not control, since it was not

PLATE 43. *A Princess Walks . . .*
Process line engraving from the pen-and-ink drawing by Howard Pyle. Reproduced here the same size as the plate facing page 52, in Pyle's The Wonder Clock *(New York: Harper, 1887), from a 1915 reissue owned by E. Jussim.*

yet recognized that transparent washes were exceedingly difficult to capture in monochrome. Technology had simultaneously offered him the illusion of being able to "reproduce anything," so that the limitations of the medium were not clear enough to enforce rigorous thinking and decorative planning. In this medium, Pyle seems a faltering hack.

When we turn to "A Princess" (Plate 43), published in the very same year as the "Thetis" (1887), it is hard to believe that the same artist is involved. Using pen-and-ink, Pyle composes freely for the process line engraving medium, presenting us with a symbolic characterization of an event, rather than a *representation.* He had been working in this medium for approximately ten years, and he was completely at home within its technological limitations. When working on "Thetis," Pyle was confronted with an inimical artistic medium and an unknown transmission medium, whereas when producing "A Princess" he was "free" to "express" himself with masterful control.

With Plate 44, "Bertha" (August, 1904), which was reproduced in pale blues, pinks, green, and brown, in very close harmony which permitted the figure to float with the wind, we see the culmination of Pyle's search for freedom of expression. Working with oils, on canvas about four times larger than what we see, Pyle could combine the decorative structure, surely the hallmark of his genius, with a modulated chiaroscuro which in no way detracts from the strength of the composition on the printed page. Comparison of the 1881 "The Lady of Shalott" with this four-color process halftone reveals that the latter process began to find its justification in color reproduction. It was not only that Pyle's talents matured along with the reproductive processes, but that he and a medium were well suited for each other. In color process halftone, Pyle was finally liberated from many of the technological strictures which had plagued him in his tonal works.

The progression of color in Pyle's illustration in the 1890s is a paradigm of the experience of all illustrators, for what was available to him was available to all the others. An example of a fake process, "The Pirate's Christmas," which appeared in *Harper's Weekly* for December 16, 1893, may be the earliest appearance of Pyle in color other than in chromolithography. This was followed by "In the Wood-Carver's Shop," in *Harper's New Monthly Magazine* for December 1895, where tints of red were arbitrarily applied to flesh tones and parts of the background, with solid red in the waistcoats of the two main figures. In April of 1897, once again in *Harper's New Monthly Magazine,* "A Banquet to Genet," reproduced in combinations of red and black tints, introduces us to Pyle as a true colorist, an artist who deployed the elements of color orchestration for the maximum effect of space and optical movement. This banquet scene was re-reproduced in black-and-white for Woodrow Wilson's *History of the American People* (Harper, 1902), and the loss of color is shocking. It is a revelation of what all black-and-white tonal reproduction destroys. It is a revelation of what limitations an artist like Howard Pyle had endured.

Unfortunately, not all color results were a product of the artist's thought or action. Illustrations originally appearing in *Scribner's Magazine* in December 1891, for Henry Van Dyke's story, "The Oak of Geismar," and in that same author's *The First Christmas Tree* (Scribner, 1897), were reprocessed with fake color for *The Blue Flower* (Scribner, 1902), with delicate results far from the melodramatic grandeur of Pyle's original conceptions. Phototechnology's ability to reduce larger works to much smaller illustrations without altering the scale of details was often disastrous, no matter what the medium. The hand engraver perforce restructured an original to

PLATE 44. ***Bertha, the Much Beloved.*** *Four-color process halftone engraving from the oil painting by Howard Pyle. Reproduced here the same size as the plate for James E. Dunning's, "The Sword of Ahab,"* Harper's Monthly Magazine, *August 1904, from a copy owned by E. Jussim.*

conform to the particular limitations of his block; the photographic engraver, whose structure was mechanically imposed in the code of the process halftone screen, had little choice.

"The Pilgrimage of Truth," by Erik Bogh, appeared in *Harper's New Monthly Magazine* for December 1900, but only after considerable technical difficulties. Emboldened by the new successes of color reproduction, Pyle painted the originals on mahogany panels, in oil colors. According to the Willard Morse scrapbooks, "They could not be reproduced, so they were done in pen and ink. Then reproductions of the pen and inks were colored in watercolors." [38] The end result was a series of illustrations in a texture resembling that of crayon lithography, in color, a technique which had proved eminently successful in some of his earlier pirate characterizations.

> About 1900, or a little after, great improvements in the method of color reproduction were made, and he began to turn his attention to paintings in full colors. These pictures with their gorgeous harmonies of brilliant colors made a lasting impression both on the publishers and on the public. Their tendency was to minimize his earlier work—the pen-and-inks and the black-and-white oils—in favor of these new and lavish creations.[39]

Now the magazines began to see full-color illustrations from Pyle, and the wonder is that he managed to preserve his distinctive styles with the new freedom. Maintaining a decorative richness in his medieval subjects for James Branch Cabell, he returned to a bleaker photographic representationalism for his American Colonial subjects.

When it was decided to republish Oliver Wendell Holmes' *One Hoss Shay* in 1905, the charming little pen-and-inks of the 1892 edition were resuscitated. Proofs of the original line plates were furnished to Pyle in the size intended for re-reproduction, and Pyle colored these with watercolors as a guide to the printer in separating for fake color process. We are fortunate in having Pyle's comments on printer's proofs:

> This is among the worst pictures of the set. The engraver seems to have made no pretense of softening the reds at all. Make him take them out where they do not belong.
> There is no red in this coat in the original nor is there any in the hat. Why has the engraver put it there? [40]

The engraver may have become anonymous, but he was still there, interfering.

What a perfectionist might have said about the continuing ruthless exploitation of Pyle's illustrations for trade editions based on stories appearing in *Harper's Monthly* is not hard to imagine. For Cabell's *Line of Love* (Harper, 1905), from the "Story of Adhelmar," of April 1904, the circles of dots produced by the yet unperfected four-color process halftone are as conspicuous as early television screen codes. The color plates from the magazine (or the color negatives) were cut down without regard for proportion or suitability of composition. Once again, we must exercise caution in judging Pyle as an illustrator if we are not sure whether or not we have something approximating his original conception before us.

We have been dealing here with Pyle as the painter of easel pictures, seemingly liberated from the narrow technological demands of earlier processes, yet he was suffering distortion of his messages (a) through approximations of originals, rather than true "reproduction"—whatever that might be, and William Ivins almost seems to be saying that there is such a thing; and (b) through an increasing lack of relationship between what he produced and the illustration on the printed page as an adjunct to typography. The technologically type-compatible medium of relief process halftone was not necessarily aesthetically type-compatible. This lack of aesthetic unity with type was as true for much of his color work as it had been for his monochrome washes.

COMMENTARY

Pyle as an easel painter was still Pyle-the-illustrator, no matter how much he longed for the economic freedom to paint what he chose, as he chose it, when he chose. Even though reproductive technology was treating him *as if* he were an easel painter, that is, by transmitting his work as if he were a painter whose creations only inadvertently became illustrations, and, at its best, treating him to the best results of fine-screen detail and the preservation of the characteristics of the original (e.g., brush strokes and opaque versus transparent passages), Pyle did not feel that he had ever succeeded in reaching the heights of self-expression. Toward the end of his life, when he was finally convinced to visit Europe, he wrote home to a friend:

Jan. 11, 1911

. . . I *wish* I had some work to do other than illustration so as to try to live up to what I have learned. Of course, I have to earn my living, but it is rather hard to be limited to illustration.[41]

The easel painter painted without giving thought to reproduction. Obviously, Pyle was too honest to abandon all considerations of appropriateness for publication, as some of his students were to affect with their enormous canvases. But the necessity to keep in mind some technological limitations prevented him always from complete freedom, as he saw it, of "artistic expression." He became even more conscious of these limitations during his visit to Europe.

Despite Pyle's early interest in Dürer, and his lifelong admiration for the narrative compositions and photographic detail of Meissonier and Gérôme, he had avoided Europe with the pretense that its art did not interest him. In particular, he had despised the Italian Renaissance painters whom the American critic James Jarves had been lauding since the Civil War. When finally he saw these paintings as originals, Pyle experienced what we should perhaps call *media shock,* a reaction similar to culture shock.

Dec. 27, 1910

You know I did not think much of the Old Masters, *seeing them in black and white* [italics added], but in color they are so remarkable that I do not see how any human being painted them as they did. . . . Two pictures of Botticelli I saw yesterday are the most remarkable pieces of work that I have ever seen in my life. . . . I kept thinking of my pupils and wishing that they could see these pictures.[42]

Poor Pyle! To have seen the "Old Masters" only through heliotype monochrome reproductions or the tonal wood engravings of men such as Timothy Cole, however marvelous they were in their day!

"Seeing them in black and white," was also, for much of Pyle's career, "seeing them" in the codes of the hand engravers. As William Ivins indicated, our opinions about art objects are determined by the medium transmitting the messages about such objects. Pyle had seen nothing in the Old Masters because, as André Malraux put it,

From the seventeenth to the nineteenth century, pictures, interpreted by engraving, had *become* engravings; they had retained their drawing (at least relatively) but lost their colors, which were replaced by an interpretation in black and white. . . . Today, an art student can examine color reproductions of most of the world's great paintings. . . .[43]

During most of Howard Pyle's career, pictures *were* engravings, hand-crafted and then mechanized. It should be obvious by this point in our discussion that photography and phototechnological media by no means eliminated all the philosophical difficulties inherent in transmitting information about originals, nor that "syntax" or codes of transmission, like magic, disappeared with the arrival of subliminal media.

The only objects in "Nature" which concerned Pyle in his preparation for transmission through either hand engraving or phototechnologies were his own original paintings or drawings. He had already codified certain characteristics of Nature, for example, textural gradients, chiaroscuro, aerial perspective, contours, and he wanted only that his transmitters should not destroy the effects he had created. His own codifications had been largely simplifications of those natural characteristics for the sake of decorative designs or for illusionism in a certain scale of final image. His primary codifications were from an imagined "reality"—sailors, maidens, whatever—onto an essentially two-dimensional surface; the only three-dimensional characteristic of his originals which mattered were brush strokes which gave direction, or a certain stylistic trick here and there of putting in the highlights. But he expected only that his own codifications were to be illusionistic; once that work was done, what he wanted from an engraver was simply to transmit his message about the fiction in his imagination.

No matter how careful Pyle was in the matter of costumes, period furniture, correct architectural backgrounds, it was not a crucial issue. Information transfer was expected to convey his creativity, not an actual message about actual realities. There would be far more complex problems when information transfer was expected to convey three-dimensional actualities, when the photograph from Nature, rather than an artistic restructuring of selections from Nature, was the medium which had to be transmitted to the public in a reliable and completely trustworthy manner.

6

William Hamilton Gibson (1850–1896): The Artist Using the Camera's Eye

Know, my friend, that that apple-tree and barn, with all their "improbabilities" in the way of posts and apple-trees, etc., were direct from a photograph which I made from nature with my little camera, and all those things were there.[1]

"EXPRESSION" OR "SCIENTIFIC FACT"

William Hamilton Gibson was an artist so perfectly devoted to the nineteenth-century Ruskinian ideal of Nature—"Every vista a cathedral; Every bough a revelation"[2]—that one of his eulogists would claim, "Three men have done more than any others to inspire our generation with the love of nature. They are Henry D. Thoreau, John Burroughs, and William Hamilton Gibson."[3] This neglected visual poet, William Gibson, has been overshadowed by his flashier cousin, Charles Dana Gibson, the originator of the "Gibson girl." To judge by his contemporaries, however, William Hamilton Gibson deserved to be ranked with the highest, for reasons which illuminate the value hierarchy of Victorian America:

> His art is pervaded with the accuracy of the lover of scientific fact, and his science glows with all the imaginative play of the artist's soul. His methods are a triumphant example of the "scientific use of the imagination," and of the imaginative presentation of science. . . . All his work is an emphatic refutation of the popular cry, as shallow as it is common, that as science advances art must decline, that a knowledge of facts tends to limit the play of the fancy, and that there is some irreconcilable contradiction between truth and imagination.[4]

Such commentary raises some pertinent questions: Can we call Gibson an *expressive* artist when his involvement was with the communication of "scientific facts"? If William Ivins was correct in his assessment that photography constituted some sort of "ultimate" communications medium, and that fine-screen process halftone engraving possessed a code so subliminal that it constituted an equivalent to photography—presumably objective and free from interference—why did Gibson have to redraw a farmyard scene, for example, "direct from a photograph which I made from nature with my little camera"? Was a potential conflict between "expressiveness" and "truthfulness" accentuated by either the literalness of photography or interference from inadequate photomechanical codes?

We propose to look first at an example of Gibson's work in which there should be no problem about identifying the elements of "expressiveness" over "scientific fact," since we can examine four other interpretations of the same subject, two in wood engraving, two in phototechnology (see Plates 45 through 49).

Here is a verbal description of "The Flume," one of the most admired natural phenomena in the White Mountains:

> Near the upper end and across the narrowest part a huge boulder was wedged until the great slide of 1883, when an avalanche caused by a cloud-burst on Mount Liberty swept through the gorge, and littered the lower end with a mass of debris, thereby upsetting Starr King's rhapsodic prediction, made only thirteen years before, concerning this great egg-shaped boulder, "As unpleasant to look at, if the nerves are irresolute, as the sword of Damocles, and yet held by a grasp out of which it will not slip for centuries." [5]

The earliest tonal wood engraving of "The Flume" (Plate 45) appeared in the 1864 edition of Thomas Starr King's rhapsody on *The White Hills*.[6] Certainly the engraving does not communicate King's feeling that the boulder was a sword of Damocles. In fact, the boulder is so poorly rendered and is so far away from the spectator that it fades rather inconspicuously into the background. We are not sure, either, how far the figure in the foreground can venture into the background, as the planks also fade away into water from which they are hardly differentiated in tone or texture.

Now let us examine a heliotype, made from Nature, as the Flume appeared in 1879 (Plate 46). This "photograph," mounted into a picture book called *Views in the White Mountains*, provides much more reliable evidence than did the first wood engraving. The graininess of the rocks, the planks, the hanging rock, and the vegetation are all portrayed with as much fidelity as could be achieved by phototechnology. No screen interferes, and the detail can be magnified probably as much as twenty times before any loss of form occurs. However, while we may be impressed with the actual shape of the distant boulder, we are not overwhelmed. We can say to ourselves, "This is how the Flume looked," yet there is hardly any excitation to awe or to a sense of danger.

Let us jump in our chronology to another edition of Starr King's *The White Hills* (1887)[7] in which there appeared, surrounded by exactly the same text as the 1864 edition, a new tonal wood engraving (Plate 47). Despite the publication date, obviously this engraving was of the Flume before the avalanche of 1883, since the boulder is still hanging in place. Comparison of this plate with the earlier Starr King edition reveals a startling change in viewpoint and rendition. Why does this engraving resemble the heliotype of 1869 more than the earlier wood engraving? Could it have been based on a photograph, specifically on one half of a stereographic double photograph? The rounded edges would tend to corroborate such an analysis, as these were almost universally used on early stereoscopic slides.[8] There is also a marked increase in textural differentiation and chiaroscuro. Textural gradients and heightened light-to-dark contrasts begin to transmit a sense of *depth*. Still, this is no "sword of Damocles" waiting for us between sixty-foot cliffs. If anything, the boulder seems even smaller here than before.

Now we are ready to study the Gibson illustration [9] (Plate 48). Have we there crossing from side to side of the ravine by primitive little bridges, that bend under the feet and that are railed by birch-poles, and then climbing the rocks again, while the spray breaks upon us from the dashing and roaring stream, till we arrive at a little bridge which spans the narrowest part of the ravine.

PLATE 45. *The Flume.* *Black-line wood engraving by Andrew from a drawing by Wheelock. Reproduced here the same size as page 123, in Thomas Starr King,* The White Hills (*Boston: Crosby & Nichols, 1864*) *from the copy in the Columbia University Libraries.*

How wild the spot is! Which shall we admire most,—the glee of the little torrent that rushes beneath our feet; or the regularity and smoothness of the frowning walls through which it goes foaming out into the sunshine; or the splendor of the dripping emerald mosses

PLATE 46. *The Flume.* *Heliotype from a photograph taken from Nature. Reproduced here the same size as the plate in M. F. Sweetser,* Views in the White Mountains *(Portland: Chisholm, 1879), from the copy owned by the Forbes Library.*

152

ascend. We go up, stepping from rock to rock, now walking along a little plank pathway, now mounting by some rude steps, here and there crossing from side to side of the ravine by primitive little bridges, that bend under the feet and that are railed by birch-poles, and then climbing the rocks again, while the spray breaks upon us from the dashing and roaring stream, till we arrive at a little bridge which spans the narrowest part of the ravine.

How wild the spot is! Which shall we admire most,—the glee of he little torrent that rushes beneath our feet; or the regularity and smoothness of the frowning walls through which it goes foaming out into the sunshine; or the splendor of the dripping emerald mosses

PLATE 47. *The Flume.* *Tonal wood engraving, probably after a stereograph. Reproduced here the same size as page 123, in Thomas Starr King,* The White Hills *(Boston: Estes & Lauriat, 1887), from the copy in the Columbia University Libraries.*

come in for a close-up, literally so in the camera sense? After all, his biographer, John Coleman Adams, tells us that in the late summer of 1880, Gibson went to the White Mountains: "He came home laden with sketches and with photographs, which were at once utilized in making the illustrations for Drake's 'Heart of the White Mountains.' " [10] Gibson made sketches and took many photographs. But where is the plankway of the Flume? And what has happened to several other topographical characteristics, like the millrace forms on the right? With the Gibson illustration, we are no longer on the outside, observing the scene dispassionately from a distance. On the contrary, we seem to be in the depths of a turbulent and potentially dangerous canyon. A large tree has recently fallen. High above the ponderous boulder, two men have crawled out to look down the awesome sixty feet to the rapids. If we ourselves are to get any closer to that boulder, we shall have to beat our way through scraggy underbrush and climb over jagged rock. But perhaps if we stand under *this* boulder, we shall finally experience "the sword of Damocles."

Something more of Gibson's accomplishment can be appreciated from the following, written about another White Mountain phenomenon, Lost River:

> The failure of photography to reproduce the strange effects of this wayward river, and its capricious bed is understood. The vague gloom of the place defies the most attentive lenses, even as the persuasive spell of the place eludes ready definition. [11]

The authors of the above statement, writing in 1930 — not in the nineteenth century — were so at a loss for some way to communicate something "as unforgettably weird as any natural phenomenon" [12] that they ended a long succession of adjectives — cavernous, menacing, spectacular — by relying on the associative power of a famous name; they called it "something out of Doré cut immortally into vast illustration of solid rock." [13] It was as Oscar Wilde had observed: Nature imitated Art. Gustave Doré was a name that could conjure up the mysterious, ghostly, terrifying: he was an artist gifted in horrific expressiveness. He was not a photographer; he was an illustrator, like Gibson.

Nothing that William Hamilton Gibson ever did surpassed *The Flume* for sheer power of statement, communicated not through phototechnology, but through a masterpiece of white-line wood engraving by John P. Davis. Surely it would be safe to say that Gibson expressed something about this natural phenomenon which all our other examples fail to transmit. It is no wonder that the general opinion in 1882 was that "Mr. William Hamilton Gibson's reputation as one of the first of modern artists for wood-engraving is established and secure." [14]

The last of these five examples of one subject, *The Flume* (Plate 49) appeared in the same 1887 Thomas Starr King edition as did Plate 47, the second of the two tonal wood engravings. Here, in the same book with a picture of the Flume with the boulder still in place, is a photograph reproduced by photogravure. The boulder is gone forever, but the sword of Damocles had been recorded for posterity — by Gibson. His was the artist's expressive contribution: "He grasps the essential fact to be shown and then his nimble imagination and artistic resources furnish him with ample devices for putting the stress upon the points he wishes the mind to catch and to hold." [15]

This is all very fine, but what would William Ivins have said about the fact that the Gibson was reproduced by a wood engraver, not by photo-

PLATE 48. *The Flume.* *Tonal wood engraving by J. P. Davis, from the illustration by*
William Hamilton Gibson. Reproduced here the same size as page 227, in Samuel Adams
Drake, The Heart of the White Mountains *(New York: Harper, 1882), from the copy*
in the Columbia University Libraries.

PLATE 49. *The Flume in 1887.* *Photogravure from a photograph from Nature. Reproduced here the same size as the plate facing page 278, in Thomas Starr King,* The White Hills (*Boston: Estes & Lauriat, 1887*), *from the copy at Columbia University.*

The Flume in 1887.

mechanical means which would have reproduced the original more authen- tically, showing us characteristics of the original drawing which we cannot now see. Was it in oils? Crayon? Ink? Was there thick impasto? Thin wash? Or did Gibson perhaps design explicitly for transmission via this type of wood engraving? Was this the way he *planned* it to look, in which case each of the strokes of the graver was plotted beforehand.

That certain nineteenth-century illustrators did indeed plan as carefully as Dürer had, drawing directly on the block as much as possible, we know from many sources. That others were poorly versed in this art, we know from many complaints of engravers. And that there was a raging contro- versy in the beginning of the 1880s is amply testified by the hullabaloo which greeted the "Scribner" prizes for wood engraving,[16] a venture on which the new magazine had embarked in an effort to oust *Harper's* as the greatest of the illustrated monthly journals. In February of 1880, *Harper's New Monthly Magazine* ran "A Symposium of Wood-Engravers," in which a number of the outstanding wood engravers of the time took sides over a dispute which had originated with an article by W. J. Linton—the one grand pundit of the trade, a trade he always insisted was a fine art—in which he had taken violent issue with Timothy Cole over his engraved ren- dering of the *texture* of a charcoal portrait. Since Gibson's work for the larger part of his short life can only be understood in terms of the repro- ductive media available for his kind of illustration, it would be useful to recall the characteristics of black-line and white-line codes while attending to the arguments presented at the Symposium.

THE SYMPOSIUM ON WOOD ENGRAVING: A REVOLUTION IN GOALS

William James Linton (1812–1897), an English wood engraver who settled in New Haven, Connecticut, in 1867, had achieved considerable reputation in his own country as a reviver of some of Thomas Bewick's concepts of white-line engraving. Yet he could not relinquish the conventionalizations of black-line engraving, and clung to them so relentlessly that when the younger men began the experimentation with textures that would lead to the New School of Engraving, Linton made a "savage onslaught."[17] They were bunglers, Juengling was "the father of meaningless textures";[18] and while Cole's "Modjeska as Juliet" (Plate 11), though "engraved from a photograph, is very perfect . . . a beautiful piece of engraving (I would call it Mr. Cole's best), one worthy of any engraver of the old time,"[19] his microscopically fine rendering of the original texture of a Wyatt Eaton "crayon" was almost a vicious act of undermining the great tradition.

The man who replaced Linton as teacher of engraving at Cooper Union was none other than the same John P. Davis who engraved *The Flume* for Mr. Gibson, and it is to his statement at the Symposium that we turn for a precise history of the conflict:

> A few years ago it was thought that beyond certain formal limits the en- graver could not venture. A certain kind of line, it was held, should be used to represent ground; another kind to represent foliage; another to represent sky, another flesh; another, drapery, and so on. Each sort of line was the orthodox symbol for a certain form, and if by chance or inexperience it was not used by the artist in his original drawing, the omission was expected to be supplied by the engraver. Of late, however, the publishers of illustrated periodicals have increased the range of their illustrations. The perpetual reoccurrence of old conventional lines became tiresome, and the use of the

works of our best known and most eminent painters was felt to be desirable. These painters, however, were not trained in the special methods employed by draughtsmen on the block; they put their conceptions upon canvas or upon paper, each in his own way, but they were not adept in the ways of the orthodox and regular draughtsman on the block. *Just here came in the assistance of photography* [italics added], by which the paintings or drawings on canvas or on paper were transferred directly to the wood. The art of wood-engraving received in consequence a fresh impulse, and entered into a new liberty, the possibilities of which it is yet too soon to estimate. . . . *Instead of merely symbolizing the work of the artist* [italics added] the engraver now makes use of all methods by which he can fix on the block, as accurately and perfectly as possible, the original picture. . . . This abandonment of conventional recipes, this enlarged liberty with respect to means, is the distinguishing characteristic of the new school. Exactly to reproduce—that is the present aim of the engraver on wood.[20]

We should note here, by the way, that although photography-on-the-block was recorded as early as 1858, according to Robert Taft, in *Photography and the American Scene,* the practice does not appear to have gained much acceptance generally until after *Picturesque America* was published in 1872–1874.

The leading question of the Symposium was directed at each of the members: "What is the first duty of the wood engraver?" A. V. S. Anthony, a die-hard disciple and co-worker of Linton's, replied that "Given the work of the artist, the engraver's first duty is to reproduce it without any change whatever."[21] On the face of it, that sounds as if he sided with Davis and Cole. On the contrary: "The only motive that can lead an artist-engraver to reproduce brush marks, washes, crayon marks, and the like, seems to be one of bread and butter."[22] Apparently, for Anthony and Linton, "reproducing" something meant "translating it." Anthony was therefore against cutting from anything but a drawing on the block: "When cutting a photograph, you are constantly compelled to refer back to the original; and besides, the cost is from ten to thirty per cent more than when engraving from the wood."[23] It would seem that, despite their disclaimers, the "Old School" was genuinely more interested in bread-and-butter questions than were their opponents.

Rising to his own defense, Timothy Cole (incorrectly called Mr. Thomas Cole here) retorted:

> . . . it would seem natural that when seeing an engraving of a drawing you should recognize the artist first and not the engraver: "Drawn by So-and-So, engraved by So-and-So." But when looking at an engraving of Mr. Linton's you say instinctively, "Engraved by So-and-So, drawn by So-and-So—" just reversing the order.[24]

But Cole does not exonerate the illustrators:

> The secret of so many recent failures of engravers to do justice to the artist lies in the fact that artists make their drawings too large, and when these are reduced by photography, and put on the block very small, the engraver is put to a great task in striving to reproduce the original effect, and he fails in the endeavor because, through the reduction in size, the effect has already been lost. Don't you see that the remedy lies with the artist? He ought to draw smaller and bolder. He had yet to learn to draw for the engraver.[25]

Obviously, unlike Howard Pyle, William Hamilton Gibson was content to learn to draw satisfactorily for reproduction through wood engraving. Unlike Pyle,[26] who always seemed to chafe at its codes and restrictions, Gibson found it a compatible language. Perhaps at least some of this difference may be charged to their early heroes: Pyle, as we recall, was devoted to the black-line effects of Dürer and developed a black-line pen-and-ink technique which was best reproduced by process line engraving. There is no evidence that he grew up admiring anyone who was either designing for or being reproduced in black-line *tonal* wood engraving. Gibson, only three years older than Pyle, grew up imbued with some of the earliest achievements of white-line engraving. For example, in 1862, when Gibson was twelve, an illustrated deluxe edition appeared of a book which had seen initial publication the same year he was born. For the boy in Sandy Hook, Connecticut, *A Treatise on Some of the Insects Injurious to Vegetation*, by Thaddeus William Harris (1795–1856), became simply "Harris on the Insects," and he was devoted to it: "It was the illustrations of Marsh which fascinated me. I never found a bug, caterpillar, or butterfly that I did not compare my specimens with the Marsh pictures. I learned this way much which I have never forgotten." [27]

We should forgive Gibson for confusing the memorable engravings by Henry Marsh with "illustrations of Marsh" or "the Marsh pictures." For it was the *engraver* who became famous, not the two illustrators, and he will figure importantly in another relationship with Gibson. Marsh not only made his reputation on this book, but he actually pleased the tyrannous W. J. Linton:

> The insects . . . drawn from nature by Sonrel and Burckhardt, needed most absolutely exact rendering, to the representation not only of form and color, but of difficult textures also; and the engraver, Henry Marsh, was therefore fully justified in his microscopic treatment. No such book has been done before, nor will it ever be surpassed. . . . It is work not only of patience and remarkable eyesight, but also of true artistic skill; showing, too, in the comparison of the steel plates with the woodcuts, that there are powers of expression in wood which cannot be equalled by the rival process. [28]

Did the two illustrators for "Harris on the Insects" draw directly on the block from laboratory specimens? Did they render large, detailed drawings which were then photographically reduced on the block? Whatever was the precise nature of their contributions, it was obliterated forever by the spectacular handwork of Henry Marsh.

Again, unlike the younger Pyle, William Hamilton Gibson had collaborated in illustrating the monumental *Picturesque America*, Appleton's gigantic and often-imitated paean to the newly explored American continent. [29] The characteristic black-line codes of the early 1870s (see Plate 57, "A Southern Plantation") were uncannily monotonous when they were encountered in hundreds of contiguous wood engravings. In the face of such monotony, it seems amusing that William Cullen Bryant, quondam editor of that great publishing venture, could rationalize the use of hand-engraved woodblocks, and their stupendous expense of more than $100,000, by claiming that "Photographs, however accurate, lack the spirit and personal quality which the accomplished painter or draughtsman infuses into his work." [30] The simple truth was that there was no technology available in 1872 which could translate photography from Nature into type-compatible channels. John Moss was only beginning to perfect his process line engravings; the messy business of mounting woodburytypes would have been prohibitively expensive; the heliotype was first beginning to be available in America; photogravure was not yet available; and, of course, mounting silver prints was out of the question in the size of edition Appleton desired. Wood engraving was the only choice among the older graphic media that was type-compatible. Yet, given the difference between the various "Flumes" which we have seen, and the Gibson version of the *The Flume*, there was unmistakable justice in William Cullen Bryant's opinion.

Picturesque America was dominated by the Linton idea of translations as opposed to reproductions. Between the Linton translations and older concepts of "universal codes" dictated by economic necessity, there was not much room for artistic expression by an illustrator. The illustrations by Gibson in *Picturesque America* are indistinguishable from those by the dozens of illustrators who contributed. Ironically, it was not until photography, that most mechanical of techniques, was widely applied as an adjunct to wood engraving, that the designer-for-the-engraver was liberated. Photography-on-the-block individualized both the maker of the original drawing and the reproducer of that drawing. It was inevitable that Linton would lose out in his attempt to remain arbiter of the "language."

Lest we overexalt photography-on-the-block, let us return to the 1880 Symposium:

> Photography often translates badly. . . . It changes blue into white, yellow into a very dark, and so on. A blue sky with white clouds becomes entirely white. When a canvas is painted thinly, its texture shows in a photograph; when it is painted thickly with heavy brush marks that throw shadows, the photograph reproduces all this too. . . .[31]

These latter two effects, of course, were precisely those vaunted by William Ivins when he claimed the superiority of fine-screen process halftone over other media. In other words, for Ivins, this faithfulness to the *an Sichlichkeit* of an object is the great virtue of any reproductive medium. We have discovered, from our Symposium, that such an idea was far from being current in 1880, and that, in fact, it took a decade of superior white-line tonal wood engraving to cultivate a taste for anything like this kind of faithfulness.

> The preservation of the original character of the picture, so that the spectator can tell whether it was in pencil, in water-color, in oil, in charcoal, or in any other substance, is what constitutes the richness of modern wood-engraving, and its superiority over engraving on steel and on copper.[32]

Again, however, the "preservation of the original character of the picture" was rendered difficult because, as another "New School" engraver put it: ". . . photography has its disadvantages. It changes the colors of the picture photographed. . . . The engraver, therefore, must continually refer to the original, else he will miss the color values; and this constant reference is a distraction."[33] So the two schools of thought were in agreement on that one drawback, constant reference to an original. John Tinkey (engraver for Gibson, Plate 50, "Moonlight in the Highlands"), after commenting that other drawbacks included the fact that the silver film on the block often discolored it, and that there were few photographers who had the knack of capturing details on the wood effectively, nevertheless remarked, "Other things being equal, give me a first-rate photograph on the wood."[34]

> It would be advantageous for the engraver, however, if the artist refrained from using yellows, browns, reds, and blues—colors which the photograph does not reproduce, and which therefore are a stumbling block to him.[35]

If the artist cooperated, then wood engraving could achieve reproductive parity with "the prince of the 'processes'"[36]—photogravure. Indeed, somewhat surprisingly, "The aim of wood-engraving is to be as faithful throughout as a photogravure is in its best parts."[37]

THE ARGUMENT BECOMES ACADEMIC:
IVES APPEARS

Even as these master craftsmen of the wood engraving were either deploring or glorying in the future of the white-line code in the new era of photo-technology, even as they were admitting only the competition of photo-gravure, Frederick Ives was preparing to introduce his first commercially viable process. By June of 1881, the Crosscup & West Engraving Company of Philadelphia, using Ives' patent, became the first concern to attempt mass production of photographically produced "dots for the eye." An ingenious system which we have previously described, combining elements of gelatin relief, the automatic application of dots on a plaster base, and the conversion of the product into *line* engraving, the steps in the procedure were so numerous that fidelity to an original illustration sometimes was very far removed. Nevertheless, as the decade continued, adventurous publishers and a few daring illustrators—the former, seeing only the economic advantages of a mechanical procedure, the latter, perhaps, far more interested in forever removing from the entire reproductive cycle precisely those very talented men at the Symposium—began to turn to half-tone process. The men of the New School of Engraving had exactly a dozen years ahead of them before the second Ives's process, through Levy's perfection of the screen, would triumph over hand media. By 1907, as we saw in the letter from N. C. Wyeth to the Pyle engraver, Albert Lindsay, the virtuoso achievements of the best work of the white-line period would seem novel and amazing.

If William Hamilton Gibson's reputation as "one of the first of modern artists for wood-engraving" was as established and secure as his critics claimed, why then did he turn from the great financial successes of *Pastoral Days* (1881), Drake's *The Heart of the White Mountains* (1882), and *Highways and Byways* (1883)—all of them white-line masterpieces—to his first adventure with Frederick Ives? If we read some of the commentary on *Pastoral Days*, for example, it is difficult to imagine that he could be dissatisfied with wood engraving:

> It was a book which yesterday would have been called "epoch-making"; today it would only be called "record-breaking." The simple truth about it is that it really touched the high-water mark in the history of nature illustration by means of wood-engraving. It was everywhere hailed as exhibiting the very best work of its kind ever achieved. . . . His engravers were applauded for the skill and spirit with which they interpreted his designs. His publishers were commended for the unstinted generosity which had balked at no pains or cost.[38]

It was a handsome book, no question, but we should note that all of its plates had previously appeared in *Harper's New Monthly Magazine,* and they were so well designed and so perfectly engraved in terms of printability that they made the book beautiful without much assistance from the publisher, whose major contribution seems to have been the sense to preserve wide margins and to provide a durable, heavy-weight paper.

After Victorian effusions of this sort, it will hardly be a surprise that, when no less a celebrity than Henry Marsh was invited to engrave several Gibson illustrations for E. P. Roe's novel, *Nature's Serial Story,* one critic's enthusiasm was simply boundless. After all, this was the same Henry Marsh whose microscopically fine work had influenced Gibson when he was a boy. This was the Henry Marsh whose white-line technique was bound to be perfection itself. There was only one slight matter which Gibson hastened to bring to the public's attention:

> I observe this evening in the current number of the "Critic" an art reference which calls for a slight correction. In a review of "Nature's Serial Story," by E. P. Roe, after paying a delicate compliment to the illustrations of the volume the reviewer goes on to say that "without detracting from the artist's mead of praise, the most remarkable thing about these illustrations is the extraordinary skill displayed by the engravers. . . . Mr. Henry Marsh, whose delicacy and precision of touch are marvelous, shows the still rarer power of taking up the theme submitted to him by the artist and adding increment after increment of meaning to it until it becomes almost wholly his own. His engraving of 'A Winter Thunder-Storm' is the finest thing in the book. We give the credit to him because we know that Mr. Gibson's forte is not in landscape."
>
> I yield to no one in my admiration of Mr. Marsh . . . and have too great respect for his interpretative genius to see attributed to him a piece of work which I am sure he would not care to claim, although it is "the finest thing in the book" and "fraught with increment after increment of meaning," and which is nevertheless nothing but a photo-engraving plate, by a purely mechanical process. Of course the "Critic"(?) will hasten to make all due acknowledgements and place the credit where it rightfully belongs, i.e. to the Ives Photo-Engraving Company, Phila., Pa., whose admirable process has reproduced not only this, but several others of the illustrations in which the aforementioned marvelous "increment" was discovered. Such is fame! . . .[39]

Gibson, here, is of course defending not only the Ives process but his own forte of landscape paintings; by praising Marsh, the critic had distinctly diminished the "mead of praise" for Gibson; by asserting the mechanical aspects of a much-praised reproduction, Gibson was inevitably praising his own capabilities, since, after all, a mechanical process could not be expected to improve upon an original. And so we return to this unsettled problem of *the characteristics of originals* which we raised earlier in connection with "The Flume."

Let us look now at several of these reproductions of Gibson paintings — or whatever — in *Nature's Serial Story* (Plates 50 through 52). First, "Moonlight in the Highlands" (Plate 50), a finely wrought Tinkey[40] white-line tonal wood engraving. Comparing this with "A Winter Thunder-Storm" (Plate 51) — which the "Critic" above had so lauded and so mistaken — we of the twentieth century are at a disadvantage. It is perhaps difficult for us to conceive of a mistake of this sort. We are so accustomed to the halftone screen and its symbolic or illusionistic transmissions of realities that it is the wood engraving which looks "different" to us.[41] Examining the wood engraving, what can we judge about the characteristics of the original? Nothing that we can be too sure about except its iconography and its mood. It has such a distinct richness that perhaps it does not seem important to know what its original was. By comparison, looking at the process halftone in question, we do begin to perceive that *something,* however vague, is beginning to come through a still awkward code: that something being, of course, the artist's picture as a message sent through a medium which is based on light reflected from an object in Nature. But this "something" is so vague, and the code is so conspicuous even to the naked eye, that the dots are quite conceivably the product of flicking boxwood with a sharp graver.

Now let us examine "Stormy Weather" (Plate 52), and compare it with "Moonlight in the Highlands" (Plate 50). Surely *this* Ives process halftone

MOONLIGHT IN THE HIGHLANDS.

Webb flushed slightly, but again proved that his brother's banter had little influence.

"If you are willing to wait a few days," he said, with a smile, "I can make clear to you, by the aid of a microscope, what father means, much better than I can explain. I can then show you the fruit germs either perfect or blackened by the frost."

2*

PLATE 50. ***Moonlight in the Highlands.*** *Tonal wood engraving by John Tinkey from an illustration by William Hamilton Gibson. Reproduced here the same size as the plate facing page 2*, in E. P. Roe,* Nature's Serial Story *(New York: Harper, 1885, 1884), from the deposit copy owned by the Library of Congress.*

thunderous report, which, though less loud than the one that preceded it, maintained the symphony with scarcely diminished grandeur.

"This is our Highland music, Amy," Webb remarked, as soon as he could be heard. "It has begun early this season, but you will hear much of it before the year is out."

"It is rather too sublime for my taste," replied the young girl, shrinking closer to Mr. Clifford's side.

"You are safe, my child," said the old man, encircling her with his arm.

"Let me also reassure you in my prosaic way," Webb continued.

A WINTER THUNDER-STORM.

"There, do you not observe that though this last flash seemed scarcely less vivid, the report followed more tardily, indicating that the storm centre is already well to the south and east of us? The next explosion will take place over the mountains beyond the river. You may now watch the scene in security, for the heavenly artillery is pointed away from you."

"Thank you. I must admit that your prose is both reassuring and inspiring. How one appreciates shelter and home on such a night as this! Hear the rain splash against the window! Every moment the air seems filled with innumerable gems as the intense light pierces them. Think of

PLATE 51. *A Winter Thunder-Storm.* *Ives process halftone engraving, from an illustration by William Hamilton Gibson. Reproduced here the same size as page 63, in E. P. Roe, Nature's Serial Story (New York: Harper, 1885, 1884), from the deposit copy owned by the Library of Congress.*

STORMY WEATHER.

wind that had been whirling the dust in clouds all night long grew fitful, and died utterly away, while the parched earth and withered herbage appeared to look at the mocking clouds in mute, despairing appeal. How could they be so near, so heavy, and yet no rain? The air was sultry and lifeless. Fall had come, but no autumn days as yet. Experienced Mr. Clifford looked often at the black, lowering sky, and predicted that a decided change was at hand.

"My fear is," he added, "that the drought may be followed by a deluge. I don't like the looks of the clouds in the southeast."

Even as he spoke a gleam of lightning shot athwart them, and was soon followed by a heavy rumble of thunder. It seemed that the electricity, or, rather, the concussion of the air, precipitated the dense vapor into water, for within a few moments down came the rain in torrents. As the first great drops struck the roads the dust flew up as if smitten by a blow, and then, with scarcely any interval, the gutters and every incline were full of tawny rills, that swelled and grew with hoarser and deeper mur-

PLATE 52. *Stormy Weather. Ives process halftone engraving from the oil original by William Hamilton Gibson. Reproduced here the same size as the plate facing page 318, in E. P. Roe,* Nature's Serial Story *(New York: Harper, 1885, 1884), from the deposit copy owned by the Library of Congress.*

cannot be confused with "Moonlight in the Highlands." The clouds, the trees, the brush, the overall texture—the difference makes itself most evident in the sudden recognition that what one is looking at in "Stormy Weather" is a thick impasto of paint, with the highlights standing out, as they do in a van Gogh, by virtue of their physical nearness to the eye. True, the effect is diminished because of the small size of the final reproduction, but it is there nonetheless. What had been three-dimensional paint on the canvas had cast a shadow and borne a highlight, both of which even this coarse version of halftone screen had been able to capture. Gibson had not been advised, apparently, to keep his work small enough to avoid loss, and all his work in *Nature's Serial Story* was too large for this scale of reduction. But we must remember that Mr. Ives was learning as much as Mr. Gibson.

THE PHOTOGRAPH LITERALLY "ENTERS THE PICTURE"

Such was fame, indeed, for Gibson that he drew down on himself many other slights, even denouncements. One newspaper writer claimed to have discovered all of Gibson's secrets:

> When Mr. Gibson sets out on a walk, he always takes a camera with him, and when an especially interesting twig or fern attracts his attention, he promptly snaps at it. On his return home, the plates are sent to the nearest photographer to be developed and from the negatives thus obtained, "bleach prints" are made. Mr. Gibson then proceeds to draw very carefully on these prints, following of course the outlines, shading, etc., of the photograph. After the drawings are finished, all traces of the photograph are quickly bleached out by immersing them in a simple solution of chemicals, leaving only the drawings on white paper. . . . It may be said without fear of contradiction that whatever excellence may exist in Mr. Gibson's published work, is due to the careful work of the photographer and the engraver.[42]

Before we can dismiss this as infamous calumny, as does his biographer, Adams, we had better take a look at another of the illustrations for *Nature's Serial Story,* "Hints of Spring" (Plate 53). Pursuing the idea of attempting to discern the characteristics of the original as the wanted artistic message, what have we here? In modern terminology, we have a silhouetted (or vignetted) drop-out, highlight process halftone; we find no black-dotted screen in the pure white at the bottom of the picture. But is there some difference in the message we receive about the trees and branches and sky at the top from what we get about the figures at the center? The two textures don't seem quite to match. The top part begins to look suspiciously like a screened photograph from Nature, while the figures seem to be added, perhaps in charcoal, soot smudges (a favorite medium with Gibson, who used it as thick charcoal dust), or in an ink wash. How do we "know" that the top is a photograph from Nature? How do we know that we are not looking at a fine-textured Henry Marsh or Elbridge Kingsley tonal wood engraving? If Gibson had not given the whole thing away, would we have been able to recognize what we are looking at? Shall we continue to scoff at the critic who confused Ives and Marsh, or shall we try to explore what assumptions basic to the history of the graphic arts might have led the critic astray?

Plates 54 to 64 represent an array of most of the major codes of the nineteenth century, with the exception of aquatint, as most of these were usually larger than the examples selected and were most often colored.

a shovel to burrow his way through the heavier drifts, drove homeward. Alf floundered off to his traps, and returned exultant with two rabbits. Amy was soon busy sketching them previous to their transformation into a pot-pie, Burt looking on with a deeper interest in the artist than in her art, although he had already learned that she had not a little skill with her pencil. Indeed, Burt promised to become quite reconciled to his part of invalid, in spite of protestations to the contrary; and his inclination to

think that Amy's companionship would be an antidote for every ill of life was increasing rapidly, in accordance with his hasty temperament, which arrived at conclusions long before others had begun to consider the steps leading to them.

Amy was still more a child than a woman; but a girl must be young indeed who does not recognize an admirer, especially so transpar-

PLATE 53. *Hints of Spring.* (*The Rabbit Trap*). *Ives process halftone engraving, from an illustration by William Hamilton Gibson, almost certainly working on a prepared photographic print. Reproduced here the same size as page 97, in E. P. Roe,* Nature's Serial Story (*New York: Harper, 1885, 1884*), *from the deposit copy owned by the Library of Congress.*

PLATE 54. *Sunset on the Hudson.*
Steel engraving by J. A. Rolph, from a painting by Weir. Reproduced here the same size as the plate facing page 92, in The Magnolia for 1837 (*New York: 1836*), *from a copy owned by Mount Holyoke College.*

The first, Plate 54, "Sunset on the Hudson," is a steel engraving, from a gift album, *The Magnolia for 1837*. Held at a slight distance from the eyes, its linear codes are distinct. Held further away, perhaps beginning at ten inches from the eyes, the codes largely disappear, and a subliminal pseudo-halftone appears. Its range of tones, textural gradients, and contour distinctions seem far greater than those of the heliotype in Plate 55, which reproduces a photograph from Nature, but its chiaroscuro is not as rich or as continuous as that of the mezzotint of "The Ambush" (Plate 56). Compared to these three media, there is almost no illusionistic, subliminal effect in the Lintonesque black-and-white-line tonal wood engraving, "A Southern Plantation" (Plate 57), or in the lithograph of "Island of St. Ignace" (Plate 58).

PLATE 56. **The Ambush.** *Mezzotint after a painting by J. G. Chapman. Reproduced here the same size as the plate facing page 91, in* The Opal for 1846 *(New York: Rilker, 1846), from the copy owned by the Forbes Library.*

PLATE 58. *Island of St. Ignace.* "*G. Elliot Cabot, from nature. Lith. of A. Sonrel. Loffler on stone.*" *Reproduced here the same size as the plate facing page 78, in Louis Agassiz,* Lake Superior (*Boston: Gould . . . , 1850*), *from the copy owned by Mount Holyoke College Library.*

If there is subliminal effect in Plate 59, "Here Flows the Stream," we are not quite so sure *why*, since at first glance this may strike us as a slightly smeared tonal wood engraving, especially since the white lines in the dark reflection of the water are graver lines such as we are used to finding in white-line codes. But if this is a tonal wood engraving, whoever produced all those dots in the sky and water by crisscrossing at right angles with a fine graver has also done the same all over the plate; in other words, he has produced all of the strange lights and darks using exactly the same texture, which would be odd for a New-School-of-Engraving man, who would be claiming liberation from any orthodoxy in pursuit of ideal reproduction. Since Plate 59 is by no means ideal, and since a magnifying glass reveals the rather characteristic crosses of the late 1880s process halftone, and, again, since external evidence reveals that John Calvin Moss made not only this plate, but the next four plates as well (Plates 60 through 64), we are forced to recognize this odd landscape as a product of Moss's competitive spirit. The date of publication for "Here Flows the Stream" is 1886, the same year that Frederick Ives announced his second patent, the "cross-line screen." Moss was refusing to be outdone.

Whoever was the Jonathan Moss whose poems served as a pretext for what we can only consider as a Moss catalog of photomechanical effects, is not important. What is important is that we are looking at the birth pangs of one of the major visual communications codes, the fine-screen process halftone; and we are looking at the competition of codes seen as *the wares of manufacturers,* just as today we are limited to certain types of color television because of manufacturer's decisions.

PLATE 59. ***Here Flows the Stream.*** *Moss process halftone engraving from a photograph from Nature; retouched either on the negative or on the metal to remove screen from the sky and water areas. Reproduced here the same size as the plate facing page 62, in Jonathan W. Moss,* Poetical Works *(Cameron, W. Va.: 1886), from the copy owned by Columbia University Libraries.*

In Plate 60, "Once More in the Deep Forest's Gloom," what looks like a tonal wood engraving is actually a photomechanical reproduction of an illustration by Gustave Doré, whose signature the photographer heedlessly lopped off. That this was reproduced from a much larger plate is unlikely. The textures are cut fine, and whatever line process is at work here, it transmits the message of the original quite well—except that we must recognize that the "original" in this case is not a painting by Doré, but a print of the wood engraving made from that painting.

PLATE 60. *Once More in the Deep Forest's Gloom. Moss process line engraving from a print of a Gustave Doré wood engraving. Reproduced here the same size as the plate facing page 89, in* Jonathan W. Moss, Poetical Works *(Cameron, W. Va.: 1886), from the copy owned by Columbia University Libraries.*

PLATE 61. *The Old Familiar Stream.*
Moss process line engraving, from a pen-and-ink drawing done in imitation of wood engraving (signed "Moss Eng. Co. N.Y."). Reproduced here the same size as the plate facing page 61, in Jonathan W. Moss, Poetical Works *(Cameron, W. Va.: 1886), from the copy owned by Columbia University Libraries.*

The next, still from Moss' *Poetical Works,* is called "The Old Familiar Stream" (Plate 61). This name is more appropriate than we might recognize, for what this is pretending to be is the old, familiar, tried-and-true Lintonesque combination of black-and-white line engraving, which was still current and which had dominated American book illustration from about 1868, when Linton had arrived in the United States, to about 1878, when the men of the New School of Engraving had revolted against its platitudes. But this is *not* a tonal wood engraving at all, but a pen-and-ink drawing, probably reproduced much as Howard Pyle's so-called wood engravings for *Robin Hood* were reproduced, by the Moss Engraving Company's line process, with a very slight possibility that this might have been inked over a photograph.

"I wandered alone far away in the woods.
On the beauties of nature to muse."

With the next, Plate 62, Moss had indeed "wandered alone far away in the woods," as the caption remarked, for he has encouraged some hopeless amateur to try his hand at a continuous-tone original. What the artistic medium was, we cannot be sure; perhaps gouache, perhaps ink, perhaps a combination, since some sections seem to be transparent and others are opaque. Is there a hint that a photograph might be underlying this abomination? Perhaps the lower foreground has some kind of continuity which even the botched white brush marks can't conceal?

Now Moss really makes it in the next, "Autumn" (Plate 63), where there can be no doubt that we are looking at a photograph of Nature reproduced by some kind of halftone process engraving. Why is there no doubt? For one, because the scale of the objects is appropriate to the code. For another, because somewhere along the progression of the graphic arts, we have *learned* how photography represents Nature. That is, we have accepted its high-density code of illusionism as a transmission about the three-dimension "real" world: the code simultaneously transmits more of the textural gradients, chiaroscuro, contour modulations, in the random patterns of Nature. In Plate 63, we see that the photograph ". . . despite all its deficiencies, was able to give detailed reports about the surfaces, with all their bosses, hollows, ridges, trenches, and rugosities. . . ." [43] As William Ivins had suggested, pre- or nonphotographic media, especially black-line codes,

PLATE 63. *Autumn. Moss process halftone engraving, from a photograph from Nature. Reproduced here the same size as the plate facing page 229, in Jonathan Moss,* Poetical Works *(Cameron, W. Va.: 1886), from the copy owned by Columbia University Libraries.*

with their formalizations based on the perspective of ruled lines and universal symbolism, ". . . were attempts, as the philosophers might say, to represent objects by stripping them of their actual qualities and substituting others for them—an undertaking which is logically impossible." [44]

We can see now that Elbridge Kingsley's "Engraving from Nature" (Plate 19), mentioned in an earlier chapter, was an inevitable development: it was a white-line wood engraving imitating the textures of process halftone, or rather, imitating the textures which process halftone produces when transmitting photographs from Nature. As we noted in our comments about Kingsley, the "Engraving from Nature" was no reproduction of some "original," but *an attempt to communicate as directly as the photograph.* It marked a kind of moment of truth in the history of the graphic arts, for by 1892—as Elizabeth Lindquist-Cock and George Ehrlich have demonstrated,[45] photography and phototechnology had usurped the representational functions of *all prior artistic media*, leaving men like Kingsley no avenue of development unless they—and their contemporary illustrators—abandoned any competition with photography and turned to more abstract and symbolic artistic pursuits.

But let us now return to 1884, and to the critic who had confused a mechanical-process halftone reproduction of a painting by William Hamilton Gibson with a hand-process reproduction. We saw that the steel engraving (Plate 54) of 1837, the mezzotint (Plate 56) of 1848, and the heliotype (Plate 55) of 1872, all had subliminal effects of a somewhat comparable kind: even at "reading distance," the sense of any intervening texture, i.e., code, is almost minimal in the mezzotint, and only barely apparent in the steel engraving. The heliotype, of course, had no texture visible above the threshold of human vision. Our critic, confronted with the Ives plate, "A Winter Thunder-Storm," had at least three prior media as references (those mentioned above) and the new white-line tonal wood-engraving codes which appeared in the same book as the Ives process plate. He had no reason to think that "A Winter Thunder-Storm" was machine produced. On the contrary, experience had taught him to believe that such effects were perfectly capable of achievement *by hand,* most particularly by the hand of Henry Marsh, wood engraver. He *had* recognized a relief process, since there was no raised ink impression on the paper, and no plate mark. If he had not been intellectually prepared for this experience, there would have been no way he could have judged such a novelty. Therefore, per se, there was nothing that Ives had accomplished *yet* that indicated that photographic process halftone differed from any of the capabilities of the other media.

However, the moment that we turn from Ives reproducing an original which is a painting by Gibson, to Ives reproducing an original created by the exposure of light-sensitive material to the actinic rays of sun reflected from natural objects in the three-dimensional "real" world, what we call "photography" registers on us as a different code; that is, we recognize it specifically *as photography.* If we compare the Ives plate, "Hints of Spring" (Plate 53), with Moss' "Here Flows the Stream . . ." (Plate 59) or the others in the series, it seems that there is a specific characteristic of photography which we have learned to recognize.[46] What we are looking at in "Hints of Spring," therefore, must be a reproduction of a photograph from Nature, with the bottom half treated in some way to permit an artist to sketch in the figures. It seems correct to assume, therefore, that the intimations of cameras and "bleach prints" in the life of William Hamilton Gibson cannot be far from the truth, especially when we have corroboration from com-

THE MOUNTAIN ROAD.

apple and other trees, with saw and pruning shears or nippers—a light little instrument with such a powerful leverage that a good-sized bough could be lopped away by one slight pressure of the hand.

"It seems to me," remarked Leonard, one evening, "that there is much diversity of opinion in regard to the time and method of trimming trees. While the majority of our neighbors prune in March, some say fall or winter is the best time. Others are in favor of June, and in some paper I've read, 'Prune when your knife is sharp.' As for cleansing the bark of the trees, very few take the trouble."

"Well," replied his father, "I've always performed these labors in March with good results. I have often observed that taking off large limbs from old and feeble trees is apt to injure them. A decay begins at the point of amputation and extends down into the body of the tree. Sap-suckers and other woodpeckers, in making their nests, soon excavate this rotten wood back into the trunk, to which the moisture of every storm is admitted, and the life of the tree is shortened."

At this point Webb went out, and soon returned with something like exultation blending with his usually grave expression.

"I think father's views are correct, and I have confirmation here in autograph letters from three of the most eminent horticulturists in the world—"

"Good gracious, Webb! don't take away our breath in that style,"

PLATE 64. *The Mountain Road.* *Tonal wood engraving by A. Lockhardt, from an illustration by William Hamilton Gibson. Reproduced here the same size as the plate facing page 130, in E. P. Roe,* Nature's Serial Story *(New York: Harper, 1885, 1884), from the deposit copy owned by the Library of Congress.*

mentators on the illustration practices of the time.[47] It may be, in the case of "Hints of Spring," that Gibson merely used opaque white and charcoal to obtain his effects without bleaching away the original photograph at the bottom of the picture. In any event, he put his usual monogram signature at the left corner of the picture, signifying that he had contributed to its artistic effect, if not, indeed, claiming what was really a photograph as a "work of art."

Comparing "Hints of Spring" with yet another illustration in the Roe book, *Nature's Serial Story,* "The Mountain Road" (Plate 64), we again see the contrast between the process halftone and a tonal wood engraving. If "The Mountain Road" was based on a photograph, we cannot be certain of it; too much "art" has happened to it, even though, like "Hints of Spring," it depends for its artistic effect on the liberal use of white paper standing for "snow."

FURTHER PROBLEMS WITH PHOTOGRAPHY

The confusion about media and the confusion about originals in Gibson's illustrations have permitted us a most fortuitous reexamination of the subliminal and illusionistic effects of photographic as well as nonphotographic media, the results of which we shall want to consider again when we come to reevaluate William Ivins. Certainly the heliotype which we examined in this series (Plate 55) offered no interfering codes. Why then did not the heliotype become the characteristic medium of reproduction for someone like Gibson? We can see the answer for ourselves by examining the volume from which our example was taken, a book of Nature chats by someone whom Gibson admired: Wilson Flagg's *The Woods and By-Ways of New England* (Boston: Osgood, 1872), published at the same time as *Picturesque America.*

The small heliotype plates are printed on a coated stock, on a page measuring 5 inches by 8 inches, and are glued along one edge to the margin of either the preceding text page or to a page left purposely blank to receive it. Each plate is further encumbered by a tissue overlay. As we open the book the heliotypes, heavier than the other pages, inevitably carry along the pages on which they are mounted, thus seriously interfering with normal scanning. Glue spots splashed during the mounting process stick up in the gutters. The plates are small on the page and the details are dark, as no orthochromatic film was available to compensate for the tendency of *green* to photograph *black.* And to what great end is this unwieldy volume dedicated? Presumably, to the reproduction of Nature uncorrupted and untranslated by human intervention. Yet, by comparison, the earlier steel engraving, from *The Magnolia for 1837* (Plate 54), makes us wonder if a little human intervention is not often useful in clarifying structure and detail.

Essentially, however, the reasons for the neglect of the heliotype for nature books as compared with the ubiquitous Lintonesque tonal wood engraving of the 1870s was that the *photograph* itself was not freed from several serious limitations: (a) it was still necessary to use a wet plate, and the equipment was infernally heavy to carry up a mountainside; (b) it made all trees look funereally dark; (c) the sharp focus practices of the day tended to supply more details from Nature than some artists or scientists might prefer for the sake of either aesthetic effect or selectivity; and (d) lacking our present system of filters, all clouds disappeared into what became monotonously gray skies. It was not the heliotype which was lacking in code capabilities; it was the originals. And it was not only the reproducing media which prevented Gibson from achieving some desired effects, but the impossibility of communicating what he wanted to communicate both artistically and scientifically *with photography* that made his first overtures with it in *Nature's Serial Story* seem covert. Gibson never hid his use of the camera from the public as Frederic Remington did.

> He was a thorough artist in his love of the technical side of his work. . . .
> He was quick to learn the special art of drawing upon wood, for the engraver.
> He had no fastidious scruples against the camera, but was swift to resort to it
> and learn its possibilities and make it into a tool to shape his thought.[48]

Probably what had kept him from utilizing photography sooner in his career was precisely the bulky and slow wet plate. When, as we mentioned before, he went into the White Mountains to obtain sketches and photographs for Drake's book in 1882, we hazard a fairly safe guess that he took with him one of the cameras of the type called "detective," as these were small and almost foolproof. He had used such a camera on a visit to Europe; one of his notebooks records, "Brought home over 300 instantaneous photographs, taken under all conditions by my detective camera."[49] With the advent of fast, easy-to-handle gelatin dry plates in the early 1880s, Gibson had the perfect tool to capture scenes and scenic detail, even miniature flora and fauna with close-up attachments. After the poor showing of Ives' first halftone process, however, and the critical furor over the confusion of media, Gibson avoided the direct use of photography for several years, and when he did begin to use it again, he was impelled—either by his memories of the Roe experience or by his recognition that the codes of photography were still new to the public as seen in the code of process halftone—to label any reproduction after a photograph clearly as such.

COMPARISONS BETWEEN TWO MODES OF COMMUNICATING

Any investigation of Gibson's work reveals several distinctions between that of the New-School-of-Engraving era and that of the advanced and presumably triumphant halftone-process era. In a single decade, a change was accomplished which, by any implication of graphic arts theory, should have liberated Gibson to do whatever he wished, however he wished it, and to have it reproduced in a medium—process halftone—which was expected to reveal his artistry rather than the ingenuity of his engravers. But, perhaps curiously, before his death in 1896, Gibson turned more and more to direct photography from Nature, offering his own photographs of flora and fauna as originals for reproduction, rather than always relying on what had been proved as his superb craftsmanship and appropriateness of artistic vision for each medium. It may be that the pressure of an excessively popular career put too many demands on his time, so that he turned to photography to ease the burden of handwork. Or it may be, as we shall see unmistakably in connection with the work of Frederic Remington (Chapter 7), that there was a public interest in photographs per se, now that there seemed some chance of having them reproduced with all their supposed scientific fact intact through the medium of the process halftone. It may be that, superb book and illustration designer that he was, Gibson was tempted by the new reproductive medium to explore new possibilities, as he was genuinely tempted to explore new artistic media during his career.

victim securely, and held him to await assistance.   It came.   The entire neighborhood had been apprised of the battle, and in less than five minutes the ground swarmed with an army of re-enforcements.   They came from all directions; they pitched upon that hornet with terrible ferocity, and his complete destruction was now only a question of moments.   I experienced a sort of malevolent delight at such a fitting expiation for a life of rapine and murder.   Already a dozen pairs of teeth were working at the joints of his wings, and those members had soon been severed from the body had I left him to his fate; but there was a problem of engineering skill connected with his capture which I wished to solve, and I concluded to come to his rescue, and

STRATEGY VERSUS STRENGTH.

even spare his life if need be, in an interesting experiment.   I therefore dislodged all the ants excepting the two original assailants.   The overwhelming attack upon the hornet had made him furious, but these pugnacious little fellows were even now more than his match, and still held him as before.   No sooner, however, did I remove from their grasp those

We can see what kinds of new expressiveness he sought between 1882 and the 1890s. His biographer remarks that "Finer illustrations, in spirit or execution, than those of 'Sharp Eyes,' or 'Highways and Byways,' it would be hard to find." [50] Looking at a characteristic vignette (Plate 65, "Strategy versus Strength") of *Highways and Byways of New England* (Harper, 1882), with its explicit black-line wood-engraving codes, it is perhaps not surprising that a book called the "marvel of delicate and poetic illustrations, that compend of rare and fascinating facts, that glory of modern illustration and book-making," [51] is not *Highways and Byways* but the entirely process-halftone *Sharp Eyes* (Harper, 1892), which included not only Gibson's wash drawings, and charcoal sketches, but Gibson's photographs from Nature (see Plates 69, 70, and 71). However impressed he may have been with Gibson's earlier achievement, his biographer, Adams, undoubtedly relished the fact that no hand engraver stood between Gibson and the printed page.

But we have only to compare the "Strategy versus Strength" of *Highways* with a white-line tonal wood engraving by Albert Lindsay for a later book, *Strolls by Starlight and Sunshine* (1891) to recognize how carefully and brilliantly Gibson could design for transmission through a hand process. "The Moth's Kiss First . . ." (Plate 66) is a masterpiece of design and texture, light and dark, superbly rendered by a master engraver. *Strolls* contains not only tonal wood engraving at the point of its highest development, but technically advanced halftone engravings, as well as pencil drawings on a prepared paper, the texture of which was so raised that the graphite strokes of a pencil across it produced a pseudo process-halftone dot structure. Plate 67, "Prehistoric Botanists," was probably produced through such a technique, a technique which permitted Gibson the luxury of an autographic medium which could be reproduced with a minimum of expense and a minimum of distortion. It is hard to say exactly what Gibson used to create "Prehistoric Botanists," yet what matters is that he could directly create a series of dots of differing size and equal in intensity for the printed page, and the plate seems to have required no visible enhancement by a handcraftsman. [52] In *Strolls by Starlight and Sunshine*, Gibson experimented freely with a variety of artistic techniques, including pencil drawings, pen-and-inks greatly reduced to a superb delicacy which the originals could not have had, wash drawing, smudged charcoal, and media which we can never know because they were transmitted via tonal wood engraving.

PLATE 65. ***Strategy versus Strength.***
Black-line wood engraving by Henry Marsh, from a drawing by William Hamilton Gibson. Reproduced here the same size as page 144, in Gibson, Highways and Byways *(New York: Harper, 1883), from a copy owned by E. Jussim.*

PLATE 66. *The Moth's Kiss First.* *Tonal white-line wood engraving by Albert Lindsay from an illustration by William Hamilton Gibson. Reproduced here the same size as page 30 in Gibson's* Strolls by Starlight and Sunshine (*New York: Harper, 1891*), *from the copy owned by the Boston Athenaeum.*

"The moth's kiss first!
Kiss me as if you made believe
You were not sure this eve
How my face, your flower, had pursed
Its petals up.

PLATE 67. *Prehistoric Botanists.* *Process line engraving, probably from a drawing on textured paper, considerably reduced from an original illustration by William Hamilton Gibson. Reproduced here the same size as page 119 in* Strolls by Starlight and Sunshine *(New York: Harper, 1891), from the copy owned by the Boston Athenaeum.*

PREHISTORIC BOTANISTS

AMONG my earliest memories associated with nature, and one that will always vividly linger, is that thrilling spectacle of a winter butterfly hovering about the farm-yard of my New England home. It was the middle of January, one of those balmy days of respite from the north wind, when the careful alder catkins are beguiled, and the puss-willow's paws first peep from beneath their snuggeries. The odors of wet twigs and sweet sap and soggy snow, tinctured with the wine of quickened loam, saturated the air. The patches of thawing drifts lay like mimic glaciers amid their melting areas on the barn and

Sharp Eyes is a revelation of Gibson's love of experimentation. The new capabilities of process halftone were strikingly demonstrated by the opening double spread. The left-hand page, "Of Eies and Seeing" (Plate 68), superimposes a process halftone insect, clearly photographed from Nature, over a paragraph of text. The right-hand page, "Through My Spectacles" (Plate 69), again permits Gibson to combine a design motif with text: type and picture were united in one metal plate by the superimposition of two negatives. This double spread must have created a sensation in its day, especially if Adams' response to it is any indication.

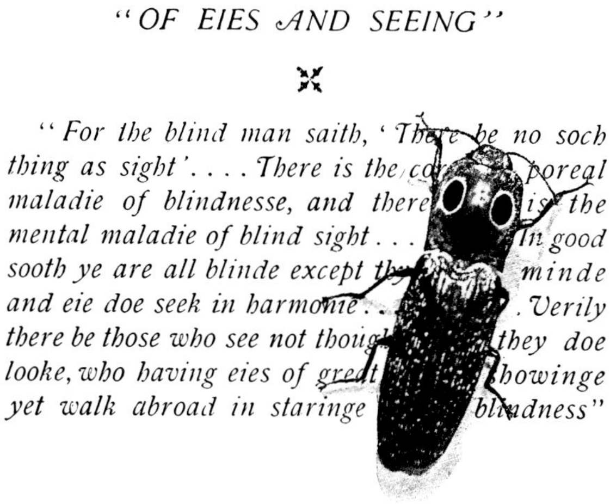

"OF EIES AND SEEING"

" For the blind man saith, ' There be no soch thing as sight'. . . . There is the corporeal maladie of blindnesse, and there is the mental maladie of blind sight . . . In good sooth ye are all blinde except the minde and eie doe seek in harmonie . . . Verily there be those who see not though they doe looke, who having eies of great showinge yet walk abroad in staringe blindness"

PLATE 68. *Of Eies and Seeing.* Combination process halftone and line engraving, superimposing a photograph from Nature over typography. Reproduced here the same size as the left-hand page of the double-spread frontispiece in William Hamilton Gibson's Sharp Eyes (New York: Harper, 1892), from the copy owned by E. Jussim.

PLATE 69. *Through My Spectacles.*
*Combination process halftone and line
engraving, superimposing either a photograph from Nature or a wash drawing,
over typography. Reproduced here the
same size as the right-hand page of the
double-spread frontispiece, in Gibson's
Sharp Eyes (New York: Harper, 1892),
from the copy owned by E. Jussim.*

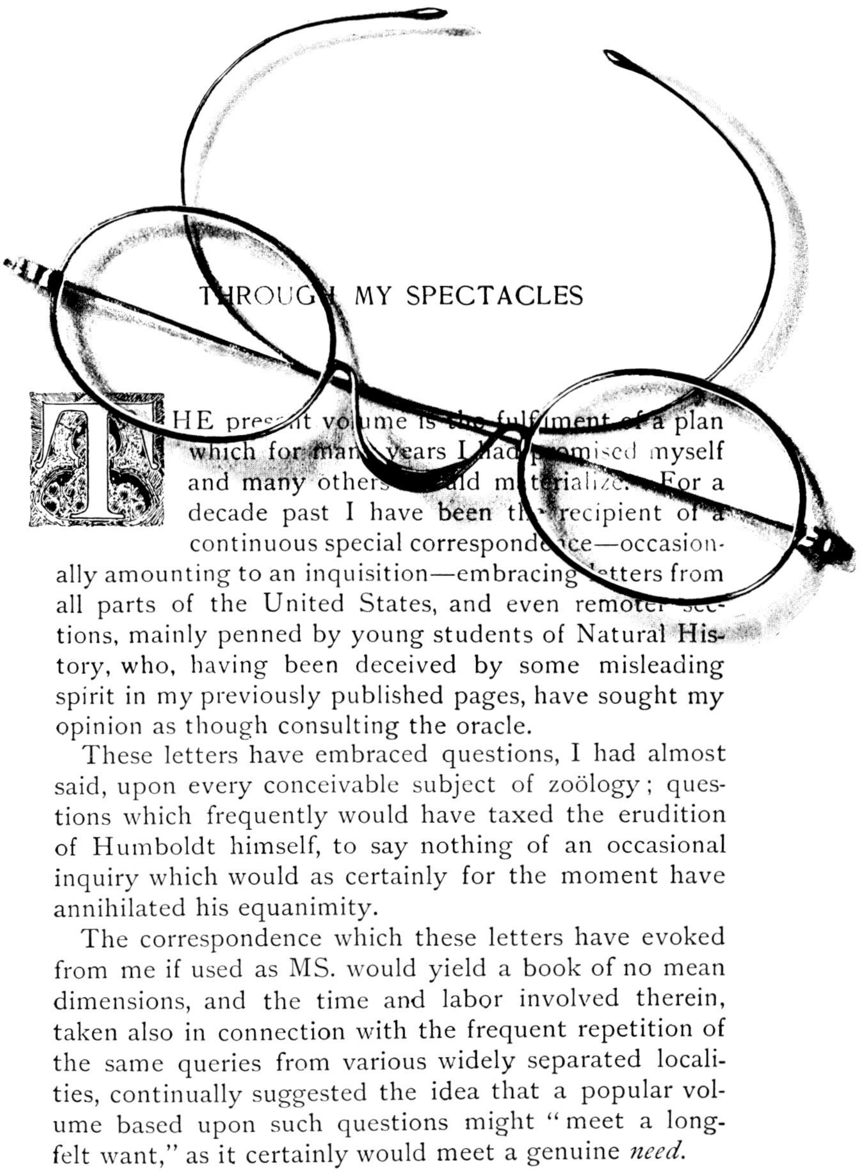

THROUGH MY SPECTACLES

THE present volume is the fulfilment of a plan
which for many years I had promised myself
and many others would materialize. For a
decade past I have been the recipient of a
continuous special correspondence—occasionally amounting to an inquisition—embracing letters from
all parts of the United States, and even remoter sections, mainly penned by young students of Natural History, who, having been deceived by some misleading
spirit in my previously published pages, have sought my
opinion as though consulting the oracle.

These letters have embraced questions, I had almost
said, upon every conceivable subject of zoölogy; questions which frequently would have taxed the erudition
of Humboldt himself, to say nothing of an occasional
inquiry which would as certainly for the moment have
annihilated his equanimity.

The correspondence which these letters have evoked
from me if used as MS. would yield a book of no mean
dimensions, and the time and labor involved therein,
taken also in connection with the frequent repetition of
the same queries from various widely separated locali-
ties, continually suggested the idea that a popular volume based upon such questions might "meet a long-
felt want," as it certainly would meet a genuine *need.*

In another illustration for *Sharp Eyes,* Gibson combined a real page of music, drastically reduced, with a superimposed initial letter, to begin a chapter on insect musicians. He was apparently delighted to try anything at least once, and the ability of the camera to enlarge or reduce elements which could be combined was a new design opportunity.

Another vignette for *Sharp Eyes,* the watercolor wash or charcoal, "Ivy," is reminiscent of one of the bugbears of the wood-engraving generation: the laid finish of the watercolor paper was used by Gibson as a horizontal decorative texture, something which the process halftone rendered to perfection. Inevitably, a wood engraver would have had to concentrate on rendering the small forms. But even in 1891, some comments by a critic reveal that the controversy over transmitting the textures of an original was by no means resolved:

> When mechanical engraving was invented, and photography began to usurp the functions of the engraver, the artists who drew the originals were still better pleased. The faithful camera not only "followed copy" with servile and literal accuracy, but it also reproduced the very brush-marks, mannerisms, "handling" of the delighted but misguided artist. This was interesting, but it is an error to suppose that a style of engraving which brings to light the "handling" of the picture is an improvement. We do not wish to see the means by which a work of art is produced, any more than we wish to know the name of the manufacturer of the brushes with which Millet painted his "Angelus." . . .[53]

Taking such an idea to its logical conclusion, the author of such illogical thinking would have to admit that, if the means by which a work of art is produced were somehow removed, all that could properly be said to remain would be an artist's conception, something about which Hamlet's words concerning "bodiless creation" might be apropos. The conceptual art of the twentieth century *has* taken as its philosophic basis the removal of the physical means so that the conception may be regarded more purely; in the nineteenth century, this was never really considered. The critic is talking balderdash, but it is balderdash originating in a serious philosophic confusion about originals, transmissions, messages, codes, and all the rest of the problems which have been concerning us here. All communication having a physical basis—whether the breath of air which carries our speech to a listener, or the marks of printer's ink by which the ideas of an author are communicated to a reader—it is absurd of the above critic to talk as if there could be something like a "pure message."

In *Sharp Eyes,* Gibson had ceased to design for reproduction through tonal wood engraving. He was using anything that came handy: watercolor washes, ink washes, pencil, charcoal, soot, and photography from Nature. From our comments on "Ivy" above, it might be expected that in *Sharp Eyes,* finally, even photography from Nature might find its perfect transmission. In one charming vignette, the results were optimistic: the screen seemed adequate to transmit a photograph of a scrap from a vireo's nest, which the bird had filled with bits of newspapers. Gibson remarked in the text, ". . . at length I came upon the sentiment which I have here reproduced by photography . . . *have in view the will of God.*"[54] Phototechnology had enabled him not only to reproduce a scrap of Nature, but, amusingly, the very typography of a message found "in Nature."

When we turn to "Winter Rosette" (Plate 70), however, we begin to wonder again what it is that we are looking at. Gibson found it necessary to inform us: "the examples which are here pictured are not drawings, but any. We find no adequate mention of these quiet resolute rosettes which are everywhere disclosed in spring upon the melting of the snow, but which might have been found as early as the previous September. Many a dried stalk or withered seed-pod protruding above the snow will point the way to them. This wiry spire of the pretty moth-mullein beset with its globular pods; these brown catkins of the rib-grass plantain; this feathery sprig of peppergrass—we may readily guess what a pretty tufted carpet is that which covers the bare earth about their feet. This brown spiny mockery of last summer's thistle reminds us of the most beautiful of all these winter decorations, the symmetrical compound star of acanthus-like leaves, guarding the root beneath, and waiting in patience for the first opportunity of sending up its stalk of bloom.

The evening primrose shows us one of the most perfectly symmetrical of all these leaf clusters—a beautiful complex spiral star, geometrical in its arrangement, and a perfect pattern for the modeller, sculptor, decorator, or wood-carver. The willow-herb, or fire-weed (*Epilobium*), is almost equally perfect; and, indeed, our art-worker may find a wide choice of ornamental types,

16

PLATE 70. *Winter Rosette. Vignetted process halftone engraving from a photograph from Nature by William Hamilton Gibson. Reproduced here the same size as page 241, in Gibson's,* Sharp Eyes (*New York: Harper, 1892*), *from the copy owned by E. Jussim.*

THE BEWITCHED
COCOONS

June 2d

N the table before me lies a letter from a
young correspondent who has been having
some perplexing entomological experiences
of so interesting a nature that I have concluded to publish her account, and my answer.

"DEAR MR. GIBSON,—I want to tell you what a funny time I
had with those three cocoons that you gave me last winter. You
remember they were quite large, and all wrapped up close in
leaves, and were very hard, like parchment. You said that they

PLATE 71. *The Bewitched Cocoons.*
*Vignetted process halftone engraving
from a wash drawing by William Hamilton Gibson. Reproduced here the same
size as page 66, in Gibson's* Sharp Eyes
(*New York: Harper, 1892*), *from the copy
owned by E. Jussim.*

are reproduced from actual photographs from the plants themselves. . . ." [55] Indeed! Looking back at the Lindsay tonal wood engraving of "The Moth's Kiss First . . ." (Plate 66), we can only wonder why he should ever have abandoned the lucidity of the artist's control.

He reproduced five of these photographic rosettes, each worse than the next. Much of this was undoubtedly the photoengraver's fault; for example, in three small rosettes, the details of the edges of the plants being too small for the screen to sustain when the vignetter came to paint away the dots around the leaves, he simply left the halftone dots where they fell. We cannot imagine Gibson being so clumsy with either his brush or his pencil, nor do the textures of the plants reassure us convincingly that they are taken "from life."

A critic, writing in the same year that *Sharp Eyes* appeared, in 1892, remarked:

> The unpleasant features of the screen processes are:—the uniformity of the textures produced by them; the mechanical regularity of the grain, to overcome which screens of other patterns, with irregular grains, have been tried; and the impossibility of rendering white, since the screen, even in the highest lights, asserts itself sufficiently to produce a light grey. This last difficulty may, indeed, be overcome by a judicious use of the graver or by the skill of the etcher; but unless these adjuncts to the process are used artistically, which they rarely are, they are more likely to mar than to help the beauty of the effect. [56]

The justice of these remarks has been amply demonstrated in our examination of Howard Pyle's early encounters with process halftone in 1887; certainly, they are just for the photographs made by Gibson for *Sharp Eyes,* as well. Nevertheless, the success of process halftone with Gibson's wash drawings in the same book reinforces our suspicions that, unlike Pyle—who, in his work in gouaches and oils, had one major objective, to produce an independent picture, an object of "fine art"—Gibson took the trouble to acquire the technical knowledge which permitted him to produce pictures which even the process halftone screen could not destroy. When Pyle blundered in process, especially in *Men of Iron,* presumably it was because he believed that phototechnology could reproduce anything perfectly; and what became an occasional blunder for Pyle became a constant flow of mediocrity from lesser talents. Gibson, on the other hand, seemed perfectly attuned to the new medium (see Plate 71, "The Bewitched Cocoons")—except when he tried to use it to reproduce his own photographs from Nature. The worst plate in *Sharp Eyes* is unquestionably that of the two boys chasing butterflies (see Plate 72, "Butterfly Hunters"). Here process, however, does not stand convicted of all the crimes which the critic Koehler enumerated above. What is at least half the problem is the lack of artistry and technical skill on the part of Gibson as photographer, and of photography from Nature in the hands of any amateur. For that was what Gibson was with the camera; with art media, he was a master craftsman. The feeble photographs in *Sharp Eyes* are inexcusable unless, perhaps, Gibson was deluded in the typical late nineteenth-century fashion, that photography was "more scientific" and "more accurate" than art.

COLOR AND THE POSTHUMOUS BOOKS

The last book prepared by Gibson before his premature death in 1896 was quite a departure from all his others. *Our Edible Toadstools and Mush-*

and vociferous exclamation of hope, defeat, or victory.
That is only half a country boy who does not know the
"swallow-tail" and the butterfly chase.

Yes, we country boys all know the velvety "black
swallow-tail" butterfly and its fluttering poise above
the clover blossoms; its two border rows of yellow
spots and cloudy band of azure blue upon the lower

6

PLATE 72. **Butterfly Hunters.** *Process
halftone engraving from a photograph by
William Hamilton Gibson. Reproduced
here the same size as page 81, Gibson's*
Sharp Eyes *(New York: Harper, 1892),
from the copy owned by E. Jussim.*

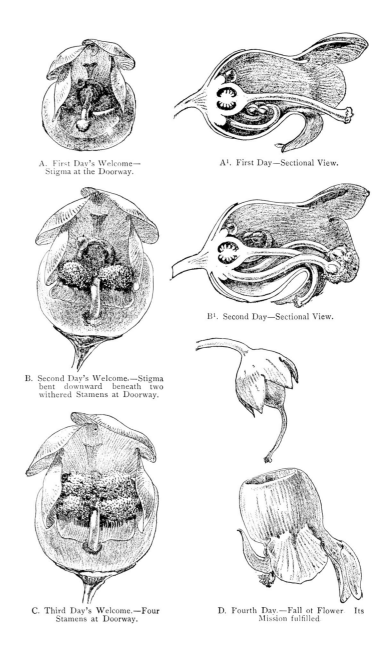

A. First Day's Welcome—
Stigma at the Doorway.

A¹. First Day—Sectional View.

B. Second Day's Welcome.—Stigma
bent downward beneath two
withered Stamens at Doorway.

B¹. Second Day—Sectional View.

C. Third Day's Welcome.—Four
Stamens at Doorway.

D. Fourth Day.—Fall of Flower. Its
Mission fulfilled.

PLATE 73. *Flower Sections.* *Process line engraving from drawings on textured paper by William Hamilton Gibson. Reproduced here the same size as page 29, in Gibson's* Eye Spy *(New York: Harper, 1897), from the copy owned by E. Jussim.*

rooms and How to Distinguish Them (Harper, 1895) contained thirty color plates reproduced by chromolithography and fifty-seven grained-paper pencil sketches. It was intended as a handbook for field use, not as a collection of picturesque views of slightly anthropomorphicized insects. The scientific integrity of the man was evident throughout. "More than one of the originals of the accompanying colored plates have been hidden in this portfolio for over twenty years . . . awaiting the further accumulation of . . . knowledge and experience. . . ."[57]

At the threshold of the three-color halftone process, he regarded the chromolithographs of his mushroom book as invaluable, for a reason which may strike the blasé twentieth century as sounding too naive:

> The addition of color to the present list [of plates] enables its extension somewhat beyond the scope of a series printed only in black and white, as in the distinction of mere form alone an uncolored drawing of a certain species might serve to the popular eye as a common portrait of a number of allied species, possibly including a poisonous variety.[58]

Here the scientist is recognizing the cruciality of color in information transfer. The artist did not live long enough to use it expressively as color book illustration.

After Gibson's death, Harper put out several more of his books, but they are largely hodgepodge assortments of field sketches and scraps from short articles in the 1890s. They are not to be regarded as books illustrated *by* Gibson, but rather as books reproducing Gibson drawings. They are disappointing after the beauties and variety of *Highways and Byways, Strolls by Starlight and Sunshine,* and *Sharp Eyes.* They are the typical products of the halftone process triumphantly reproducing anything, cheaply and efficiently, but not, perhaps, always beautifully or in the spirit of an artist's original.

These later books with Gibson drawings as illustrations, however, demonstrate the accuracy of one of William Ivins' observations:

> For many purposes . . . drawing, as for instance in such a science as anatomy, preserved its utility because it could schematically abstract selected elements from a complex of forms and show them by themselves, which the photograph could not do because it unavoidably took in all of the complex. The drawing, therefore, maintained its place as a means of making abstractions while it lost its place as a means of representing concretions.[59]

In the multitude of informational drawings which appeared in these posthumous books, for example, Plate 73, which is from the 1897 *Eye Spy,* "it is hard to say whether Gibson was first a naturalist and afterwards an artist, or first an artist and afterwards a naturalist."[60] Perhaps he could be best characterized as a teacher, a communicator, who put his artistic skills at the service of explicating complexities so that others could better understand. A naturalist, an artist, a communicator who turned courageously to any new medium which might help him to transfer information, by experimenting with photography and phototechnology he was helping to define the limitations of all mechanical media.

7

Frederic Remington
(1861–1909):
The Camera
or the Artist

. . . I think every great draftsman sees Nature first through the eyes
of some other man, until by and by Nature reveals herself to him
direct.[1]

I will get such photos as I can and send them to you by express. . . .[2]

Artist of the Old West, reporter of the wars with the Apache as well as of
the Cuban campaigns of the Spanish-American War, recorder of the pass-
ing ways of the cowboy and the pioneer, Frederic Remington retains a
secure place in the esteem of historians, art critics, and an action-loving
public.

It would be perfectly possible to examine the career of this prolific
artist, whose oeuvre totals more than 3000 illustrations, much as we did
that of Howard Pyle (1853–1911), his close contemporary. We could, for
example, trace the development of his relationship to the graphic processes through, say, his "actinics"[3]—mistaken, as were those of Pyle, for
"wood engravings" (see Plate 74, "Bringing Home the Game"). We could
study his early appearances in tonal wood engravings, which we shall do
shortly in another connection, or his first photogravures in *Picturesque
California* (1888)—(see Plate 75, "Miners Prospecting for Gold"). We could
compare these with process halftones reduced from magazine illustrations
into book illustrations (see Plate 76, "The Guide") and note that "The
Guide" was prepared for Francis Parkman's *The Oregon Trail* (Boston:
Little, Brown, 1894). The first hint that we might want to watch for something different in Remington's career would be that it was Parkman who
commented, "I will get such photos as I can and send them to you by
express. . . ."

Otherwise, such general comparisons would prove reasonably instructive and would confirm the development of Howard Pyle through these
same steps. For example, this Remington comment will certainly remind
us of Pyle in his dissatisfaction with hand reproduction:

The pen was never natural with me . . . I worked with it in the early days
only to get away from the infernal wood-engravers. Do not misunderstand
me, I have no quarrel with the *good* engravers of the block, the men who

195

PLATE 74. ***Bringing Home the Game.*** *Process line engraving from the pen-and-ink draw-ing by Frederic Remington. Reproduced here the same size as page 135, in Theodore Roosevelt,* Ranch Life and the Hunting Trail *(New York: Century, 1888), from the copy owned by the Amherst College Library.*

are as much artists as those whose drawings they interpret. But those clumsy blacksmiths turned woodchoppers, who invariably made my drawings say things I did not intend them to say—those were the fellows who made my youthful spleen rise up and boil. Pen and ink is a splendid medium for pre-senting familiar, every-day subjects, but my stuff was utterly strange to most people when I began picture-ing [*sic*] Western types.[4]

This last sentence is a complaint we certainly did not hear from Mr. Pyle. His "stuff," mythological or not, never seemed "strange to most people." What Remington indicates here is that he believed *an engraver was bound to have problems rendering the details of a drawing if he were thoroughly unfamiliar with the three-dimensional objects about which a message is being transmitted.* The truth of this is at least partially evident in one of the early

PLATE 76. *The Guide.* *Kurtz process halftone from the illustration by Remington. Reproduced here the same size as the plate facing page 10, in Francis Parkman,* The Oregon Trail *(Boston: Little Brown, 1894; author's edition), from the copy at Mount Holyoke College.*

tonal wood engravings (see Plate 83, to be discussed later in detail) where the inadequacy of rendering details like the hubs of wagon wheels suggests either a faulty photograph-on-the-block from Remington's original, or an engraver who was unfamiliar with such objects. Remington's actinics ("Bringing Home the Game") were at least under his own control.

We can study the autographic quality of his work by examining the textures of the photogravure ("Miners Prospecting for Gold") where the reproducing medium has captured the impasto of heavy paint on the "rocks" of the original. The nature of the original is almost too evident here, for all the broad strokes which build up the three-dimensionality of the forms are captured by the camera down to the last crudity.

We could then go into a comparison of the compression ratios between the reduced process halftone ("The Guide") and, say, those of a former journalistic medium, lithography (see Plate 77, not by Remington, of "Stanley's March in Africa" of 1875); lithography, after all, had become the most popular medium for book illustration dealing with newsworthy items, travels, and so on.

We could even go on, as we did with Pyle, to evaluate the effect of color reproduction on Remington. It was clearly of major importance: "Color process printing did for Frederic Remington and his art what the incandescent lamp did for Edison, and the telephone for Bell. . . ."[5] We know that he confined himself to monochrome for the early years of his career, as all of his work was produced for magazines: "Although Remington did most of his work in his New York studio, he did not experiment with colored oils until the early 1890's, and it took him several years to master the technique." [6]

We can certainly tell from the reproduction of his "An Old-Time Plains Fight" (Plate 78), a fine-line developed process halftone of 1904—characteristically hand-retouched by one of the old-timers—that we can enjoy little of the brilliant yellows or any other colors in a black-and-white transcription, and that the reduction has obliterated much significant detail.

But all of these useful comparisons would bypass the far greater significance of Remington for our purposes as we try to understand the full impact of photography on visual communication. However useful, they

PLATE 77. *Stanley's March in Africa. Crayon lithograph, artist unknown. Reproduced here the same size as the plate facing page 257, in John S. Roberts,* The Life and Explorations of David Livingstone *(Boston: Russell, 1875), from a copy owned by E. Jussim.*

PLATE 78. *An Old-Time Plains Fight.*
Process halftone engraving hand-high-
lighted by Chadwick from the oil painting
in full color by Frederic Remington. Re-
produced here the same size as the plate
facing page 808, in Agnes C. Laut, "The
Fights of the Fur Companies," Century
Magazine *(new series) (March 1904),*
from the copy at Mount Holyoke College.

would not even begin to answer questions which arise even in the first quotation about his pen-and-ink techniques. Why, for example, was his stuff "strange" to most people if photography had been available since 1840? Was there no widespread distribution of pictures of the West? Certainly Matthew Brady had circularized thousands of albums of Civil War photographs, most of them mounted prints. Certainly the stereoscope and stereographic slides had made almost any subject available to the back-Easters. Was there any truth in this implication by Remington that information about half-breeds, cavalry officers, cowboys, and wild horses, had not been circularized? Or was he simply indulging in self-aggrandizement — a characteristic of Remington for most of his life?

REMINGTON AS TRANSMITTER OF "HISTORY"

We encounter several factors in communications processes by attempting to find some answers to the above questions. The first discovery is a simple one. The subjects which Remington tended to draw — coarse, unshaved, unromanticized, ornery types — were not considered to be fit subjects for refined people. Therefore, according to Poultney Bigelow,[7] who was the first to introduce large amounts of Remingtonia into the magazine field, book and magazine editors had seen fit to withhold distribution of this sort of picture. However, once the public saw his work, it became used to the idea of such subject matter, and even became used to the "unrefined" way he drew his characters. To put it another way, the public first accepted *what* he saw, then accepted *how* he transmitted what he saw. In performing both actions, the public could then incorporate this new vision as its own, acceptable, and normal.

The second discovery comes as a result of examining hundreds of magazine and book illustrations in the areas of Wild West stories and articles from the 1860s through the 1880s, and it, too, is deceptively simple: the inability of the photograph to transmit itself through photomechanical media appropriate to the graphic needs of publishing had effectively limited the widespread transmission of certain types of information.

Until the mid-1870s and 1880s, when photography-on-the-block became commonplace, tonal wood engraving had failed to transmit authentic, reliable information of a caliber comparable to photography itself. To an audience becoming more and more used to the presence of photography in their lives, outside of publication, the haphazard details and generalizations of, say, an F. O. C. Darley illustration for Hiawatha (see Plate 79, "Hiawatha's Fishing") were becoming less and less acceptable as reliable information about the Indian, however acceptable as artistic expression. Beyond that, as we shall see, there were certain aspects of Nature which photography itself could not transmit until the invention of faster and more responsive emulsions, electric shutters, and orthochromatic photomechanical codes. The types of people, the types of activity which Remington recorded in his illustrations, were only beginning to be available as information for the general public, who obtained most of their information through the pictorial press which had sprung up after the Civil War.

It is probable that we are so familiar with the paintings of Remington now in major museums that we have forgotten that the largest portion of his work was produced for illustration purposes, as originals *intended* for reproduction in periodicals and books. It is surely ironic that the rough, masculine art of Frederic Remington, with its roots deep in pictorial journalism, should have succeeded in escaping from the critically inferior

PLATE 79. *Hiawatha's Fishing.* *Black-line wood engraving by Bogert from the illustration by F. O. C. Darley. Reproduced here the same size as the plate facing page 158 in Henry Wadsworth Longfellow,* Poems, *new rev. ed. (Boston: Houghton Mifflin, 1894) from the copy at the Forbes Library.*

pigeonhole called "illustration," out into the esteemed category of "fine art," while the lyrical magniloquence of Howard Pyle, evolved in the grand manner from the Renaissance German masters and the French academics, failed to achieve for him precisely that greatest ambition of his life, to be known as an easel painter. That this differentiation continues to be true is partly, at least, the choice of the Wilmington Society of the Fine Arts, owner of the largest collection of superb original Pyle paintings and drawings, which discourages considering Pyle as anything other than purely an illustrator.

In terms of their contemporaries, both Howard Pyle and Frederic Remington were performing the same task: to visualize history, each in his own fields of interest. Yet few today would go to a Pyle painting to see "how it was when Washington lived"; we would go to Benjamin West, Trumbull, or Copley, contemporaries of the great General. We reserve a little mistrust for the fictive artist's re-creation of men of epochs long past. For no matter how scrupulous Pyle was in his attention to authentic historical costumes and furniture, in his study of the colonial artists and their graphic representations, he had to rely upon his imagination. He could — and did — take photographs of his costumed models to save them from posing long hours, he could take photographs of museum rooms full of period furniture, but he could not take photographs of men who had died before the advent of photography. One of the measures of the accuracy of Ivins' contentions that photography changed our vision in so many ways is precisely that we no longer trust noncontemporaneous or noncamera images.

PLATE 80. ***Long Sat Waiting for an Answer*** (*Hiawatha's Fishing*). *Photogravure on heavy wove paper from the oil monochrome painting by Frederic Remington. Reproduced here the same size as the plate facing page 76, in Longfellow,* The Song of Hiawatha (*Boston: Houghton Mifflin, 1892*) *from the copy owned by the Forbes Library.*

Unlike Pyle, the man who ". . . made the picture-loving public reconstruct its ideas of the cow-puncher, the Indian, the army scout, the pioneer and even the bucking broncho and the pack-mule" [8] was in a vastly different situation. Remington was called upon to re-create "instant history," to transmit to readers back East all the excitement of the continuing wars with the Indians, the advance of the American cavalry into hostile territories, at a time when the massacre at Little Big Horn (1876) was fresh in memory. There are few documented examples of Remington's having to rely upon his imagination; indeed, this is exactly what the publishers and the public did *not* want him to do. *What was expected of Remington was the literal reportage of specific "real" events.* Even at his most expressively imaginative, in the Hiawatha [9] illustrations of 1892 (see Plate 80, "Long Sat Waiting for an Answer"), we can compare his literalness with the earlier Darley "Hiawatha's Fishing." The Darley is romantic and generalized; Remington's muscular Indian sits in a canoe specifically of birch, with struts which make us believe we could measure them. This is what was expected of Remington: to make us believe that we are looking at a representation of three-dimensional reality. We expect to trust Remington's reports as we trust the reports of the camera.[10] In the *Memoirs* (1907) of General O. O. Howard, for example, copies made from Remington's illustrations were used interchangeably with photographs, as if they were photographs. In their introduction to these *Memoirs,* which largely concentrated on photographs supplied by the Bureau of Ethnology and on colored plates of Indian artifacts, the publishers remark:

> The old method of having artists seize the general outline of a scene, and by a few rapid strokes of a pencil preserve the general idea, until, in the studio, leisure was found to enlarge the hasty sketch . . . has passed away; the modern camera has taken its place, and is the basis of most of the illustrations in this volume.[11]

We are accustomed to thinking about Remington's later color paintings as "artistically expressive" works, and so they are, often masterpieces of design and striking color. But in another respect, they are like color snapshots of history. They intend, like the movie western, to permit us to experience vicariously a certain way of life. The more authentic the representation in all its details, the more transfer of information occurs. As we examine the entire oeuvre of Remington, it becomes obvious that the greatest part of his role as an illustrator was dedicated to the transmission of information under the guise of artistic expression, and that he was essentially an intermediary between the informational content of photography and the printed page.

THE CAMERA OR THE ARTIST

As Ivins hypothesized,

> Up to that time very few people had been aware of the difference between pictorial expression and pictorial communication of statements of fact. The profound difference between creating something and making a statement about the quality and character of something had not been perceived.[12]

In order to make his "pictorial communication of statements of fact" when the facts were not immediately available in the form of three-dimensional contemporaneous events, Remington could rely on the camera recording the event through the eyes of another man. The philosophical implications of this extraordinary state of affairs were prophesied with unusual clarity as early as 1859 in a perceptive commentary by Oliver Wendell Holmes:

> *Form is henceforth divorced from matter.* In fact, matter as a visible object is of no great use any longer, except as the mould on which form is shaped. Give us a few negatives of a thing worth seeing, taken from different points of view, and that is all we want of it. Pull it down or burn it up, if you please. We must, perhaps, sacrifice some luxury in the loss of color; but form and light and shade are the great things, and even color can be added, and perhaps by and by may be got direct from Nature. . . . Matter in large masses must always be fixed and dear; form is cheap and transportable. We have got the fruit of creation now, and need not trouble ourselves with the core. Every conceivable object of Nature and Art will soon scale off its surface for us. Men will hunt all curious, beautiful, grand objects, as they hunt cattle in South America, for their *skins*, and leave the carcasses as of little worth.[13]

Holmes here was eulogizing the stereoscopic slide and the stereograph; he had invented his own version of the stereoscope, and wrote enthusiastically about the three-dimensional illusions obtainable through it. But even the flatness of ordinary nonbinocular photography represents a symbolic divorcement of "form" from "matter." In an extraordinary way, Holmes foresaw what André Malraux would observe in the twentieth century: that looking at photographs would be substituted for looking at the so-called "real thing."

Remington very rarely admitted that he "hunted" with the camera, or even relied upon photography in any way, until the prevailing expectation of such admission forced his hand. He has to be read very carefully, although he is cautious in his statements:

> I remembered that the year before a Blackfoot on the Bow River had shown a desire to tomahawk me because I was endeavoring to immortalize him. After a long and tedious course of diplomacy it is at times possible to get one of these people to gaze in a defiant and tearful way into the eye of a camera; but to stand still until a man draws his picture on paper or canvas is a proposition which no Apache will entertain for a moment.[14]

It is typical of the approach taken by Harold McCracken, his biographer, that he makes no comment on Remington's statement, nor does he anywhere acknowledge Remington's profound relationship with photography. Apparently, Remington's biographers have not taken into account the fact that, by the 1880s, "detective cameras" and other such deviously disguised cameras—including complex "watch cameras," "vest cameras," and other hidden photographic equipment—were widely distributed, were inexpensive to own, and that, with a little looking, numerous public and private admissions by Remington concerning his dependence on photography can be found. As shown in a previous chapter, William Hamilton Gibson had a detective camera and carried it through Europe on one of his trips.

But Remington does not need to be caught using the camera itself. This was precisely the point that Oliver Wendell Holmes was making: "*Form is henceforth divorced from matter.*" Anyone could take a photograph of an event, bury the print in his attic, and revive it to send to Mr. Remington as possible source material. His friends, complete strangers, his authors, his publishers, anyone could—and did—supply him with authentic material for his illustrations. Typical is a letter from Elizabeth B. Custer, the General's wife, who wrote to Remington as late as 1908:

> In the autumn, whatever I can do with photographs and anything that I have that pertains to the General, I shall be so glad to offer you. . . . There is

an old Seargeant of the 7th Cavalry . . . who served in the Regiment. . . .
He has all the pictures of the 7th Cavalry officers, newspaper clippings,
pictures of the scouts, an account of an interview with "Sitting Bull," pictures of the Indian Chiefs. . . .[15]

It is possible that Mrs. Custer had supplied Remington with materials
for her life of General Custer, published in 1887, at a time when Remington was first beginning to be published as an illustrator. He and another
artist were asked to provide visual re-creations for the book, but they
were tonal wood engravings from photographs. One such is Plate 81,
"A Buffalo at Bay," a thoroughly uninspired picture which bears a subtitle
in parenthesis: "From a photograph taken on the spot." No name is given
in connection with this illustration; that is, no one is credited with having
redrawn the photograph for engraving. It seems obvious, then, that either

A Buffalo at Bay.
(*From a photograph taken on the spot.*)

PLATE 81. *A Buffalo at Bay. Wood
engraving by "Harley, N.Y." after a
photograph from Nature, undoubtedly
via photography-on-the-block. Reproduced here the same size as page 573, in
Elizabeth B. Custer,* Tenting on the
Plains *(New York: Webster, 1887), from
the copy at Mount Holyoke College.*

the original negative or a print was transferred to the wood block and the engraver, "Harley," took it from there. We can compare this wood engraving (Plate 81) with a later Remington of 1892, Plate 82, "Water," which appeared originally in *Harper's Weekly* and was reduced for use in a book by Richard Harding Davis. In Plate 82, we have Remington admitting, after his signature, that "Water" was drawn "after photo." (In another of the Davis illustrations, he scribbled on the illustration, "after a bad photo.") There is little difference between the two examples we have here: "Buffalo at Bay" and "Water" are both *after photographs;* in the first case, a hand engraver rendered the photograph; in the second case, an illustrator was called in to render a photograph for the new mechanical medium of process halftone engraving. Since there is no appreciable amount of "artistic expression" in the rendition of the mounted cavalry, it seems logical to assume that Remington was simply redrawing a poor photograph for purposes of mechanical reproduction, just exactly as skilled staff artists had redrawn his own—or Howard Pyle's—early sketches for hand reproduction. We find this role of Remington's repeated throughout his career, except that in some cases he was forced to acknowledge his dependence on photographs, and in other cases, curiously, he hides this fact as much as possible.

PLATE 83. *Conestoga Wagon.* *Wood engraving by "Harley, N.Y." from the illustration by Frederic Remington. Reproduced here the same size as the plate facing page 250, in Elizabeth B. Custer,* Tenting on the Plains *(New York: Webster, 1887), from the copy at Mount Holyoke College.*

It was partly the medium itself which dictated his admission. In the Custer biography (1887) in which "A Buffalo at Bay" appeared, we find a Remington, mentioned previously: "Conestoga Wagon, or Prairie Schooner" (Plate 83). We find a similar subject in the Richard Harding Davis book as well, in 1892: "One of Williamson's Stages" (Plate 84). Although there is no stated evidence that either of these was based on photographs, there is no evidence that they were not. In both cases, Remington is presenting specific information which presumably could be checked by a reader who could find the "real" three-dimensional objects and the animals used as bases for these pictorial transmissions. We can pause for a moment, and recognize further that the medium for the early Remington, "Conestoga Wagon," tells us very little about the original of the reproduction. If indeed Remington did copy it from a photograph, either he copied it very poorly or the engraver, as we suggested earlier, did not understand what he was looking at. "Conestoga Wagon" looks as if the original models had literally been carved out of wood. In the second picture of this comparison, "One of Williamson's Stages," a process halftone, the illustration resembles the denser textures of "Nature" much more. This success would seem to depend on both the nature of the artistic medium (watercolor or ink wash) and the direct reproduction medium which permitted Remington to indicate speed and motion. Here he reveals that he has learned how to portray motion, or at least, that no engraver has prevented him from portraying it. What is curious about the two pictures is that it is the *earlier* which resembles the stop-motion action of what was called "instantaneous photography"—with a speed that could freeze an action in midcourse, and which was available in the 1880s—while the later illustration has incorporated the lessons taught by painters such as Thomas Eakins on the visual depiction of motion as an illusion, as opposed to the literal stoppage of it by the camera.[16]

Comparing these two illustrations (Plates 83 and 84, "Conestoga

PLATE 84. *One of Williamson's Stages.* *Kurtz process halftone engraving from the painting by Frederic Remington. Reproduced here the same size as the plate on page 159, in Richard Harding Davis,* The West from a Car Window (*New York: Harper, 1892), from a reissue in 1903 owned by E. Jussim.*

Copyright, 1890,
By
Frederic Remington

PLATE 85. *Jockeys.* *Tonal white-line wood engraving by Albert Lindsay, from an illustration by Frederic Remington. Reproduced here the same size as the plate in Theodore Dodge, "Some American Riders,"* Harper's Monthly, *August 1891, page 373; from the engraver's proof, courtesy of Mrs. Margaret Van Brunt, Wilmington, Del.*

210

Wagon" and "One of Williamson's Stages") with "Jockeys" (Plate 85), which appeared in *Harper's Monthly* for August 1891, we discover that an inventive and skillful wood engraver, here, Albert Munford Lindsay, who had done so well for both Pyle and Gibson, could manage to invent a successful code for translating Remington's indications of motion and speed. Lindsay ingeniously blurred the forms of forelegs and even interrupted the whip to symbolize speed. That tonal wood engraving of this excellence surpassed all the process halftone work up to 1892 can hardly be disputed. The play of dots and sworls of textures are not uniformly stamped on an original, but assist in the interpretation of the perspective of surfaces. Held at a further distance from the eye than is usual for reading, the effect of motion in "Jockeys" is unmistakable.

"Jockeys," like the Hiawatha, represents the side of Remington which falls more into the category of "artistic expression" than "Conestoga Wagon," "One of Williamson's Stages," or "Water," all of which, as we saw, were involved in the transmission of journalistic information. It seems probable that one of our judgments of what constitutes the element of artistic expression in an illustration is at least partially based on what we consider could *not* have been supplied by a camera image. If this is so, then Ivins again would be justified in his contention that up to the time of the successful utilization of the photograph, "very few people had been aware of the difference between pictorial expression and pictorial communication of statements of fact." [17] That is, photography supplied, for the first time, a visual measure of authenticity; and it was by this standard that statements of fact began to be judged. This was true to such an extent that, by the end of the 1890s, it was expected that statements of fact would be made *only* by photography, and not by artists. Thus we see a literal diminishing of the role of the illustrator as a "packager of information" in Plate 86.

Plate 86, "Philippine War — Double Spread" was filled with photographs reproduced in process halftone, depicting camp scenes of U.S. Army field forces seeing action in the Spanish-American War. In the center of the page was a lone Remington "sketch" of a rainy-day scene. It seems reasonable to conjecture that the photograph originally taken in the rain was very poor, untransmittable, and *Harper's Weekly* (for May 20, 1899) asked its noted war artist, Frederic Remington, to render the scene fit for halftone process reproduction. This double-page spread, in a journal which had once been noted for its encouragement of the artist and its dependence on top-quality reporter-wood engravers, represents the triumph of the halftone process as a means of transmitting the information contained in photographs. Certainly no hand-engraving process could succeed so well in securing our trust in its informational content, with the possible exception of photographs transmitted by photography-on-the-block and rendered by illusionistic wood-engraving techniques (recall the Cole "Modjeska").

There is no question about Remington's recognition of what was expected of him in terms of literal, factual, reliable transmission of information. In hitherto unpublished correspondence between the artist and his publisher, Mr. Harper, about the possibility of bringing a law suit against another publisher for plagiarizing one of Remington's illustrations, Remington begs off in the following note:

New Rochelle, N.Y. Dec. 1 (1899)

Letter to My Dear Captain —
In thinking over that infringement of my drawing I should not like to testify on the stand to the fact that the "block-house" which I drew "was not

right" because such testimony would be bad for both myself and the interest of the weekly.

I think the reaction of such testimony would be worse than the benefits which might be gained from it.

I could say on the stand that I thought the drawing was *made after mine* but don't believe it would be a good thing to *prove it* as I explained to you I could.

The fact that I *faked* the block house—having lost my sketch book & having no photograph at the time—might give the public the idea that such a thing is habitual to me.

Yours faithfully,
Frederic Remington.[18]

The "block-house" referred to here is one which appeared in an illustration of the Spanish-American War. Remington, like the true war-hound that he was, went down to Cuba at the same time as his friends and authors, Richard Harding Davis and Theodore Roosevelt. One of the most famous illustrations that came out of his experiences in Cuba was *The Charge Up San Juan Hill*, which he characterized in his usual hardy, realistic style. The picture is credited with no less an accomplishment than helping to make Theodore Roosevelt President of the United States, but it is cautiously admitted that Remington was probably not in the thick of that particular battle or even quite possibly not there at all, and that he most probably relied upon composite photographs, as he did for so many others of his war pictures.

As Remington's career progressed, we find that it was only after the success of the process halftone in transmitting photography per se that there was any public acknowledgment by him of particular works based on photography. As the readers of the periodicals became visually more sophisticated and demanding of authenticity, obviously they could not believe that Remington, then in Cuba and sending back written and visual reports, could have been sending out reports and drawings simultaneously from the Philippines and from South Africa, both areas which he later illustrated. From about 1892 on, it would be possible to draw up a specific list of the pictures for which he acknowledges reliance on photography, those which he seemed careless about specifying (or else was claiming as the work either of on-the-spot recording or of his imagination), and those few which are genuinely dominated by characteristics of "artistic expression." For every sketch like the Philippine rainstorm previously noted (Plate 86),

PLATE 86. *Philippine War* (*double spread*). *Four process halftone engravings from photographs from Nature (two at the top, two at the bottom) with a process halftone (center) from a rendering by Frederic Remington. Reproduced here greatly reduced from the double spread in* Harper's Weekly, *May 20, 1899, pages 502–503. Courtesy of the Free Library of Philadelphia.*

in which he did not add "after photo" under his signature, there are dozens of pictures produced for *Harper's Weekly* at this time which are so signed. The public had begun to want its information pure, uncontaminated by artistic idiosyncracies. The artist was suspect, willy-nilly, simply because he was not, and could not be, a camera. It had been a slow progress, perhaps, between the incorporation of etching or engravings based on daguerreotypes to the transmission of photography by screened process halftones, but there can be no doubt that by the time Remington came to be famous, he was competing with the camera. ". . . the new pictorial processes filled the pictorially informative needs far more accurately, far faster, and far more cheaply, than was possible with the other, older techniques." [19]

Remington's relationship to the graphic arts reflects positively on Ivins' hypothesis: "by conditioning its audience, the photograph became the norm for the appearance of everything." [20]

Beyond this, and in a specific way, Remington's work documents Ivins' assertion that photography had other conditioning effects:

> Not only has it vastly extended the gamut of our visual knowledge, but through its reproduction in the printing press, it has effected a very complete revolution in the ways we use our eyes, and, especially, in the kinds of things our minds permit our eyes to tell us. [21]

This documentation is part of the story of Remington's relationship to the instantaneous photographs of Eadweard Muybridge, where we shall see that Remington not only carried out his role of acting as an intermediary between information captured by the camera and the printed page, but that he participated in a revolution of vision in which his role as illustrator was both explicitly and implicitly influential.

REMINGTON AND MUYBRIDGE: THE CAMERA IS QUICKER THAN THE EYE

It was in the course of systematically checking out conflicting assertions about Remington and Muybridge that the present writer discovered Remington's essential role as an intermediary. Some of these assertions, crediting Remington with supernatural vision, are epitomized in the following passage from Harold McCracken's biography of 1947:

> Frederic Remington was by no means the first artist who loved to portray horses. . . . Nor was he the first to portray a horse racing with all four feet off the ground. . . . [But] The manner in which he pictured this noble animal was, at the time, considered the most unconventional aspect of his work. Previously for centuries . . . most of those who dared to portray a horse supposedly running at full speed or taking a jump, pictured it as skimming over the ground with all four legs spread out horizontally—like a frozen rabbit. But Remington's horses were different. . . . He drew them standing almost erect on their hind legs, or on their front feet, or even doubled up with their legs jack-knifed under their bellies "like crabs." And he made a bold habit of picturing them with all four feet off the ground. For this revolutionary boldness, he was criticized and ridiculed, not only by critics of art but by authorities on horses. *His vindication, however, was not long in coming* [italics added]; and it came in a manner which even the most incredulous could not dispute. Professor Muybridge's discoveries made through instantaneous photography demonstrated beyond all argument the fact that horses did at times travel with *all four feet off the ground* [McCracken's italics]. But Remington's keen eye had already been his own instantaneous camera. [22]

Of the many articles and books available at this date on Remington, only two seemed to have questioned the implications of the above myth. Perriton Maxwell did so in 1907 in the Pearson's article already cited, and Robert Taft, in *Photography and the American Scene* (1938). Taft could not seem to satisfy his own doubts about the sequence of events—Muybridge first or Remington first—apparently because he did not have time to make a strict chronological sequence, which we shall do here. As he could not, for example, ascertain whether or not Remington's library had contained any of the Muybridge books soon to be discussed, he did not come to grips with the logic of the situation, a surprising eventuality, given the scrupulous scholarship of Robert Taft.

In any event, the origin of the specific character of McCracken's representation—that Remington had been able to see what previous artists through the centuries had not been able to see—is most probably a single source of confusion, F. Hopkinson Smith's *American Illustrators* of 1892:

> If Muybridge taught us the true movements of animals, as illustrated by his discoveries through instantaneous photography, Remington is the first man who has utilized these discoveries in his work, and made us feel the absurdity of the Sheridan-ride-kind-of-gallop, with all four legs stretched out even with the ground, the tail flying straight in the wind. *And yet Remington saw these movements in a horse long before he ever heard of Muybridge or his discoveries* [italics added]. His own eye was the lens of the camera, his brain the dry-plate, and his pencil the developer. In doing this, remember, he was doing unconsciously what no other painter, either here or abroad, had ever conceived or attempted. I have heard that the great Meissonier lay awake all night after Muybridge showed him a negative of some hunters taking a five-barred gate. He had been doing the Sheridan-ride-gallop himself all his life, and the shock to his sense of truth—for if Meissonier was not truthful he was nothing—must have been tremendous. . . . And yet there is more movement, rush, whirl, in one of Remington's swooping Indian ponies with his legs doubled up under him like a crab, than in the whole troop in Meissonier's famous picture of "1807." [23]

Now, here we have an enthusiastic fellow-artist eulogizing Remington without documentation; for if F. Hopkinson Smith had even casually mentioned the known facts—that Meissonier had devoted a long life to the study and painting of horses in action, that there had been a great international controversy over animal locomotion which only the photographs of Eadweard Muybridge had settled, and that Muybridge had visited Paris and talked with Meissonier (and other startled animal painters) in 1879, when Frederic Remington was still an undergraduate playing football at Yale University—we would have dismissed his deification of Remington as so much poppycock. Smith's hyperboles have permitted a long line of adoring writers to credit Remington with what it is exceptionally difficult to believe, unless, truly, he had been born with superhuman vision.

Fortunately, as noted before, the investigation of this myth proved extremely rewarding, providing unexpected insights into the role of the illustrator in transferring information. In order to verify or disprove the statements claiming such extraordinary powers for Remington, it was necessary to establish a chronology of events, particularly the chronology of the publication and distribution of information of *visual* knowledge which might have been available to Mr. Remington. In doing so, a publishing sequence was discovered which so perfectly demonstrates the development of information transfer techniques in the nineteenth century that it could serve by itself as the paradigm of the entire publishing experience.

THE PROBLEM OF MOTION

As we saw with William Hamilton Gibson, the transmission of photography from Nature presented a curious paradox, whereby the very technology by which illustration was made reproducible could not succeed in reproducing its own characteristics, at least not in the general context of book and periodical publication. The basic reason for this failure was the need for a subliminally textured code of type-compatible transmission which could match the subliminally textured character of photography from Nature. All processes, no matter how subliminal—like the mezzotint or the daguerreotype—which relied either upon idiosyncratic coding by an illustrator or on a nonconvertible positive copy, could not serve to transmit photography via the printed page. The economic, aesthetic, and technological problems inherent in mounting prints, or woodburytypes, or incorporating heliotypes, militated against their continuing competition with type-compatible media. Until the development of fine-screen, typographically compatible halftone processes and inexpensive rotary forms of photogravure, periodicals—which constituted the largest bulk of American publishing—were especially dependent upon *translations* of photography-from-Nature, especially on tonal wood-engraving translations via photography-on-the-block.

The Symposium on Wood-Engraving, however, reminded us that photography-on-the-block had the same drawbacks as all other photography of that era, namely, lack of orthochromatic fidelity (distortion of greens, yellows, and reds into blacks, and the complete loss of blues), lack of appropriate exposure when foreground and background of subjects were in contrasting degrees of light, and other problems inherent in the photographic processes themselves affected in due course the reproduction of photography from Nature.

Most importantly, there was one aspect of Nature which photography found exceedingly difficult to capture. That was, simply, Nature itself: the world in flux, the world which is every moment moving, changing, and never at rest. If iron clamps could hold heads still enough for portraits, nothing prevented brisk winds from transforming would-be panoramas of stately trees into illegible black blurs of branches, while foaming brooks became slippery vacuities. Nature, photographers discovered to their dismay, *moved.*

The slowness of emulsions in the early days of photography had made it possible to manipulate the length of exposures merely by removing and replacing the camera cap. The itinerant tintype man, still occasionally

PLATE 87. *The Horse in Motion* (*1878*) (*detail*). *Wood engravings from a full-page series, based on photographs by Eadweard Muybridge, reproduced here the same size as the front page,* Scientific American, *Oct. 19, 1878. Courtesy of the Free Library of Philadelphia.*

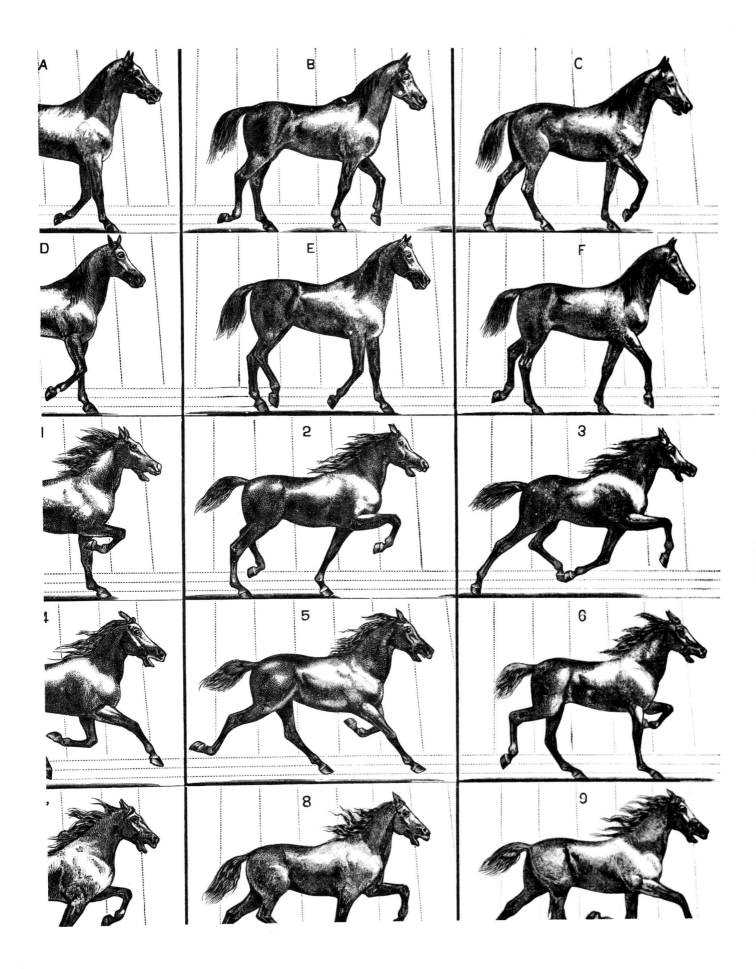

encountered in public parks, does not employ a shutter, a comparatively late development, perfected around 1878. It was only by speeding up the. early emulsions that some miracles of photography were achieved as early as 1860, when Oliver Wendell Holmes enthused about a stereoscopic slide:

> This is Mr. Anthony's miraculous instantaneous view in Broadway. . . . It is the Oriental story of the petrified city made real to our eyes. . . . Every foot is caught in its movement with such suddenness that it shows as clearly as if quite still. . . . And what a metaphysical puzzle have we here in this simple-looking paradox! Is motion but a succession of rests? All is still in this picture of universal movement. Take ten thousand instantaneous photographs of the great thoroughfare in a day; every one will be as still as the *tableaux* in the "Enchanted Beauty." Yet the hurried day's life of Broadway will have been made up of just such stillnesses. Motion is as rigid as marble, if you only take a wink's worth of it at a time.[24]

Taking a wink's worth of it was exactly the problem, for what could be "stopped" in one tenth of a second, or in one twenty-fifth of a second, did not include all of the speeds of natural motion, nor did it answer some harassing scientific questions.

One of these questions proved so provocative that it demanded solution, and, since the story is well known, it will be summarized here very briefly. To satisfy an argument then current among artists and scientists as to the actual positions of a horse's legs in full gallop, Governor Leland Stanford of California, owner of a vast stable of racers, encouraged a photographer then working in San Francisco to invent some means of using the camera to settle the dispute once and for all. Muybridge claimed that it was he who went to the Governor, not the other way around. Be that as it may, Eadweard Muybridge (1830–1904) made his first motion experiments in 1872. Since he lacked a fast shutter, these first tries were somewhat inconclusive, and he pushed on to develop an electrical shutter that managed a two-hundredths-of-a-second exposure.[25] On October 19, 1878, at about the time that the first experiments in the New School of Engraving were appearing in the periodicals, the *Scientific American* devoted its front page to a series of stop-motion studies (see Plate 87, "Horse in Motion"), and published the following article; we quote this at length because it is crucial not only to the history of photography in America, and to understanding how scientific disputes may be settled with the camera, but because the date and the content of the article have great importance in our understanding of the context in which Remington appeared:

PLATE 88. *Conventional Positions of Quadrupeds in Motion*. *Heliotype from schoolbook pictures, printed on lithographically tinted background. Reproduced here the same size as Plate 25, in J. D. B. Stillman,* The Horse in Motion *(Boston: Osgood, 1882), from the copy owned by the Mount Holyoke College Library.*

A short time since the *Scientific American* briefly noted the fact that Mr. Muybridge, of San Francisco, had perfected an automatic electrophotographic apparatus, Mr. Muybridge courteously responded by forwarding a series of instantaneous photographs, showing with absolute accuracy the motion of the horses when walking, trotting, and running. From these we have selected two series, the first showing the movement of the horse, "Abe Edginton," while walking at a 15-minute gait; the second showing the same horse while trotting at a 2:24 gait. These—omitting the driver and his sulky—we have had enlarged and skillfully engraved, as shown by the illustration on the first page. . . .

The most careless observer of these figures will not fail to notice that the conventional figure of a trotting horse in motion does not appear in any of them, or anything like it. Before these pictures were taken no artist would have dared to draw a horse as a horse really is when in motion, *even if it had been possible for the unaided eye to detect his real attitude* [italics added]. At first sight an artist will say of many of the positions that there is absolutely no "motion" at all in them; yet after a little while the conventional idea gives way to Truth. . . .

Mr. Muybridge's ingenious and successful efforts to catch and fix the fleeting attitudes of moving animals thus not only make a notable addition to our stock of positive knowledge, but must also effect a radical change in the art of depicting horses in motion. . . .

Our drawings, though admirable and instructive as such, are necessarily inferior to the photographs in scope and variety of detail; and they lack also that element of indisputable accuracy which belongs to the sun pictures. However truthful, an artist's work cannot have the convincing force of a photograph.[26]

Among the important implications of the preceding report, most obviously, the prediction was made that Mr. Muybridge's instantaneous views would revolutionize the art of portraying horses and that his electrophotographic apparatus would provide access to other scientifically useful motion studies. We also discover that his photographs could not be transmitted directly to the many readers of the *Scientific American* because there was no suitable means other than mounting prints, and that, therefore, the standard newspaper method of transmission was employed, i.e., the coarse tonal wood engraving (Plate 87). There is also a hint in the *Scientific American* report that *if some means could be found of transmitting a photograph directly, artists could be dispensed with as packagers of information,* a role which they had performed since the beginnings of graphic communication in paleolithic art. In one sense there was some means: at the end of the above report, readers of the *Scientific American* were informed that, by writing to Muybridge in San Francisco, they could obtain postcard size reproductions of the photographs. Thus, in 1878, small photographic copies of Muybridge's first success were available to the general public, if they took the trouble to obtain them.

Artists, from Paul Delaroche—the academic French painter who is reported to have exclaimed, at first sight of a daguerreotype in 1839, "From now on, painting is dead!"—to Jean Meissonier, had been variously stunned by the ability of the camera to transcend first the artist's hand and then the artist's eye. But the lack of "that element of indisputable accuracy which belongs to sun pictures" now put insistent pressure on the graphic arts to find some means whereby the information content of photographs could be transmitted more directly.

The publication sequence of Muybridge's photographs provides us with the steps whereby the graphic arts succeeded in this task.

PLATE 89. *Mohammed—Running Stride* (1882). *Heliotype from "instantaneous photography" from Nature by Eadweard Muybridge Reproduced here the same size as Plate 13, in J. D. B. Stillman,* The Horse in Motion (*Boston: Osgood, 1882*), *from the copy owned by the Mount Holyoke College Library.*

THE HORSE IN MOTION

When Muybridge completed his Palo Alto researches in 1879, he had already deposited with the Library of Congress a "number of sheets of photographs, each one of which illustrated . . . a horse while walking (etc.). They were published under the general title of 'The Horse in Motion.'"[27] Muybridge explained later that

> A number of these subjects were, a few years afterward, copied, and republished in a book bearing the same title as that originally used by this author Muybridge, without the formality of placing his name on the title-page.[28]

Unlike the originals, however, this "republication" was certainly not a "number of sheets of photographs." As Muybridge indicated, his work was copied. Why and how the originals were copied is elaborately reported by the putative "author" of the book[29] presenting the copies, J. D. B. Stillman, who contributed a lengthy essay to what was otherwise bound sets of pictures, Muybridge's instantaneous views transformed into the primary material of the volume.

The illustrations in the Stillman-Muybridge *The Horse in Motion, as Shown by Instantaneous Photography* (Boston: James Osgood, 1882) utilized at least four of the major reproductive processes available in America in 1881–1882:

(1) Full-page heliotypes on calendered stock; these reproduced both "artwork" and photographs from Nature, for example, Plate 88, "Conventional Positions of Quadrupeds in Motion," which demonstrated the older and false ideas of animal motion, and the stop-action study, Plate 89, "Mohammed—Running Stride" which was by Muybridge.

(2) Full-page, anatomically schematicized chromolithographs on heavy wove stock.

(3) Full pages of black-and-white lithographs in two media: (a) crayon textures, these being simultaneous multiple views of horses and riders in motion, from all of five angles; and (b) black silhouettes of motion studies printed on lithotinted color areas. These two kinds of photolithographs constituted the major portions of the book's illustrations.

(4) Text outline drawings reproduced by process line engraving (see Plate 90, "The Horse in Motion"), here reproduced from an article about Muybridge's work.

In the attempt to reproduce Muybridge's instantaneous exposures, the publisher encountered so many difficulties that Stillman found it advisable

PLATE 90. *The Horse in Motion (1882). Process line engravings, based on Muybridge photographs, used to illustrate George Waring's review of the Stillman book cited above. Originally printed in the Stillman book. Reproduced here the same size as page 383, in Waring, "The Horse in Motion,"* Century Magazine, *July 1882, from the copy owned by E. Jussim.*

FIG. 10.

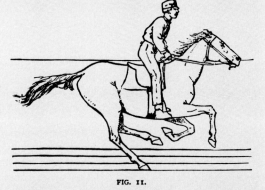

FIG. 11.

of the pastern, is continued after the foot leaves the ground, so that in Figure 9 the croup and shoulder have been thrown quite to the gauge line. In Figure 10, the horse being still off the ground, the croup has gone an inch above the line. It has hitherto been the general belief that when the horse descends from his bound he lands on one of his

both fore feet being still more than a foot from the ground, both hind feet are in firm contact with it. In Figure 14, the right hind foot is ten inches from the ground and far to the rear. The left hind foot is performing the functions of the right in Figure 12, and the right fore foot is on the ground. The leading fore leg is extended to its utmost in Figure 15.

FIG. 13.

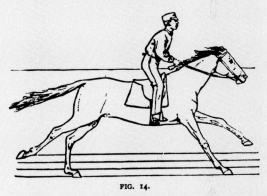

FIG. 14.

fore feet. Figure 11 shows that the right hind foot first reaches the ground, the other three feet being more that twelve inches above it. As this hind leg passes to the rear in Figure 12 the pastern is parallel with the ground, the left hind foot is preparing to take its position, and both fore feet are moving to the front. At the next position, Figure 13,

The two hind legs are extended, and the left fore leg is still four inches from the ground (Figure 16), when the right, the only one in contact, is nearly at the end of its stroke. In Figure 17, eighteen feet in advance of Figure 1, the left fore foot is still somewhat in advance of the position there shown. Figure 18, as above stated, finishes the stride, the leg,

FIG. 17.

FIG. 18.

to explain how these had been finally resolved. The following is quoted at length from Stillman's Chapter VII, "Illustrations of the Paces":

> The series of plates which follow are intended to show more fully than was possible in the silhouettes that precede them, the action of the horse in every possible position. . . . The time of the exposure of the negatives was so immeasurably small that few of the pictures were perfect in all the details; and as red appears as black in the photograph, so all bay horses were without any details of light and shade, simply as silhouettes, and even when the horse was light or grey there would be some defect in some part of every one of the series.
>
> Experiments were made with various processes to reproduce them with all their defects; but it was found that the making of the necessary transfers from the originals, while they reproduced accurately all the defects of the original photographs, reproduced them with diminished sharpness, and these methods were abandoned. Under the direction of the Heliotype Printing Company another plan was adopted.
>
> From the original photographs, by the heliotype process, copies were produced on gelatine magnified, and prints were taken on Bristol board in blue ink in the same manner as in the ordinary heliotype process. These prints, with the originals, were put into the hands of artists skilled in drawing on wood for engravers, who drew them with a pen and india ink, under careful supervision of the writer, so as to preserve the outlines as they were rendered by the camera and avoid reproducing the blotted defects of the originals. These drawings were then reproduced on stone by the camera, reduced to their original size, and the prints given in the volume were printed from these stones as in ordinary lithography.[30]

We have already seen evidence in Plate 14, "The Courtin' " by Winslow Homer, that a heliotype could be produced from solid black silhouettes with no difficulty.

Elsewhere in the Stillman-Muybridge volume, the presence of outline drawings, like those in Plate 90, in the text is explained as follows:

> In order to avoid the abstract study of the coordination of the limbs in locomotion, figures are given to aid the mind in following the movements. They were executed by a process called photoengraving, after drawings made with great care from a series of photographs . . . . The cuts are not introduced for their accuracy; they have been subjected to too much manipulation to lay claim to that precision of outline that will be found in the heliotype and silhouettes in photolithography given in illustration of the paces.[31]

The need for faithful reproduction is again underscored in this explanation of the plates used by Stillman to demonstrate the older, inaccurate methods of representing the horse in full gallop (see Plate 88):

> Plates XXV and XXVI represent sketches taken from elementary drawing-books manufactured in London and Berlin and used in the schools. They are heliotyped, on a reduced scale, in order that there should be no suspicion of inaccuracy in the copies.[32]

And again (see Plate 89):

> Examples have been selected of the two principal paces, when the horses were light-colored, to reproduce in heliotype—a process which furnishes an exact transcript of the original photograph by the same agency, namely, the sun.[33]

Despite the difficulties inherent in both the color blindness of the wet-plate emulsions and the small size of the negatives, the expenses of having the silhouettes redrawn and the multiple views transferred to stone, the Stillman book registered an enormous scientific success, and it received thoughtful and extensive reviews in major periodicals, particularly in the *Century Magazine*[34] of July 1882, from which the outline drawings of Plate 90 are taken. It happened that the author of the *Century* review, George Waring, Jr., had for some years been publishing articles in that magazine on the horse, and he began his review with some paragraphs which confirm us in the prior distribution of Muybridge's motion studies:

> Those curious in such matters were much interested, a few years ago, by the circulation of a few sets of photographs, taken at the private race-course of Governor Leland Stanford, by Mr. Muybridge, a photographer of San Francisco. The consecutive positions of the legs in the stride of a running horse, as revealed by these photographs, seemed ludicrous and almost impossible. Indeed, it required the combination of the positions given by the reproduction of the pace in the zoetrope to convince the skeptical that the analysis of the movement was correct. . . . Since the first appearance of these photographs, the processes for securing them have been much improved, and Mr. Muybridge's public and private representations, here and abroad, have been received with the greatest favor. Meissonier, who has made a specialty of the action of the horse, is announced as an adherent of the new theory, and it is said that he has recently modified a painting in conformity with it.[35]

Waring was an honest man. He conceded that "not only art but man is conventional."[36]

> We are accustomed to seeing certain things represented in a certain way. When an attempt is made to represent them in another way our conventional natures revolt at the innovation. A familiarity of some years with Muybridge's photographs, while it has not enabled me to see in them the activity of the old type of picture, has unquestionably modified the view with which I regard them.[37]

Waring concluded a prolonged discussion of the propriety of the new views in terms of art with these remarks:

> It may be that, as our ideas become trained to the analysis of quadrupedal movement, we shall accept the new light in its fullness; but let us not, in our enthusiasm over a new discovery, and in our devotion to a purely-theoretical "truth," lose sight of the limitations which must always surround every attempt to represent action by passive objects and lines.[38]

From some of Stillman's remarks quoted by Waring, we learn that Muybridge's photographs had occasioned a great deal of scorn and ridicule, as if (like the scientist friend of Galileo's who refused to look at the moons of Jupiter through the telescope lest it shake his faith in God) by pretending the photographs were wrong, the truth would go away. In order to demonstrate the validity of his motion studies, Muybridge had recourse to a toy "based on the principle of the persistence of vision"[39]—the zoetrope, which had been on the market since 1867. With the zoetrope, a collection of transparent projection slides, and with a refinement called the zoopraxiscope, he toured the country, lecturing and demonstrating the scientific accuracy of his views. He commenced his lecture tour in 1879 in San Francisco, and eventually went to Europe, where the news of his discoveries had preceded him.[40]

THE CHRONOLOGY OF
FREDERIC REMINGTON'S WORK

Before we continue with the progress of the publication of Muybridge's instantaneous motion studies, let us catch up with Mr. Remington.

Born in 1861 in upper New York state, Frederic Remington was the son of a Civil War Cavalry officer who became a successful newspaper publisher, and who remained an aficionado of both horses and horse racing. In 1872, when Muybridge's first attempts were made to settle the controversy for Governor Stanford, Remington, age eleven, was just beginning to doodle. In 1877–1878, when Muybridge deposited the successful motion studies with the Library of Congress, and when *Scientific American* published its front page full of wood-engraved translations of Muybridge stop-action photographs, young Remington, age seventeen, was at the Yale University Art School. Here, despite a well-documented, seemingly total commitment to football instead of studying, he was almost certainly exposed to either heliotype or photogravure reproductions of Detaille, DeNeuville, Meissonier, Gérôme, and other French academics who were widely admired for their detailed panoramic paintings of military maneuvers, especially of the flamboyant French cavalry.[41] There seems little reason to doubt that Yale University may have acquired a set or a partial set of the large prints which Muybridge had circulated to magazines, scientific institutions, and individuals—all those, as Waring put it, "curious in such matters," in the hope not only of increasing his fame but of increasing sales of prints from the series, especially to artists. It seems extremely unlikely that an art student at Yale University, no matter how devoted he was to rugged outdoor sports, especially an art student who was fascinated by his father's career in cavalry and in horse races, could have missed hearing about and seeing some news items about Muybridge's experiments, at least the front-page story in *Scientific American*, 1878. Yet there is no direct evidence that young Remington paid any attention to the ensuing furor, or was yet even aware of Muybridge's achievements.

When his studies were interrupted by the death of his father in 1880, Remington took his inheritance, and—like Theodore Roosevelt and Owen Wister, who were doing the same thing at about the same time—he went West to seek his fortune, *not* as an itinerant artist, like George Catlin or John Mix Stanley or Karl Bodmer, all of whom had painted and drawn the American Indian before Frederic Remington was born, but as a sheep rancher. He settled in Kansas in 1881 after a long trip to Montana, where he visited the site of the Custer massacre of 1876, then still recent and heroic history.

Although he had gone to Kansas specifically with the intention of making his fortune at ranching, Remington found time not only to make a few side trips, but to draw a few sketches to send back East to the big illustrated journals, finally succeeding—much as had Howard Pyle, and by the same route—in having a drawing of his see print in *Harper's Weekly*, February 25, 1882. This was called "Cow-Boys of Arizona: Roused by a Scout. Drawn by W. A. Rogers from a sketch by Frederic Remington."

On the first page of this chapter appears this quotation from W. A. Rogers: "I think every great draftsman sees Nature first through the eyes of some other man, until by and by Nature reveals herself to him direct." In Remington's case, we hope to demonstrate that the eyes were those of the photographer, Muybridge, and that Remington did not take conspicuous advantage of those eyes until later in the 1880s.

In 1882, the Stillman-Muybridge book, *The Horse in Motion,* came out with extensive plates reproduced as heliotypes, lithographs, line engravings, and silhouettes of the Muybridge instantaneous motion studies; and, in July of 1882, the George Waring, Jr., review appeared in *Century Magazine,* reproducing all of the outline engravings and a smattering of the other plates. In Remington's first published sketch, redrawn by another artist for the block, there are no galloping horses, in fact, no horses of any kind. Apparently, it was still too soon for him to have come to grips with the significance of the Muybridge achievement.

For the next two years after 1882, nothing by Remington appeared in any of the magazines. He drew, but, if we are to judge by later reports, he was considered too inept and crude by the refined tastes of the back-East dude editors. In the aftermath of a boyish prank, Remington gave up his ranch in 1884, setting out into the Southwest among the Apache and the Mexicans, in his first serious attempt to study and to sketch the Indians, army scouts, and "breeds" who would later form his stock in trade. When the refusal of his newlywed wife to remain in the wild West sent Remington back East in 1885, he shipped home myriad types of gear, guns, trappings, feathers, blankets, moccasins, saddles, and all the other paraphernalia which the journalistically inclined artist relies upon for accurate and realistic details in his illustrations.[42]

The famous T. de Thulstrup, an outstanding portrayer of horses and soldiers in action, was called upon to redraw Remington's next published sketches for tonal wood-engraving reproduction, first in *Harper's Weekly* for March 28, 1885, and again on May 29, 1886. The latter illustration, "Shot on Picket," demonstrates a sharp contrast between Thulstrup's fully developed, sure draughtsmanship, and the still amateurish efforts of the inexperienced Remington (see *Harper's Weekly* for January 9 and 30, and April 24, of 1886). "His early pen-and-ink sketches undoubtedly showed lack of training for they did not exhibit the anatomical skill and technical finish expected of a graduate of the art schools." [43]

Clearly no Raphael astonishing the world with his artistic capabilities as an infant prodigy, Remington tried to increase his facility by studying at the Art Student's League in New York. Finally, in 1887, came the publication of a momentous work which was to supply him with a solid structure of knowledge on which to base new portrayals of horses and riders in action.

PHOTOTECHNOLOGY TRANSMITS MUYBRIDGE

At the same time that Remington was struggling to establish himself as an illustrator, Eadweard Muybridge had become so encouraged by "so much attention in the artistic and scientific worlds" [44] as a result of the Stillman book, that he was convinced he could perfect his experimental equipment by using the newly successful dry plates which Eastman and other companies had perfected by 1883. Between 1884 and 1885, then, under the auspices of the University of Pennsylvania, Muybridge once again set to work.

> More than a hundred thousand plates were used in the preparation of the work for the press . . . the results were published in 1887, with the title of "Animal locomotion." The work contains more than 20,000 figures of moving men, women, children, beasts and birds, in 781 photo-engravings bound in eleven folio volumes.[45]

We should correct this comment. In the original folios, printed by the Photogravure Company of New York, these were not photoengravings (a term usually reserved for relief process halftone plates, and already here mentioned in connection with the line relief plates used in Waring's article) but *photogravures.*

A large proportion of these plates represented simultaneous multiple exposures of mounted horsemen from the side, three-quarter front, and three-quarter back (see Plate 91), which provided artists with almost every conceivable position of horses in motion.

Since the cost of manufacture was enormous, the University limited the elephant folio edition to a few complete copies, now among the rarest items ever published, but,

> With a view of supplying the demand of art and science students . . . it has been decided to select a number of the most important plates made at the university, and to republish them on a reduced scale in a more popular and accessible manner. . . . These plates . . . are chemically-executed engravings, and are reproduced with all the original defects of the photographic manipulation, precisely as they were made in the camera.[46]

The "original defects" were now attributes of fidelity to Nature, unlike the "original defects" which had mandated such reproductive distortions for the Stillman book, valuable as these had been. Fifteen years had passed between Muybridge's first experiments in 1872, using the wet-plate process and slow shutters, and these triumphant dry-plate, electrically controlled multiple exposures, reproduced by photogravure and process halftone engraving, in 1887.

PLATE 91. *The Horse in Motion* (*1887*). *Photogravure from simultaneous multiple exposures from Nature, by Eadweard Muybridge. Reproduced here about one third the size of the original Plate 579, vol. 9,* Horses, *in Muybridge,* Animal Locomotion, an Electro-Photographic Investigation of Consecutive Phases of Animal Movements, 1872–85 (*Philadelphia: published under the auspices of the University of Pennsylvania, 1887*). *Courtesy of the Free Library of Philadelphia, Rare Book Dept.*

PLATE 92. *The Midday Meal.* *White-line tonal wood engraving by R. C. Collins, from a painting by Frederic Remington based on a photograph by Theodore Roosevelt. Reproduced here the same size as page 498, in Roosevelt's series on "Ranch Life and the Far West" in the* Century Magazine, *Feb. 1888, from the copy owned by E. Jussim.*

The year *following* the appearance of *Animal Locomotion,* in other words, in 1888, there began a series of articles by Theodore Roosevelt, called *Ranch Life and the Far West,* illustrated by Frederic Remington using both monochrome gouache (see Plate 92, "The Midday Meal"), reproduced by tonal wood-engraving and pen-and-ink (see Plate 93, "Branding a Calf"), reproduced by process line engraving. In this same series, the March issue of *Century Magazine* carried what might be called the original of all the "like a crab" Remington horses, four feet off the ground and with legs doubled up—just as Muybridge had captured the animal. (See the detail of the monochrome original, Plate 94, and the tonal wood engraving, "In with the Horse Herd," Plate 95.) The most likely source for this illustration, "In with the Horse Herd," is plate 624, frame 8, vol. IX, of *Animal Locomotion*, as Robert Taft believed. However, there are very similar pictures in both the line engravings and the silhouettes in Stillman's *The Horse in Motion*.

It would be difficult to dispute this chronological evidence that the Muybridge views of horses in all cases preceded works by Remington. Both visual and verbal information concerning Muybridge's discoveries had been widely circulated since the *Scientific American* article of 1879. The Stillman book, *The Horse in Motion* (1882), had provided ample information for artists who knew the horse at all, and even the line engravings reproduced in George Waring's review documented these instantaneous views by Muybridge, who was then world famous. Yet it is not until after the publication of *Animal Locomotion* in 1887, the most comprehensive and detailed of Muybridge's publications, that we find Remington producing gouache drawings of horses answering the description of the F. Hopkinson Smith eulogy on his prior vision.

As if this were not enough to deflate poor Mr. Remington, evidence has just been uncovered which reveals that he not only had Muybridge to follow for his horse drawings, but that the author whom he had illustrated in "Ranch Life and the Far West," Theodore Roosevelt, had supplied many photographs to him, including the sources for the Remington drawing "Branding a Calf" and the gouache "The Midday Meal." Action pictures taken by Roosevelt and by C. D. Kirkland, and W. G. Walker, all appear in James D. Horan's *The Great American West: A Pictorial History from*

PLATE 93. *Branding a Calf. Process line engraving from a pen-and-ink drawing by Frederic Remington; based on a photograph by Theodore Roosevelt. Reproduced here the same size as page 861, in Roosevelt's series on "Ranch Life and the Far West,"* Century Magazine, *April 1888.*

PLATE 94. **In with the Horse Herd** (detail).   *Monochrome oil painting on composition board, by Frederic Remington, 1888, the same size as the original. From the collection of Francis A. Herrington, Jr. Courtesy of the Worcester Art Museum, Worcester, Mass.*

Coronado to the Last Frontier (New York: Bonanza Books, 1959). Roosevelt's photograph called "Branding Calves," and another called "The Midday Meal" appear on page 180 of the Horan book. According to Horan, all the pictures he reproduced had been taken by Roosevelt in 1882.

Now the question is, how could F. Hopkinson Smith have believed that a seventeen-year-old student at Yale, with his mind on football, could have accomplished what a master like Meissonier—who had devoted so much of his life to observing the horse and whose major intent had been to depict it realistically—had not been able to accomplish? How could anyone assume for a moment that a man unaided by the camera could "see" what it took the sophisticated electric shutter and fast film to "stop" in one thousandth of a second? Is there any clue to an answer to these questions in Remington's already noted link in the communications system between photography and the printed page? We believe there is. We could dismiss the F. Hopkinson Smith claims for Remington as either ignorance or willful cooperation in myth-making, but we have preferred to consider what might have given rise to such a misconception.

THE ANSWER TO THE PUZZLE

Possibly the simplest explanation, although perhaps a somewhat startling one, is that *Remington*, rather than Muybridge, served as the prime distributor of information about the real motion of the horse between 1888 and 1893. Note that although F. Hopkinson Smith wrote *American Illustrators* in 1892, it was the following year which should be viewed as the true threshold year for the universal acceptance and conquest of process half-tone engraving; it was the year of the Columbian Exposition in Chicago, which will be discussed in Chapter 9. Remington's illustrations nevertheless continued to be prime sources of knowledge about the real motion of the horse for the following reasons.

Let us recall what transmission codes were available for photography per se in this period, and consider the large circulation of periodicals as opposed to books during the same years. Muybridge's elephant folios of the 1887 *Animal Locomotion* are known to have been sent to very few institutions. The smaller version was published for a specialized audience of art and science students, and it was in book form. But Remington's innumerable illustrations appeared in *Century Magazine, Harper's Weekly, Outing Magazine, Scribner's, Cosmopolitan,* month after month, issue after issue, accompanying either his own articles or stories and articles by famous authors. Remington and these authors were reporting the exciting news of the closing of the American frontier to a public clamoring for details. Remington, as he put it himself, was "picture-ing" events of momentous interest to the "folks back East." Out of these numerous articles for the periodicals came dozens of books, increasing the general circulation of Remington's illustrations. The obvious truth was that a Muybridge photograph, however scientifically correct and valuable, could not very well be adapted to use *as illustration*, since a picture of a naked man on a horse (and the preponderance of Muybridge's models were, for the sake of scientific accuracy, naked) could not very well be adapted to use, say, as a mounted cavalry officer of the Mexican Army.

We recall that F. Hopkinson Smith began his statement with an admission that Muybridge "taught us the true movements of animals . . ." and that Remington had been "the first man who has utilized these discoveries in his work." These statements are true, if we limit "the first man" to American illustration rather than to painting, where Meissonier preceded him by a decade. But the statement, "And yet Remington saw these movements in a horse long before he ever heard of Muybridge or his discoveries," can be true only if (a) we admit the possibility of superhuman eyesight; (b) we disregard the chronological evidence; or (c) we discover that Remington himself had been busy in Kansas (1881–1883) with his little detective camera and dry plates—and even that circumstance would still not place him before Muybridge, whose experiments were published as early as 1878. Yet, if Remington were the most prevalent source of visual experience with the Muybridge discoveries, rather than the other way around, it is possible to understand Smith's confusion, especially since it is obvious that Smith investigated nothing and documented less.

If Remington's career was essentially that of an intermediary between photography from Nature and the printed page, and if this career was at least partially dictated by the exigencies of photomechanical developments, with the coming of photogravure and process halftone as subliminal media, we must ask ourselves why photography itself eventually replaced Remington's role as a packager of information and why it did not replace Remington's role as an expressive artist.

THE PHOTOGRAPH OR THE ARTIST

One of the major objections to photography as illustration was voiced by the "Critic" in Philip Gilbert Hamerton's dialogue on "Book Illustration" (1889). When the "Artist" at the imaginary conversation asks the "Scientist" about his preference for illustrations to accompany a book of travels,

> *Artist.* Why not resort to instantaneous photography at once?
> *Critic.* The only practical objection to the photograph, considered as a means of obtaining *useful* illustrations, is that it does not detach one thing from another as a skillful artist can. The artist can take what the reader wants, and that only, and he can make the needed facts very plain and intelligible, whilst in a photograph they may be entangled with many other details that are not wanted. The traveller largely uses this power of selection in writing an account of what he has seen and done, so the illustrations of an artist are better in harmony with his work than the photograph can ever be. In fact, a pure photograph from nature is out of place in any book whatever.[47]

There is no doubt that Remington had been useful in "detaching" things one from the other, for example, to make the details in the army camp in the Philippines downpour more intelligible. The critic and the scientist in Hamerton agree that they do not want photography as book illustration because it cannot simplify information sufficiently to transfer it usefully to a reader. We have seen that William Hamilton Gibson surpassed photography for this purpose in the field of nature study, where it was necessary to provide a symbolic *generalization* of structure for purposes of identification.

But, as mentioned in an earlier chapter, there was always a certain *specificity* about photography which George Bernard Shaw aptly described:

> There is a terrible truthfulness about photography that sometimes makes a thing ridiculous. . . . Take the case of the ordinary academician. He gets hold of a pretty model, he puts a dress on her, and he paints her as well as he can, and calls her "Juliet," and puts a nice verse from Shakespeare underneath, and puts the picture in the Gallery. It is admired beyond measure. The photographer finds the same pretty girl; he dresses her up and photographs her, and calls her "Juliet," but somehow it is no good—it is still Miss Wilkins, the model. It is too true to be Juliet.[48]

Even a would-be proponent of photography as illustration found serious difficulty:

> Everyone will admit that, granted the best technical result, a photograph of a landscape may now be made which will approach, in the estimation of most persons, a monotint drawing of the same scene under similar conditions. It is true that the credit lies with the man equally if not more than with the instrument, but that is true of the sketch or painting. But the composing of groups before the camera is a different and undoubtedly higher undertaking. Men are regarded as better than machines because they have brains and can think. But in some situations men, and specially women, are the better for not thinking, or at any rate for not discriminating; and one of these situations is when they are placed before a camera to help tell a story in the dumb show of a genre composition, or some sort of personification. Then self-consciousness stiffens limbs that are never so willing, and stamps the countenance with a certain anxiety, though it be so faintly that the all-revealing lens alone detects it. . . .[49]

Clearly, photography from Nature employs a code which transmits much of the three-dimensional reality of an original: the real, the inescapably densely textured, intractable, overly detailed, all-revealing real. It can only be that it was because photography possesses this characteristic, as Ivins suggests, that we began to differentiate between the real and the fictive. Since this is so, the place of the fictive artist as illustrator is permanently assured. No matter how much Remington relied upon photography, or how much photography came to replace him in certain types of information transfer involving *generalization* or for communication concerning *subjective states expressed artistically*.

Evidence of this general condition, and for the phasing out of the illustrator as information packager and the continuing of the illustrator as picturemaker, is found in Remington's relationship with *Collier's Magazine*, where he was placed under contract in 1905 to produce, not illustrations for any particular story, but easel paintings suitable for color reproduction and sale as individual framing prints. Liberated from illustration for other authors, Remington at one stroke became a painter, paid for the reproduction rights to his works. It is no wonder that he entered into his most creative period, suddenly developing as a creator of magnificent color scenes. He met his untimely death at the height of his reputation, at a time when phototechnology had liberated illustrators from many of the chores of information transfer.

The New Technologies and the History of Art History

From the seventeenth to the nineteenth century, pictures, interpreted by engraving, had *become* engravings. . . .[1]

Were we sure that photographs of pictures would last, we are not
sure that we should not be content to see engraving numbered among
the extinct arts. . . .[2]

We have now reached a fresh area of consideration: that of the transmission of messages about originals which were never intended to be "book
illustrations." Such messages have predominated over those explicitly
prepared for reproduction in books, since they have been employed in all
fields where visual information about an object is desired for itself.

Thus far, we have been concerned with the effects of reproductive media
as they distort the work of illustrators. Now we shall see how individual
objects in the natural world fare in the hands of primary and secondary
codifiers of information.

According to William Ivins, Talbot's discovery of a "Process by which
Natural Objects may be made to Delineate Themselves without the Aid of
the Artist's Pencil,"[3] was the liberation of the communicative processes
from "the omissions, distortions, and the subjective difficulties that are
inherent in all pictures in which draughtsmanship plays a part."[4] In other
words, the "artist"—the illustrator who is the primary codifier of information—was the first of two culprits in the faulty transmission of messages
about art objects. The draughtsman clearly and necessarily interposed his
own codes, manner of drawing, accidents of visual capacity, between the
original and the recipient of the message. To document his contention,
Ivins reproduced ten versions of a detail of the famous Laocoön statue,
each demonstrating the subjective analysis of the draughtsman as a distortion of the original. For Ivins, the additional interference by the engraving medium—in his examples, etching, line engraving, primitive black-line
wood engraving, and combination stipple-and-line—was secondary to the
major argument. The "artist" drew what he saw; but what he saw was
dictated by the customs of his "school" of draughtsmanship; any hand
process of necessity interfered with the transmission of accurate and reli-

PLATE 96. ***Death of General Wolfe.*** *Mezzotint on steel by John Sartain from the painting by Benjamin West. Reproduced here the same size as the plate apparently cut from a copy of the* Eclectic (*a gift annual*), *n.d.* (*probably ca. 1850*), *owned by E. Jussim.*

able messages. According to Ivins, not even the various *machines à dessiner*[5]—the *camera obscura* or the *camera lucida*, the vertical screens of Dubreuil used in the seventeenth century for perspective drawings from Nature, the pantograph and the physiognotrace of the eighteenth centuries, and the many other devices used by artists for centuries as aids in obtaining correct proportion or perspective or even in simple copying—could bypass this necessary evil of the subjective eye and the conventionalizing hand.

A simple comparison between two reproductions of a well-known painting should assist us here: Plates 96 and 97 of "The Death of General

PLATE 97. ***Death of General Wolfe.*** *Black-line wood engraving in imitation of metal line engraving; unknown engraver. Reproduced here the same size as page 53, in Edward Strahan,* Art Gallery of the Exhibition (*Philadelphia: 1877*). *Courtesy of the Free Library of Philadelphia, Rare Book Dept.*

Wolfe," by Benjamin West. Plate 96 is a mezzotint from the prodigal producer of mezzotints, John Sartain. Plate 97 is a black-line tonal wood engraving by an unknown, done in imitation of metal engraving codes. For the sake of argument, let us assume that the mezzotint, probably published in the 1850s, was assisted by some nonphotographic copying device, or even copied from a paper photograph (unlikely, but possible). Let us assume that the wood engraving was produced with the aid of photography-on-the-block when it was cut in 1876 or thereabouts. In each case, it is unmistakable that two separate sets of pictorial codes have interposed their own characteristics between the original of a message and the transmission of that message, and that those two codes were (1) that of the artist-copyist, and (2) that of the manipulator of the medium, the engraver; this is true even if the artist-copyist and the engraver were the same person, as they probably were in the Sartain mezzotint. The demands of copying the West painting and the demands of a specific channel like metal or wood represent two different sets of problems, each subjectively defined.

Each version of the West painting tells us a somewhat different story. Overall tonality, the effects of the atmosphere, facial expression and specific identities, the number of ships and men in the background, the texture of the foreground grass, details of costume—which of these two stories is correct? We have only to examine the expressions on the faces of Wolfe and the men around him to recognize the extent to which subjective discriminatory acts of interpretation can distort a message about a work of art. And what, if anything, has, of necessity, been omitted from these messages about the West painting? With all the dramatic chiaroscuro of the mezzotint, which the linear and conspicuous codes of the wood engraving destroy, is there anything about the painting which has been omitted or neglected in both of these messages?

> Suppose we take an oil painting which it is intended to reproduce in chromo. Let us suppose each tint to have been conscientiously rendered, and the proof to be unexceptional as to colour, yet we shall be obliged to confess that there is something wanting—in short, there is "flatness." In the original there is a valuable relief where the paint has been laid on thickly; very slight and scarcely perceptible shadows are cast by these projections, which have the effect of redeeming it from flatness and a sort of tea-tray smoothness.[6]

Even with color, this "tea-tray" smoothness was objectionable not only in itself, but because it was false to the original. Anyone who has looked at a van Gogh painting knows how important each stroke of the brush was in conveying the artist's vision of the world. In our examples of the mezzotint and the wood engraving of the "Death of General Wolfe," nothing is conveyed about the thing-in-itself characteristics of the original. They are both alike in this obliteration of the surface characteristics of the painting, because they lack (a) mechanical and automatic transcription in a sufficiently condensed scanning code; and (b) duplicative three-dimensional qualities, as they are both merely ink on paper.

Now, it was William Ivins' contention that the most crucial differences between two subjects painted in a similar choice of light, models, inconographic design, would be in the subjective manipulation of the paint and surfaces of the canvas. To try to represent real objects by substituting the characteristics of engraving codes for their own qualities is a philosophical non sequitur; yet that is exactly what engravers did when they transmitted only the iconography of a work of art. As we might expect, Ivins saw photography as the solution to this problem:

> The photograph, to the contrary, despite all its deficiencies, was able to give detailed reports about the surfaces, with all their bosses, hollows, ridges, trenches, and rugosities, so that they could be seen as traces of the creative dance of the artist's hand. . . .[7]

We know that Ivins, to all intents and purposes, equated the fine-line process halftone with "photography" itself. It should, therefore, be possible to test his assertion that the "photograph" was, "despite all its deficiencies," superior as a transmitter of messages, by examining a series of phototechnological reproductions of a single painting. We shall be looking for some evidence that the fine-line photomechanical equivalent of a "photograph" was able to give "detailed reports about the surfaces, with all their bosses, hollows, ridges, trenches, and rugosities. . . ." We may find that this does not obtain in all cases, may not be appropriate, or may actually prove less important than the transmission of iconographic detail.

Let us examine four versions of Raphael's painting, "The Ecstasy of St. Cecilia," Plates 98, 99, 100, and 101.

Plate 98: Crossline process halftone on text paper, 1888.

Plate 99: Black-line wood engraving, c. 1889.

Plate 100: Heliotype reduction of an engraving of the painting, 1883.

Plate 101: Fine-line process halftone, 1899.

Without having the original Raphael before us, on what basis can we judge the fidelity of these four messages about an unknown original?

The crossline process halftone of 1888 (Plate 98) obliterates almost all detail, yet there can be no question that it transmits different information about the expressions on the saints' faces, qualities of hair and clothing, from what is transmitted by the wood engraving (Plate 99). The wood engraving, in turn, transmits information about the facial expressions which more closely resembles information in the heliotype reduction (Plate 100), while both of these plates differ again from the fine-line process halftone (Plate 101).

The latter resembles the earlier halftone, however, particularly in the upturned face of the St. Cecilia. Yet the halos, to pick one small but important detail, can be seen in Plate 101 only upon close examination, while they are quite clear in the heliotype. Is it possible that a hand product — namely, the engraving which the heliotype reduced — can transmit more information than a mechanical (photographic) product? It would seem so. The crux of the problem is that, once again, Ivins ignored *scale* as a primary factor in the adequacy of graphic arts transmissions. While the orthochromatic fidelity of transposition of colors into black and white is most conspicuous in the fine-line process halftone, the extreme reduction has obliterated the pattern of St. Cecilia's brocade and other textures or details. Not only does the extreme reduction deny us any sense of the "surfaces, with all their bosses, hollows, ridges . . ." but we are denied any sense of what the original might be: is it a fresco? an easel painting? a miniature in tempera? is it a photograph of a group of actors in a tableau?

Are we not dealing, then, with a symbolic transfer of meaning, in the same sense as the wood engraving symbolizes — without giving us an illusionistic replica — namely, the original iconography of the Raphael painting? Even the exceptional fine-line screens of today, in four-color process halftone, suffer from problems of extreme reduction in size from originals.

On the other hand, there can be no doubting the justice of Ivins' evaluation of the primary codifier's or secondary codifier's subjective eye. The cupid's-bow lips and vacant stare of St. Cecilia, in both the hand-products we have examined, are clearly at odds with one of the few facts about which the photomechanical products agree: that Raphael's Cecilia was listening, not simpering. The failure of the phototechnologies to transmit other iconographic details may be considered as less important than this conveyance of mood.

PLATE 98. *St. Cecilia* by *Raphael* (*1888*). *Crossline process halftone engraving printed on text paper from a photograph of the painting. Reproduced here the same size as Plate 154, in W. H. Goodyear,* History of Art, *1st ed.* (*New York: Barnes, 1888*). *Courtesy of the Library of Adelbert College of Western Reserve University.*

PLATE 99. ***St. Cecilia*** *by Raphael (1889). Wood engraving, or pen-and-ink over a bleached photograph in imitation of wood engraving, after the painting. Reproduced here the same size as Plate 204 in W. H. Goodyear,* History of Art, *2nd ed. (New York: Barnes, 1889), from the copy owned by E. Jussim.*

PLATE 100. *St. Cecilia* by *Raphael.
Heliotype from a photograph of a line
engraving reduced to about half its original size. Reproduced here the same size
as the plate facing page 78, in M. F.
Sweetser,* Raphael *(Boston: Osgood,
1883; Artist-Biographies Series), from a
copy owned by E. Jussim.*

244

PLATE 101. *St. Cecilia* by *Raphael.*
*Process halftone engraving on white
coated stock. Reproduced here the same
size as the plate facing page 266, in Clara
Erskine Clement,* Saints in Art *(Boston:
1899) from a copy owned by E. Jussim.*

RAPHAEL. — THE ECSTASY OF ST. CECILIA.

NINETEENTH-CENTURY VISUAL CONDITIONING

When Howard Pyle wrote to his friends from Europe that he was astonished by the color and beauty of the Old Masters, he acknowledged that he had not thought much of them when he saw them in black and white. What seems curious about Pyle's response to, say, the cool beauty of an original Botticelli, was that he had never, apparently, challenged or questioned the validity of the monochrome messages he had been receiving all of his life through wood engravings, heliotypes, photogravures, and process halftones. He had, obviously, accepted these *messages* about original paintings as equivalent to the paintings themselves. He had believed he *knew* what Botticelli's paintings looked like.

While it may be argued that Pyle's unthinking acceptance of information about color via black-and-white messages was the outcome of centuries of painterly argument over the primacy of form and contour or color and atmosphere, there can be little question that Pyle and his generation had been thoroughly conditioned by monochrome graphic representations. The acceptance of black-and-white codes was an unconscious rationalization of technological limitations which the early history of photography did little to alter.

On the face of it, Ivins' contention that "despite its deficiencies," photography was superior for the transmission of art information, tends to ignore the entire area of color. Early photographic emulsions were color-blind, sensitive to only a few of the actinic rays of the sun. As we have noted, yellow and red became black, blue disappeared into white, green darkened into unintelligible shadow. Paper photography had interposed the texture of the paper negative into the finished print. Excessive slowness of the early emulsions, coupled with the inadequacies of pre-electric light, prohibited the direct photography of many originals in situ in their darkened chapels or baronial halls.

It was no wonder, given these difficulties, that the very first art book illustrated with mounted paper prints, Sir William Stirling's *Talbotype Illustrations to the Annals of the Artists of Spain* (London: 1847) contained "sixty-six calotypes of engravings of paintings," [8] *rather than calotypes of the paintings themselves.* This was certainly a humble beginning for what André Malraux has described as our present capabilities:

> A museum without walls has been opened to us, and it will carry infinitely farther that limited revelation of the world of art which the real museums of art offer us within their walls: in answer to their appeal, the plastic arts have produced their printing press. [9]

Malraux believed that photography had opened doors which had never been opened before, since the objective character of photography made it possible to capture the essence of primitive art objects—so influential in the development of the modern arts—without the intervention of ethnocentric primary codifiers of information, whose visual training was so culturally skewed that it could only prove inadequate to the subtle distinctions of form in totally foreign originals.

Lest we interpret Malraux's statement as implying that the plastic arts lacked a "printing press" prior to photography, let us remember that the graphic arts have been bound up with the transmission of messages about works of art since their inception. Stirling's *Annals of the Artists of Spain,* using paper photography, was merely reproducing the old medium, metal line engraving, which had been the medium of reproduction and the main transmitter of messages about oil paintings, sculpture, architecture, and all objets d'art for four centuries. The "old" medium functioned as much as a *mass medium* as the new:

> In America . . . between 1815 and 1860 line engraving on steel almost completely superseded copper engraving for cheap book illustration.
>
> The process was often regarded with contempt, perhaps because of the very fact that it enabled reproductions of pictures and works of art to be circulated cheaply to rich and poor alike. This offended the exclusive attitudes of the well-to-do connoisseur, who was liable to discuss steel-engraving as being so coarse as to debase the whole art of engraving.[10]

To the connoisseur, the engraving had become far more interesting and important than the original; as Malraux noted, for the twentieth century, color photography had come to replace the visit to the art museum. To the nineteenth-century public, eager for "culture," even the economical large editions of steel engravings could not satisfy the demand for some equivalent to originals. The labor and time expenditures needed in the manufacture of steel engravings were enormous and they therefore could not be produced quickly enough to keep up with the market.

> Frith's "Railway Station" occupied the engravers for four years, and Raphael Morgan needed six years to engrave Raphael's "Transfiguration." Consequently . . . prints from hand-engraved plates had to be priced at several guineas, whereas prints from photo-engraved plates could be sold for a shilling or so.[11]

Even if steel engraving was a type of mass medium, it was still far beyond the pockets of the nineteenth-century poor, for whom the meanest photographically duplicated picture was as precious as the cheap woodblocks of the sixteenth century had been to that public. Just as soon as an inexpensive means of duplicating the content of the old graphic media became available, the public's demand encouraged what was to the connoisseur nothing but cheap fakery.

PHOTOMECHANICS VERSUS AUTOGRAPHIC EXPRESSION

> Messrs. James R. Osgood & Co. have the pleasure of announcing that by the desire of the President and Fellows of Harvard College they have published Heliotype reproductions of the principal art treasures of the "Gray Collection of Engravings," owned by Harvard College. This Collection is one of the most complete and perfect in the country. It contains the choicest and most costly proofs of many of the best engravers of the world. . . . The publishers are enabled, by means of the rapidity, faithfulness, and artistic quality of the Heliotype Process, to offer to the public beautiful reproductions from the choicest and most costly works of art at the lowest possible prices. Rare etchings or artist-proof engravings, worth hundreds of dollars each, may be reproduced and sold at prices varying from fifty cents to two or three dollars; thus bringing the treasures of the art-galleries within the reach of all, and affording a means of art-education hitherto unattainable.[12]

In some ways, the publication of Ernest Edwards' *The Heliotype Process* by James Osgood in 1876 was an American event comparable to the publication of Fox Talbot's *The Pencil of Nature.* Despite the aegis of Harvard, hardly a mob-oriented institution, the fright of connoisseurs of the graphic arts was an understandable response to the heliotype. What, after all, could prevent a general devaluation of all the limited editions of "original" graphic works if photographic reproductions became universally available? By a curious quirk of fate, artists—who had turned to the graphic arts for the multiplication of their originals—now were fighting to restrict the multiplication of graphic arts originals. As we noted in an earlier chapter, artists were immediately driven to demonstrate that they could "reproduce" their own paintings in an autographic medium—by etching or lithography—so that the public would not cease to want their services. The autographic beauties of etching, dormant since the advent of lithography, were revived by Manet, Whistler, Winslow Homer, and many other artists, in a short-lived attempt to offer the public an alternative to photoreproduction which would put coin in their own pockets.

The plaints of the connoisseurs and the fears of artists notwithstanding, the most influential of the teacher-etchers in the 1880s, Philip Gilbert Hamerton, was not loathe to take advantage of new media for the sake of high-quality information transfer in his *Etching and Etchers:*

> All plates marked with an asterisk in this list are copies etched on copper by M. Amand-Durand's process of heliogravure, and printed as ordinary etchings. They are of the same size as the originals, which they resemble very closely, and are incomparably superior to poor impressions from the original plates themselves.[13]

Unfortunately, Amand-Durand's and other manufacturers of heliogravures, a type of photogravure, left embossed or raised impressions of ink, similar to original etchings. It therefore became an easy matter for forgers to duplicate plates and pass them off as original prints.

Hamerton's famous book on etching included no examples of one of the world's most important etchers, for reasons which bear upon our understanding of prephotographic communication:

> . . . the answer is because, although Piranesi was an etcher of great force, his plates are simply powerful representations of material objects, and are not conceived as independent works of art. . . . Such representation of things is perfectly legitimate in itself, but whatever the force and skill displayed in it, the difference between simple representation and the artistic conception of new unities is wide indeed . . . ever since the invention of photographic engraving object etching may still be practiced. In Piranesi's time, when there were no photographs, such skill as his was the best means for diffusing architectural and archaeological information.[14]

While it may be difficult to forgive Hamerton for neglecting to even mention Piranesi's magnificent series, *I Carceri,* in which purely imaginary and fantastic prison architecture becomes the vehicle for the artist's expression, we must acknowledge that Hamerton's was a comparatively early recognition of the Ivins hypothesis that there is a "difference between creating something and making a statement about the quality and character of something"; it was photography which had made the distinction inescapably clear. What Hamerton failed to admit, and what Ivins scanted in his constant emphasis on the destructive aspects of the illustrator's subjective vision, is that there are certain types of visual information which benefit from precisely the artist's subjective discrimination for the purposes of transmission.

In S. R. Koehler's book on *Etching* (1885), further complications of media evaluation arose. The plates were: "Phototypes by the Moss Engraving Company, of New York, with the exception of Nos. . . . which are by the Heliotype Printing Co., Boston. Etchings printed by Mssrs. Kimmel & Voigt, N.Y." [15]

Writers on art were now forced to explain exactly what reproductive processes had been used in their works to transmit messages about original works of art; here is Koehler's elaborate explanation:

> So far as they are original plates they need no apology. The heliogravures—which show that we are beginning to do good work of this kind in the United States—likewise carry with them their own justification. It may seem strange, however, that so many etchings are given in phototypic reproductions, which, naturally, must fall far behind the originals from which they were made, as even the best work of this kind, which involves surface printing, cannot reproduce the effects attainable by printing from etched plates. The alternative presented itself, however, of no illustrations at all (beyond the thirty etched plates), or these phototypic reproductions, since the immense cost of making heliographic facsimiles of all the plates, and the additional cost of printing, would simply have made the publication of the book an impossibility. To avoid as much as possible the deterioration in quality and to preserve their technical character, the illustrations have been reproduced full-size (with a few unimportant exceptions), even at the risk of admitting some plates which are manifestly too large for the size of the page. [16]

Koehler was to be congratulated for his recognition that *scale* in the transmission of messages about originals is of prime importance. With the wood engraver, or other hand engraver (who perforce had to preoccupy himself with the scale necessary to translate an original into a suitable printing surface, and who was now increasingly pushed aside in favor of photographic media which could reduce, enlarge, recopy directly onto a printing plate) such considerations of appropriate scale of re-reproduction were often neglected. While the photographic media had crystallized the difference between artistic expression (the creation of a "something") and information transfer (making a statement about the character of a "something"), the unthinking mechanical response of the camera was beginning to blur the differentiation between certain types of originals, to obliterate the distinctions between the graphic arts, to expand the zone of interchangeability to the point where original etchings and engravings had to be protected from exploitation, since intaglio plates could be prepared—as in the case of Hamerton's book on etching—ostensibly and legitimately as messages about originals (more accurately, duplication) which could be misinterpreted as being the originals themselves. Furthermore, phototypic (mechanical process line engravings, as in the Moss line processes) relief engravings could reproduce the flat pattern characteristics—that part of the ink deposit which lies closest to the paper—of intaglio plates quite cheaply. These phototypic plates were therefore increasingly substituted in books about etching or other graphic arts, reproducing only the flat characteristics and not the depth of ink or shadows produced by high embossing, or the delicate ink smears used by artists such as Rembrandt to veil or to enhance chiaroscuro effects. A student of art depending entirely on phototypic line reproductions in books for the study of the history of etching would be totally misled as to the importance of three-dimensional effects in a medium such as etching.

There was a heated exchange between Koehler and the publishers of the *American Art Review* in 1880, concerning Koehler's review of a book published in 1878. The publishers asked: "what were typographic etchings?"

That is, how could etching (an intaglio process) appear in the text of a book when the text was type, a relief process?

> . . . Therefore, apparently, the originals were in *relief,* and the printing done as if from woodblocks or electro-types of wood-blocks. We object and still object to the fashion of coining names for new processes which tend to confuse people as to these processes.[17]

"Typographic etching" certainly sounded like a contradiction in terms. However, the publishers of the *American Art Review* had forgotten about William Blake's expedient of drawing with the acid resist and etching away the negative space around the desired positive forms. This was precisely the way the new relief line plates were produced, and precisely the way in which the later screened halftone plates were manufactured. As Koehler explained, "These illustrations, as I know of my own personal knowledge, were produced by *etching,* that is to say, the 'corrosive power of acid, acting on metal.' "[18] "Typographic etchings" were the opposite of what was ordinarily considered as "etching," and the attempt to capitalize on the snob appeal of an older graphic medium only resulted in serious media confusion. The public, which had never been able to afford limited edition etching in any event, could not have cared less. What it wanted was cheap pictures, both in its books and to hang on walls.

With the advent of photogravure, it did not have to limit its tastes to the engravings which the heliotype process reproduced so well, but now the public could begin to discover the delights of photographic reproductions of paintings themselves.

THE FIDELITY TRANSMISSION OF HALFTONE ORIGINALS

At the Philadelphia Centennial, when the heliotype was also presented to the public, Amand-Durand and Goupil exhibited examples of the very new and secret process of photogravure and heliogravure. Compared with any other process of its day, photogravure walked off with the honors for compression of information. The photogravure of the Chartran painting (Plate 102) which appeared as the frontispiece for Edward Strahan's *Masterpieces of the Centennial International Exhibition,* must have been a visual shock in a volume otherwise devoted to black-line wood engraving and stipple. Goupil's successes were accorded many testimonials, among them the following "puff":

PLATE 102. ***Painting by Chartran.*** *Photogravure (either by Amand-Durand or by Goupil) from an oil painting by Chartran. Reproduced here the same size as the plate facing page 14, in Edward Strahan,* Masterpieces of the Centennial International Exhibition *(1877), vol. 1,* Fine Arts. *Courtesy of the Free Library of Philadelphia, Rare Book Dept.*

It is said that Mr. Edouard Detaille, the eminent war-painter, was lately struck by seeing a water-colour drawing of his own in a shop-window day after day as he went to his studio. Sometimes it would disappear for a day or two, but it would always re-appear. At last, unable to bear this irritating apparition any longer, he burst brusquely into the shop one morning and said, "Since you can't persuade anybody to buy that drawing, I will buy it myself." "Oh, but sir," they replied, "it is having a very large sale." "What do you mean?" said the painter. "How can a watercolour drawing have a large sale?" "It is the Goupil facsimile of your drawing, sir." And when he examined it closely in his hands he found that it really was the facsimile.[19]

Such eulogies for the subliminal characteristics of photogravure should include recognition of the efforts of the hand engravers whose retouching made possible such exquisite detail. Even Ernest Edwards had admitted that considerable handwork augmented photography for the heliotype process:

It is true, as in all processes depending on photographic negative for their base, that color is unfaithfully reproduced. Hence, oil-paintings depending on color for their effect, require an intermediate translation. A copy must first be produced wherein the defects so arising must be corrected; and this copy must then again be reproduced for issue. It seems to me probable, that as progress is made there will be a distinct class of artists, who will be "translators of color into light and shade," for use in this and analogous processes. Where paintings depend for their effect on light and shade, or form, and not on color, this intermediate translation is not necessary.[20]

The procedure to which Edwards referred apparently involved providing an artist with a monochrome paper positive made from the original negative. The "artist" retouched this monochrome with a special range of warm or cool-hued opaque paints, to correct the failure of blues to register and the loss of detail. His corrected print was rephotographed for heliotyping. Obviously, there was great subjective discrimination and as great craft. It will be evident from a discussion of a reproduction of "The Farnese Bull" later in this chapter how abysmal were the results of such retouching when inappropriately added to positive prints.

Edwards, talking about 1876, had not realized that in another medium, wood engraving, a "distinct class of artists who will be translators of color into light and shade" was already available; they had developed the process out of photography-on-the-block, and in the same year that the Goupil-gravure appeared, produced Timothy Cole's Modjeska portrait (Plate 11). The white-line wood engraver, encouraged by the mechanical reduction of large images such as easel paintings to the small size of his woodblock, was beginning to develop the greatest handcrafted translation of color into light and shade which the relief graphic arts had ever known.

Edward Strahan himself noted that the camera would give hard competition to the hand processes:

To gain an idea of the care and tact with which French experts now conduct the business of copying paintings by photography, one should enter the establishment of Bingham, of Paris, who makes a specialty of this process. It is true that American painters often get their pictures photographed by the nearest camera to be had, as a memorandum or souvenir of their work; and it is equally common to see in the shops photographs of the paintings of old masters, whether from Venice, or Munich, or London; but these are generally false and unequal in tone, with a despairing blackness settling down gradually upon them towards the corners—hopeless misstatements, vulgar things, country copyists, bungling counterfeiters, and not fit to come within a mile of the aristocratic society of the metropolitan photograph-forgery. The latter gives the threads of the canvas, the relief of the impasto, the counterfeit of the general tone, and you have, in all but the color, the precise aspect of the paints laid on by the original artist. . . .[21]

To achieve this perfection, very slow emulsions were used in conjunction with a system of screens to deflect excess light from the glossy surfaces of oil paintings. The utmost attention was paid to the surface texture, for this was recognized as specifically the characteristic of a particular work of art. Obviously, the size of the Bingham copies must have been in a decent ratio to the size of the original in order to capture such minutiae. Strahan does not state certainly whether "Bingham" was producing photogravures or carbon prints from photographic negatives, but it is extremely likely that the slow emulsion implied a preparation of a printing plate rather than a glass negative for paper prints, or so it seems from other descriptions of the secret processes. In any event, it was the transcription of the textures of what had previously been considered merely "flat originals," that is, oil paintings on canvas, which was simultaneously tantalizing the wood engravers and had already led them into questioning the older syntaxes or codes of the graphic arts.

It should not be surprising that it was Elbridge Kingsley who was one of those who began the transition from the concept of art objects as merely being a starting point for a statement by the engraver to the consideration of art objects as demanding fidelity messages. In his autobiography, he documented in detail the early years of the post-*Picturesque America* era.

> . . . for a year or two after I began, the ordinary illustrated article would have as much crayon and pencil to reproduce as the drawings of sepia or gouache on Bristol board. The practice of working directly from paintings as a method of illustration had hardly begun then. . . .[22]

When Kingsley entered the field of tonal wood engraving, the "universal" code of line engraving was in command; any combination of wood engravers was expected to be able to work together, simply because they had all learned the basic code of wood engraving. Kingsley writes, for example, that ". . . we came out with a Mills-Drake-Shirlaw-Kingsley combination. This effort was called a 'Hunters' Fright.'. . ."[23] within the universal code, which was developed for each channel—for example, the painter Durand worked with three steel engravers to reproduce one painting, "The Capture of Major André"[24]—each engraver had his own specializations. But if wood engravers in the 1870s had to pitch in and somehow make a block come out all right, Kingsley was intrigued by new aesthetic realities and new transmission opportunities:

> A photographic artist by the name of Saroney [sic] was having a great success in the enlargement of portraits of celebrated characters. He used a combination of charcoal and crayon in working up his pictures. I was attracted by the variety of his textures. . . . What a sensation it would have made in the Engraving world to have reproduced one of the Saroney [sic] drawings, textures and all, in imitation of charcoal.[25]

We have already noted W. J. Linton's excoriation of any attempt to reproduce the texture of an original illustration, as if there were some impropriety involved. When men like Juengling defied him, and made "a sensation" with as faithful copies of the originals of drawings as could be made with a white-line negative code relief medium, it was possible for J. Comyns Carr, in 1882, to write:

So closely does the work accord with the original it has undertaken to imitate, that I have often heard it asserted, even by artists, that these American woodblocks are in fact not woodblocks at all, but are mechanical reproductions of drawings or paintings. . . . Although these American illustrations are genuine works of wood-engraving, there would seem to be little doubt that the efforts of their authors have been largely stimulated by the success with which various mechanical processes have lately been developed.[26]

This was not merely a copying of the superficial characteristics of other media, but a profound change in the philosophy of reproductive engraving. It was no longer to be symbolic abstraction à la Linton, but high-fidelity transcription of a three-dimensional object (albeit that object was a "flat" painting). When Kingsley finally essayed a Sarony drawing,

The size was half page, and about right to do justice to the detail. Here again there was no chance for line engraving. It was simply reproducing the quality of charcoal in stipple. And so I picked away and enjoyed myself, all the time destroying the traditions in which I had been trained, and getting away from the old engravers.[27]

The new values were those of fidelity of transmission, but, perhaps inevitably, as the old orthodoxy was shattered, a new subjectivism arose. In place of the old textures of the "universal" code, which were essentially meaningless for the reporting of the surfaces of originals so crucial in art reproduction, the men of the New School of Engraving made up new rules as they went along. Kingsley himself comments frequently on the specific differences among engravers.

The natural line and textures that became an unconscious habit with me, was better suited to color and atmospheric effects than anything else, and I think my near-sighted eyes had something to do with the fineness of the textures. . . .[28]

Timothy Cole wrote:

Now a vigorous and enthusiastic lot of young American painters returned to New York fresh from the Paris ateliers, imbued with the new truths of the great Barbizon school of painters; and it became apparent that the old conventions were inadequate to a sympathetic rendering of their works. The line had to be tampered with in order to faithfully render the qualities characteristic of each artist's manner. In other words, the painting came to be deemed more important than the exploitation of the engraver's skill in the production of lines. The engravers discovered that no one valued lines except themselves. All the old conceptions of producing textures—a certain sort of line for this and another sort of line for that—had to go.[29]

It was Kingsley's set of textures, "better suited to color and atmospheric effects than anything else," which was put in the service of transmitting messages about the Barbizon painters to the American public. "I knew well enough the tremendous influence of the Barbazon [*sic*] men on the foremost of the American painters. I did not know whether my textures would be fitting for the task or not." [30]

These textures of Kingsley's were partly the result of a simple technological change:

The new men got down to one tool mostly, or perhaps two or three. This was called the square graver for all tints and shades, and perhaps we had a fine elliptic graver for stippling. . . . New requirements demanded a nearer approach to expressing light, and more blending of light and shade than any previous work known.[31]

These new requirements were a combination of factors, most substantially the influence of the Barbizon painters themselves and the plein air schools of painting, and a growing public consciousness of the difference between the Linton symbolic linear conceptions and the surfaces of reality, especially as the photograph was accustoming the human eye to nuances of light and shade as converted into flat plane codes. Truly, as Ivins observed,

> Up to that time very few people had been aware of the difference between pictorial expression and pictorial communication of statements of fact. The profound difference between creating something and making a statement about the quality and character of something had not been perceived.[32]

The men of the New School of Engraving understood this difference. Juengling and Cole and Kingsley and Closson and Davis, all would have agreed with Ivins:

> Objects can be seen as works of art only in so far as they have visible surfaces. The surfaces contain the brush marks, the chisel strokes, and the worked textures, the sum totals of which are actually the works of art.[33]

But none of these innovators could have agreed with Ivins that "the hand made prints after objects were never able to report about their surfaces." [34] This, precisely, was their revolution.

The first of several articles illustrated by Kingsley on the Barbizon painters was for an article about Corot, in *Century Magazine* for June 1889. The article opened with a pen-and-ink drawing of Corot by the visual biographer of this period, Wyatt Eaton, whose Lincoln portrait (Plate 12) had been so skillfully facsimiled by Timothy Cole in 1882. This time, process line engraving has replaced Mr. Cole's genius, briskly and emphatically, and ever so cheaply and quickly, duplicating the spikey pen lines. The rest of the article is devoted to Kingsley white-line tonal engravings of Corot's oil paintings, each reproduction more subtle and delicate than the next. The reader is urged to examine this issue of *Century Magazine,* as it is a prime example of multimedia effects and attendant visual confusion. In this same issue are immensely fine tonal wood engravings in imitation of the textures of crayon and charcoal drawings; a J. P. Davis rendering of a bas-relief which, at first glance, resembles nothing less than a photograph; process line engravings of pen-and-inks by Harry Fenn, a rival of William Hamilton Gibson's in the Nature field; one of Timothy Cole's "Italian Old Master" series—of which, more later—and the somehow ominous and unexpected presence of a silhouetted process halftone engraving of a watercolor drawing. In the August 1889 issue, we find more process half-tone engravings, at least two white-line tonal wood engravings which closely resemble the effects of the photomedia on adjoining pages, a process line engraving attributed to "After Photograph," and other illustrations for Frederic Remington's "Artist Wandering Among the Cheyennes." A few pages beyond this portentous mélange of reproductive media and the confusing resemblance of effects, we encounter a series of lively articles by the men of the New School of Engravers, now banded together in the American Society of Wood Engravers. They were visiting Kingsley as "Wood-Engravers in Camp." Kingsley had gone out into the countryside with his photographically equipped cart, and had begun to experiment with painter-engraving directly from Nature.

Not surprisingly, we encounter another symposium, reminiscent of the Society's 1882 answer to Linton. Kingsley, writing as leader of the group, commented on the controversy between the process screen and handcraft:

Many artists may justly feel that they are better reproduced by mechanical means than by engraving. This may be true if they can make the textures necessary entirely themselves; if not, they are dependent on a monotonous texture that is entirely mechanical, thus antagonizing one of the most important principles of their daily teaching and practice—that is, that "nature does not repeat herself, and no one given surface of a picture should be like another." Thus, how can a harmony, made up of many notes, be best produced by a machine having only one note or texture? The result can only be a shadow of the original—a mere lifeless corpse.[35]

W. B. Closson remarked on the difficulties of the craft:

In relief engraving there are but two values to work with, absolute black and absolute white. A white touch remains always a white touch without modification, and all effects, textures, tones and values are secured by shaping and arranging those white touches or lines and the black spaces between them. Every touch retains its shape as first made and its relation to every other touch with the utmost obstinacy, so that the engraver has but one shot; he must either by acquired knowledge or by intuition know what relation each touch made will bear to its fellows and what influence it will have on them, and secure his tones, values, and textures the first time, for no radical change can be made.

The engraver therefore works under much greater nervous strain than the painter. . . .[36]

In addition to all these feats of intellectual and artistic ability, the tonal wood engraver in this *ménage* was also seeking to make pleasing textures, suitable textures, and struggling for the relative subliminality of the photographic media.

In the graphic arts there is no method which makes use of granulations so minute as to be indistinguishable to the eye, excepting photogravure. The similarity in size of the particles of color and the granules of ink would make it seem possible that photogravure is akin to painting, but for this reason it is not: multitudes of particles of varied and harmonious color have a charm for the eye which multitudes of granules of ink of one color have not; and where only one color is to be used some charm of treatment must be substituted for the lacking charm of color, if an equal degree of interest is to be maintained.[37]

Even photogravure, in other words, was to be considered as outdone by the brilliant execution, the variety of "textures," or codes of transference, the addition of the autographic qualities of the engraver to make up for the loss of those autographic qualities in greatly reduced transmissions about oil paintings.

"The best, or ideal, results in reproductive engraving can be achieved only when the painter and the engraver are thoroughly in sympathy."[38] In 1880, Kingsley had wanted to engrave a picture of Homer Martin's at the painter's studio, "but that was before such reproduction was thought of."[39] As the decade wore on, Kingsley became more and more dissatisfied with copying either what was on the block or in a corrected black-and-white photograph beside the block, all that he had to go by. "The feeling was growing that I could do best with the color before me rather than just a black and white drawing. It was the growing impulse to transpose color values directly from the painting itself."[40] This impulse, of course, exactly matches Kingsley's impulse to transpose the values in a real landscape scene directly from that scene, rather than from a photograph of it copied in a studio.

By the end of the decade, for it was only ten years or so until photography forced the issue, it was considered mandatory to consult with the artist. Thus Kingsley could at last happily visit the studios of George Inness and Albert Pinkham Ryder before rendering their subtle and difficult works into tonal wood-engraving "textures."

> A certain orchestration of color was demanded — greater depth, breadth, softness, flatness of planes, brilliancy, luminosity, and atmosphere — all involving a more subtle sense of tonal gradations and a completer apprehension of values than was ever displayed by the old school. In a word, wood-engraving became no longer engraving per se, but painting.[41]

As we have already observed, the ironic result of all this creative search for meaningful "textures" — codes of transcription — was that the increased costs of such craftsmanly ardor could not compete with the cheapness of the improved process halftone engraving. But all of this encounter with transmitting painting was another indication of a changing conditioning of visual expectation and visual understanding on the part of artist, public, and engraver alike.

THREE-DIMENSIONAL FORMS IN TRANSMISSION

Turning from the problems of messages about originals on flat surfaces — whether or not intended as book illustration — to the problems of free-standing, three-dimensional objects about which information was desired, we find that James Gibson's formulation of the concept of texture gradients is more important than ever.

Here are two typical examples (Plates 103 and 104), culled from Edward Strahan's *Masterpieces of the Centennial Exhibition,* of the kinds of statements which the nineteenth-century public was conditioned to accepting as valid messages about "objects of statuary."

The engravers of "The Genius of Electricity" (Plate 103) and "The Young Grape Gatherer" (Plate 104) had the problem of transmitting information about textural gradients, chiaroscuro, modulations of contour and outline, and color, as their urgent tasks. Yet, if we were not accustomed to accepting the visual convention that a representation of a figure on a pedestal, lacking a specific background, is supposed to be that of a piece of sculpture, we might conceivably respond to these plates as if they were details from paintings. The ability to transmit chiaroscuro demonstrated by the stipple engraving (Plate 103) is certainly not matched by any information that this "Genius" was a bronze statue. Certainly, the Linton-esque linearly symbolic wood engraving of "The Young Grape Gatherer" (Plate 104) in no way tells us that its subject was cut in marble.

Photography-on-the-block was an improvement in some respects, and unquestionably exceeded the Moss line process based on drawing with ink on bleached photographs. The "Head of Bacchus" (Plate 105A) is clearly a white-line wood engraving via photography-on-the-block;[42] the "Head of Antinoüs" (Plate 105B), a pen-and-ink on a photographic print. The comparison suggests that the technique of adding black to white (Antinoüs) failed to match the illusionism of removing white from black (Bacchus). Cross-hatching with the pen could not achieve the fine highlights of the graver.

The vast assistance which photography-on-the-block provided for wood engravers is most evident in complex materials like "The Bronze Doors of the Florence Baptistery" (Plate 106), where Ghiberti was rendered in

PLATE 103. *The Genius of Electricity.*
Stipple engraving, possibly after a photo-
graph from Nature (in this case, a bronze
statue); reproduced here the same size as
the plate facing page 108, in Edward
Strahan, Masterpieces of the Centennial International Exhibition *(1877),*
vol. 1, Fine Arts. *Courtesy of the Free*
Library of Philadelphia, Rare Book
Dept.

PLATE 104. *The Young Grape Gatherer.* *Black-line wood engraving, possibly via photography-on-the-block (from a marble statue). Reproduced here the same size as page 105, in Edward Strahan,* Masterpieces of the Centennial International Exhibition *(1877),* vol. 1, Fine Arts. *Courtesy of the Free Library of Philadelphia, Rare Book Dept.*

PLATE 105A. ***Head of Bacchus.***
Wood engraving via photography-on-the-block. Reproduced here the same size as the plate in W. H. Goodyear, History of Art, *2nd ed. (New York: Barnes, 1889), from the copy owned by E. Jussim.*

PLATE 105B. ***Head of Antinoüs.***
Process line engraving, possibly from pen-and-ink drawing over a bleached photoprint. Reproduced here from the same page as Plate 105A.

PLATE 106. *Bronze Doors of the Florence Baptistery* (detail), Ghiberti. *Wood engraving via photography-on-the-block. Reproduced here the same size as the lower portion of Plate 148, in W. H. Goodyear,* History of Art, *2nd ed. (New York: Barnes, 1889), from the copy owned by E. Jussim.*

261

astonishing detail. The author of the book reproducing this plate was well pleased:

> The most satisfactory representations of the Italian art of the 15th century are the reliefs of the Ghiberti Gates. This is not only on account of their individual perfection, but also because engravings of reliefs are more satisfactory illustrations than engravings of paintings.[43]

Why were engravings of reliefs more satisfactory illustrations than engravings of paintings? Perhaps because form transmits more easily than color. We receive a certain kind of information about the Ghiberti doors which is a fair representation of the innumerable details of each panel. These details were not in polychrome: the entire door is essentially monochrome. The engraver could concentrate on transmitting chiaroscuro. Nevertheless, to convey even monochrome three-dimensional forms, with all their particularities of the light and shade which define them, using only black lines on white paper, is no mean trick. If the conspicuous code of the Ghiberti is subdued by moving the eye back to about twenty inches, the three-dimensional effect can only be considered remarkable.

Publishers were willing to underwrite the costs of such painstaking work just so long as there was no type-compatible alternative. But the very moment that it began to seem possible that a photomechanical relief process might prove viable, publishers hastened to try any experiment which promised to bypass the expensive and slow secondary codifier of information. What happened to one such publisher—economically eager and technologically brash—is related in the following section.

THE TWO EDITIONS OF GOODYEAR'S HISTORY OF ART

In 1888, the same year that Elbridge Kingsley was busily transmitting Corot to the American public, the enterprising A. S. Barnes published the first art book in the English language to be illustrated entirely by process halftone engravings. A year later, when the American Society of Wood-Engravers was debating the virtues of wood engraving over process and as compared to photogravure, Barnes published a *second* edition of William Henry Goodyear's *A History of Art.* The two editions together present an almost unique experience in the history of the graphic arts, for while the *first* edition was illustrated by process halftone engravings, so many technological difficulties were encountered that the *second* edition reverted to black-line or white-line tonal wood engravings intermixed with occasional great improvements in screened halftones. We have already seen several of these plates. The crossline "St. Cecilia" (Plate 98) was from the first edition of Goodyear; the wood engraving "St. Cecilia" (Plate 99) was from the second. Let us keep these two versions of the Raphael painting in mind as we read the following explications from the introduction to the first edition of Goodyear:

> The unsatisfactory character of the engravings which have so far been used for illustration in all histories of art, whether published abroad or republished in this country, is notorious to all experts in the subject. The few independent compendiums and abridgements of the subject which have appeared in this country are still more unsatisfactory in the quality of wood-cut illustration. It is also well understood by experts that this inferiority in the quality of illustration results from the impossibility of producing a history of art with satisfactory wood-cut illustration at any price below that of an *edition de luxe.*

To escape the dilemma which has so far beset every publisher of similar works, recourse has been had in this book to process reproductions of photographs, as it is conceded that the worst photograph has some peculiar advantages over the best engraving for the reproduction of ancient works of art, especially paintings and statues. The fidelity and veracity of photographs are conceded, and the process inventions of the last few years have made it possible to present an amount of illustration which has not been previously offered even by works of much larger size and corresponding expense. As regards the quality of the process photographs, the publishers of this work will spare no pains in subsequent editions to make all possible improvement, and beg leave to call attention to the difficulty of reaching perfection on this head in a first edition *especially in view of the present experimental character of all photography* [italics added]. They also beg leave to say that this is the first history of art printed in the English tongue which has taken the line, as regards illustration, which all subsequent works of the kind are ultimately to follow. The illustration of the book is a *successful experiment* [italics added] as regards the use of photography, and as regards the effort to illustrate adequately a history of art in number and choice of objects. As regards the process itself, there are many shortcomings which they hope to remedy in the next edition.[44]

In the first edition, there were 205 process halftone illustrations. They are printed on text paper, in black ink, and they are all extremely poor. The promise of relief process halftone had seemed to the publishers to be type-compatibility and cheapness. The cheapness was evident in the attempt to print the whole book in process halftone when the first few impressions must have told them that *the paper was wrong.* If we examine and compare several sets of photographs and wood engravings from this work by Goodyear, we will see what a remarkable recovery was made *in one year* for the screened halftone, and what a strange mixed-media book resulted.

The first edition's "Belvedere Apollo" (Plate 107) an "Diana of Versailles" (Plate 108) appeared on separate pages as we here indicate. The first edition process screens converted the photographs of these two sculptures into sharply black-and-white images, with the screens obliterating any softness of halftone chiaroscuro and partially obliterating information about details and surfaces. (In the originals in the book, the screen is even more markedly noticeable than in our own reproductions of them here.) The same confusion which attended William Hamilton Gibson's first use of screened halftones could very well have accompanied the appearance of these strangely brilliant plates, which have so much resemblance to a television screen set for too much contrast. Yet let us only compare even these two primitive plates with the standard outline approach of another general history, by N. d'Anvers,[45] and it is questionable which set of distortions we would prefer (see Plates 109A and B). Published in the same year as the second edition of Goodyear, in 1889, the d'Anvers offers us these simpering outlines, a "restored" Apollo Belvedere (Plate 109A), holding a conjectural but not proven head, with muddled hair, a torso which has misunderstood the abdominal muscles of the original, legs which have lost all the arrow grace and tension of the ponderated pose, and a face whose features are strangely small. This latter "refinement" of the original is evident in the Diana (Plate 109B). In the d'Anvers, the Diana has turned into a Nymph of Fontainebleau, a mannerist creation as far from the forthright original as can be imagined. Even in the "noisy" Goodyear transmission, we can see that the neck of the original is short, and the feet large.

The d'Anvers incorporates the worst features of the pen-and-ink type of packaging of information which the invention of process line engraving

PLATE 107. *Belvedere Apollo* (1888). *Crossline process halftone engraving. Reproduced here the same size as Plate 87 in W. H. Goodyear,* History of Art *1st ed. (New York: Barnes, 1888). Courtesy of the Library of Adelbert College of Western Reserve University. Originally it was the right-hand plate on the page with a similar halftone engraving of the "Farnese Hercules."*

PLATE 108. *Diana of Versailles* (1888). *Crossline process halftone engraving. Reproduced here the same size as Plate 89 in W. H. Goodyear,* History of Art, *1st ed. (New York: Barnes, 1888). Courtesy of the Library of Adelbert College of Western Reserve University. Originally it was the right-hand plate on the page with a similar engraving of the "Medici Venus."*

PLATE 109A. *Apollo Belvedere.* *Process line engraving most probably from a pen-and-ink drawing on a bleached photoprint — of another drawing. The head in Apollo's hand is an imaginary reconstruction. Reproduced here the same size as Plate 154, in N. d'Anvers,* An Elementary History of Art *(New York: Scribner and Welford, 1889), 3rd ed., from the copy owned by E. Jussim.*

PLATE 109B. *Diana with the Stag.* *Black-line wood engraving by Pannemaker, possibly from a photograph. Reproduced here the same size as Plate 155, in N. d'Anvers,* An Elementary History of Art, *3rd ed. (New York: Scribner and Welford, 1889), from the copy owned by E. Jussim.*

PLATE 110A. *Belvedere Apollo* (1889). *Fine-screen process halftone printed on coated paper from a photograph of the statue. Reproduced here the same size as Plate 118, in W. H. Goodyear,* History of Art, *2nd ed. (New York: Barnes, 1889), from the copy owned by E. Jussim.*

PLATE 110B. *Diana of Versailles* (1889). *Wood-engraving via photography-on-the-block. Reproduced here the same size as Plate 119, in W. H. Goodyear,* History of Art, *2nd ed. (New York: Barnes, 1889), from the copy owned by E. Jussim.*

PLATE 111. ***Head of the Belvedere Apollo*** and ***Head of the Diana of Versailles*** (*1889*). *Both wood engravings via photography-on-the-block. Reproduced here the same size as the plates printed together in reddish brown ink, in W. H. Goodyear,* History of Art, *2nd ed. (New York: Barnes, 1889), from the copy owned by E. Jussim.*

had made possible. Sloppy workmanship, coupled with inadequate verbal explanation in the text concerning the restored head-in-Apollo's hand, together transmit what can only be called a fabrication. The Diana is not as serious a lie, although it has been restructured according to the Victorian ideal of graceful necks, small hands and small feet. Artists are culture-centric, and the amateur or hack illustrator of textbooks probably relies more upon the visual clichés of his time than does the creative artist.

The first edition of the Goodyear history had offered screened process halftones printed in black ink. The second edition not only reverted to wood engraving in more than half the book, but printed many of the plates in the garish hues of the multimedia books of the time. Thus, while the vastly improved "Apollo" and the monstrous version of the "Diana" appeared side by side in the new edition, printed in black (Plates 110A and B), the tonal wood engravings reproducing details of each (Plate 111) were printed in terra cotta. In Plate 111, note the conventionalizing of details and the arbitrary decision to convert the statues into busts. It can hardly be disputed, however, that these two tonal wood engravings have a surprising amount of Gibsonian data. The code, since it is not a mechanical crossbar grating imposed on every detail, but a sensitive modeling of surfaces following the convexity or concavity of hollows and planes, uses the kind of illusionistic perspective of lines advocated by Harland and attempted by Timothy Cole in his "Modjeska" of 1879. Photographed on the block, the "heads" of the Apollo and Diana are far superior to the first edition halftones of the full statues, always keeping in mind the difference in scale.

In the second edition (Plates 110A and B), the Diana is as poorly cut as the St. John in the Raphael's "St. Cecilia," and possibly by the same hand—or is this, indeed, a wood engraving? Is this one of those damnable hasty pen-and-inks converted into an imitation woodblock by bleaching out a photographic print and making a process line engraving? Toward the end of the century, as Ivins remarked, it is frequently impossible to tell exactly how a plate was produced. Yet there is no doubt at all about the Apollo. We have at last reached the perfected process halftone, still a bit heavy-handed, but more than worthwhile for the reproduction of three-dimensional objects. There can be little doubt now which of these transmissions about the "Apollo" offers the greatest fidelity to the original —within, of course, the ever severe limitations of transposing a three-dimensional object into the symbolic structures of the printed page.

Two more sets of comparisons from the Goodyear editions provide further insights into the problems of transmitting information. The "Farnese Bull" group, probably one of the most complicated pieces of sculpture ever to come out of the Rhodian school, needs some explanation before we can even attempt to decipher the Goodyear plate (see Plate 112, from the second edition):

> The myth in question describes the punishment of a jealous woman by the sons of a mother whom she had designated for a like punishment. Amphion and Zetheus bind Dirce to the horns of a bull. Their mother, Antiope, stands in the background.[46]

Plate 112 is a fairly typical example of a retouched photograph, as differentiated from a retouched metal plate. The original photographic print used to make this plate was gone over by an "artist" (one of that distinct class of artists whom Ernest Edwards had predicted would rise to fill the need for translators into light and shade) who has drawn in, with a brush and opaque Chinese white, all those strong white lines which appear somewhat miraculously on the far side of the blackest shadows, for example, on the left side of the dog, around his legs, around the outstretched arm of the girl seated at the lower right, on the right leg of the bull, and in several other places which will be readily found on examination of details. In addition, the "artist" rectified certain other defects of contrast by coming back again with thin lines of opaque black,[47] as we see on the face of the uppermost figure, on the face and spear of Antiope, and possibly along the bull's muzzle. The pure whites popping where they do not belong, and the pure blacks confusing the eye — since they cannot belong to "Nature" — contribute to an extremely confusing optical catastrophe, where the message might almost be described as seething with contradictions. Contrast this hodgepodge of effects with a tiny tonal wood engraving of almost identical viewpoint ("The Farnese Bull," Plate 113) and we may wonder if the process halftone was really an improvement. The wood engraving appeared in *St. Nicholas* for March 1881, in an article by Clara Erskine Clement, a well-known writer on art. The only one of five illustrations for the Clement article which is unmistakably photography-on-the-block, the small Farnese Bull group contains an astonishing amount of information, despite the high visibility of its codes. At least these codes are unified in terms of light and shadow, while the feeble photography, which required such hack retouching for reproduction in the larger process halftone, has lost almost all of its virtues, namely, subliminality and faithfulness of surface transmission.

The last comparison from the Goodyear editions involves one of the ancient world's most famous buildings, the Pantheon. The first edition (Plate 114) presented a delightful and rare blooper: it "flopped" the negative, thus producing a positive on the plate which could only print the reverse of what it was supposed to print. In the second edition (Plate 115B), exactly the same original was used, rescreened with a finer screen, and printed right way around. The amount of interference, which the original transmission suffered from the inadequacy of the code and the paper, is nowhere more clear than in these two examples. In the second edition, a finer screen *and* appropriate super-calendered paper stock promoted a doubling of information transfer capacity. But what is this information which we receive? A Roman scissors-grinder and a sweet-drink stall? Little sense of the giant dome is conveyed; we see only a rather tawdry Italian street with an old building. Is the information contained in this process halftone superior for study purposes to the outline drawing of the Maison Carrée (Plate 115A), a wood engraving published on the same page in the second edition? For the purposes of art history, were the scissors-grinder and the sweet-drink stall advantages (perhaps of scale?) or disadvantages (of distraction?)? We have already mentioned the absurdities of such pictures in the Hawthorne *Marble Faun* (*Transformations*) of 1860! We might say that no medium can redeem a faulty original, and no amount of rectitude in the transmission of messages can redeem inadequate or inappropriate choices of originals.

The second Goodyear edition must be seen to be believed, as its range of purple and brown and blue inks, with all-green paintings and all-brown sculpture, blue cathedrals and a bright red "Head of the Venus di Milo," represents a vain attempt to compete with the increasing progress in color, especially the advance of chromolithography by the Prang Company of Boston, and the imported color heliogravures which were arriving in increasing numbers from Paris. Even the black-and-white Chartran painting (Plate 102) reproduced in photogravure for the Philadelphia

PLATE 112. *Farnese Bull Group.*
Process halftone engraving, from a re-touched photoprint of the statue. Re-produced here the same size as Plate 124, in W. H. Goodyear, History of Art, *2nd ed. (New York: Barnes, 1889), from the copy owned by E. Jussim.*

Centennial (1876), with its subliminal excellence, soft chiaroscuro, and crisp detail, indicates how stiff the competition was from foreign firms.

ATTEMPTS AT COLOR FIDELITY

Color was a major component of *The Art of the World Illustrated in the Paintings, Statuary, and Architecture of the World's Columbian Exposition* (Appleton, 1893), and, thanks to the shift in visual expectations caused by years of photographic and phototechnological conditioning, there was a general understanding of the goals of fidelity transmission. If Elbridge Kingsley had been considered dangerously avant-garde in the 1870s when he first suggested that messages about artists' paintings should be coded in the presence of the originals, by 1893 such an approach was mandatory. For the *Art of the World*, for example, the publishers went to great lengths:

> Appreciating the magnitude and beauty of this work, many of the leading artists of France, Holland and America *have painted replicas of the pictures selected* [italics added], which have been sent to Boussod, Valadon, & Co. of Paris, the successors of Goupil & Co., whose processes are conceded to be unapproached, in order to insure exact reproduction in color. For no art work ever published has this been done before, and the preparation of these costly color models for this work marks a new departure in the making of art books.[48]

THE FARNESE BULL.

PLATE 113. *The Farnese Bull. Wood engraving via photography-on-the-block. Reproduced here the same size as page 405, in* St. Nicholas Magazine, *March 1881. Courtesy of the Free Library of Philadelphia, Rare Book Dept.*

PLATE 114. *The Pantheon* (1888). *Crossline process halftone engraving from photograph from Nature. Note that the negative was "flopped" and that the lettering appears in reverse. Reproduced here the same size as Plate 29, in W. H. Goodyear,* History of Art, *1st ed. (New York: Barnes, 1888). Courtesy of the Library of Adelbert College of Western Reserve University.*

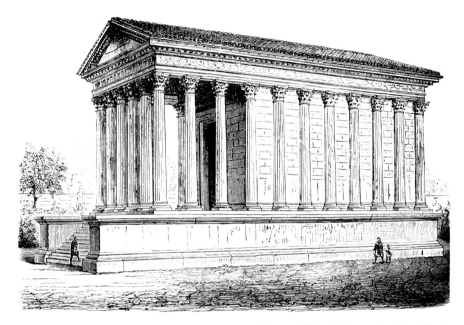

PLATE 115A. *Maison Carrée.* *Black-line wood engraving possibly via photography-on-the-block.* (*See caption for Plate 115B.*)

PLATE 115B. *The Pantheon* (1889). *Fine-screen process halftone engraving from the same photograph as the previous edition. Reproduced here the same size as Plate 39, in W. H. Goodyear,* History of Art, *2nd ed.* (*New York: Barnes, 1889*)*, from the copy owned by E. Jussim.*

It was possible to offer "Goupil Photogravures, Facsimiles in Color, and Typogravures" at prices which were not exorbitant, and some of the plates may still please twentieth-century eyes; nevertheless, ". . . comme toutes choses, la production mécanique contient ses bienfaits et son mal. Ses bienfaits, on les conçoit facilement. Son mal, c'est l'automatisme auquel condamne la machine." [49] It was the same story all over again: "la machine" was only a mechanical automaton. In many of the color plates for this monumental series of thirty parts, the grain or screen impinges on the message, colors die an insipid three-color process death, fake effects make viewers wonder what kind of "costly color models" had been provided, especially since handwork is visible even in the best of these reproductions.

No evidence seems available as to the specific characteristics of the "costly color models," but their existence raises some important questions: what was their size? were they intended as duplicates of the original? did the artist "improve" upon originals for the sake of reproduction, or even simplify them, as we suspect from some of the results? If an artist provided a "color model" of his own work, does that not constitute a new message? And is this new message not an aspect of *illustration* rather than of "fine art"? If the *Art of the World's* three-color, partly mechanical, partly subjective reinterpretations of originals were repackaged by the artist for a specific use, we must judge the results by very different standards from those we might use to evaluate messages about originals never intended for reproduction.

Art reproductions, even prepared from "costly color models," could not escape the technological limitations of scale, size, subjective evaluations of color differentiation, or the lack of a direct one-to-one relationship of printing inks to original art media. The art reproductions in the *Art of the World* were a species of hoax, extremely useful for some purposes, extremely misleading for others. Like black-and-white wood engraving, they were simply "maps" of originals, not duplications of originals, as indeed are even the finest of today's full-color reproductions.

"SPIRIT" RATHER THAN "FIDELITY": TIMOTHY COLE

Even after the three-color halftone process had been perfected, and color heliogravures had been on the American scene for at least ten years, *Century Magazine* continued to employ the famous wood engraver, Timothy Cole, to produce black-and-white monochrome wood engravings for a series of "Old Masters," which occupied the greater part of his considerable talents from 1884 to 1910.

> It was a memorable enterprise. His range of sensibility to various styles and the beauty of his own style constitute one of the glories of modern art. His immense resourcefulness in method is alone of the essence of genius. No such spirituality has been displayed in any other reproduction of great painting.[50]

Now, this is an extraordinary statement on the face of it. We are talking about a reproductive engraver, are we not? How can we then talk about "spirituality" in the reproduction of great paintings?

It may be that Timothy Cole recognized the "message" characteristics of all media. Or perhaps he was simply undaunted by the increasing capacity of various photomechanical technologies to transmit messages—however misleading—in color as well as in black-and-white. In either case, he insisted on engraving his series of "Old Masters" in the presence of the originals, or, at the very least, consulting the originals in situ, whether they were in Italy, Spain, England, Holland, Belgium, or France.

Cole's interest for us is not simply as a master craftsman, a surviving anachronism from the original New School of Engraving. If we study one of his later engravings (Plate 116), we find that the "Philip IV as Sportsman," after the painting by Velasquez, and published in the *Century* in 1903, indicates that something significant had altered his whole approach to wood engraving. This change is especially marked if we compare the "Philip" with the "Modjeska" of twenty-five years before. The change can be described as a shift from descriptive attention to the textures of surfaces—so vaunted by the men of the New School—to the painterly organization of large masses seen with an eye that had become a scanning instrument. The dot of the halftone screen is here being produced by a subjective, discriminating eye rather than by a mechanical device. The sensitivity to nuances of tones, of overall approximations to the values of colors, is achieved by scanning the overall light which is reflected by colors of materials, rather like a TV scanner. With a few exceptions, notably in the hair, the sleeve, the gloves, small areas of the trees, and the general differentiation of the dotted effect of the foreground from the diagonals of the background, the overall effect of the "Philip" is that of an intelligent, unmechanical, discriminating halftone screen. If the "Philip" is viewed from a distance of from four to five feet, the range of codes becomes subliminal and the overall effect, remarkably varied. Prephotographic effects like this had been attempted with mezzotint, stipple etching, and lithography, but no positive codes achieved the density and control of this negative picking away at lights.

This effectively, handsomely decorative plate had come out of photography-on-the-block as it evolved in competition with photogravure and process halftone engraving. Its original aim had been to place the subjective interpretative intelligence of the wood engraver at the service of fidelity transmission. If we are beginning to suspect that fidelity transmission of visual material may be judged by the adequacy of the transmission in terms of a specific communications goal, and not simply on the basis of *mechanical/objective* versus *human/subjective*, it may be because men like Timothy Cole turned themselves into intelligent machines. The goal was to capture the "spirit" of the original of a message in such a way that minimum distortion was wreaked upon it. In that sense, certainly, it may be justly said of Cole that "no such spirituality has been displayed in any reproduction of great painting."[51]

Compare any of the "St. Cecilia" series (Plates 98 through 101) with this "Philip IV" by Cole and judge for yourself whether or not Cole's technique might not suffice or even excel in the transmission of certain types of messages. Compare the "Philip" with almost anything in the illustrations accompanying this text—with the exception of the photogravures and the mezzotints—and quite possibly a renewed respect for the defunct art of reproductive wood engraving may counter any practical considerations. For, despite its beauty, the Cole must stand accused of being expensive, subjectively discriminating, and nonsubliminal at a reader's ordinary viewing distance. As a framing print, it is a "work of art." As the reproduction of an oil painting for a magazine, the overpowering visibility of its codes may be judged as distracting.

In 1910, when editorial policy changed at the *Century Magazine*, the

PLATE 116. *Philip IV as Sportsman. Velasquez. White-line wood engraving by Timothy Cole, via photography-on-the-block and direct study of the original painting by Velasquez. Reproduced here the same size as the plate facing page 576, in* Century Magazine (*new series*) *45 (Dec. 1903), from the copy at the Mount Holyoke College Library.*

series by Cole was abandoned as a hanger-on from the days when all reproduction was hand-crafted, when no gentleman or lady would admit to
hanging a mechanically reproduced picture in the living room. Now the
graphic arts came to a great separation of function: *they became either photographic and reproductive, or autographically artistic.* The "art" was removed
from engraving; information transfer was almost completely in the realm
of the phototechnologies. As the phototechnologies waxed more and more
successful in transmitting information more economically than could be
accomplished through handcraft, it was, as Ivins observed, "obvious that
most of the work that had been done in the past by the painters, draughtsmen, engravers and etchers, had basically been informative or reporto-
rial rather than artistic in purpose." [52] We assume here that Ivins defined
"artistic" as having the goal of creating an aesthetic object. But concerning his statement about this late nineteenth-century recognition that there
was a difference between information transfer and artistic communication, we need to go beyond it. At the beginning of this chapter, an 1870
remark by G. Wharton Simpson is quoted: "Were we sure that photographs
of pictures would last, we are not sure that we should not be content to see
engraving among the extinct arts. . . ." Simpson attributed this remark to
"An acute art critic, by no means favorable to the recognition of photography as a fine art, but fully sensible of its value in literal faithfulness of
reproduction." [53] (We should recall that the permanence of photographs
was still debatable in 1870.) The permanent acceptance of the information
transfer tasks of communication by the photomechanical media can be
said to have liberated the autographic "graphic arts" to return to their role
in artistic expression, and certainly the renaissance of the graphic arts in
the twentieth century was the direct outcome of the success of the phototechnologies. Yet it was precisely because the photographic technologies
were relatively successful at assuming the workhorse role of information
transfer, that photography as a medium was long an outcast from the inner
circle of the "fine arts." It has by no means been completely accepted even
to this day, despite the admirable achievements of the great photographers
of both the nineteenth and the twentieth centuries. The paradox implicit
in the remarks of Simpson's "acute art critic" above is that he would have
been content to see *engraving* disappear if photographs of pictures proved
permanent; he had totally forgotten or overlooked the fact that engraving
had also served as a vehicle for artistic expression. Once a medium became
identified as useful for information transfer, it lost survival value among
arts.

On the other hand, the quotation from André Malraux's *Museum without
Walls* which begins this chapter, also contains a paradox. Malraux observed:
"From the seventeenth to the nineteenth century, pictures, interpreted by
engraving, had *become* engravings. . . ." In a very real sense, as the import
of Malraux's own book demonstrates, we have not progressed very far.
Pictures interpreted by engravings in the prephotographic days had become engravings; that is, the codes of engravings were regarded as if they
were the original pictures themselves, which, of course, they were not. In
photographic times, pictures interpreted by photomechanical engravings
still become engravings; that is, the codes which result from diminished
size, loss of a sense of scale, artificial color approximations, obliteration of
crucial detail, transformation of three-dimensional objects to the two dimensions of ink on paper, are all still being regarded as if they were the pictures themselves, which, of course, they are not. In *Museum without Walls*,
Malraux observes that this fact will lead to students of art history ignoring

the originals in museums, as they will remain deluded by the illusionism of projected slides or reproductions in books and believe that they are equivalents to the originals. Photography did not liberate humanity from the false and mistaken substitution of the codes of a particular medium for the original of a message; it may be said merely to have made it easier and more pleasant to make the substitution.

9

Expositions: History Captured by Photography

Now that manual engraving has surrendered and photo-mechanical engraving occupies the field. . . .[1]

Probably, no single event influenced the subsequent course of photography as a medium of communication more than the Great Exhibition held at London in 1851. It was "not only the first international exhibition, but also included the first important display of photography."[2] Photographic societies were formed as a result of the stimulus of international exchanges of ideas. The Queen of England saw, and was delighted by, the stereoscope. American daguerreotypists were hailed as the most advanced in the world. Those who could not attend the Exhibition could learn about it through the new medium of stereoscopic daguerreotypes:

> A selection of these photographs was sent to the Czar of Russia, who, unable to visit London, was so delighted to be able to form a correct impression of the Exhibition that he presented Claudet with a diamond ring accompanied by a letter complimenting him on the effect of relief obtained in the stereoscope.[3]

As Oliver Wendell Holmes observed, "Form is henceforth divorced from matter."[4] A reliable message could be transmitted at great distances from the original through the channel of molecular changes in salts deposited on metal, produced by exposure to the light modeling the chiaroscuro of the original forms, in codes which could be identified as having many of the condensed scanning characteristics of the real, three-dimensional world.

We ourselves can "see" some aspects of the Great Exhibition of 1851 in London through the medium of photography. As paper photography was still largely undependable at the time, and as Talbot still held the reins of the calotype process firmly in patent, the most usual way for us to "see" the Great Exhibition today would be through engravings made from daguer-

PLATE 117. *Great Exhibition Main Avenue* (*1851*).   *Metal line engraving by H. Bibby, from a daguerreotype by Mayall. Note that the figures were almost certainly added by the engraver. Reproduced here the same size as the plate facing page 51, in J. G. Strutt, ed.,* Tallis' History . . . of the Crystal Palace (*London: 1851*), *vol. 3. Courtesy of the Free Library of Philadelphia.*

reotypes. The "Great Exhibition Main Avenue," engraved by H. Bibby from a daguerreotype by Mayall (Plate 117) shows us at least the overall perspective of the main hall, the relative size of some of the objects and statues, the kinds of pillars utilized as supports, the relative amounts of light on each story, and perhaps even several of the individuals who were there, although this is extremely unlikely. Comparison with other contemporary views of the Main Hall indicates the probability that many of the people in the Mayall original moved, or that the light was insufficient, and that the engraver cheerfully supplied any defective forms. The hybrid character of the picture is the result of combining a specific moment of lighting, in a specific hall, with generalized people, oversimplified statuary, and purely linear architectural details. Nevertheless, we may assume that we are receiving some basic information about the Great Exhibition which no succession of purely verbal images could succeed in rivaling.

THE PHILADELPHIA CENTENNIAL AND ITS ERA

For the International Centennial Exhibition celebrating the first century of American Independence, held in Philadelphia in 1876, the daguerreotype was a memory of the past, still individually represented in parlors or in lockets or as framed wall portraits, but gone from the repertory of professional photographers, to whom the wet-collodion glass negative and the paper print were standard media. In the Photographic Exhibition Building there were offered an impressive variety of carbon prints, transparencies, stereoscopic views, and other photographic exhibits, including John Carbutt's "Photo-lithographic reproductions," Charles Bierstadt's "Photographs, in printing-ink, by Albert's process," Mason's "Photographs of the Moon," Osgood's "Photographs in printing-ink, by heliotype process," and several "specimens of photo-engraving." These extensive listings in the official catalogue do not prepare the reader for the following paragraph from Edward Strahan's *Masterpieces of the International Exhibition* (1877):

> As these pages are to form an *Illustrated* Catalogue of Masterpieces, it would have been an anomaly to let the present portion of our criticisms go to the public without illustrations; but the manner of embellishment presented a difficulty; we were unwilling to deface our work with photographic mounts; and we hope our readers will acknowledge that the best style we could adopt was to present illustrations of some of the most notable and extensive of the art photographs included in the Exposition, executed in the usual methods selected for the embellishment of other portions of our work. They will understand, then, that *the engravings we present in this portion are simply given as likenesses of some of the largest and most artistic photographs displayed* [italics added].[5]

What this paragraph describes is the core problem of the 1870s: the inability of photography to reproduce itself in a medium suitable for type-compatible printing. We therefore read this absurdity: the artistic photographs described above as part of the Photography Exhibit were not from "Nature," but were from paintings. What we have, then, in Strahan's book, are *reproductions in wood engraving of photographs of paintings.* In other words, we have messages about messages about originals.

When we attempt to see for ourselves what the Philadelphia Centennial buildings looked like, we discover that the most usual medium of communication was that of the Lintonesque and pre-Linton black-line engraving, rather like our earlier "Major Ringgold." A typical engraving, "The

Central Aisle of the Main Exhibition Building" (Plate 118) cannot compare with the illusionism of the daguerreotype-based "Main Avenue" (Plate 117) of the 1851 Exhibition. Details are crude. Light and shade have been largely abandoned to a symbolic, generalized, and schematic rendition. If we can judge that metal posts and glass were used, we cannot be sure that the giant flags were not cardboard or wood; we make a verbal as-if leap and translate the symbol: "flags are of cloth; therefore *these* flags are of cloth." The transmission code helps us very little in assessing the textures of various stalls, and the smallest units of information in this picture seem generally much larger than in "The Main Avenue." It may well be that the engraver of "The Central Aisle" was using a photograph-on-the-block, but it is extremely difficult to see any remains of it.

James McCabe's *Illustrated History of the Centennial Exhibition* is a basic text for the event, and it is from this work, "Embellished with nearly 400 fine engravings . . ."[6] that "The Central Aisle" has been taken. The word "embellished" or "embellishment" also appeared in Strahan's paragraph, quoted above; the term signified pictorial decoration. McCabe, however, recognizes that "embellishment" was not the purpose of an illustrated history. "Those who saw the Exhibition will, it is believed, admit the truthfulness of the picture herein presented, whatever they may think of the manner in which the work is executed."[7] McCabe here is talking about the total "picture" which he was presenting in the book, not about "individual pictures." "The engravings in this work have been prepared especially for it, and at great expense. It is sufficient to say that they were engraved by Messrs. Van Ingen & Snyder, Philadelphia, Harper & Bros., New York, and other well-known houses."[8] The engraver of "The Central Aisle" is unknown, but his work is no better and no worse than the rest of the larger "embellishments" in the *Illustrated History*. What McCabe meant by "it is sufficient to say" is conjectural, at best; we presume he meant that the engravings were therefore of high excellence and truthfulness. What he perhaps should have said was that all the engravings conformed to the standards of execution of the wood-engraving codes of 1876, that time and place had dictated the development of these codes, and that they were certainly no improvement over earlier codes.

One of the two frontispieces for the McCabe book was a stipple-and-line engraving, probably steel or steel-plated copper, of "G. Washington, Taken from life in 1794." The credits read, "Painted by Stuart. Engraved by Illman Brothers." Here again we have a message about a message, this time, about a real person, for the Stuart painting cannot be regarded solely as a "work of art" in such a context. "Taken from life" indicates to us that the legend writer wanted us to know that a contemporary had painted the portrait, and that, therefore, we are expected to accept it as a genuine message about "reality"; the engraver, nevertheless, considered his task sufficiently important to merit a signature, in the same way that a translator of a poem into another language signs his translation and offers to the world the opportunity of judging how well or how poorly he caught the spirit of the original. Obviously, to judge the merits of a message about a message, when we no longer have the *original* of the primary message to compare, we should at least have before us the *primary message* for the sake of comparison with the *secondary* message, recognizing all the while that what we are seeing is an optical illusion in black ink on a flat surface which purports to convey information about a man named Washington.

A much poorer engraving accompanied this Washington portrait, a rendition of Trumbull's painting of "The Declaration of Independence."

PLATE 118. *Central Aisle of the Main Exhibition Building* (1876). *Black-line wood engraving, folded and tipped into text. Reproduced here the same size as in the unnumbered front matter, in James D. McCabe,* The Illustrated History of the Centennial Exhibition *(Philadelphia: National Publishing Co., 1876), from the copy owned by E. Jussim.*

Here the codes are so conspicuous that almost every surface is rendered in crosshatched, parallel diagonal lines of high visibility. These two frontis-pieces were the only concession to the past glories of metal line engraving. The rest of the illustrations were in black-line tonal wood engraving.

If the reader wishes to see how low were the standards for art repro-duction in the ordinary trade book of the Centennial generation, he is advised to examine the hack work inflicted on Eastman Johnson's "Old Kentucky Home," or Alma Tadema's "The Vintage Festival" from the Memorial Hall exhibits at the Philadelphia Centennial, as McCabe's vaunted engravers have rendered them. The McCabe book, printed on cheap text paper, offers a glimpse of the standard publishing practices of the period, in contradistinction to Strahan's deluxe *Masterpieces.* In terms of sheer numbers, of course, it is almost certain that the one-volume McCabe reached a larger audience, an audience well accustomed to such books and to the linear symbolism of their messages.

Looking at the engraving of "The Central Aisle" (Plate 118), so typical of the 1876 era, it is almost impossible to imagine the revolution which photography-on-the-block and the developed "textures" of Kingsley and Cole and Juengling would bring about in the next few years. The com-petition from the heliotype, the woodburytype, and the mounted photo-graph now began to pressure the codifiers of information to condense information, push their codes toward subliminality, and begin to describe the textures of the three-dimensional world rather than predefined abstrac-tions.

In other books of the Centennial of 1876, lithography (often black on tinted backgrounds), etching, chromolithography, steel engraving—both stipple and line—appear, but the predominant medium of the generation of 1876 is unmistakably the black-line wood engraving. We have remarked on the isolated appearance of the first goupilgravure of the Chartran painting (Plate 102). In addition, a few Moss line engravings may be scattered through the dozens of guidebooks, commentaries, exhibition mementos, and journal articles, as well as photo-zincographic maps or floor plans. The black-line wood engraving was at its zenith; nevertheless, except for the cheapest of children's books and trade reissues, it was on the way out. With the appearance of the photogravure, the heliotype, the process line engraving, and white-line tonal wood engraving based on photography-on-the-block, the old symbolic order was dying and the new was born. The Centennial, with its extensive exhibition of photography and photomechanical devices, seen by hundreds of thousands of people, was the catalyst.

Photolithography, or photo-zincography—or even, as Stephen Horgan called it, photoplanography—was very much a part of the Centennial generation. Horgan's work for the New York *Daily Graphic* is well known. The "first illustrated daily newspaper in the world,"[9] the *Daily Graphic* began publication in 1873, produced by the application of photography to lithography in both type and illustration.

> Photolithography . . . was the first of the photomechanical reproductive processes to be commercially profitable. It was the basis of a big business in New York, when, in the eighties, it was crowded out by the photorelief processes that came into use at that time. Had the offset press then been perfected, photolithography would have been applied to the offset press, and would have continued to be the most practical method for reproducing maps, diagrams, charts, catalogues, and much of the illustrative matter of today in which the high lights are desired to be as clear as in lithography. . . . Photo-

lithography in the old days was practiced in secret, and the few who were best acquainted with the methods have passed away and their secret processes have been buried with them.[10]

This secrecy was typical of many establishments. Even Daguerre had recognized that to publish his secret process was effectively to render it unpatentable. The *Daily Graphic*

> . . . startled the whole printing world, for it demonstrated that photography was going to usurp the place of wood engraving, which at that time was the only method of preparing illustrations for the printing press. So carefully were the secrets of the *Daily Graphic* guarded that the writer was under heavy bonds not to divulge even what he saw in their extensive photographic establishment.[11]

Ultimately, however, such secrecy could not prevail in the face of the upsurge of relief processes. The lithographic presses of those days were slow, with an impression capability of "about 700 to 800 an hour." [12] Writing in 1913, Stephen Horgan was convinced that "the quantity of illustrative work that went through the *Graphic* establishment could not be handled by any of the photoengraving plants of our day." [13] Slow or not on the press, the photolithograph was so easy for the artist to exploit, that the *Graphic* plant turned out: ". . . reproductions of the regular weekly issues of patent drawings, Government and real-estate maps; art reproductions; catalogues; booklets; cigarette and other labels; book illustrations, and several weekly newspapers." [14]

As we have noted in an earlier chapter, lithography was the medium preservative of all media—with the exception of the photograph itself—prior to the development of the screen halftone. Horgan himself adapted a screen to an albertype from Nature and processed it into the photoplanographic methods for his famous "Shanty Town," which appeared on March 4, 1880, and used a screen of only 70 lines per inch. The daily journalistic capturing of "history," live events as they happened, was on its way. Very probably, if the modern offset press—a planographic press using fast rotary action—had been available at the time, it is possible that the New School of Engraving might never have developed, and that our visual conditioning and the war of the media as it developed in the 1880s would have come out very differently.

The war between competing media sometimes seemed to undergo a kind of nervous truce, or even an acculturated series of compromises. Between the Philadelphia Centennial and the Columbian Exposition of 1893, there came a neglected series of "multimedia" communications, in which the modes of communication were combined, in a single book or crammed together on a single page; worse still, crushed into an often ludicrous octopus of an illustration, where its body might be a process halftone engraving and its peculiar arms a succession of other media. Publishers seemed unconcerned about the visual ambiguities and confusions thus obtained, some, in fact, attempting rather pretentiously "arty" effects with half-moons of wash drawings transmitted in process, combined with full moons of pen-and-inks rendered in line engraving.

A fascinating example of this kind of menagerie of the media was John Muir's *Picturesque California* (1888), which was to the multimedia book what the monumental *Picturesque America* (1872) had been to the wood engraving and the steel engraving. *Picturesque California* was a ten-volume extravaganza which saw simultaneous publication of a condensed two-volume edition and a one-volume trade edition. "Containing about four hundred etchings, photogravures, wood engravings, etc., by eminent American artists," [15] and printed in a variety of inks which particularly characterize this generation of books (as, for example, the second edition of the Goodyear *History of Art* of the same year: purples, blues, dark greens, acid reds, occasional terracottas), too heavy because of its size to drag from the parlor table, the trade edition of *Picturesque California* was a superlative example of the communications practices of the late 1880s. Etchings by Thomas Moran, photogravures from paintings by Thomas Hill and Frederic Remington, among many other notable Western illustrators and painters, process halftone (phototypic) full-page reproductions of photographs from "Nature," surrounding innumerable smaller vignettes and combinations, made for multimedia pages within a multimedia book (Plate 119).

Plate 119, for our purposes called "Multimedia Combinations," contains (a) a process line engraving transmitting a pen-and-ink drawing; (b) a process halftone engraving with some odd looking details and some of the characteristics of a photograph from "Nature"; and (c) a black-line tonal wood engraving, reproducing some fictive artist's packaging of "a scene"— presumably this would have been rendered in opaque gouache and photographed on the block.

What is amusing about the part of Plate 119 called "Interior of the Oakland Depot" (lower left of Plate 119) is that it has been obviously retouched; figures have been drawn onto the photograph, others have been manipulated, and these photographic fakeries are conspicuous to the trained eye by their lack of coordination with either the lighting scheme of the depot or the linear differentiations which would have been added to make the message intelligible. Undoubtedly, the "artist" counted on the halftone screen to break up the blacks and fill up the whites sufficiently to blend the painted anomalies into the other dots. But his fraudulent behavior is easily discovered. And it is ridiculous to even ask which of these three schema of reality we should accept as transmitting reliable characteristics of the originals. To have to choose between the linear symbolic, the painted photograph, or a comic wood engraving is to put our credulity and our visual adaptability to the utmost strain.

On other pages of *Picturesque California,* tonal wood engravings were morticed into line engravings, or crayon textures intermingled with photography. Only the etchings, photogravures, and steel engravings remained pure, as they were printed separately, and were, in effect, "prints" bound into the body of the book rather than printed simultaneously with the type.

These hodgepodges of smaller effects mixed with the text were partly the result of putting together odd "cuts" and woodblocks which might happen to be available on a subject, while the etchings and photogravures were commissioned, or rights to original paintings purchased specifically for reproduction in this work. Since there were now three major media which could be used type-compatibly—the process line engraving, the screened process halftone engraving, and the wood engraving—more and more amalgams of publisher-illustrated books found their way to the public. They were as much collages of available pictorial effects as the fantasies of Max Ernst. Like the gift albums and ladies' annuals which were the parlor adornments and keepsakes of much of the nineteenth century, the editorial policy of many of these multimedia books seems to have been: find us a (type-compatible) picture and we'll get someone to write a paragraph about its message. [16]

THE MOLE.—OAKLAND IN THE DISTANCE.

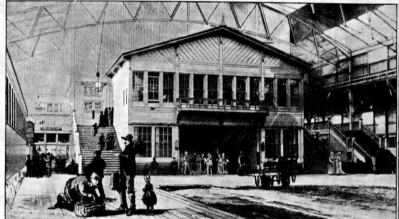

INTERIOR OF THE OAKLAND DEPOT.

ferry-boats ply on the routes, carrying daily some twenty-five thousand passengers, and the great freight-boats, like floating bridges, transfer an entire freight train at a single trip.

PLATE 119. *Multimedia Combinations.* *Slightly reduced multimedia engravings, discussed in the text. From John Muir,* Picturesque California *(1888), vol. 2 of the 3-volume edition. Courtesy of the Free Library of Philadelphia, Rare Book Dept.*

Any reader who is not familiar with *Picturesque California* or the children's annuals of this period may easily see some of these multimedia effects by examining the more widely available publication, *Harper's New Monthly Magazine* for 1887. A typical article, "Here and There in the South," has the following illustration sequence:

a wood-engraving vignette, half page
a white-line tonal wood engraving, half page; engraver, Tinkey
a full-page process halftone, in which most of the picture is obliterated
    by black ink; from a gouache
a full-page tonal wood engraving; engraver, Lindsay
a one-third page process halftone, in which the routing out of highlights
    with a graver is conspicuous
a two-thirds page tonal wood engraving, by Hellawell

These do not have the interchangeable aspects we mentioned in connection with William Hamilton Gibson; the process work is poor.

When Robert Taft summarily announced in his *Photography and the American Scene* that the screened process halftone "began" to be used in American publishing about 1892, he unwittingly dismissed a most important period of transition.[17] After all, the process halftone began to appear in books and periodicals from the moment Frederick Ives patented his first process in 1881. The decade of the 1880s was its proving ground; while it often failed, its progress was inexorable, and its pressure on all other media, enormous. The shock of media confusion, already noted in connection with Gibson, cannot be measured directly, for the individuals who might have been questioned have taken most of their immediate responses with them into history. But the revolution in communications which was taking place in the 1880s deserves our serious attention, as it represented a crossing over from symbolic representations based largely on specific rules of graphic delineation to an "itness," a specific encounter with what was actually supposed to have existed or continues to exist.

The linear outline of, say, the "Apollo Belvedere" (Plate 109A) was only a *sign* that if you went to Rome, you might see a statue by such a name. The process halftone of the Apollo (Plate 110A) had lost its "sign-function" and had become an optical illusion with surrogate power. These optical illusions have been so successful that people today express disappointment when they, like Howard Pyle, go abroad to see the originals of works of art. Unlike Howard Pyle, they have "seen it all" already, and the prediction of Oliver Wendell Holmes has sadly come true: *Form is henceforth divorced from matter.* The public has been conditioned to using the photograph as a substitute for direct experience. The psychological consequences of such conditioning have never been adequately measured, although Daniel Boorstin, William Ivins, and their popularizer, Marshall McLuhan, have contributed enormously to the understanding of what might have happened.

A NEW ERA: THE COLUMBIAN EXPOSITION OF 1893

The contrast between the old and new modes of thought, after several decades of exposure to the photographic image, was already present even in the generation of the Philadelphia Exhibition. In Benson Lossing's *Centennial History* (1876), the author advises the reader:

The engravings are introduced not for the sole purpose of embellishing the volume, but to enhance its utility as an instructor. Every picture is intended to illustrate a fact, not merely to beautify the page. Great care has been taken to secure accuracy in all the delineations of men and things, so that they may not convey false instruction.[18]

"Great care" *must* be taken by subjective human packagers of illustration. No such proviso was necessary in Charles Kurtz's comments on the Columbian Exposition:

To those who may not visit the Exposition, the illustration of the art exhibits will convey an idea of them that could be obtained in no other manner so effective or adequate. Being engraved directly from photographs of the works, the illustrations are absolutely accurate in detail. They lack only size and color.[19]

By 1893, the screened process halftone or the photogravure reproducing photography was accepted as equivalent to seeing the originals. There could be no question of "embellishment" versus "instruction." The photograph unquestionably stood for the thing itself. It was not viewed as a message about reality, but as reality itself, somehow magically compressed and flattened onto the printed page, but, nevertheless, equivalent to, rather than symbolic of, three-dimensional reality.

In Kurtz's *Official Illustrations* for the fine arts displays, technology had solved the problems which had plagued the aesthetic sensibilities of Edward Strahan in 1876, when he had been forced to permit the reproduction of photographs of paintings to be transmitted through black-line wood engravings. Every plate in the Kurtz book is monotonously process halftone, reducing all sizes and shapes of paintings to the handbook size.

We can compare McCabe's *Illustrated History of the Centennial Exhibition* with a one-volume standard history of the Columbian Exposition by Trumbull White and William Igleheart. A trade book, meant for mass consumption, and "Fully-illustrated with halftone and wood engravings and pen drawings by the best artists,"[20] it included an early chapter on the history or prior world exhibitions.

Reviewing the history of international exhibitions, it seems almost incredible that the first effort in that direction was instituted less than half a century ago. In the forty odd years that have intervened the art of exhibiting has grown into a science as exact in its general rules and as far-reaching in its effect on civilization as its antithesis, the science of war.[21]

White and Igleheart's historical recapitulation reveals the startling differences in vision which photography had wrought. Beginning with the Crystal Palace Exhibition of 1851, we are introduced to a series of pictures of expositions and exhibitions—New York in 1853, Florence in 1861, Paris in 1867, Vienna in 1873, Philadelphia in 1876—all of these transmitted via the symbolic, linear codes of black-line wood engraving. Suddenly, with the Paris Exposition of 1889, we "see" a night view, transmitted via photography reproduced by process halftone. We can also "see" the Eiffel Tower. For the Columbian Exposition itself, we can "see" the dedication ceremonies of October 1892, through the advanced photo-technology, now fast enough to capture large indoor crowds with a minimum of blur, now reproducible through the halftone screen, with subliminality of codes sufficient to preserve recognizable details. Unfortunately, the publishers chose to print the plates and the text on the same paper, much the same mistake as was made in the first edition of Goodyear. The result is that the halftones are muddy and blurred, the screen conspicuously interferes, and the stamping character of relief processes is all too evident.

No such error interfered with the messages of the four-volume *History of the World's Columbian Exposition* published in 1898. Both text and visual communications were printed on coated stock, so that small process halftone vignettes could be used to good advantage by the book designer. In contrast to the monotonous Kurtz handbook, with its page after page of identical sizes and overall grayness, the deluxe four-volume history freely utilized horizontal and vertical pictures, interspersed with small portraits whose edges had been "artistically retouched" by former wood engravers, now working for their nemesis. It was a considerable advance over the bookmaking and design characteristics of the White and Igleheart book of 1893.

Although the four-volume work purports to be the complete history of the Columbian Exposition, it is from White and Igleheart that we learn more about certain exhibits of relevance to our discussion. For example, the later, larger book dismisses Eadweard Muybridge's zoopraxigraphical exhibits in one sentence. White and Igleheart tell us:

> The first [of three small concessions] is the Zoopraxiscopic exhibit and lecture room which is of vast interest to artists and scientists. Animal locomotion is a new study, pursued chiefly by electro-photographic investigation. Instantaneous photographs, taken with the aid of the electric shutter, show all preconceived opinions as to the method of representing animals in action to be utterly false. Here lectures on animal locomotion are given, and by an ingenious apparatus there is an exhibit of illustrations of the movements of men, women, and children, and many sorts of animals. The investigations which have resulted in this excellent display are those of Eadweard Muybridge, of the University of Pennsylvania.[22]

Accompanying this paragraph are two process line engravings: one is a pen-and-ink drawing of the building itself, and the other, what is almost certainly an outline redrawing of the old wood engravings which had appeared in *Scientific American* in 1879, reduced to about one quarter their original size.

Muybridge's zoopraxographical hall was one of the many sideshows at the Midway Plaisance of the Columbian Exposition, where it shared attention with, among other attractions, the Electric Scenic Theatre.

> It consists of a display of scenery shown by the latest methods of effects by electricity. The scenery was executed in Germany, and is considered a triumph of art. It represents "A Day in the Alps," which begins with sunrise, and over the mountain top appears the ruddy glow of early sunlight . . . the volume of light increases, the beauties of the mountain become more apparent until their full glory flashes upon the beholder. . . .[23]

And so on, through an entire day of storm and night of stars. This description of the Electric Scenic Theatre almost exactly matches descriptions of the Diorama of 1822, which had led its inventor, Louis Daguerre, into his obsession with capturing three-dimensional lighting effects through the artist's tool, the camera obscura. Now electricity made all his beloved illusionistic displays a simple matter of switches and dimmers, and it had speeded up the shutter of the camera so that information never dreamed of in Daguerre's day could be stopped by the ingenuity of Muybridge's electric apparatus.

No one came forward, as had Oliver Wendell Holmes in his commentary on the new medium of stereoscopy, to prophecy that the Electric Scenic Theatre and the zoopraxigraphical hall were together the archetypes of the motion picture palace where science and art were to join in a new rivaling of the printed word, of the still photograph, and of all other phototechnological processes.[24]

As in the earlier exhibition, the Columbian Exposition's Fine Arts displays also housed an extensive showing of American photography and processes, and the publishers outdid each other in the number and variety of exhibitions of the new communications media. The publishers of *Scribner's Magazine,* which had given such impetus to the New School of Engraving in the early 1880s, exhibited the old and the new side-by-side.

> To show the process of illustrating a modern magazine, there are the original drawings, the same reproduced by photo engravings, by wood engravings, also the prepared wood block, the block upon which the picture has been photographed for the engraver, and the block after being engraved, but before being electrotyped.[25]

The New School of Engraving, now officially active as "The American Society of Wood Engravers," contributed an exhibit, about which Elbridge Kingsley reported:

> Unfortunately, I have no catalogue for reference, so I do not know whether original, reproductive, or general work predominated. I think it was supposed to represent all classes. I had no official connection whatever with the Exhibition and did not see it after it was arranged at Chicago. . . . So I must rely upon memory and what I was told by others. I have no doubt that it was a complete showing of the engravers up to that time, and this on the eve of their livelihood being taken away from them by the process plate.[26]

Kingsley, himself technologically unemployed by 1893, was quite right. Of all the books published for the Columbian Exposition which are still extant, perhaps only twenty-five percent contain any reproductive medium other than process halftone (reproducing photography from Nature in type-compatible form) and process line engraving (reproducing pen-and-ink with such facility): the phototechnologies had won out.

The most typical of the Columbian Exposition books were those published by the Shepp Brothers, "Authors of 'Shepp's Photographs of the World,' the most famous book of modern times."[27] Printed on coated paper, using a fine-screen halftone, *Shepp's World's Fair Photographed* was a "Collection of Original Copyrighted Photographs,"[28] in which all vestiges of technological ineptitude have been overcome. A night photograph of fireworks is reproduced with utter ease, instantaneously stopping the action of the soaring shower of sparks and capturing the glow of lights across the water. Interiors are almost all sharply defined in these large square halftones, one to each double spread, all the same size and of approximately the same excellence. The photograph had come into its own as a communications channel, using the code of the fine-screen halftone to transmit its own molecular codes. *Shepp's* is the picturebook of modern times in every respect save color, the beginning of the picturebooks which record history with such illusionism that we have come to believe that all we need of an event is its visual "skin" in order to know it.

Reviewing these exhibition pictures—the Mayall daguerreotype-based "Main Avenue" (Plate 117) of the Crystal Palace of 1851 and the black-line wood engraving of the "Central Aisle" (Plate 118) of the Philadelphia Exhibition of 1876, and then turning to a plate like "General View in the

PLATE 120. *General View in the Shoe and Leather Building* (1893). *Process halftone engraving from photograph from Nature. Reproduced here the same size as the plate facing page 324, in R. Johnson, ed.,* History of the World's Columbian Exposition Held in Chicago in 1893 *(New York: Appleton, 1898), vol. 3. Courtesy of the Free Library of Philadelphia.*

Shoe and Leather Building" (Plate 120) of the Columbian Exposition of 1893 — we have a capsule of the communications progress of the nineteenth century. The "General View" (Plate 120), like the halftones in Shepp's book, is unmistakably what we accept as "real." Flags are of cloth, partially transparent; metal standards and tin floors have different textural characteristics; we have little difficulty in imagining ourselves moving through the spaces around the cabinets. From another book we have selected a fairly typical photogravure, taken either on an exceptionally sunny day or overexposed by the photographer and therefore exhibiting too much contrast. This view, Plate 121, "Interior of the Manufactures and Liberal Arts Building," like Plate 120, is clearly illusionistic, while the "Central Aisle" (Plate 118), in the Lintonesque symbolism of the 1870s, is not. If any human subjectivity has entered into either the photogravure or the process halftone, it was primarily through choice of vantage point, so that the photogravure makes the interior of the Manufactures and Liberal Arts Building seem somewhat taller than the same building in a similar halftone in *Shepp's*. There can be no question in either that the photographic technology has succeeded in transmitting a message about an original photograph which is sufficiently subliminal to resemble *the original of the photograph,* namely, three-dimensional objects at a particular moment on a particular day.[29]

In describing the "Puck" building at the Columbian Exposition, the *Shepp's* comments:

> We have before us an illustration of how the great pictorial papers are made; we see the clean white paper go through the lips of the great rollers, and come out lined with the black letterpress; then, passing through another roller, dainty little black vignettes appear, and in others, we see the ground tone of larger pictures gradually built upon with various colors until all is complete. . . . It seems only yesterday that such a feat seemed impossible, while now the Sunday issues, and many also of the weekly papers, are regarded as imperfect without these illustrations. Those who remember the old-fashioned books and souvenir volumes, in which our grandmothers delighted, will think of the old plates carefully lithographed in but few colors, which once awakened admiration; now any journal can produce better illustrations and by a much simpler process. It used to be the custom to give away chromos with newspapers and magazines, and some of them were thought so good that we may find them framed in many of the farm and country houses throughout the land; now our illustrated papers are full of much better prints. . . .[30]

While photography had momentarily not only succeeded in ousting all other originals of printed messages but had ousted all other means of transmission through its applications, the multimedia book lingered on, and, of course, still appears today when reproductions of differing chronological periods must be used to transmit messages about those periods. At the turn of the century, books were still being published with "cuts" out of the old grab-bag of the nineteenth-century's discards. Such a book, *The New Century History of Our Country and Island Possessions,* by Henry Davenport Northrop (Philadelphia: Moore, © 1900), was "Embellished with over 500 superb engravings," some of which can be recognized as the work of men such as Thomas Moran, which had appeared twenty-five years before in *Scribner's* and *Harper's Monthly* or in *Picturesque America* when the current events of western expansion were the most exciting history in the making. Now a curious thing had occurred. Since its "death," wood engraving had achieved a certain "antique" desirability, very necessary for the embellishments of history books. Therefore, for the Northrop book, *imitation* "wood engravings," produced by pen-and-ink via process line engravings, compete for attention with the "Major Ringgold" reissue of a genuine wood engraving, either photographically reproduced from a print or electrotyped from the original block. Duotoned (fake process) halftones resurrect F. O. C. Darley drawings, Trumbull paintings, and photographs of the General Staff of the Spanish-American War. Fake process in four colors provides some contrast with the black and whites. With the exception of the full-page process halftones, the book could have been issued in the 1870s, under the enterprising entrepreneurship of someone like John Calvin Moss. Yet the existence of such cheap-jack rehashes using the codes of now obsolete technologies does not alter the truth that these execrable pictures were emanations out of the past, not specifically produced or even chosen for this book. The book was one of the Pandora's box phenomena of phototechnological facility.

By 1904, when the St. Louis Exposition opened, even very ordinary little trade books carried process halftones correctly printed on coated paper. Color backgrounds or fake process in three or four colors abound. The twentieth century was on its way, with photographic technology firmly embedded in the communications matrix of publishing and illustration, and, more importantly, permanently a factor in the thinking processes of human beings.

Photographic Technology and Visual Communication: Summary and Conclusions

. . . the photograph, with all its applied discoveries and its applications to the service of the printing press, may be said to be as important a discovery in its effects on art and books as was the discovery of printing itself. . . .[1]

In applying several concepts of information theory to an investigation of the characteristics of nineteenth-century American illustration, we have been attempting to discover in what ways the introduction of photographic technologies altered the artistic and informational capacities of the graphic media. To do this, we have had to explore the ways in which the capabilities for artistic expression and information transfer of the photographic technologies differed not only from the pre- or nonphotographic processes, but from each other.

The terminology of message, channel, code, transmission, distortion, interference, and other information theory constructs, not only has proved valuable in simplifying the examination of William Ivins' pioneering theories but may prove of further value in investigations of what Charles Biederman has described as the evolution of visual knowledge.

Before we present our conclusions and an analysis of some of the broader implications of our investigations, we should reconsider Ivins in the light of specific evidence uncovered or discerned in the course of our explorations.

WILLIAM IVINS AND "PHOTOGRAPHIC" THEORY RECONSIDERED

It may be recalled that the primary hypothesis offered by Ivins was that photography was the first and only graphic medium in which images

. . . were not subject to the omissions, the distortions, and the subjective difficulties that are inherent in all pictures in which draughtsmanship plays a part. Here were exactly repeatable visual images made without any of the syntactical elements implicit in all hand-made pictures.[2]

In our terms, Ivins hypothesized that photography is not dependent upon either the primary or secondary "packager of information"—that is, the illustrator or the hand engraver—and that photography is, therefore, a superior channel of information transmission which revolutionized visual communication. Despite his recognition that photography had "deficiencies," [3] he maintained that the subjective distortions of the primary codifier, the illustrator, were completely bypassed by the mechanical objectivity of the camera, and similarly, that the arbitrary, technologically or culturally determined routines of the secondary codifier, the hand engraver, were made obsolete and unnecessary by lens and the emulsion. "Inescapably built into every photograph were a great amount of detail, and, especially, the geometrical perspective of central projection and section. The accuracy of both depended merely on the goodness of the lens." [4]

We must argue with Mr. Ivins here. *Nothing* is built inescapably into every photograph, precisely because everything depends on "the goodness of the lens" and on the individual manipulating it. The type of lens is equally important. The "blur-beautiful" of the illustrator-photographer, Julia Cameron, resulted

> . . . from her use of a lens of unusually long focal length (30 in.) which obliged her to work at open aperture to arrive at exposures of manageable length. This resulted in differential focusing—sharp in the parts on which she focused, and rapidly falling off in the receding and projecting parts of the sitter. [5]

The whole of the school of so-called "Naturalistic Photography," founded by P. H. Emerson in the 1880s, in admiration for Mrs. Cameron's technologically induced blur,

> . . . advocated a certain degree of softness . . . in the negative through differential focusing . . . . Differential focusing, Emerson claimed, enabled the naturalistic photographer to give *a subjective rendering of nature* [italics added], whereas the realistic photographer recorded with objective, soulless precision. [6]

Gernsheim claims that Emerson was mistaken: ". . . subjective photography as opposed to mechanical photography is dependent on the artistic ability of the photographer and not on soft or sharp rendering." [7]

It is not our intention to argue the merits of this case here, but rather to use the implications of these comments in terms of Ivins. If there is a possibility that "photography" can be *subjective*, that what it records can be manipulated by an individual or restricted either by the technological limitations of lens or emulsion or by "artistic," i.e., subjective, manipulations in the making of photographic positives on paper, then we must admit that the purely objective character of photography as posited by Ivins is a fiction. We could just as easily say that "inescapably built into every artist's eye and hand were a great deal of detail . . . the accuracy of both depended merely on the goodness of the lens and of the fingers."

If, however, we redefine Ivins' hypothesis so as to convey a more accurate definition of what photography is to begin with, we may be able to salvage his ideas. Let us first define "photography." Photography results from the molecular changes in light-sensitive materials which have been exposed to the light reflected from three-dimensional real objects through the lens of a camera focused on a surface, and, ordinarily (except where the surface is round, as in photography on ceramics) represents the amount of actinic stimulation from the real world by the compression of that information on a flat, rather than on a three-dimensional, surface. Using a lens which approximates the normal range of human vision, and a light-sensitive emulsion which has condensed scanning characteristics approximating normal human differentiation of textures, the process of photography can supply a closer approximation to three-dimensional reality, as transposed through molecular codes on a flat surface, than any other graphic technology. With a sharp-focus lens, and a molecular light-sensitive emulsion with a wide exposure latitude, it is probable that the compression index for photographically transmitted information is greater than any hand process, even including the mezzotint. Since photography—as we describe it here—is posited as imitating the characteristics of human vision, with the notable and all-important distinction that it represents the world as flat rather than as three-dimensional, the recording made of a message about an original must be understood to be as much a *coding* of a message about an original as that used by any other graphic process. The difference is simply that photographic coding is subliminal (except where it is too greatly enlarged from a small negative; then the grain shows distinctly), conveying what amounts to an optical illusion which we learn to accept as a surrogate of reality.

Since the original of the message may be grossly large compared to the message as received on paper, our interpretation of the forms and textures is based on an "as-if" response. We behave with photographic messages as if they were the original, since we can intellectually equate a small paper image with the tiny retinal image of a far object. If our eyes could "see" no more than two feet away from our noses, it is quite possible that we could not interpret photographic images of large objects or events, since we would never be able to see the totality of an object by moving back from it until we saw all of it. The ordinary photographic image might then have the tremendous impact on our knowledge systems that the electron microscope now has.

What Ivins is saying about the *primary* codifier of information, the illustrator who is communicating "facts," is that culture and the technology of artistic media influence and structure his vision. He *cannot* deliver to us a means for the reproduction of what Ivins called "an exactly repeatable printing image" because he can only draw *one* original (in our terms) with a positive code which does not match the subliminality of the textures of Nature. If he copies this original, he may make small mistakes. If someone else hand-copies this original, there will be further mistakes resulting from inevitable differences in vision and hand expertise. This one-time, subjective artist's coding can be multiplied if the artist can work directly in an autographic code of high-density scanning characteristics, as, for example, an original scraper of mezzotints might work. But that code would not result from the transformations caused by light falling directly on the objects about which a message is to be transmitted. Therefore it cannot equal photography, which not only transmits messages originating in this way, but has a molecular subliminality of code which somewhat resembles the originals of messages.

What Ivins is saying about the *secondary* packager of information, the hand engraver who recodifies the artist's codes of representation into the technological channel, is that culture and the limitations of media, as well as purely arbitrary considerations of economics, tend to structure this second step in the communications process. Ivins affirms (in our formulation) that messages of fact transmitted in this manner are received at third remove from reality. He indicated that photography bypassed this secondary codification as well, for light transmitted from the original is the source of the molecular change in the emulsion, thus light has drawn (*photo-*

graphos) the original and simultaneously prepared the duplicating medium.

The fact that the primary codifier might be needed to make certain kinds of statements which photography cannot reliably make, that his manipulations of "reality" might be for the purpose of clarifying it, or even explaining it, seemed unimportant to Ivins because he was profoundly concerned with the accurate transmission of information about art objects. Overlooking the acute problems of scale of transmission, he did not look hard enough at some of the accomplishments of hand engravers.

More importantly, he confused the issue of the nature of photography by equating a single photomechanical reproducing medium with photography itself.

> At last men had discovered a way to make visual reports in printer's ink without syntax, and without the distorting analyses of form that syntax necessitated. Today we are so accustomed to this that we think little of it, but it represents one of the most amazing discoveries that man has ever made — a cheap and easy means of symbolic communication without syntax.[8]

If we were to turn back to the first and second Goodyear editions of *The History of Art,* and examine the clear texture of crossed lines visible in the first edition Apollo Belvedere, and then examine the second edition version of the same statue, we can only come to the conclusion that Ivins is mistaken in thinking that there is *any* means of symbolic communication *without syntax,* i.e., without some transmitting structure. What we see in the first edition Apollo, the visible crosslines, are still present in the second edition, transformed into subliminal dots. The dots are there. The transmitting structure is there. One has only to apply a magnifying glass to the second edition Apollo to see how clear those dots are, distinctly separated from each other, individual blobs of ink representing specific amounts of light admitted through the apertures of a screen.

With the electron microscope, it is possible to see the molecules which structure the photographic transmission. With an ordinary microscope, it is possible to see the grains which structure the transmission in gravure or in extremely fine contemporary process halftones. To this day, photogravure has so vastly outdistanced the optical richness of all but four-color, finest density process halftone that it is extensively used for art reproductions and art books, where the quality of the typography is sacrificed for the greater perfection of the intaglio ink image for the pictures. Yet it was not even photogravure which made the first transition into printable images, but the heliotype and the woodburytype which bridged the technology of paper photographic positives to the book. The heliotype, a gelatin process produced by direct exposure of the ultimate printing surface to an original, and printed by lithographic or planographic means, more closely approximated the messages sent by "photography."

By no means, then, is the "great importance of the halftone . . . its syntactical difference from the older hand-made processes of printing pictures," as Ivins claimed, for the halftone process engraving was but one of many phototechnologies which differed from the older, hand-made ones. Its great importance was that in a screen coarse enough to print on ordinary text paper, it was type-compatible at moderate cost. Increase the fineness and therefore the subliminality of the screen and the cost becomes greater because of the need for better and more expensive paper, which usually must have a coated surface to accommodate the delicate dot structure. But this has nothing to do with the virtues which Ivins propounded for it. In another context, Ivins acknowledges that the type-compatibility of process halftone was its major asset for *publishers*. Other phototechnologies were clearly superior in subliminality and richness of detail. Thus Ivins must be contradicted when he repeats:

> . . . the invention of the ruled cross-line halftone screen, a device which made it possible to make a printing surface for a pictorial report in which neither the draughtsman nor the engraver had had a hand. Its great importance lay in the fact that the lines of the process as distinct from the lines of the visual report could be below the threshold of normal human vision.[9]

The importance of the crossline halftone was that it was cheap, a relief process that could be used interchangeably from book to book as could the other relief processes, and it offered to the publishers an opportunity of bypassing the expense of commissioning either an artist-illustrator or an artist-engraver to transmit a message from Nature. What is so paradoxical in the situation is that publishers soon realized that an inept photograph, unsuited to transmission via any phototechnological medium, was no better than an inept illustrator. If they wanted accurate, attractive, technologically appropriate photographs, they had to hire a professional photographer, whose subjective eye and professional training made him every bit the equal of the old primary codifier. Without going into the more arcane depths of the sociology of knowledge, or the psychology of perception, it should suffice here to say that communication seems to have a material basis in any transaction, and that all communication, visual or otherwise, seems to involve at least some subjective factors. The choice of the point of view of a photograph, its lighting, its exposure, the kind of lens, the type of film, the printing paper, the length of development, and all the other variables in the production of one photograph, must make us recognize that photography does not represent some miraculously "pure" communication which transmits the textural gradients, chiaroscuro, contours, and colors, of events and objects in Nature in a perfect one-to-one relationship.

PHOTOTECHNOLOGIES AND ARTISTIC EXPRESSION

We have attempted to show that both the fictive illustrator and the factual illustrator depend, for their effectiveness in either role, on the correct transmission of messages about their originals.

We saw, in our discussion of William Hamilton Gibson and the Flume series, that "artistic expression" enters into many "information transfer" situations, and that an artist may be able to express precisely what photography cannot.

For the fictive artist, such as Howard Pyle, whose originals were supposed to be planned for transmission through a specific channel, the advent of the phototechnologies seemed to offer liberation from the arbitrary or subjective distortions of secondary codifiers, the hand engravers who "translated" artistic media into printing media. At first, the fictive illustrator was narrowly restricted to black-and-white pen-and-ink drawings ordinarily no larger than twice the finished reproduction, as the Moss process and other process line methods depended upon an absolute distinction between black and white, permitting no grays or continuous halftones. Pyle's *Robin Hood,* one of the most famous children's books produced in this manner, at least bypassed the codes of the wood engravers and preserved many of the autographic characteristics of the artist's creative handwork. Once the adherence to the technological requirements of process line engraving became habitual, a host of great illustrators, such as Pyle and Edwin Austin Abbey, were freed to develop a decorative style of widely accepted aesthetic worth. The characteristics of the artistic medium of pen-and-ink, as reproduced in process line engraving, offered much potential for overall page design as type-compatible as the wood engraving, but not, actually, differing to any considerable degree from the achievements of traditional wood engraving.

While geniuses of the graver continued for a time to facsimile pen-and-ink drawings, as did Timothy Cole with the cited Wyatt Eaton portrait of Lincoln (see Plate 12), the increasing dependability of the Moss and similar line processes bested such virtuoso performances economically and in speed of execution. The illustrator was considerably freer to design his pen strokes for the facility of the new processes than he had been in the facsimile days of F. O. C. Darley, whose drawings for facsimile wood engraving were often drawn directly on the block. With the advent of line photo-technology, the connection between the block and the artist was severed.

The separation was even more sharply demarcated with the development and acceptance, after the Philadelphia Centennial, of almost universal photography-on-the-block for wood engraving in tones. The fictive artist then became aware that he was free to create in larger sizes than the finished reproduction, although he discovered that if his original medium was watercolor wash or gouache or oils, even the most competent wood engraver had perforce to translate the details of his originals into a scale which suited the printing limitations of a relief surface. The artist therefore faced the dilemma of increased freedom on the creative side, and a seemingly absolute limit of capability of wood engraving, since the codes of wood engraving were white areas routed out from black, with very few tricks of the trade (such as lowering the entire relief surface in the background or building up the block to increase pressure for blackness in other areas) to produce any differentiation in ink deposit. Whether assisted by photography-on-the-block or not, the wood engraving limited the artist to the particular textures which each hand engraver had developed as his own style.

Despite a few monumental works, such as Elihu Vedder's *Rubaiyat of Omar Khayyam*, produced like a block-book with Vedder's hand-lettered text and drawings on one heliotype per page, the collotype processes like the heliotype did not enter into the communication capabilities for any of the three artists we considered. Expensive, noncompatible with type, and somewhat weak in ink impression despite the two inkings for each planographically printed plate, the heliotype made its dual impact on American communication through the production of art reproductions as *prints* (individually manufactured, later added to a book or left as separate plates in art folios) and through information transfer, the transmission of messages about "reality" rather than about fictive originals. Other collotype processes suffered from the technological limitations placed on all gelatin methods by the excessive climatic dampness of the various printing centers in the United States, and collotype to this day is largely manufactured in Europe. The woodburytype, another process using permanent printing ink, simultaneously with the heliotype made the first successful permanent transmissions of photographs from Nature, but although mounted pictures had been used to illustrate fictive literary works (such as Nathaniel Hawthorne's *Transformations*, Plate 20), the expense of the hand labor of mounting individual prints on text paper in books militated against the adoption of so-called "permanent photography" as standard transmission for the work of fictive illustrators. This was especially true since the fictive illustrator could rely upon symbolic linear codes as well as illusionistic statements, and therefore was not pushed as hard as he might have been if he had only one artistic avenue open to him.

The desire for illusionism, so marked in nineteenth-century painting and theatrical display, increased the desire to find a satisfactory channel for illusionistic reproduction of illusionistic originals. The photogravure, which in its early days was simply an application of photography to aquatint, was the first intaglio channel to provide an opportunity for artistic illusionism. Possessing a subliminal code which printed with a rich ink impression, it was nevertheless so slow and expensive, and required so much hand finishing, that it could not offer the ordinary trade book illustrator any advantage. Where photogravure did enter the mainstream of American fictive communication was with the deluxe edition—the Remington illustrations for *Hiawatha*, for example, or the Pyle plates for *The Autocrat of the Breakfast Table*. In such editions, photogravure was unmatched in its perfection of detail, range of tonal equivalences from white to black, and pleasing texture. Printed on heavy wove stock, separately from the text, the photogravure necessarily remained a "print" grafted onto the body of the book or even into the run of a periodical, and it was, therefore, in the early days of its use, primarily a luxury for only the most sumptuous publications.

Photogravure, offering the fictive artist such compressed transmission characteristics, tempted the artist into painting originals which were much too large for their ultimate reduction. Thus Howard Pyle pushed the capabilities of the medium to such limits that details of tiny faces, while perfectly transmitted, are so small that they are difficult to interpret in casual examination. The necessity for close scanning of such detail for the subtleties which Pyle designed into the message, e.g., a look of horror on a face whose total area is perhaps one sixteenth of a square inch, is tiring. Pyle's love of illusionistic detail, an artistic compulsion which he shared with many of the French academics who had been profoundly influenced by the aesthetics of the camera, was stimulated by the ease of reproduction by the phototechnologies; but such insistence on minutiae was perhaps more a demonstration of his skill than an appropriate response to the needs of book illustration. Typography, which usually prints flat on a page and is a symbolic translation from speech into visual codes, may suffer in legibility or design in context with an illusionistic illustration. We are, of course, used to this multimedia experience which greets us every time we open an illustrated journal, newspaper, or textbook, but we have never measured the strain of responding to such psychologically disjunctive stimuli, nor are we sure what effects the overall combinations of vision-for-sound and vision-as-if-for-real have had on our culture and our modes of thinking and responding to reality.

The first type-compatible phototechnology, the screened process halftone engraving, was no solution to this dilemma. The screen, mechanically imposing its crosslines and its overall dot structure, was so difficult a challenge that many great illustrators floundered when they encountered it. Pyle's *Thetis*, for example (Plate 42) demonstrated that it was by no means a simple matter for the illustrator to adjust to new technological methods. If anything, the hand engraver was at least in a position to assist the illustrator by translating details into appropriate printing patterns and scale, while the process engraver could only hope that the illustrator had prepared his original with sufficient contrast and sufficient freedom from the small niggling brushwork so dear to perfectionists, that his copperplate would etch without serious defect. The Moss Company's attempts to rival Frederick Ives in process halftone engraving bred a class of illustrators who were the clumsiest amateurs; and, unlike the Moss line engraving processes, which had encouraged a technical proficiency of ultimate aesthetic worth, the production of these early halftones deluded artists into thinking that technological facility ensured success.

By 1892, the imaginary dialogues of F. Hopkinson Smith's *American Illustrators* could serve as a summary of what had happened and as a forecast of what was to come. The complaints about the steamroller effect of process halftone were numerous, but resigned. The wood engravers, whose genius had rivaled the process halftone in the mid-eighties, were technologically unemployed, or had themselves turned to illustrating, becoming "painter wood engravers" like Elbridge Kingsley, going out into the field, working directly from Nature. The chromolithograph had reached a high state of technical perfection, and was in stiff competition with imported heliogravures in color. The illustrating artist seemingly had innumerable avenues for self-expression. Each avenue of reproduction, however, was discovered to have its own specific limitations. Each illustrator had to discover for himself which of the new media were compatible with his own creative styles. Ultimately, with the perfection of the fine-screen halftone process engraving, and with the introduction of orthochromatic film for color correction, the subliminality and compression of the code permitted a certain "isness" to be transmitted. At this point, the artist-illustrator became increasingly tempted to produce, not the originals of illustrations, but easel pictures which could be reproduced from almost any medium.

Reproduction in black and white from color originals was so difficult during the transitional period of the 1880s that monochrome painting in gouache became the rule. The fictive artist was forced to characterize his imaginary scenes with the same monochromatic range as black-and-white photography. Gradually, artists discovered that duochrome originals, using reds to differentiate certain types of forms and textures, would reproduce adequately. But even with the advent of color processes, the innate differences between artists' media and printing inks prevented high-fidelity transmission. Until the development of the color-separated negative process, the color in the final reproduction was a product of tints selected by the photoengraver after consultation with an artist's colored "dummy" or original sketch. They were not reproduced by photography, but were percentages of colored printing inks determined by percentage-rated mechanical devices.

The developed three-color process halftones of the early 1900s eliminated many of the restrictions which had hamstrung creative illustrators. A color genius like Pyle was now enabled to design originals boldly and with a rich interplay of color and form. Remington emerged as a colorist of considerable force, although many of his *Collier's* spreads were publisher-colored, not Remington-painted. John Whitfield Harland's idea that black-and-white codes had been more than adequate to the transcription of the multicolored world now seemed more a technologically motivated absurdity than a philosophical profundity. And if certain students of Pyle completely neglected any relationship of size of original to size of printed message, the code capacities of the new halftones transmitted considerable numbers of details.

Generally, if not always, the artist was economically happier with the phototechnologies than he had been with the hand media. With the expense of hand engraving minimized, speedy execution and increasing availability of pictures created a market for more and more illustration. The professional illustrator became a notable figure of American life. No longer merely an adjunct to some wood-engraver's mass-production line, the illustrator was now recognized for himself, just as the Cruikshanks and John Leeches of England who had worked in the autographic etching medium had been appreciated for their particular eccentricities. The illustrator was no longer merely the provider of the visual idea for the technicians to "work up," no longer transfigured by inadequate and arbitrary codes, now more free than at any time in history to be judged for himself. He was not limited to the autographic media such as etching or lithography, in which his hand might have proved inadequate and his vision inappropriate. If he kept within certain limitations of the new media, he could work loosely or tightly, use an impasto which would reproduce, or a thin glaze that might barely, plan for a certain compression of final message which could be produced on a larger scale in his original, and generally operate as a free agent.

Unfortunately, the very facility of the phototechnologies made possible books "illustrated" by publishers rather than by illustrators. While this publisher-illustrated book had been a fact of life since the earliest days of the incunabula (cuts wandered from book to book and from page to page), the new "persona" of the illustrator suffered in the worst of this practice. Illustrations designed for one medium, and successful in that medium in that size, could be cheaply and swiftly reproduced in a greatly reduced size, to fill up the text of a quick trade reissue of a popular magazine tale. The fact that there was now an artist-illustrator's *original* preserved from direct onslaught by the graver presented publishers with carte-blanche use of it in ways not intended by the artist.

The fictive, illusionistic illustrator, aided and abetted by the increasing capacity of the media to transmit his illusions with high fidelity to his original, in any artistic medium, was no less at the mercy of the photo-mechanical engraver than he had been with the hand engraver. An inadequately trained phototechnician could wreak as much havoc on an original as the hand engraver had with his arbitrary codes. An incorrect choice of printing paper or ink still destroyed any chance of proper transmission. Totally extraneous economic considerations, like the price of copperplate or zinc, influenced publication decisions.

Freed in so many ways from the confining codes of the past, the fictive illustrator, desiring complete artistic freedom of expression, was still bound by the technological limitations of each new medium.

PHOTOTECHNOLOGIES AND INFORMATION TRANSFER

In the enormous area of information transfer, or the transmission of "facts," the phototechnologies made a still-underestimated impact on the total culture and on the expectations of transmission fidelity. We have attempted to demonstrate the justice of William Ivins' observations:

> Up to that time very few people had been aware of the difference between pictorial expression and pictorial communication of statements of fact. The profound difference between creating something and making a statement about the quality and character of something had not been perceived.[10]

When we recall that the exactly repeatable visual statement was merely five hundred years old, and that ". . . it was through the engraved picture that the world received its visual notions about most of the things it had not seen and studied with its own eyes — which is to say about most of the things in the world . . ." [11] we begin to understand what an important step in the development of human communications systems this distinction between creation and reporting has become.

That information transfer and artistic creation were distinct processes, and that the subjectivity of an artist's judgment about what to communicate in a given situation was an inevitable distortion of the original message, and that the photographic technologies tended to distort least, was admitted by even so pure an aesthete of the book as Walter Crane. In his influential *The Bases of Design* (1898), Crane prefaced his text with the following:

> It may be noted that I have freely used both line and tone blocks in the text and throughout the book, although I advocate the use of line drawings only with type in books wherein completeness of organic ornamental character is the object. Such a book as this, however, being rather in the nature of a tool or auxiliary to a designer's workshop, can hardly be regarded from that point of view. The scheme of the work, which necessitates the gathering together of so many and varied illustrations as diverse in scale, subject, and treatment as the historic periods which they represent, would itself preclude a consistent decorative treatment, and it has been found necessary to reproduce many of the illustrations from their original form in large scale drawings on brown paper touched with white, as well as from photographs which necessarily print as tone-blocks. [12]

We should recognize that "a consistent decorative treatment" would imply a translation of any original into an artist's view of aesthetic compatability with certain assumptions about flat paper and ink, rather than fidelity transmission of the characteristics of the original. As a designer, Crane was, of course, an advocate of the William Morris school; as a teacher, in the example of his many books on design, he had realized the inappropriate aspects of artistic transmission, and had abandoned subjective or aesthetic considerations in favor of information transfer of a reliable kind. That phototechnology represented a kind of culture shock to someone like Crane is obvious in the emphasis he places on an explanation for a practice — the phototechnological reproduction in his book of photolithographs, "Punch" line drawings, actual blocks which had been electrotyped rather than rephotographed, crayon sketches, and photographs from Nature, all creating a monstrous multimedia menagerie of effects — which he saw in complete conflict with his aesthetic ideals. Obviously, Walter Crane had come to the revolutionary conclusion that it was far more important to transmit accurate information than to adhere strictly to some predetermined aesthetic effect.

William Ivins must have recognized the basic materiality of communication, despite his confusions over it, otherwise it is difficult to see how he could have arrived at any of his conclusions. He said, for example:

> Whatever may be the psychological and physiological processes which we call knowing and thinking, we are only able to communicate the results of that knowing and thinking to other men by using one or another kind of symbolism. [13]

The "symbolism" idea, however, may be confusing to some readers who see "symbolism" as involved in *meanings* rather than in specific structures for the transfer of meanings whose sense is predetermined by cultural ideologies, whether implicit or explicit. What Ivins perhaps should have used here was the word "code." We communicate meanings by transmitting them through culturally approved and acceptable codes, whether these are of speech or of vision. Using the term "code" assists us in recognizing how much of our education and all of our communication depends on the development of codes which permit maximum reliability and where possible, compression of information. We can never forget that the characteristics of a code depend on the physical characteristics of a channel.

> It is doubtful that any much more intricate intellectual process can be imagined than the translation of a linear series of verbal symbols, arranged in an analytical, syntactical time order, into an organization of concrete materials, and shapes, and colours, all existing simultaneously in a three-dimension space. If this is true of such simple abstract forms as those of can-openers, it takes little thought to realize what the situation is in regard to the infinitely complex and accidental shapes that occur in nature and in art.[14]

If *Webster's New International Dictionary* (2nd edition) lists "can opener" as "a special tool for opening cans, or tins," that is a major generalization and provides absolutely no specific information. Even a verbal description of this nature is inadequate to a non-can-opener culture. To a culture which has only baskets, or which opens its plastic envelopes with a laser beam, much more verbal description is needed. Even photographs of various types of can openers will not necessarily convey the total "organization of concrete materials, and shapes, and colours, all existing simultaneously in a three-dimensional space." If we are not in a museum situation and cannot examine a can opener for ourselves, perhaps the closest approximation of the reality of can openers could be conveyed by photography; not *still* photography, but *motion* photography, transmitted by whatever means, is perhaps the only nonduplicative, symbolic—that is, codified—medium which could show us visually what can openers are *in terms of the process they carry out.*

When artists like Frederic Remington attempted to transmit information about horses through the medium of instantaneous photography, they ran the risk of exceeding not only the cultural norms of representation and illusionism, but of physiological norms as well. The "freezing" of action, which Oliver Wendell Holmes had noted in a picture of Broadway at noon, is not a method of conveying "motion." It *locates* an object in motion at a particular moment along the particular trajectory of its motion, but it does not represent "motion," any more than a diagram of a can opener conveys its *function.* Instantaneous photography, now the popular game of sports enthusiasts and reporters who like to catch, say, a basketball player seemingly standing stock still with his feet in the air, has proved to be an enigmatic servant of science, explaining nothing and misrepresenting the world-in-flux as a world-in-stasis. It does not contribute to our understanding of living as a process, but merely isolates the fragments for study; isolating a "moment" for study in the laboratory may prove useful for the rationalizing of scientific knowledge, but scientists recognize today that the laboratory is an artificial environment which contaminates and distorts the object studied.

For all its subliminal codes, and increasing compression of information, the photograph, as Ivins described it, has serious drawbacks. Some of these are recognized in our space program, for the astronauts used stereoscopic photography rather than single-focal-plane photography, wherever possible, just as they use motion photography, rather than still photography when they can. However much an advance they may be over hand-engraved, subjectively codified informational pictures, the flat-plane photograph and even the stereographic picture still represent communications limitations which we may hopefully surpass. The science of holography would seem to be leading us in a three-dimensional direction, and it is only for maximum illusionism which transmits as many of the characteristics of Nature that we need to go that way.

When the daguerreotype astonished the world with its minute and accurate detail, a pathway had been established for the further pursuit of physicochemical transformations of light-sensitive materials. The paper photograph, the "permanent photograph" in printer's ink, the heliotype, photogravure, process line and halftone, and color codes, all of these represent a continuing—not a completed—search for the perfection of media to transmit information. William Ivins believed,

> The seriousness of the role of the exactly repeatable pictorial statement in all the long development since about 1450 has escaped attention very largely because the statement has been so familiar that it has never been subjected to adequate analysis. Having been taken for granted it has been overlooked. The photograph, as of today, is the final form of that exactly repeatable pictorial statement or report.[15]

Fortunately, he qualified his last statement: *as of today.* It is, therefore, no "final" form.

Because it is not final does not mean that we should ignore the photograph. On the contrary, it has had such a profound effect on our lives just because it has been regarded as some kind of miraculous final form of "truth." That this is a serious danger has not been mitigated by the arrival of television, for, as Ivins was one of the most anxious to point out, ". . . at any given moment the accepted report of an event is of greater importance than the event, for what we think about and act upon is the symbolic report and not the concrete event itself."[16]

GENERAL IMPLICATIONS

If it is true that what we think about and act upon are "symbolic reports" (in our terms, codified transmissions of messages about originals), rather than "concrete events" (in our terms, originals in Nature), then the importance of studying the nature of visual codifications of information can hardly be overestimated. Obviously, both *words* and *pictures* are "symbolic reports"; both stand for, but do not replicate or duplicate "concrete events." It is only recently that the coding aspects of visual symbols have begun to be investigated, with perhaps the contributions of Rudolf Arnheim in *Visual Thinking* (London: Faber & Faber, 1969) as most important and worth much further exploration. But we should give honor where honor is due: to Marshall McLuhan. For whether or not we respect his oracular style, it is difficult to avoid paying homage to someone who has attempted to awaken us from an unconscious acceptance of messages as identical with originals. He has perhaps done more than anyone else to stimulate interdisciplinary interest in media research.

It seems almost inconceivable that McLuhan's observation that "the medium is the message" is still rejected without inspection by individuals who may not even accept the simpler concept, that the medium is a message. At the very least, this book should have helped to demonstrate that *the medium can interfere so seriously with the message that the only message which is transmitted is that of the medium itself.* Information theory simplifies our understanding of this phenomenon. If a medium can constitute a message, even on the most trivial level of "noise," then further investigation of McLuhan's seemingly extremist statement can be justified.

When McLuhan puns at his readers, saying "the medium is the *Massage*," [17] rather than the *message,* he is trying to emphasize the impact of *the message of the medium* as apart from the meanings which the medium transmits, as these meanings exist prior to and outside the particular transmission of a message. When we want to receive correct information about original events, perhaps for the urgent purpose of decision-making, presumably we need to receive such information without being manipulated by the characteristics of a medium. Yet we cannot receive *any* information about originals without the intervention of a channel and a code. *Therefore we are inevitably manipulated by the characteristics of media.*

If our expectations concerning "truth" and "reality" have been conditioned along certain lines by our having accepted the characteristics of a specific medium as the model for thought, we may lessen our general ability to differentiate between "reality" and communications codes. We may lose the ability to respond directly to original events. Conversely, we become conditioned to expect certain characteristics of communications media to occur in "Nature." Thus, television, for example, presents several interesting paradoxes. On the one hand, if life is process, and if, even as we blink, our own electrons are shifting and our planet hurtles a thousand miles through the sky, then perhaps the constant barrage of shifting images from television (and film) are increasing our ability to comprehend *flux,* and to rid ourselves of any lingering notions of *fixity.* On the other hand, there seems to be serious evidence that these media may be conditioning us to expect, want, and seek *only* flux, to expect, want, and seek *only* constant stimulation.

Speculation along these behavioral lines is receiving increasing attention from social scientists, in particular, social psychologists. Applications of information theory and less mechanistic adaptations of such theory can perhaps make their greatest contribution through the resolution of some age-old semantic difficulties, especially in the areas of aesthetics and art history and in any discussion of older ideas of *form* and *content.* Perhaps the greatest hope for assistance in investigating and understanding the complex interconnections between our techniques and our societies would be the legitimation of Media Analysis as an interdisciplinary focus for the study of the technologies of culture. Such a focus may be needed to establish the study of visual information on a par with the verbal.

Notes

INTRODUCTION

1. Victor Strauss, *The Printing Industry* (Washington, D.C.: Printing Industries of America, 1967), p. 13.
2. William M. Ivins, Jr., *Prints and Visual Communication* (Cambridge, Mass.: Harvard University Press, 1953), p. 180.
3. Abraham Moles, *Information Theory and Esthetic Perception;* trans. by Joel E. Cohen (Urbana, Ill.: University of Illinois Press, 1968), p. 197.
4. Ivins, *op. cit.,* p. 136.
5. Access to the stacks of Columbia University Libraries, the New York Public Library, the Free Library of Philadelphia, and the Wilmington Public Library, revealed that there are more books extant in connection with the two expositions than can be discovered through the Library of Congress or any other bibliographical source.
6. Strauss, *op. cit.,* pp. 13–14.

CHAPTER 1

1. Jagjit Singh, *Great Ideas in Information Theory, Language and Cybernetics* (New York: Dover, 1966), p. 29.
2. Marshall McLuhan, *Understanding Media: The Extensions of Man* (New York: McGraw-Hill, 1964), p. 190.
3. William M. Ivins, Jr., *Prints and Visual Communication* (Cambridge, Mass.: Harvard University Press, 1953), p. vii.
4. *Ibid.,* p. 1.
5. *Ibid.,* p. 3.
6. *Ibid.*
7. George Iles, *Flame, Electricity and the Camera,* deluxe edition (New York: J. A. Hill, 1904), p. 265.
8. *Ibid.,* p. 267.
9. *Ibid.,* p. 273.
10. Ivins, *op. cit.,* p. 3.
11. *Ibid.,* p. 122.
12. *Ibid.,* heading of Chapter VI: "Pictorial statement without syntax; the nineteenth century," p. 113.
13. *Ibid.,* p. 128.
14. *Ibid.*
15. *Ibid.*
16. Abraham Moles, *Information Theory and Esthetic Perception;* trans. by Joel E. Cohen (Urbana, Ill.: University of Illinois Press, 1968), p. 200. Moles is here primarily concerned with perceptions of originality and banality in music, using Shannon's statistical approach, but he recognized the validity of his theories in the visual field as well.
17. Ivins, *op. cit.,* p. 177.

18. Moles, *op. cit.,* p. 79.
19. Ivins, *op. cit.,* p. 177.
20. *Ibid.,* p. 133.
21. *Ibid.,* p. 126.
22. *Ibid.,* p. vii.
23. Moles, *op. cit.,* p. 192.

CHAPTER 2

1. Philip Gilbert Hamerton, *The Graphic Arts* . . . (London: Seeley, Jackson & Halliday, 1882), p. 1.
2. Lack of visual education or awareness may be the primary cause of some apparent difficulties which prevent many individuals from recognizing even the concept of "visual languages." The subject of representation is complex. Any image on the retina, for example, is actually quite small when compared to either original natural objects or representations of them.
3. James J. Gibson, *The Perception of the Visual World* (Boston: Houghton Mifflin, 1950), p. 77.
4. *Ibid.,* p. 78.
5. *Ibid.,* p. 85.
6. *Ibid.,* p. 92.
7. *Ibid.,* p. 94.
8. Gibson further notes that "The order of shading is a stimulus for depth . . . only in relation to the orientation of the observer to his total visual world." *op. cit.,* p. 98.
9. Gibson, *op. cit.,* p. 99.
10. The creative artists who were engaged in direct artistic expression through printmaking were not concerned with the mass medium of the book. Those creative artists who drew specifically for the mass reproduction media were perforce less concerned with the autographic freedom of their printmaking colleagues than with the hard economic facts of paper, ink, and press runs; they became, therefore, a subservient class whose imagination was literally at the mercy of the publishing technicians, the hand engravers. Even when the illustrator learned to make symbolic statements suited to the limitations of a specific medium, he was still at the mercy of the duplicative skills of the hand engraver.
11. See Chapter VIII of E. H. Gombrich's *Art and Illusion: A Study in the Psychology of Pictorial Representation,* 2nd ed. rev. Bollingen Series XXXV-5 (Princeton, N.J.: Princeton University Press, 1969).
12. Hamerton, *op. cit.,* p. 5.
13. We must emphasize that our formulation for the idea of *illusion* in a medium is its potentiality for the successful imitation of the texture gradients, chiaroscuro, modulations of surface and contour which characterize our visual world.
14. By an irony which tends to corroborate many of Ivins' basic hypotheses, it is phototechnology which here makes it possible to duplicate, however imperfectly, the original effect of ink on paper in reproducing the original illustrations.
15. Hennessy was described as an industrious illustrator specializing in sentimental genre scenes; see Henry T. Tuckerman, *Book of the Artists* (New York: Carr, 1966; originally published 1867), pp. 453–454.
16. William M. Ivins, Jr., *Prints and Visual Communication* (Cambridge, Mass.: Harvard University Press, 1953), p. 44.

17. *Ibid.,* p. 60.
18. *Ibid.*
19. Frank Weitenkampf, *American Graphic Art* (New York: Holt, 1912), p. 107.
20. Frank Weitenkampf, *How to Appreciate Prints,* 3rd, rev. ed. (New York: Scribner, 1927), p. 94.
21. *Ibid.,* p. 95.
22. Weitenkampf, *American Graphic Art,* p. 107.
23. Elbridge Kingsley, "Originality in Wood-Engraving," *Century Magazine* 38 (August 1889): 578.
24. Television manufacturers may recognize this relationship but we have found no previous statement which applies specifically to the graphic arts.
25. William M. Ivins, Jr., *How Prints Look* (Boston: Beacon Press, 1958), p. 148.
26. Note how this closely approximates our discussion of James Gibson's "textural gradients" and the perspective of textures.
27. Charles Blanc, *The Grammar of Painting and Engraving;* translated from the French of Blanc's *Grammaire des arts du dessin* by Kate Newell Doggett, with the original illustrations (New York: Hurd and Houghton, 1874), pp. 248–249.
28. John Whitfield Harland, *The Printing Arts* (New York: Ward Lock Bowden, 1892), p. 60.
29. *Ibid.,* p. 63.
30. *Ibid.,* p. 73.
31. Often incorrectly called stipple engraving.
32. Weitenkampf, *How to Appreciate Prints,* p. 149.
33. *Ibid.,* p. 157.
34. Ivins, *How Prints Look,* p. 144.
35. E. S. Lumsden, *The Art of Etching* (New York: Dover, 1962, 1924), p. 24.
36. Blanc, *op. cit.,* pp. 273–274.
37. John Mollett, *Etched Examples of Paintings Old and New* (London: n.p., 1885), p. 26.
38. Ivins, *Prints and Visual Communication,* p. 180.
39. Philip Gilbert Hamerton, *Etching and Etchers* (London: Macmillan, 1880), p. 15.
40. Frank Mather, ed., *The American Spirit in Art, The Pageant of America,* vol. 12 (New Haven, Conn.: Yale University Press, 1927), p. 225.
41. Weitenkampf, *How to Appreciate Prints,* p. 132.
42. *Ibid.*
43. *Ibid.*
44. Weitenkampf, *American Graphic Art,* p. 128.
45. Mather, *op. cit.,* p. 240.
46. Wilhelm Weber, *A History of Lithography* (New York: McGraw-Hill, 1966), p. 17. Rudolf Mayer, quoted on this same page, offers a molecular explanation of the process.
47. Robert Routledge, *Discoveries and Inventions of the 19th Century,* new ed. rev. (London and New York: Routledge, 1876), p. 465.
48. *Ibid.*
49. Joseph Pennell, *Lithography and Lithographers* (London: Unwin, 1898), p. 260. "Formerly, steel-engravings and etching for a large edition were transferred to lithographic stones, when they could be printed far more rapidly, though they lost their character. . . . Much of the work of Cruikshank and 'Phiz' was printed in this way for the books

they illustrated." It was not only speed which was valued by the publishers, however, but the cheaper paper which the planographic process of lithography permitted them to use.

50. Weber, *op. cit.,* p. 30.
51. *Ibid.,* p. 65.
52. Mather, *op. cit.,* p. 242.
53. Weitenkampf, *American Graphic Art,* pp. 195–196.
54. Chapter title for Chapter V of Ivins, *Prints and Visual Communication,* p. 93.
55. Ivins, *Prints and Visual Communication,* pp. 110–111.

CHAPTER 3

1. Philip Gilbert Hamerton, *Thoughts About Art,* a new edition, rev. by the author (Boston: Roberts, 1871), p. 114.
2. William M. Ivins, Jr., *Prints and Visual Communication* (Cambridge, Mass.: Harvard University Press, 1953), p. 94.
3. See note 1.
4. David Bland, *A History of Book Illustration,* 1st ed. (Cleveland: World, 1958), p. 209. See also p. 212: "Illustrations during this century were distinguished from prints by imitation picture frames." Obviously, the print for the real wall would receive a real frame; in a book, the picture was made ornamental by receiving a printed imitation frame.
5. Alfred T. Story, *The Story of Photography* (New York: University Society, 1909), p. 32.
6. Helmut Gernsheim, *The History of Photography* . . . (London: Oxford University Press, 1955), p. 36.
7. Lithography was first called *Polyautography,* or the means whereby "the artist is sure of a perfect autographic multiplication of his design, without the intervention of an engraver." From Joseph Pennell, *Lithography and Lithographers* (London: Unwin, 1898), p. 54.
8. This can be clearly observed with the television medium as well, where the primary content is the earlier medium, film.
9. Pennell, *op. cit.,* p. 54.
10. Story, *op. cit.,* p. 39.
11. From a letter by Morse dated March 9, 1839; quoted in Beaumont Newhall, *The Daguerreotype in America,* 1st ed. (New York: Duell, Sloan & Pearce, 1961), p. 15.
12. *Phototyp nach der Erfindung des Prof. Berres in Wien* (1840), an edition of 200, illustrated with five plates. See Gernsheim, *History of Photography,* p. 358.
13. Published jointly by the optician, Lerebours, and three others, in 1841–1842, *Excursions daguerriennes* represents the swift exploitation of a new medium made available to a group of artists who consented to travel primarily for the purpose of capturing "views."
14. Josef M. Eder, *History of Photography,* trans. by Edward Epstean (New York: Columbia University Press, 1945), p. 578.
15. The instrument continues in use by artists today for enlarging or reducing art to be copied.
16. Gernsheim, *op. cit.,* p. 61.
17. This point can be disputed by those who argue that the widespread sale of printed playing cards or individual prints preceded the use of pictures in books. The chronology is moot.
18. Niépce had failed to capture an image in less than eight hours of

exposure time. Daguerre's great contribution was that he discovered that a short exposure could capture a latent image which would respond to later development in further chemical manipulation.

19. Gernsheim, *op. cit.*, p. 62. The first surviving photograph was taken by Niépce in 1826.

20. Daguerre knew that patenting his invention would be useless. To publish such a process would be, in effect, permitting its use, as he saw it. The French government's hand was forced by the catastrophic burning of the Diorama—Daguerre's livelihood—on the very afternoon when Samuel F. B. Morse was visiting Daguerre, who lost everything but a few plates and his chemicals.

21. To all intents and purposes, Talbot's restrictions and the lack of a guaranteed permanent paper process delayed American use of paper until the 1850s.

22. Gernsheim, *op. cit.*, p. 64.

23. As for the question of "first," see Vernon Snow's article in the *Times Literary Supplement,* Thursday, December 23, 1965, "The First Photographically-Illustrated Book," for comments on a small commemorative volume preceding Talbot's *Pencil of Nature,* which Talbot's own workshop produced for John Walter III.

24. Gernsheim, *op. cit.*, p. 127.

25. John W. Harland, *The Printing Arts* (New York: Ward Lock Bowden, 1892), p. 119.

26. Gernsheim, *op. cit.*, p. 127.

27. Photogenic, as distinct from photographic, illustrations are the result of a process whereby objects are placed directly on prepared light-sensitive paper and their silhouettes captured by exposing them to light. In the twentieth century, the Surrealist Man Ray revived this process for his Photograms.

28. Gernsheim, *op. cit.*, see reproduced advertisement, p. 125.

29. The copy of *The Pencil of Nature* owned by the New York Public Library Rare Books Division, for example, is badly yellowed, and every exposure to the sulfur dioxide of city air assists in its further decay.

30. According to Dr. R. S. Schultze, of Harrow, who is mentioned in Vernon Snow's "The First Photographically-Illustrated Book" (see note 23 above).

31. Gernsheim, *op. cit.*, p. 367.

32. Stephen H. Horgan, *Horgan's Half-tone and Photomechanical Processes* (Chicago: Inland Printer, 1911), p. 41.

33. Gernsheim, *op. cit.*, p. 368.

34. Boston, Museum of Fine Arts. Print Dept. *Exhibition Illustrating the Technical Methods of the Reproductive Arts . . . With Special Reference to the Photo-Mechanical Processes; January 8 to March 6, 1892* (Boston: Mudge, 1892), p. 85.

35. Horgan, *op. cit.*, p. 47.

36. *Encyclopaedia Britannica,* 11th ed. (1911), vol. 22, p. 412.

37. Horgan, *op. cit.*, p. 47.

38. Gernsheim, *History of Photography,* p. 363.

39. *Ibid.*, p. 277.

40. *Ibid.* The woodburytype was invented by the Englishman Walter Bentley Woodbury (1834–1885), who patented it in September of 1864.

41. Henry B. Wheatley, ed., *Modern Methods of Illustrating Books* (London: Stock, 1887), p. 46.

42. S. R. Koehler, "The Photomechanical Process," *Technology Quarterly* 5 (October 1892): 196.
43. Robert Taft, *Photography and the American Scene . . .* (New York: Dover, 1964), p. 422.
44. *Ibid.*
45. Elbridge Kingsley, unpublished autobiography (Northampton, Mass.: Forbes Library), from the typescript, p. 87.
46. Ivins, *op. cit.,* p. 136.
47. W. J. Linton, *The History of Wood-Engraving in America* (London: Bell, 1882), p. 51.
48. Item in *Scribner's Monthly* 15 (April 1878): 891.
49. J. Comyns Carr, *Book Illustration, Old and New* (London: Trounce, 1882; Cantor Lectures, Society for the Encouragement of Arts, Manufactures, and Commerce, delivered before the Society of Arts, May 1882), p. 17.
50. R. R. Bowker, "A Printed Book," *Harper's Monthly,* July 1887, p. 184. This is the best source for a description of the first Ives patent.
51. *Ibid.*
52. Harland, *op. cit.,* p. 61.
53. Oliver Wendell Holmes, *Soundings from the Atlantic* (Boston: Ticknor & Fields, 1864), p. 172. This was originally published in the *Atlantic* in the article "Sun-Painting and Sun-Sculpture."
54. Bland, *op. cit.,* p. 250.
55. Typical examples are in the books by Benson J. Lossing, e.g., *The Pictorial Field-Book of the War of 1812* (New York: Harper, 1869).
56. Charles Blanc, *The Grammar of Painting and Engraving* (New York: Hurd and Houghton, 1874), p. 306.
57. *The Chromolithograph; A Journal of Art, Decoration, and the Accomplishments with which it Incorporated "Nature and Art"* (London: Zorn, 1868; 2 vols.), vol. 1, December 28, 1867, p. 91.
58. *The Chromolithograph, loc. cit.*
59. R. M. Burch, *Colour Printing and Colour Printers* (New York: Baker and Taylor, 1912), p. 118.
60. Harland, *op. cit.,* p. 78.
61. Burch, *op. cit.,* p. 222.
62. Horgan, *op. cit.,* p. 112.
63. Burch, *op. cit.,* p. 232.
64. *Ibid.,* p. 233.
65. Horgan, *op. cit.,* p. 113.
66. Burch, *op. cit.,* p. 255.
67. See the back cover of Part I, *The Art of the World,* cited in the text.
68. The notorious inadequacies of the cheap lens used by Mrs. Julia Cameron, which sometimes promoted genius and other times obliterated everything with the "blur beautiful," may have stimulated the movement toward imprecision of focus. The controversy was furthered by P. H. Emerson in *Naturalistic Photography* (1889).
69. Ivins, *op. cit.,* p. 128.
70. *Ibid.,* p. 177.
71. *Ibid.*

CHAPTER 4

1. Comment by the "Scientist" in Philip Gilbert Hamerton's dialogue on "Book Illustration," in his *Portfolio Papers* (Boston: Roberts, 1889), p. 357.

2. Comment by "an Illustrator" in F. Hopkinson Smith's imaginary dialogues in *American Illustrators* (New York: Scribner, 1892), part I, p. 8.

3. Quoted in William M. Ivins, Jr., *Prints and Visual Communication* (Cambridge, Mass.: Harvard University Press, 1953), p. 122.

4. *Ibid.*

5. For discussions of the photographic impulse in Western art, and of the takeover by photography of representationalism, see *Dutch Painting* by R. H. Wilenski (New York: Beechhurst Press, 1955), and the Elizabeth Lindquist-Cock and George Ehrlich theses cited in the Bibliography.

6. Ivins, *op. cit.*, p. 136.

7. Eugene Exman, *The House of Harper*, 1st ed. (New York: Harper, 1967), p. 28.

8. Quoted in Beaumont Newhall, *The Daguerreotype in America*, 1st ed. (New York: Duell, Sloan & Pearce, 1961), p. 74. See also John L. Stephens, *Incidents of Travel in Yucatán*, illustrated by 120 engravings (New York: Harper, 1843), vol. I, p. 174: "Mr. Catherwood . . . made all his drawings with the camera lucida, for the purpose of obtaining the utmost accuracy of proportion and detail. Besides which, we had with us a Daguerreotype apparatus, the best that could be procured in New York."

9. Victor Wolfgang Von Hagen. *Maya Explorer: John Lloyd Stephens and the Lost Cities of Central America and Yucatan* (Norman, Okla.: University of Oklahoma Press, 1947), p. 259.

10. *Ibid.*, p. 26.

11. Presently at the Massachusetts Institute of Technology.

12. Gyorgy Kepes, ed. *Education of Vision* (New York: Braziller, 1965), p. ii. From his own introduction to the book.

13. Ivins, *op. cit.*, p. 44.

14. *Encyclopedia of World Art* (New York: McGraw-Hill, 1959–1969); vol. I, p. 289.

15. Helmut Lehmann-Haupt, "English Illustrators in the Collection of George Arents," *Colophon*, New Graphic Series, no. 4, vol. I, 1940; n.p.

16. *Ibid.*

17. Theodore Bolton, *American Book Illustrators: Bibliographic Check Lists of 123 Artists* (New York: Bowker, 1938), p. 45.

18. *Ibid.*

19. Walter Montgomery, *American Art and American Art Collections* (Boston: Walker, 1889), title page.

20. Frank Weitenkampf, *American Graphic Art* (New York: Holt, 1912), p. 101.

21. *Ibid.*, p. 147.

22. Joseph Pennell, *Pen Drawing and Pen Draughtsmen* (London: Macmillan, 1889), p. 301.

23. W. A. Rogers, *A World Worth-While* (New York: Harper, 1922), p. 14.

24. *Ibid.*, p. 15.

25. Elbridge Kingsley, unpublished autobiography (Northampton, Mass.: Forbes Library), from the typescript, p. 87.

26. *Ibid.*, p. 192.

27. Miscellaneous item in *Printers' Circular* 3 (December 1868): 301.

28. Kingsley, *op. cit.*, p. 87.

29. J. Comyns Carr, *Book Illustration, Old and New* (London: Trounce, 1882), p. 21.

30. F. Hopkinson Smith, *American Illustrators* (New York: Scribner, 1892), vol. I, p. 10.
31. *Ibid.*
32. Review of "Holiday Books," *Atlantic Monthly* 67 (January 1891): 121.
33. John W. Harland, *The Printing Arts* (New York: Ward Lock Bowden, 1892), p. 81.
34. Quoted in Carl Weber, *The Rise and Fall of James Ripley Osgood; A Biography* (Waterville, Maine: Colby College Press, 1959), p. 243.
35. Weitenkampf, *American Graphic Art*, p. 229.
36. Quoted in Carl Weber, *op. cit.*, p. 221.
37. Charles G. Harper, *A Practical Handbook of Drawing for Modern Methods of Reproduction* . . . 2nd ed., rev. (London: Chapman & Hall, 1901), p. 9.
38. *Ibid.*, p. 10.
39. *Ibid.*, pp. 10–11. This condition prevails even today.
40. Exman, *op. cit.*, p. 111.
41. Joseph Pennell, *The Illustration of Books: A Manual for the Use of Students; Notes for a Course of Lectures at the Slade School, University College* (New York: Century, 1896), pp. 82–83.
42. *Ibid.*, p. 85.
43. *Ibid.*, pp. 87–88.
44. *Catalogue of the Works of Elbridge Kingsley* . . . Compiled & Arranged for Mt. Holyoke College, 1910. Both Mount Holyoke College and the Forbes Library of Northampton, Mass., have complete sets of Japan proofs and other memorabilia of Kingsley, including his experiments with making his own process halftone blocks and his color experiments.
45. See note 32.
46. Théophile Gautier, a famous French critic, quoted in Albert Ten Eyck Gardner, *Winslow Homer: American Artist* . . . (New York: Bramhall House, 1961), pp. 167–168.
47. *Ibid.*, pp. 184–185.
48. See note 32.
49. See note 32; p. 122.
50. See note 32; p. 123.
51. Ibid.
52. See note 32; p. 122.
53. Walter Crane, *Of the Decorative Illustration of Books Old and New* (London: Bell, 1896), p. 178.
54. See note 12.
55. Richard P. Wunder, "18th and 19th-Century Paintings in the National Collection of Fine Arts," in *Highlights of the National Collection of Fine Arts* (Washington, D.C.: Smithsonian Institution Press, 1968), p. 27.
56. Victor Strauss, *The Printing Industry* (Washington, D.C.: Printing Industries of America), p. 13.
57. Stephen Horgan, *Horgan's Half-Tone and Photomechanical Processes* (Chicago: Inland Printer Co., 1911), p. 111.
58. R. G. Hunt, *The Reproduction of Colour* (London: Fountain Press, 1957), p. 15.
59. Horgan, *op. cit.*, p. 112.
60. Patricia Sloane, *Colour . . . Basic Principles, New Directions* (London: Studio Vista, 1968), p. 29.
61. R. M. Burch, *Colour Printing and Colour Printers* (New York: Baker and Taylor, 1912), p. 261.
62. There was an entrepreneur recently who planned to market color reproductions of paintings made by some sort of mold impression

taken from the originals, then printed; thus, the problem has never, and probably can never, be fully solved to everyone's satisfaction.

63. Joseph Pennell, *Modern Illustration* (London: Bell, 1895), pp. 33–34.

64. *Ibid.*, p. 34.

65. *Ibid.*

66. Joseph Pennell, *The Graphic Arts: Modern Men and Modern Methods* (The Scammon Lectures for 1920. Published for the Art Institute of Chicago by the University of Chicago Press, 1921), p. 130.

67. *Ibid.*

68. *Ibid.*, p. 131.

69. *Ibid.*, p. 132.

70. A. C. Austin, *Practical Half-Tone and Tri-Color Engraving* (Buffalo, N.Y.: Professional Photographer Publishing Co., 1898), pp. 59–60.

71. Royal Cortissoz, "Frederic Remington: A Painter of American Life," *Scribner's Magazine* 47 (Feb. 1910): 184. Remington is used here as an example because the chapter devoted to him concentrates largely on other problems of his work.

72. Charles Harper, *op. cit.*, p. 2.

73. *Ibid.*

74. Philip Gilbert Hamerton, "Notes on Aesthetics," in his *Portfolio Papers* (Boston: Roberts, 1889), p. 223.

75. Ivins, *op. cit.*, p. 164.

76. Joseph Pennell, *op. cit.*, p. 19.

77. See note 75; p. 165.

CHAPTER 5

1. Boston, Museum of Fine Arts, Print Dept. *Exhibition Illustrating the Technical Methods of the Reproductive Arts from the XV Century to the Present Time, with Special Reference to the Photo-Mechanical Processes;* January 8 to March 6, 1892 (Boston: Mudge, 1892), p. 53.

2. Remarks of George Hawling, in *Report of the Private View of the Exhibition of Works by Howard Pyle at the Art Alliance* (Philadelphia: January 22, 1923), n.p. Limited edition of 25 copies, available at the Wilmington Society of the Fine Arts.

3. Letter of Pyle to his mother, quoted in Charles Abbott, *Howard Pyle, A Chronicle* (New York: Harper, 1925), p. 23.

4. Letter of Pyle to his mother, dated Nov. 18, 1876; quoted in Abbott, *op. cit.*, p. 26.

5. Benson J. Lossing, in his "The Graphic Arts," *Scribner's,* May 1871– Oct. 1872 volume, p. 413, commented on the early success of the actinic process, seeing any mechanical process as destined to supersede wood engraving: "because cheaper, and allowing the plates to be printed typographically. . . . More recently the Photograph has been employed for the same purpose; and what is called 'Actinic-Engraving,' or Photo-Engraving by the 'Moss Process' has apparently more nearly approached the desired goal than any other similar method. It reproduces upon metal plates an exact representation of all kinds of pictorial work, done in lines or dots."

6. Letter of Pyle to his mother, Dec. 15, 1876; quoted in Abbott, *op. cit.*, p. 41.

7. Abbott, *op. cit.*, p. 15.

8. Letter of Pyle to his mother, quoted in Abbott, *op. cit.*, p. 48.

9. Abbott, *op. cit.*, p. 88.

10. *Ibid.*

11. Charles Blanc, *The Grammar of Painting and Engraving,* translated from the French of Blanc's *Grammaire des arts du dessin* by Kate Newell Doggett; with the original illustrations (New York: Hurd and Houghton, 1874), p. 307.
12. See especially the plates for "Judith," "Rachel," and "Leah."
13. Abbott, *op. cit.,* p. 88.
14. Willard Morse and Gertrude Brinckle, compilers, *Howard Pyle, A Record of His Illustrations and Writings* (Wilmington, Del.: Wilmington Society of the Fine Arts, 1921) offers such misleading or inadequate information about methods of reproduction that it deserves to be redone from scratch.
15. See Joseph Pennell, *Pen-Drawing and Pen-Draughtsmen* (London: Macmillan, 1889), p. 92.
16. Quoted in Abbott, *op. cit.,* p. 118.
17. *Ibid.*
18. Many of these are on view at the Willard Morse Collection of Pyle at the Wilmington Society of the Fine Arts.
19. Arthur M. Hind, ed. *Albrecht Dürer: His Engravings and Woodcuts* (New York: Stokes, n.d.), p. 7.
20. Pyle's "The Emperor Commodus," a wood engraving which first appeared in the size reproduced herein *Wide Awake* (May 1886); then it was used for Elbridge S. Brooks' *Storied Holidays* (Boston: Lothrop, 1887) and it is here reproduced from C. Thaxter, *Verses* (Lothrop, 1891); it was then reused for another Brooks' work in 1895, *Great Men's Sons.* Are we to consider that Pyle "illustrated" these books?
21. The plates were used afterwards for Mary E. Burt's *Odysseus* (New York: Scribner, 1898). The originals have not been located as yet, if they still exist.
22. Copper remained the primary material for process halftone work of fine screen; zinc is used for coarser screens and for pure line work.
23. Letter in this writer's possession, by courtesy of the granddaughter of Lindsay, Mrs. Margaret Van Brunt, of Wilmington.
24. This second letter is still owned by Mrs. Van Brunt.
25. From a letter owned by Mrs. Margaret Van Brunt.
26. Quoted in Abbott, *op. cit.,* p. 121.
27. From a letter owned by Mrs. Van Brunt.
28. This kind of plate, common today, is called a combination plate, and may literally be made of two sections of different metal, zinc for line, copper for screen.
29. Available at the Wilmington Society of Fine Arts.
30. In the original, this sentence is in upper and lower case, but is twice underscored; therefore the liberty was taken to put it in capitals.
31. These notes are on a proof sheet mounted into a study scrapbook at the Wilmington Society of the Fine Arts
32. One of Pyle's illustrations for Woodrow Wilson's *George Washington* (New York: Harper, 1897) elicited from the then Princeton professor what was probably a supreme compliment: "it reminds one, in its subtle touches of character, of Gérôme." Letter quoted in Abbott, *op. cit.,* p. 159.
33. Plate was retouched rather poorly by some photoengraver who scraped out a few highlights (the earring, collar, etc.) and who seems to have run a roulette rather haphazardly over the foreground to liven the screen. See the discussion of the illustrations for *Hugh Wynne,* for more concerning this method.

34. Thomas A. Janvier, "The Evolution of New York," *Harper's New Monthly Magazine* (June 15, 1893).

35. Letter owned by Mrs. Margaret Van Brunt.

36. Introduction to Abbott, *op. cit.,* p. xiv.

37. An oil painting at the Wilmington Society of the Fine Arts, in which Pyle uses red and black despite the fact that red registers as black in most phototechnologies, even with color-corrected film. The blood running down the gladiator's raised arm is in red in the original, of course, but once it was translated into the black of ink it became somewhat difficult to interpret in this small size.

38. Original panels owned by the Wilmington Society of the Fine Arts; the comment was written into one of Pyle's scrapbooks on a reproduction.

39. Abbott, *op. cit.,* p. 122.

40. At the Wilmington Society of the Fine Arts.

41. Letter to Stanley Arthurs, quoted in Abbott, *op. cit.,* p. 244.

42. Letter to Ethel Penniwell Brown, quoted in Abbott, *op. cit.,* pp. 242–243.

43. André Malraux, *Museum without Walls,* translated from the French by Stuart Gilbert and Francis Price (Garden City: Doubleday, 1967), pp. 11–12.

CHAPTER 6

1. Quotation from a letter by Gibson in answer to a criticism that he was "not being truthful," in John Coleman Adams, *William Hamilton Gibson: Artist — Naturalist — Author* (New York: Putnam, 1901), p. 223.

2. From the title page of Gibson's *Highways and Byways in New England* (New York: Harper, 1882).

3. John Coleman Adams, "William Hamilton Gibson," *New England Magazine* (new series) 15 (February 1897): 643.

4. *Ibid.,* p. 650.

5. John Anderson and Stearns Morse, *The Book of the White Mountains* (New York: Minton, Balch & Co., 1930), p. 49.

6. Thomas Starr King, *The White Hills: Their Legends, Landscape and Poetry* (Boston: Crosby and Nichols, 1864). The sixty illustrations were "engraved by Andrew from drawings by Wheelock."

7. Thomas Starr King, *The White Hills* (Boston: Estes and Lauriat, 1887). Illustrated with eleven photogravures and sixty woodcuts.

8. The writer is indebted to Professor Elizabeth Lindquist-Cock for her prior and extensive work on the use by Thomas Moran of stereographs for his graphic work and magazine illustration.

9. From Samuel Adams Drake, *The Heart of the White Mountains: Their Legends and Scenery* (New York: Harper, 1882).

10. Adams, *op. cit.,* p. 55.

11. Anderson and Morse, *op. cit.,* p. 41.

12. *Ibid.,* p. 40.

13. *Ibid.*

14. Quoted in Adams: *op. cit.* in note 1, page 57.

15. Adams, obituary article on Gibson, *op. cit.* in note 3 above, p. 650.

16. See "Wood-Engraving and the 'Scribner' Prizes," in *Scribner's Magazine* 21 (April 1881): 937–945.

17. Elbridge Kingsley, unpublished autobiography (Northampton, Mass.: Forbes Library), from the typescript, p. 89.

18. *Ibid.*

19. William J. Linton, *The History of Wood-Engraving in America* (London:

Bell, 1882), p. 50. Linton's book reproduced one of the crayon portraits rendered by Cole as well as the Modjeska; see plates bound between pages 50 and 51.

20. "A Symposium of Wood-Engravers," *Harper's New Monthly Magazine* (February 1880), p. 447.

21. Remarks of A. V. S. Anthony in "A Symposium," *op. cit.* in note 20, p. 443.

22. *Ibid.*

23. *Ibid.*, p. 444.

24. Remarks of Timothy Cole in "A Symposium," *op. cit.* in note 20, p. 446.

25. *Ibid.*

26. It is sometimes difficult to understand Pyle's complaints. In the same issues of *Harper's New Monthly Magazine* in which Gibson was making his reputation, Pyle appears handsomely reproduced; see April and May issues, 1880, vol. 60. Perhaps his real complaints should have been directed at *Harper's Weekly*, where the demands of printing made a coarse, heavy-handed reproduction mandatory.

27. Quoted by Barnet Phillips in his obituary introduction to Gibson's *Eye Spy* (New York: Harper, 1897), p. xiv. The Harris book was published in Boston by Crosby and Nichols.

28. Linton, *op. cit.*, p. 34.

29. See Robert Taft, *Photography and the American Scene*, and the Lindquist-Cock Ph.D. thesis cited in the Bibliography for an excellent presentation of the background of railroad exploration and its relationship to the graphic arts of the late nineteenth century.

30. Introduction to William Cullen Bryant, ed., *Picturesque America* (New York: Appleton, 1872–1873), vol. 1, p. iv.

31. Remarks of Henry Wolf in "A Symposium," *op. cit.* in note 20, p. 453.

32. *Ibid.*

33. Remarks of John Tinkey in "A Symposium," *op. cit.* in note 20, p. 451.

34. *Ibid.*

35. *Ibid.*

36. Remarks of Richard A. Muller in "A Symposium," *op. cit.* in note 20, p. 450.

37. *Ibid.*

38. Adams, *op. cit.*, p. 51.

39. Quoted from the memoirs of Roe by Adams: *op. cit.* in note 38, p. 220.

40. The Tinkey engraving is much more closely comparable to "A Winter Thunder-Storm," and its codes are exactly those of Mr. Marsh; therefore it was selected for illustration here over one of the two small Marsh vignettes in the book. Tinkey, the reader may recall, spoke of the disadvantages of photography-on-the-block at the Symposium.

41. Several readers outside the graphic arts area, including several librarians, could not, when asked, identify the wood engraving as specifically that.

42. Quoted in Adams, biography of Gibson, *op. cit.* in note 1, p. 168.

43. William M. Ivins, Jr., *Prints and Visual Communication* (Cambridge, Mass.: Harvard University Press, 1953), p. 144.

44. *Ibid.*

45. See their doctoral dissertations cited in the Bibliography.

46. Psychologists would say we were conditioned to recognize it. See Ivins' comments on this in Chapter VII of *Prints and Visual Communication*.

47. Charles G. Harper, *A Practical Handbook of Drawing for Modern Methods*

of Reproduction, 2nd ed., rev. (London: Chapman & Hall, 1901), pp. 114–115.

48. Adams, biography of Gibson, *op. cit.* in note 1, p. 81.
49. Quoted in Adams; see note 48, p. 115.
50. Adams, obituary article on Gibson, *op. cit.* in note 3, p. 650.
51. *Ibid.,* p. 647.
52. Ivins had warned of this kind of confusion, without providing specific examples of media or illustrators. Yet he failed to recognize that he thereby diminished the case for process halftone.
53. William H. Downes, "Photographic Illustration of Poetry," *New England Magazine* (new series) 4 (March 1891): 91.
54. William Hamilton Gibson, *Sharp Eyes: A Rambler's Calender* (New York: Harper, 1892), p. 222.
55. *Ibid.,* p. 243.
56. S. R. Koehler, "The Photomechanical Process," *Technology Quarterly* 5 (October 1892): 197.
57. William Hamilton Gibson, *Our Edible Toadstools and Mushrooms . . .* (New York: Harper, 1895), p. 6.
58. *Ibid.,* p. 7.
59. Ivins, *op. cit.,* p. 137.
60. Adams, biography of Gibson, *op. cit.* in note 1, p. 81.

CHAPTER 7

1. W. A. Rogers, *A World Worth-While* (New York: Harper, 1922), p. 248. Rogers was here referring to another artist's work, but we are all familiar with the Oscar Wilde dictum that "Nature imitates Art" as a jest about the fact that we *learn* to see.
2. Letter from Francis Parkman to Frederic Remington, dated Jan. 7, 1892, Boston, offering to send the artist appropriate photographs for his forthcoming illustrations for *The Oregon Trail.* Original in Ogdensburg, Remington Memorial; copied from microfilm of these archives at the New York Public Library.
3. The term "actinics" was explained in relation to the early pen-and-inks of Howard Pyle. While Darley's "Dutch Fisherman" had to be reproduced by wood engraving, the work of Remington and Pyle did not, at least not in their pen-and-inks.
4. Quoted in Perriton Maxwell, "Frederic Remington—Most Typical of American Artists," *Pearson's Magazine* 18 (July 1907): 403.
5. Atwood Manley, *Frederic Remington's North Country Associations* (Canton, N.Y.: 1961), p. 37.
6. Richard P. Wunder, "18th- and 19th-Century Paintings in the National Collection of Fine Arts," in *Highlights of the National Collection of Fine Arts* (Washington, D.C.: Smithsonian Institution Press, 1968), p. 27.
7. Poultney Bigelow, *Seventy Summers* (New York: Longmans, Green, 1925), 2 vols. Bigelow, at Yale with Remington, became editor of *Outing Magazine* and made it possible for Remington to make a start.
8. Maxwell, *op. cit.* in note 4, p. 404.
9. The outstanding critical success of the photogravures for the *Hiawatha* may have been instrumental in convincing Pyle's publishers to try the medium for *Autocrat of the Breakfast Table* (1894). Remington's reputation soared with the publication of the *Hiawatha*, not only for the few photogravures, but for hundreds of authentic details he provided as marginalia, details he drew from his own collection of Indian costumes.

10. We know the camera lies, but we have become accustomed to those lies about perspective and focus, and as Ivins suggested, we now seek those lies as the truth in other graphic media.

11. O. O. Howard, *My Life and Experiences among Our Hostile Indians* (Hartford, Conn.: Worthington, 1907).

12. William M. Ivins, Jr., *Prints and Visual Communication* (Cambridge, Mass.: Harvard University Press, 1953), p. 136.

13. Oliver Wendell Holmes, "The Stereoscope and the Stereograph," in his *Soundings from the Atlantic* (Boston: Ticknor & Fields, 1864), pp. 161–162. The article appeared first in the *Atlantic Monthly,* June 1859.

14. Quoted in Harold McCracken, *Frederic Remington, Artist of the Old West,* 1st ed. (Philadelphia: Lippincott, 1947), p. 44, from Remington's article, "On the Indian Reservation," *Century Magazine,* July 1889.

15. Elizabeth B. Custer, *Tenting on the Plains, or, General Custer in Kansas and Texas* (New York: Charles Webster, 1887).

16. The writer is indebted to Professor Lindquist-Cock for her comments on this aspect of motion-in-art; the review of *The Horse in Motion, Century Magazine* 24 (July 1882), by George Waring mentioned later in the chapter also discusses these problems.

17. Ivins, *op. cit.,* p. 136.

18. From correspondence mounted at the front of vol. I, the Merle Johnson scrapbooks of Remington, New York Public Library.

19. Ivins, *op. cit.,* p. 130.

20. *Ibid.,* p. 138.

21. *Ibid.,* p. 134.

22. McCracken, *op. cit.,* pp. 83–84.

23. F. Hopkinson Smith, *American Illustrators* (New York: Scribner, 1892), p. 24.

24. Oliver Wendell Holmes, "Sun-Painting and Sun-Sculpture," in *Soundings from the Atlantic* (Boston: Ticknor & Fields, 1864), pp. 181–183. The article appeared originally in the *Atlantic Monthly* in 1861.

25. According to Gernsheim, *History of Photography,* pp. 326–327, Muybridge ultimately managed exposures of one two-thousandth of a second in the University of Pennsylvania series, using the new dry gelatin plates. With the earlier wet-collodion emulsions, Gernsheim suggests that exposures of between one two-hundredth and one five-hundredth of a second were probably all that could register. The wet-collodion process was unpredictable and slow, but it did contribute to Muybridge's success in producing superb plates of Yosemite.

26. *Scientific American* (new series) 39 (Oct. 19, 1878): 241; illustrations, front page.

27. Eadweard Muybridge, *Animals in Motion . . . an Electro-photographic Investigation of Consecutive Phases of Muscular Actions . . . Commenced 1872. Completed 1885* (London: Chapman Hall, 1925; 1899 by Muybridge), p. 1. This is a later edition of the work titled *Animal Locomotion* (1887), reproducing a selection from the original photogravures in considerably smaller process halftones.

28. *Ibid.,* p. 5.

29. J. D. B. Stillman, *The Horse in Motion, as Shown by Instantaneous Photography, with a Study on Animal Mechanics* (Boston: James Osgood, 1882). The full title included: "Founded on anatomy and the revelations of the camera. In which is demonstrated the theory of quadrupedal locomotion. Executed and published under the auspices of Leland Stanford."

30. *Ibid.,* pp. 117–119.
31. *Ibid.,* p. 87. The process line engravings were reproduced in the Waring review.
32. *Ibid.,* p. 115.
33. *Ibid.,* p. 119.
34. Formerly *Scribner's Monthly.*
35. Waring, *op. cit.* in note 16, p. 381.
36. *Ibid.,* p. 387.
37. *Ibid.*
38. *Ibid.,* p. 388.
39. C. W. Ceram, *The Archeology of the Cinema,* translated by Richard Winston (New York: Harcourt, Brace & World, 1965), pp. 72–73.
40. See review by George Tissandier, in *La Nature,* 1879, pp. 23–26. "Nous recevons de M. E. L. Muybridge de San Francisco (États Unis) une série de photographies d'un intérêt peu commun. . . . Si un artiste en avait donné la représentation par le dessin, on l'accurserait assurement de s'être livré aux fantasies de son imagination. . . ." *La Nature* reproduced several views, "par les procédés d'heliogravure en relief."
41. For further discussion, see the section on art history in Chapter 8. Correspondence with Yale University has produced no absolutely certain evidence that these sets were present, but if we are to believe Oliver Larkin in *Art and Life in America* (1960), the art departments of colleges and universities were quick to take advantage of phototechnological reproductions, for obvious reasons. The Yale Art Department librarian and the Curator concur in this opinion.
42. For perhaps the only trustworthy account of Remington's Kansas experiences, see Robert Taft, *Artists and Illustrators of the Old West* (New York: Scribner, 1953).
43. R. W. G. Vail, "Frederic Remington—Chronicler of the Vanished West," in *Bulletin* of the New York Public Library, February 1929, p. 72.
44. Muybridge, *op. cit.,* p. 5.
45. *Ibid.*
46. *Ibid.*
47. Philip Gilbert Hamerton, *Portfolio Papers* (Boston: Roberts, 1889), pp. 334–335.
48. Quoted in Helmut Gernsheim, *Creative Photography; Aesthetic Trends 1839–1960* (Boston: Boston Book & Art Shop, 1962), p. 76. From a Shaw lecture, "Photography in Its Relation to Modern Art," October 1909.
49. T. Dwight Parkinson, "A Difficulty in Art-Photography," illustrated from photographs by A. N. Lindenmuth, *The Monthly Illustrator* 5 (third quarter, 1895): 207. (New York: Harry Jones, 1895.)

CHAPTER 8

1. André Malraux, *Museum without Walls* (Garden City, N.Y.: Doubleday, 1967), p. 12.
2. G. Wharton Simpson, "On Heliotype as a Means of Reproducing Works of Art," *Art Pictorial and Industrial* 1 (1870–1871): 74.
3. From the subtitle of Fox Talbot's *Pencil of Nature* quoted in William M. Ivins, Jr., *Prints and Visual Communication* (Cambridge, Mass.: Harvard University Press, 1953), p. 122.
4. *Ibid.*

5. The writer is indebted to Dr. Elizabeth Lindquist-Cock for directing her attention to several sources of information concerning these inventions.

6. John W. Harland, *The Printing Arts* . . . (New York: Ward Lock Bowden, 1892), p. 98.

7. Ivins, *op. cit.,* p. 144.

8. Helmut Gernsheim, *The History of Photography* . . . (New York: Oxford University Press, 1955), p. 128. Albert Boni, in his *Photographic Literature,* calls the Stirling book "the first book in which photography is utilized to illustrate the text," thus differentiating it from *The Pencil of Nature* and Talbot's ensuing picture view book of Scotland, the former using mounted prints as examples of a process rather than as illustrations of a text or story, the latter having no text at all.

9. Malraux, *op. cit.,* p. 12.

10. Francis D. Klingender, *Art and the Industrial Revolution* ed. and rev. by Arthur Elton (New York: Kelley, 1969; Reprints of Economic Classics), p. 66.

11. Gernsheim, *op. cit.,* p. 360.

12. Ernest Edwards, *The Heliotype Process* (Boston: Osgood, 1876), p. 13. The prices listed ranged from fifty cents to a dollar and a half. A list of the subjects in the Gray Collection was published on pp. 15–16 of the book.

13. Philip Gilbert Hamerton, *Etching and Etchers,* 3rd ed. (London: Macmillan, 1880), p. xiv.

14. *Ibid.*

15. S. R. Koehler, *Etching: an Outline of Its Technical Processes and Its History* (New York: Cassell, 1885), verso of title page.

16. *Ibid.,* p. v.

17. *American Art Review,* bound volume for 1880, p. 222. This is in the John Sloan Collection of the Wilmington Society of the Fine Arts.

18. *Ibid.*

19. H. Trueman Wood, *Modern Methods of Illustrating Books* (London: Stock, 1887); from an advertisement for Goupil in the end papers.

20. Edwards, *op. cit.,* p. 11.

21. Edward Strahan, ed., *Masterpieces of the International Exhibition* (Philadelphia: Gebbie & Barrie [1877]), vol. 1, p. 336.

22. Elbridge Kingsley, unpublished autobiography (Northampton, Mass.: Forbes Library), from the typescript, p. 91.

23. *Ibid.,* p. 93.

24. Alfred Jones for the figures, James Smillie and Hinshelwood for the landscape.

25. See note 22, p. 47.

26. J. Comyns Carr, *Book Illustration, Old and New* (London: Trounce, 1882), p. 15.

27. Kingsley, *op. cit.,* p. 95.

28. *Ibid.,* p. 140.

29. Timothy Cole, *Considerations on Engraving* (New York: Rudge, 1921), p. 11. The writer is indebted to Mr. Kenneth Lohf of Columbia University for bringing this item to her attention.

30. Kingsley, ms. of autobiography, p. 194.

31. *Ibid.,* p. 96.

32. Ivins, *op. cit.,* p. 136.

33. *Ibid.,* p. 143.

34. *Ibid.*

35. Elbridge Kingsley, "Originality in Wood-Engraving," *Century Magazine* 38 (August 1889): 578.
36. W. B. Closson, "Painter-Engraving," *Century Magazine* 38 (August 1889): 587.
37. *Ibid.*
38. *Ibid.,* p. 584.
39. Kingsley, ms. of autobiography, p. 112.
40. *Ibid.,* p. 127
41. Timothy Cole, *op. cit.,* p. 12.
42. Note that single-line process "halftone" screens could also produce the thick-and-thin chiaroscuro lines in the "Bacchus" face and chest.
43. William Henry Goodyear, *A History of Art for Classes, Art-Students, and Tourists in Europe,* 2nd ed., rev. with new illustrations (New York: Barnes, 1889), p. 257.
44. Goodyear, *History of Art,* 1st ed., 1888, pp. v–vi.
45. N. d'Anvers, *An Elementary History of Art, Architecture, Sculpture, Painting* (New York: Scribner and Welford, 1889), 3rd ed.
46. Goodyear, *History of Art,* 2nd ed., 1889, p. 177. The copy offered here is somewhat blacker in the shadows than the original plate in Goodyear, but it is close enough for our purposes.
47. Opaque brush retouching on a photograph is unlikely to reproduce correctly, as the intensity and surface qualities of the paints must match the print exactly, and, furthermore, blend in as subliminally as the true microscopic codes of photography. The airbrush, which sprays minute particles of paint with somewhat the texture of early photogravures, is the best technique for chiaroscuro rendering.
48. Back cover of *The Art of the World,* Part I.
49. Preface by Victor Breton for Jules Pinsard, *L'illustration du livre moderne et la photographie* (Paris: Mendel, 1897), p. 23. This is commendable for its extensive reproduction of different media, and its fine record of technological achievements on the continent and in England.
50. Foreword by Robert Underwood Johnson to the Print Club of Philadelphia's *Memorial Catalog* of the Timothy Cole Exhibition, n.p.
51. Johnson, *op. cit.* See note 50.
52. Ivins, *op. cit.,* p. 130.
53. See note 2.

CHAPTER 9

1. Stephen Horgan, *Horgan's Half-Tone and Photomechanical Processes* (Chicago: Inland Printer Co., 1911), p. i.
2. Helmut Gernsheim, *The History of Photography . . .* (New York: Oxford University Press, 1955), p. 134.
3. *Ibid.,* p. 189.
4. Oliver Wendell Holmes, "The Stereoscope and the Stereograph," in *Soundings from the Atlantic* (Boston: Ticknor & Fields, 1864), p. 161.
5. Edward Strahan, ed., *Masterpieces of the International Exhibition* (Philadelphia: 1876), vol. 1, p. 334.
6. James D. McCabe, *The Illustrated History of the Centennial Exhibition* (Philadelphia: National Publishing Co., 1876), title page.
7. *Ibid.,* p. 6.
8. *Ibid.*
9. Horgan, *op. cit.,* p. 11.
10. *Ibid.*

11. *Ibid.,* p. 12.
12. *Ibid.*
13. *Ibid.*
14. *Ibid.*
15. John Muir, *Picturesque California* (New York: J. Dewing, 1888), 1 vol. ed. title page.
16. For a discussion of such practices see Thompson's *American Literary Annuals and Gift Books, 1825–1865* (New York: H. W. Wilson, 1936).
17. See his chapter on reproductive media in *Photography and the American Scene* (New York: Dover, 1964).
18. Benson J. Lossing, *A Centennial Edition of the History of the United States . . .* (Hartford, Conn.: Belknap, 1876), p. vi. Illustrated with 12 steel engravings, 388 wood engravings, and one chromolithograph.
19. Charles M. Kurtz, ed., *Illustrations (three-hundred and thirty-six engravings) from the Art Gallery of World's Exposition,* 1st ed. (Philadelphia: Barrie, 1893), p. 8.
20. Trumbull White and William Igleheart, *The World's Columbian Exposition,* Chicago 1893 (Philadelphia: Monarch, 1893), title page.
21. *Ibid.,* p. 21.
22. White and Igleheart, *op. cit.,* pp. 574–575.
23. *Ibid.,* p. 564.
24. See G. W. Ceram, *The Archaeology of the Cinema* (New York: Harcourt, Brace & World, 1965), for further details.
25. White and Igleheart, *op. cit.,* p. 395.
26. Kingsley, unpublished autobiography (Northampton, Mass.: Forbes Library), from the typescript, p. 246.
27. James W. Shepp and Daniel B. Shepp, *Shepp's World's Fair Photographed . . .* (Chicago: Globe Bible Publishing Co., 1893), title page.
28. *Ibid.* The photographs were copyrighted by the Columbian Exposition, not by the publishers.
29. The reproduction of Plate 121, "Interior of the Manufactures and Liberal Arts Building," cannot transmit the soft grain and intense blacks of the original photogravure, and since it here undergoes a reproduction, loses its specific characteristic, that of yielding up enlarged detail, while process halftone yields up only its screen.
30. Shepp and Shepp, *op. cit.,* p. 270.

CHAPTER 10

1. Walter Crane, *Of the Decorative Illustration of Books, Old and New* (London: Bell, 1896), p. 177.
2. William M. Ivins, Jr., *Prints and Visual Communication* (Cambridge, Mass.: Harvard University Press, 1953), p. 122.
3. *Ibid.,* p. 144.
4. *Ibid.,* p. 138.
5. Helmut Gernsheim, *Creative Photography* (Boston: Boston Book and Art Shop, 1962), p. 120.
6. *Ibid.,* p. 119.
7. *Ibid.*
8. Ivins, *op cit.,* p. 128.
9. *Ibid.,* p. 177.
10. *Ibid.,* p. 136.
11. *Ibid.,* p. 172.
12. Walter Crane, *The Bases of Design* (London: Bell, 1898).

13. Ivins, *op. cit.*, p. 158.
14. *Ibid.*, p. 160.
15. *Ibid.*, p. 180.
16. *Ibid.*
17. The title of McLuhan's book written with Quentin Fiore, *The Medium Is the Message: An Inventory of Effects* (New York: Bantam Books, 1967).

Selected Bibliography

BOOKS

Abbott, Charles. *Howard Pyle: a Chronicle.* New York: Harper, 1925.

Adams, John Coleman. *William Hamilton Gibson; Artist—Naturalist—Author.* New York: Putnam, 1901.

Anderson, John, and Morse, Stearns. *The Book of the White Mountains.* New York: Minton, Balch, 1930.

Aranguren, José Luis. *Human Communication.* Translated by Frances Partridge. New York: McGraw-Hill, 1967.

Arnheim, Rudolf. *Visual Thinking.* London: Faber & Faber, 1969.

Austin, A. C. *Practical Half-Tone and Tri-Color Engraving.* Buffalo: Professional Photographer Publishing Co., 1898.

Beiderman, Charles. *Art as the Evolution of Visual Knowledge,* 1st ed. Red Wing, Minn.: 1948.

Bell, Quentin. *Victorian Artists.* Cambridge, Mass.: Harvard University Press, 1967.

Benjamin, S. G. W. *Contemporary Art in Europe.* New York: Harper, 1877.

Bernheimer, Richard. *The Nature of Representation; a Phenomenological Inquiry,* ed. by Horst W. Janson. New York: New York University Press, 1961.

Bigelow, Poultney. *Seventy Summers.* New York: Longmans, Green, 1925. 2 vols.

Blackburn, Henry. *The Art of Illustration.* London: Allen, 1894.

Blanc, Charles. *The Grammar of Painting and Engraving.* Translated from the French of Blanc's *Grammaire des arts du dessin* by Kate Newell Doggett, with the original illustrations. New York: Hurd and Houghton, 1874.

Bland, David. *A History of Book Illustration,* 1st ed. Cleveland, Ohio: World Publishing, 1958.

Bolton, Theodore. *American Book Illustrators.* New York: Bowker, 1938.

Boni, Albert, ed. *Photographic Literature.* New York: Morgan and Morgan, 1962.

Boston, Museum of Fine Arts, Print Dept. *Exhibition Illustrating the Technical Methods of the Reproductive Arts from the XV Century to the Present Time, with Special Reference to the Photo-Mechanical Processes; Jan. 8 to March 6, 1892.* Boston: Mudge, 1892.

Brown, F. H., and Rankin, H. A. *Simple Pictorial Illustration.* London: Pitman, 1913.

Bryant, William Cullen, ed. *Picturesque America.* New York: Appleton, 1872–1873. 2 vols.

Burch, R. M. *Colour Printing and Colour Printers.* New York: Baker and Taylor, 1912.

Carr, J. Comyns. *Book Illustration, Old and New.* London: Trounce, 1882. (The Cantor Lectures)

Ceram, C. W. *The Archeology of the Cinema.* Translated by Richard Winston. New York: Harcourt, Brace & World, 1965.

Cherry, Colin. *On Human Communication.* New York: Wiley, 1961.

Cole, Timothy. *Considerations on Engraving.* New York: Rudge, 1921.

Crane, Walter. *Of the Decorative Illustration of Books Old and New.* London: Bell, 1896.

Crane, Walter. *The Bases of Design.* London: Bell, 1898.

Custer, Elizabeth B. *Tenting on the Plains; or, General Custer in Kansas and Texas.* New York: Webster, 1887.

D'Anvers, N. *An Elementary History of Art—Architecture—Sculpture—Painting,* 3rd ed. New York: Scribner and Welford, 1889.

Drake, Samuel Adams. *The Heart of the White Mountains; Their Legends and Scenery.* New York: Harper, 1882.

Dunlap, William. *A History of the Rise and Progress of the Arts of Design in the United States,* new ed., illustrated. Boston: Goodspeed, 1918.

Duplessis, George. *The Wonders of Engraving.* London: Sampson, Low . . . 1871.

Early American Book Illustrators and Wood Engravers, 1670—1870. The Sinclair Hamilton Collection of American Illustrated Books, at Princeton University. Princeton, N.J.: 1958.

Eder, Josef M. *History of Photography.* Translated by Edward Epstean. New York: Columbia University Press, 1945.

Edwards, Ernest. *The Heliotype Process.* Boston: Osgood, 1876.

Emerson, P. H. *Naturalistic Photography for Students of the Art,* 3rd ed., rev., enl., and rewritten in parts. New York: Scovill & Adams, 1899.

Encyclopedia of World Art. New York: McGraw-Hill, 1959–1969. 15v.

Exman, Eugene. *The House of Harper,* 1st ed. New York: Harper, 1967.

Gardner, Albert Ten Eyck. *Winslow Homer, American Artist.* New York: Bramhall House, 1961.

Gernsheim, Helmut. *Creative Photography.* Boston: Boston Book and Art Shop, 1962.

Gernsheim, Helmut, in collaboration with Alison Gernsheim. *The History of Photography, from the Earliest Use of the Camera Obscura in the Eleventh Century up to 1914.* New York: Oxford University Press, 1955.

Gibson, William Hamilton. *Eye Spy.* New York: Harper, 1897.

Gombrich, Ernest Hans. *Art and Illusion: A Study in the Psychology of Pictorial Representation.* New York: Pantheon Books, 1960.

Gombrich, Ernest Hans. *Meditations on a Hobby Horse.* London: Phaidon, 1963.

Goodyear, William Henry. *A History of Art for Classes, Art-Students, and Tourists in Europe,* 1st ed. New York: Barnes, 1888.

Goodyear, William Henry. *A History of Art for Classes, Art-Students, and Tourists in Europe,* 2d ed., rev. New York: Barnes, 1889.

Gregory, Richard L. *Eye and Brain: The Psychology of Seeing.* New York: McGraw-Hill, 1966.

Hamerton, Philip Gilbert. *Etching and Etchers,* 3rd ed. London: Macmillan, 1880.

Hamerton, Philip Gilbert. *The Graphic Arts.* London: Seeley, Jackson & Halliday, 1882.

Hamerton, Philip Gilbert. *Portfolio Papers.* Boston: Roberts, 1889.

Hamerton, Philip Gilbert. *Thoughts about Art,* new ed., rev. Boston: Roberts, 1871.

Harland, John Whitfield. *The Printing Arts; An Epitome of the Theory, Practice, Processes, and Mutual Relations of Engraving, Lithography, & Printing in Black and in Colours.* New York: Ward Lock Bowden, 1892.

Harper, Charles G. *A Practical Handbook of Drawing for Modern Methods of Reproduction*, 2d ed., rev. London: Chapman & Hall, 1901.

Hind, Arthur M. *A History of Engraving and Etching from the 15th Century to the Year 1914 . . .* , 3rd and fully revised ed. of "A Short History of Engraving and Etching." New York: Dover, 1963, 1923.

Hind, Arthur M. *Albrecht Dürer, His Engravings and Woodcuts.* New York: Stokes, n.d.

Hodson, James Shirley. *An Historical and Practical Guide to Art Illustration.* London: Low, 1884.

Hogben, Lancelot. *From Cave Painting to Comic Strip; A Kaleidoscope of Human Communication.* New York: Chanticleer Press, 1949.

Horgan, Stephen. *Horgan's Half-Tone and Photomechanical Processes.* Chicago: Inland Printer Co., 1911.

Howard, O. O. *My Life and Experiences Among Our Hostile Indians . . .* Hartford, Conn.: Worthington, 1907.

Hunt, R. G. *The Reproduction of Colour.* London: Fountain Press, 1957.

Iles, George. *Flame, Electricity, and the Camera; Man's Progress from the First Kindling of Fire to the Wireless Telegraph and the Photography of Color*, New York: Hill, 1900.

Ivins, William M., Jr. *How Prints Look.* Boston: Beacon Press, 1958, 1943.

Ivins, William M., Jr. *Prints and Visual Communication.* Cambridge, Mass.: Harvard University Press, 1953.

Jarves, James Jackson. *The Art-Idea; Sculpture, Painting, and Architecture in America*, 3rd ed. New York: Hurd & Houghton, 1866.

Kepes, Gyorgy, ed. *Education of Vision.* New York: Braziller, 1965.

Kilburn, S. S. *Specimen of Designing and Engraving on Wood.* Boston: 1872.

Klingender, Francis D. *Art and the Industrial Revolution*, ed. and rev. by Arthur Elton. New York: Kelley, 1969. (Reprints of Economic Classics.)

Koehler, S. R. *Etching: An Outline of Its Technical Processes and Its History.* New York: Cassell, 1885.

Kurtz, Charles M., ed. *Illustrations . . . from the Art Gallery of the World's Exposition*, 1st ed. Philadelphia: Barrie, 1893.

Larkin, Oliver. *Art and Life in America*, rev. and enl. ed. New York: Holt Rinehart and Winston, 1960.

Lehmann-Haupt, Helmut. *The Book in America: A History of the Making and Selling of Books in the United States.* In collaboration with Lawrence C. Wroth and Rollo G. Silver. 2d ed. New York: Bowker, 1951.

Linton, William J. *The History of Wood-Engraving in America.* London: Bell, 1882.

Lossing, Benson J. *A Centennial Edition of the History of the United States.* Hartford, Conn., Belknap, 1876.

Lumsden, E. S. *The Art of Etching . . .* New York: Dover, 1962.

McCabe, James D. *The Illustrated History of the Centennial Exhibition.* Philadelphia: National Publishing Co., 1876.

McCracken, Harold. *Frederic Remington, Artist of the Old West.* Philadelphia: Lippincott, 1947.

McLean, Ruari. *Victorian Book Design and Colour Printing.* New York: Oxford University Press, 1963.

McLuhan, Marshall. *Understanding Media: the Extensions of Man.* New York: McGraw-Hill, 1964.

Malraux, André. *Museum without Walls.* Translated from the French by Stuart Gilbert and Francis Price. Garden City, N.Y.: Doubleday, 1967.

Manley, Atwood. *Some of Frederic Remington's North Country Associations.* Canton, N.Y.: 1961. (Cover-title: *Frederic Remington in the Land of His Youth.*)

Mather, Frank, ed. *The American Spirit in Art.* New Haven: Yale University Press, 1927. (Pageant of America, vol. 12.)

Moles, Abraham. *Information Theory and Esthetic Perception.* Translated by Joel E. Cohen. Urbana, Ill.: University of Illinois Press, 1968.

Montgomery, Walter. *American Art and American Art Collections.* Boston: Walker, 1889. 2 vols.

Morse, Willard S., and Brincklé, Gertrude. *Howard Pyle, a Record of His Illustrations and Writings.* Wilmington, Del.: Wilmington Society of the Fine Arts, 1921.

Mount Holyoke College. *Catalogue of the Works of Elbridge Kingsley.* South Hadley, Mass.: 1910.

Mumford, Lewis. *Art and Technics.* New York: Columbia University Press, 1960.

Mumford, Lewis. *The Brown Decades: A Study of the Arts in America, 1865–1895,* 2d rev. ed. New York: Dover, 1955.

Muybridge, Eadweard. *Animals in Motion . . . An Electro-Photographic Investigation of Consecutive Phases of Muscular Motions . . . Commenced 1872, Completed 1885.* London: Chapman Hall, 1925; 1899 by Muybridge.

Newhall, Beaumont. *The Daguerreotype in America.* 1st ed. New York: Duell, Sloan & Pearce, 1961.

Pennell, Joseph. *The Graphic Arts: Modern Men and Modern Methods.* Published for the Art Institute of Chicago by the University of Chicago Press, 1921. (Scammon Lectures for 1920.)

Pennell, Joseph. *The Illustration of Books: A Manual for the Use of Students; Notes for a Course of Lectures at the Slade School, University College.* New York: Century, 1896.

Pennell, Joseph. *Lithography and Lithographers . . .* London: Unwin, 1898.

Pennell, Joseph. *Modern Illustration.* London: Bell, 1895.

Pennell, Joseph. *Pen-Drawing and Pen Draughtsmen.* London: Macmillan, 1889.

Pettit, James S. *Modern Reproductive Graphic Processes.* New York: Van Nostrand, 1884.

Pinsard, Jules. *L'illustration du livre moderne et la photographie.* Paris: Mendel, 1897.

Print Club of America. *Timothy Cole; Memorial Exhibition, November Ninth to Twenty-Eighth Nineteen Thirty-One.* (n.p., n.d., Publication no. 6.)

Roger-Marx, Claude. *Graphic Art; the 19th Century.* Translated by E. M. Gwyer. New York: McGraw-Hill, 1962.

Rogers, W. A. *A World Worth-While.* New York: Harper, 1922.

Routledge, Robert. *Discoveries and Inventions of the 19th Century,* new ed., rev. New York: Routledge, 1876.

Singer, Hans W., and Strang, William. *Etching, Engraving, and the Other Methods of Printing Pictures.* London: Kegan Paul, Trench, Trubner, 1897.

Singh, Jagjit. *Great Ideas in Information Theory, Language, and Cybernetics.* New York: Dover, 1966.

Sipley, Louis W. *The Photomechanical Halftone.* Philadelphia: American Museum of Photography, n.d.

Sloane, Patricia. *Colour: Basic Principles, New Directions.* London: Studio Vista, 1968.

Smith, F. Hopkinson. *American Illustrators.* New York: Scribner, 1892. 5 parts.

Stephens, John L. *Incidents of Travel in Yucatan.* New York: Harper, 1843. 2 vols.

Stillman, J. D. B. *The Horse in Motion, as Shown by Instantaneous Photography, with a Study on Animal Mechanics . . .* Boston: Osgood, 1882.

Story, Alfred T. *The Story of Photography.* New York: University Society, 1909.

Strahan, Edward, ed. *Art of the World, Illustrated in the Paintings, Statuary, and Architecture of the World's Columbian Exposition.* New York: Appleton, 1893.

Strahan, Edward, ed. *Masterpieces of the Centennial International Exhibition.* Philadelphia: Gebbie & Barrie, 1877. 3 vols.

Strauss, Victor. *The Printing Industry.* Washington, D.C.: Printing Industries of America, 1967.

Taft, Robert. *Artists and Illustrators of the Old West, 1850 to 1900.* New York: Scribner, 1953.

Taft, Robert. *Photography and the American Scene: A Social History, 1839–1889.* New York: Dover, 1964, © 1938.

Talbot, Henry Fox. *The Pencil of Nature.* London: Longman, Brown, Green & Longmans, 1844–46.

Thompson, Ralph. *American Literary Annuals and Gift Books, 1825–1865.* New York: H. W. Wilson, 1936.

Tuckerman, Henry T. *Book of the Artists.* New York: Putnam, 1867.

Von Hagen, Victor Wolfgang. *Maya Explorer: John Lloyd Stephens, and the Lost Cities of Central America and Yucatan.* Norman, Okla.: University of Oklahoma Press, 1947.

Weber, Carl. *The Rise and Fall of James Ripley Osgood: A Biography.* Waterville, Maine: Colby College Press, 1959.

Weber, Wilhelm. *A History of Lithography.* New York: McGraw-Hill, 1966.

Weitenkampf, Frank. *American Graphic Art.* New York: Holt, 1912.

Weitenkampf, Frank. *How to Appreciate Prints,* 3rd rev. ed. New York: Scribner, 1927.

Weitenkampf, Frank. *The Illustrated Book.* Cambridge, Mass.: Harvard University Press, 1938.

White, Trumbull, and Igleheart, William. *The World's Columbian Exposition, 1893.* Philadelphia: Monarch, 1893.

Wilmington Society of the Fine Arts. *Catalogue of Pictures by Howard Pyle, 1926.*

Wilmington Society of the Fine Arts. *Report of the Private View of the Exhibition of Works by Howard Pyle at the Art Alliance,* Philadelphia, Jan. 22, 1923. (Only 25 copies published.)

Wood, H. Trueman. *Modern Methods of Illustrating Books.* London: Stock, 1887.

Woodberry, George E. *A History of Wood-Engraving.* New York: Harper, 1883.

Worringer, Wilhelm. *Abstraction and Empathy: A Contribution to the Psychology of Style.* Translated by Michael Bullock. New York: International University Press, 1953.

UNPUBLISHED MATERIALS

Dissertations

Ehrlich, George. "Technology and the Artist: A Study of the Interaction of Technological Growth and 19th-Century American Pictorial Art." Ph.D. dissertation, University of Illinois, 1960.

Lindquist-Cock, Elizabeth Maria. "The Influence of Photography on American Landscape Painting, 1839–1880." Ph.D. dissertation, New York University, 1967.

Manuscripts

Kingsley, Elbridge. Unpublished autobiography and other papers. Northampton, Mass.: Forbes Library.

Letters from the editors, publishers, and artists for whom Albert Mumford Lindsay worked as an engraver; collection in the possession of Mrs. Margaret Van Brunt, Wilmington, Delaware.

Miscellaneous papers from the Remington Memorial, Ogdensburg, New York. Files on microfilm at the New York Public Library.

Scrapbooks

Johnson, Merle. Scrapbooks of the Works of Frederic Remington. New York Public Library, Art Reference Room.

Morse, Willard. Scrapbooks of the Works of Howard Pyle. Wilmington, Delaware: Wilmington Society of the Fine Arts.

(The scrapbooks above include manuscript materials as well as reproductions of the works of the illustrators.)

ARTICLES

Adams, John Coleman. "William Hamilton Gibson." *New England Magazine* (new series) XV (February 1897): 642–655.

"The Artists' Model." *Metropolitan Magazine,* July 1886.

Closson, W. B. "Painter-Engraving." *Century Magazine,* XXXVIII (August 1889): 583–587.

Hawthorne, Julian. "Howard Pyle, Illustrator." *Pearson's,* XVIII (1907): 261 ff.

"Holiday Books." *Atlantic Monthly* XVII (January 1891).

Holmes, Oliver Wendell. "The Stereoscope and the Stereograph." In his *Soundings from the Atlantic.* Boston: Ticknor & Fields, 1864.

Holmes, Oliver Wendell. "Sun-Painting and Sun-Sculpture." In his *Soundings from the Atlantic.* Boston: Ticknor & Fields, 1864.

Ivins, William M., Jr. "Photography and the Modern Point of View: A Speculation in the History of Taste." *Metropolitan Museum Studies* I (October 1928): 16–24.

Kingsley, Elbridge. "Originality in Wood-Engraving." *Century Magazine* XXXVIII (August 1889): 576–583.

Koehler, S. R. "The Photomechanical Process." *Technology Quarterly* V (October 1892).

Lehmann-Haupt, Helmut. "English Illustrators in the Collection of George Arents." *Colophon* (new graphic series) I (1940).

Maxwell, Perriton. "Frederic Remington—Most Typical of American Artists." *Pearson's* XVIII (July 1907).

Muybridge item. *Scientific American* (new series) XXXIX (October 19, 1878): 241 and front page.

Parkinson, T. Dwight. "A Difficulty in Art-Photography." *The Monthly Illustrator* V, Third Quarter (1895). New York: Jones.

Scribner's Monthly XV (April 1878): 891 (editorial note).

Simpson, G. Wharton. "On Heliotype as a Means of Reproducing Works of Art." *Art Pictorial and Industrial* I (1870–1871).

Snow, Vernon. "The First Photographically-Illustrated Book." *Times Literary Supplement* (December 23, 1965).

"A Symposium of Wood-Engravers." *Harper's New Monthly Magazine* LX (February 1880): 442–453.

Syndenham, Alvin H. "Frederic Remington . . ." (Reprint from August, 1940 *Bulletin of the New York Public Library*, pp. 609–613.)

Tissandier, George. "Muybridge Review Item." *La Nature* (1879).

Vail, R. W. G. "Frederic Remington — Chronicler of the Vanished West." *Bulletin of the New York Public Library*, February 1929.

Waring, George. "The Horse in Motion." *Century Magazine* XXIV (July 1882): 381–388.

"Wood-Engraving and the 'Scribner' Prizes." *Scribner's Magazine* XXI (April 1881): 937–945.

Wunder, Richard P. "18th- and 19th-Century Paintings in the National Collection of Fine Arts," in *Highlights of the National Collection of Fine Arts,* Washington, D.C.: Smithsonian Institution Press, 1968.

Glossary

actinics   An early name applied to process line engravings produced with the aid of photography. The first company, established in 1871, of John Calvin Moss (1838–1892) was called the Actinic Engraving Company. The pen-and-inks of Howard Pyle, for example, long thought to be wood engravings, were "actinics."

aquatint   An intaglio process whereby a metal plate receives a coating of an acid-resistant resinous powder. Heated, the resin melts, attaching itself as reticulated available message units to the metal. Since the resin is acid proof, the blacks and whites to be printed on paper are produced by controlling the areas of and the amount of etching. Capable of considerable subliminality, it was the forerunner of photogravure.

autographic medium   Any combination of channel and code which permits direct and rapid working by an illustrator (primary codifier). Etching and lithography are two outstandingly autographic media, whereas the slow and tedious labor of metal engraving or wood engraving tended to require the development of secondary codifiers who specialized in the technical application of printing knowledge.

black-line wood engraving   Like its progenitor, the black-line woodcut, this method of producing a printing surface excavates from the block all that is to be white and leaves standing all that is to print black. The difference between black-line and white-line wood engraving is primarily that black-line is cut with a knife on the outer contours of a positive (black) area, whereas in white-line the engraver uses a graver to flick out tiny specks or lines to model an area. Black-line was used largely to reproduce pen-and-ink or pencil drawings, and its messages were conceived in units of contour rather than of textural gradients, outlines rather than chiaroscuro.

camera lucida   A hand copying tool of the early nineteenth century, still in use, offering a prism on a metal stalk which could be raised or lowered depending on what size the final image to be traced was to appear on the paper. Not a camera in the photographic sense.

camera obscura   Essentially, a box of some sort containing a tiny hole which permits light and images to enter, upside down and reversed, so that they can be copied on tracing paper over glass by artists who have used such means for centuries. Eventually equipped with photographic means for permanently capturing an image, it became our contemporary camera.

channel   The physical means whereby an encoded message can be transmitted carrying information about an original to a receiver or viewer.

chiaroscuro   Modeling the illusion of the volume and mass of natural objects by light and dark gradations, usually in smooth transitions called continuous halftones.

chromolithography A process reproducing color via planographic plates. Before the application of photographic screened techniques for halftones, considerable numbers of plates were needed, each bearing an individual tint or hue and requiring precise registration. Combined with phototechnologies, the chromolithographies could manage to transmit moderately grainy or solid colors and can now transmit photography per se.

code The organizing structure by which a message is transmitted through a physical channel. In the graphic arts, physical channels tend to dictate the structural possibilities, such as the size of the dots, lines, irregular subliminal areas, or the autographic options. Codes can be imitated, but the peculiarities of each channel usually, not always, impress distinct characteristics on the message units. The molecular, subliminal code of photography simplified the transmission of other codes but could not transmit all characteristics or all codes.

collotype A fine arts reproduction process by which a film of gelatin is light-sensitized with a bichromate, given a grain, made responsive to either greasy ink or water, and treated like lithographic stone. Because it provides a subliminal code, it excels at the transmission of photography and is considered one of the processes of "permanent" photography.

contour The visible boundary between the volume or mass of an object or individual and the surrounding atmosphere. The surface of an object or individual as seen in profile or outline. Contour is one of the four clues to the nature of visible objects.

crossline screen process An early process halftone engraving method, using two line screens at right angles to each other, creating apertures which restructure a visible image viewed through a camera into dots of different size but of similar intensity, thereby providing a code transmittable by relief printing. Still in use. In a special meaning used in this book, the earliest screen process wherein the crossed lines were visible to the naked eye as a squared mesh.

daguerreotype The outcome of discoveries by Joseph Nicéphore Niépce and Louis Jacques Daguerre, this was the first successful method of "photography," made public in 1839. Using a camera obscura fitted with a lens, and a copper plate coated with light-sensitive silver salts, a latent image was developed with the aid of vapors of metallic mercury. A densely coded, one-time, nonprinting compatible process viewable only from a certain angle.

dot structure Refers either to the coding of an image in ink via dots imitating the textural characteristics of visible objects, or to the physical structures in metal or wood which have been prepared for ink by relief process photoengraving, in which case the dots are of equal intensity but of different sizes, or by the intaglio process of photogravure, in which the irregular "dots" are not only of different sizes but of differing intensities.

engraving The preparation of a printing surface by removing lines or dots from the surface of a metal plate. The ink is deposited in these subsurface excavations, the surface wiped clean, and the image transferred to paper by pressure. An intaglio process, not type-compatible. Current usage has shortened the term "photoengraving" to "engraving," but a "photoengraving" is a *relief* plate, and the two processes should not be confused.

etching An autographic chemical process. A metal plate having been coated with an acid-resistant ground, the artist-codifier lays bare the metal beneath the lines and dots or masses of these message units to be transmitted, and exposes the plate to acid, which "bites" the exposed areas to desired depths. The intaglio plate is then inked and subjected to pressure, usually in a special etching press.

facsimile wood engraving The exact duplication of a line drawing, usually with an original in pen-and-ink, through excavating all wood around the code elements (message units) for relief printing. The invention of "actinics," or process line engravings, in the 1870s, made such labor unnecessary, although facsimile remained the false standard by which the craftsmanship of wood engravers was judged until the 1880s.

fake process halftone In the late nineteenth century and early twentieth century, the imitation of multicolor printing by the application of screened tints (dots of equal size and equal intensity) over screened process halftones (dots of unequal size but equal intensity) often in only one or two additional colors. Also used to describe a variety of color processes which transmitted black and white originals as if they had been photographed in color, either by flat tints or by shooting three or four plates from the black and white original and printing them in superimposed printing inks to imitate a full-colored original.

fine-screen halftone relief process The restructuring of images into densely packed printing codes of considerable subliminality, in which many characteristics of the screening procedures are not available to the naked eye, although the characteristic of an overall evenness is visible. Demands high-quality, coated papers, unlike metal relief type which can print on ordinary text papers.

halftones The entire range of tonal gradients between pure black and pure white; by extension, any photomechanical process which is capable of reproducing such gradients.

halftone process engraving See *process halftone engraving.*

heliotype A modified collotype process (which see) invented by Ernest Edwards and introduced into America in the early 1870s. Requiring two printings, one for shadows and one for light tones, the heliotype was widely used for art reproductions and for transmitting photography, but it was not type-compatible.

illusionism The goal of much Western art; *trompe l'oeil.* Refers to the fooling of the human eye into believing that what is essentially a codes transmission or original communication is similar to, or identical with, real objects, individuals, or events in "Nature." Illusionism depends on the transmission of textural gradients, chiaroscuro, modulations of contour and surface, and color. See the works of James J. Gibson.

illustrator A primary codifier of either artistic communication or information transfer intended specifically for transmission via the printed page. The profession of illustration was the outcome of the alteration of the relationships of the primary and secondary codifiers achieved by phototechnology.

information transfer   The communication of data or the transmission of a space/time complex from a source of a message, which may be either a coded message itself or an object, individual, or event in "Nature." Requires coding of message units (speech, print, images) into physical channels (air, wood, metal, silver salts), its excellence being judged by how closely the transmitted message approximates the original.

intaglio process   Printing plates which hold ink below the surface, as, for example, in the bitten lines or dots of etching, aquatint, or the excavated lines of engravings, or the rocked and then scraped surfaces of mezzotint. Characteristically, the impression of ink is slightly raised on the surface of the paper, most conspicuously in etching.

Ives process   One of several inventions of Frederic Eugene Ives (1856–1937), and the name may be used to describe either his 1878 patent covering a gelatin and plaster process of obtaining halftone dots, his 1886 crossline screen halftone process, or his Photochromoscope process in which true separation of color originals in separate printing plates was achieved by using red, green, and blue-violet filters. Ives is credited with the first practical method of creating relief halftone plates, although other European inventors were also working at the same time in the 1880s.

line engraving   A confusing term, as it can mean one of several things: (a) an intaglio metal printing plate wherein ink is held in message units below the surface; (b) a relief printing surface where the negative white space which is not to print is etched with acid to remove it from the raised portions; (c) any printing plate, either photographic or non-photographic, in which the message units are pure black lines (or dots) containing no halftones.

lithography   A planographic process, permitting total autographic control by the artist. Using a treated stone, it depends on the mutual repulsion of oil and water when greasy ink is applied. The principle was discovered by Aloysius Senefelder in 1796, and the process, first called "polyautography" in England, was popularized by the second decade of the nineteenth century. With transfer paper, lithography was capable of transmitting almost all the codes of other media with the exception of photography, which necessitated the invention of methods to restructure the halftones into dots of different sizes. While not compatible with metal relief typography, fresh ink impressions from text type could be transferred to stone, and pictures jointly printed.

medium   The combination of a code and a channel. Motion pictures, for example, use photographic molecular codes on a transparent acetate film channel, sprocketed to travel through a projector at a certain rate. While each medium tends to have unique characteristics, codes can be imitated if the message units are subliminal or if the channel permits of similar manipulations.

message   According to some sources, a message is merely a selection from a repertory of previously established meanings. In one sense, it is the communicated data or the transmitted space/time complexity containing information concerning an original object, individual, or event in "Nature." In reproducing an artist's work, his painting, for example, is the original about which we wish to send a message to the public. In transmitting scientific data, a scientist's coding of information concerning Nature is the message we seek to transmit. The term should not be confused with "meaning."

message unit The smallest code element of a transmission through a channel. In the case of the halftone screen, the dot is the message unit.

mezzotint An intaglio printing plate prepared by pitting the entire surface with a special "rocker." Highlights are then removed by burnishing away or scraping down the overall burr produced by the rocking. Capable of considerable subliminality and illusionism.

Moss process halftone Invented by John Calvin Moss (1838–1892), it attempted to restructure continuous halftones into relief printing surfaces of dots of different size but the same intensity. It did not compete successfully with the Ives process, in contrast to the success of the Moss line process. Despite this early failure, the Moss Company eventually became one of the most influential photoengraving companies in New York and still survives today under another name.

Moss process line engraving One of the most successful of all early photoengraving processes, providing typographically compatible plates which could transmit pure blacks perfectly. The supposed Düreresque "wood engravings" of Howard Pyle were pen-and-inks reproduced by Moss line photoengravings.

mounted photographic print The first method of transmitting the information contained in paper photographs. Paper positives were glued onto text pages and steam ironed for flatness. The process gained widest acceptance through the albumen prints of Louis-Désiré Blanquart-Evrard (1802–1872) who published giant travel books illustrated with photographs by Francis Frith and others during the 1850s.

negative/positive photography The invention of Sir William Henry Fox Talbot (1800–1877), one of the most significant in the history of photography, as it established the principle of a negative from which innumerable positives can be obtained. He published his process in *The Pencil of Nature* (1844–1846), the first major publication to utilize mounted paper prints.

"noise" Any aspect of a signal or code which interferes with the transmission of an intended message.

original The object, individual, or event in "Nature" about which information is collected and transmitted via a message sent through a medium.

paper photography As differentiated from metal photography, where the light-sensitive emulsion is on a metal support. Originally involved a paper, rather than a film, negative by which a paper positive was obtained.

"permanent" photography Processes not relying upon silver salts in the light-sensitive emulsion, as these salts were discovered to deteriorate with the passage of time. Usually refers to the carbon tissue process, collotype, gum prints, woodburytypes, heliotypes, and any other process whereby pigments rather than silver salts were the final print-making medium. See Helmut Gernsheim's *History of Photography* for further details.

photo-aquatint   A name given to the photogravure process at a historic exhibition at the Boston Museum of Fine Arts in 1892, but quickly abandoned.

photoengraving   A general term for any photographically assisted relief process printing surface, whether of line or halftone originals. The printing code is transferred to metal and the message units produced by etching away what is to be white on the printed page, leaving the metal standing clear where it is to be black. The entire surface of the plate is inked and it prints simultaneously with metal type.

photoetching   Sometimes misused for "photoengraving" because the latter is etched with acid to produce a relief printing surface. In the strictest sense, the term "photoetching" should be restricted to plates in which the camera has assisted in the transfer of message units which are to be printed by the intaglio process, whereby what is to be black on the printed page is below the surface, and what is white remains at the surface plane; in other words, the converse of photoengraving.

photography-on-the-block   A means of producing a relief printing plate by transferring a photographic image from a negative to the surface of a woodblock (usually boxwood) which has been prepared with light-sensitive materials. First used in the mid-1850s, the technique did not achieve widespread use until the early 1870s in response to the rise of the popular pictorial press.

photogravure   Called the most beautiful of all phototechnologies, it depends for its effects on the richness of ink available to all intaglio processes. The message units of photogravure are so small that ordinarily a photogravure of the 1876–1900 epoch could be enlarged to reveal even more detail than had been visible to the naked eye before the underlying code began to be discerned. Based on the properties of aquatint, in which reticulation of a powder on a metal plate provides a variety of dot structures, photogravure is etched and produces a "print" in terms of book illustration.

photolithography   An application of phototechnology to the production of lithographic plates in which the printing is achieved by chemical means, planographically.

photomechanical process   Any process which produces printing plates with the assistance of the camera. Today, generally used as synonymous with "photoengraving," although technically the term applies to both intaglio and planographic plates.

phototechnologies   All methods of producing printing surfaces which incorporate photography and photomechanical techniques.

planographic printing   Usually applied to lithography where the printing ink is applied to a support in which the message units are neither *above* (relief printing) or *below* (intaglio printing) the surface, but remain on the surface and are differentiated from the rest of the printing area primarily by chemical separation.

primary codifier   The illustrator/artist who creates messages concerning objects, individuals, and events in Nature and who structures this information in such a way that a secondary codifier is ordinarily required to impose printable codes for purposes of mass transmission. In our century, phototechnologies are the secondary codifiers and, quite often, photographers rather than artists are the primary codifiers of messages.

print (a) as a noun, a "print" is an individually manufactured image produced by any process (intaglio, relief, planographic) differentiated from "illustration," which is presumed to be manufactured specially as a part of a book for mass distribution. Many illustrations are, strictly speaking, "prints," even when produced by phototechnologies, if they are inserted separately from or printed on paper different from the text; (b) a photographic print is a positive image on paper, produced from a negative on film (or paper) capable of producing multiples of the same print; (c) as a verb, to transfer images from any of the three basic ink-bearing surfaces (relief, intaglio, planographic); (d) as a verb, specifically and exactly, the act of transferring images from a surface on which the message units are in relief to paper or another receiving surface intended to transmit images.

print-compatible A relief medium amenable to simultaneous manufacture with metal or wood relief typography.

process halftone engraving A metal relief plate in which dots of different sizes and of the same intensity are produced by photographic manipulation of an image through some screening or other device which restructures tones between pure black and pure white into printable message units. The area not to be printed is ordinarily etched away to produce dots standing in free relief.

process line engraving A metal relief plate produced by photographic transfer of pure black-and-white images, such as pen-and-ink drawings.

relief printing The transmission of images via ink-bearing surfaces in which the positive (pure black) message units are raised and separated from their negative areas (pure white) or background support. Requires considerable pressure, often a kind of stamping, to transfer the ink images to paper.

screened engraving A process engraving produced by restructuring the continuous halftones of an original photograph or art illustration into printable message units through the device of the meshes of a screen interposed between the camera and the original. The finer the screen, the finer the message units and the greater the capacity for subliminality. The dot size resulting from the size of the meshes determines the finish of the paper required for the final transmission, as a rough-surfaced paper cannot transmit fine dots. See Victor Strauss' *The Printing Industry* for more detail.

secondary codifier The technician who structures the message created by a primary codifier into printable message units. Today the secondary codifier is most often a photoengraver or a phototechnician.

stereographs Based on the observations of Sir Henry Wheatstone and his inventions in the 1830s covering the illusion of three-dimensional reality which results from our brains fusing two slightly dissimilar optical images which our two eyes separately receive. This principle was applied to photography by Sir David Brewster in the late 1840s and made widely popular in the 1850s by paper photography. Two similar photographs, taken from slightly different angles by a stereographic camera, mounted on cardboard, were placed in an instrument called a lenticular stereoscope which provided the illusion of a single fused image seen in separate planes, hence illusionistic.

stipple engraving   Although a metal plate can be punched or flicked by gravers, the technique was not as popular as stipple etching, for which the term stipple "engraving" is a misnomer.

stipple etching   As with any etching process, a metal plate is covered with an acid resist. Two or three finely pointed needles are bound together and minute openings in the coating produced by rapid puncturing in the act of amassing of dots which are to create the illusion of continuous halftones by how far apart or how close together they are. The dots are then etched with acid to the desired depth.

subliminal effects   Those aspects of message units which are smaller than can be seen with the unaided human eye, and which often depend on the distance over which a message is viewed. Framing prints which seem to have gross textural effects, for example, engraved "lozenge" shapes, when seen close up, demonstrate considerable subliminality when viewed from a distance.

texture gradients   As formulated by James J. Gibson, this refers to the characteristic units of any surface which can be perceived in a perspective which makes them smaller or larger as they are seen from varying positions and distances. One of the major elements which must be present in any graphic arts presentation of the illusion of three-dimensionality.

transfer process   Permits the printing of relief typography or relief visual images, or of intaglio messages, via lithography—a planographic process—by accepting a freshly inked impression on transfer paper which is then applied to the lithographic stone or plate.

transmission   The carrying or sending of a message about an original via a medium. By extension, the message itself.

visual syntax   The term used by William Ivins in *Prints and Visual Communication* to describe the formal structures by which the graphic arts order and transmit messages, analogous to the structure of language. See "code."

white-line wood engraving   A relief process block in which the negative (white) message units are the primary structurers of information, created by flicks and dots made by the graver. As significantly finer dots and lines could be created by this method than by the more difficult method of carving out a positive black line or black dot, the process could be more illusionistic because more subliminal. It also imitates more successfully the opacity of light falling on surfaces.

wood engraving   A relief process in which a block of boxwood (or other hard wood) is prepared by gluing together the small end-grain units into a larger surface. The message units may be conceived of as white (negative) or black (positive). See also black-line and white-line wood engraving.

woodburytype   A true halftone process, perfect for the duplication of photography and used extensively for photographic book illustration from the 1870s to the 1890s; a "permanent" photographic method creating gelatin molds under extreme pressure, where the thickest part of the final image was the darkest and the thinnest, the lightest. Not type-compatible. Also called "Photoglyptie" in France.

xylographic book   The so-called "block book" was produced by cutting both verbal and visual message units out of the same plank of wood, thereby producing a complete relief plate. Similar attempts to unify text and illustration were made by engraving, by chromolithography, by heliotype, by photography.

Index